2 · 2011

D1480968

The "Good War" in American Memory

THE "GOOD WAR"
IN AMERICAN MEMORY

JOHN BODNAR

The Johns Hopkins University Press
Baltimore

© 2010 The Johns Hopkins University Press
All rights reserved. Published 2010
Printed in the United States of America on acid-free paper
2 4 6 8 9 7 5 3 1

The Johns Hopkins University Press
2715 North Charles Street
Baltimore, Maryland 21218-4363
www.press.jhu.edu

Library of Congress Cataloging-in-Publication Data
Bodnar, John E., 1944–
The "Good War" in American memory / John Bodnar.
p. cm.
Includes bibliographical references and index.
ISBN-13: 978-0-8018-9667-5 (hardcover : alk. paper)
ISBN-10: 0-8018-9667-3 (hardcover : alk. paper)
1. World War, 1939–1945—Social aspects—United
States.   2. Collective memory—United States.   3. Memory—Social
aspects—United States.   4. War and society—United
States.   5. National characteristics, American.   I. Title.
D744.7.U6B635 2010
940.53'73—dc22   2009052695

A catalog record for this book is available from the British Library.

Special discounts are available for bulk purchases of this book.
For more information, please contact Special Sales at 410-516-6936 or
specialsales@press.jhu.edu.

The Johns Hopkins University Press uses environmentally
friendly book materials, including recycled text paper that is
composed of at least 30 percent post-consumer waste, whenever
possible. All of our book papers are acid-free, and our jackets
and covers are printed on paper with recycled content.

For Sophie and Francesca

Contents

Acknowledgments

When my mother and father talked about World War II, they always did so in bits and pieces. I never recall them saying anything about Fascism or the Four Freedoms. Those were things I learned in school. Their remembrance was about how the war affected them personally. They had scheduled their wedding ceremony in Pennsylvania in 1943 early enough in the morning so they could catch a train to Texas, where my father was stationed in the Army Air Corps near Victoria. And they talked a great deal about the friends they made in Victoria and the fact that I was born there. My mother would often recall the long train rides she took with me as an infant and how busy the rail stations were during the war years. I can still see my father's army hat and shirt with sergeant stripes hanging in the family garage in Forest City, Pennsylvania, where I grew up. At some point the hat and shirt disappeared, but my memory of what they told me never did. I would not have written this book if it had not been for the stories they told.

I benefited from the cooperation and support of many others. At Indiana University, Claude Clegg was one of the first individuals to encourage me to write this book, and Jeff Wasserstrom stirred my early interest by getting me to write an essay on war movies. Ed Linenthal read early drafts of my manuscript and made numerous suggestions for revisions. I received a good deal of assistance from Martha Norkunas in locating materials related to Norman Mailer. I also thank Alan Brinkley, Nancy Cott, Gaines Foster, Carol Oja, John Grabowski, and Robb Westbrook. Graduate students at Indiana helped me collect materials and discuss many of the central issues discussed in the book, especially Karen Dunak, Keith Eberly, Jim Seaver, Jennifer Stinson, Chris Stone, and Jamie Warren. Barbara Truesdell offered generous help in processing and saving photographic images. Jo Ellen Fitzgerald's help was indispensable in obtaining research materials and saving various versions of the manuscript. The History Department at Indiana University is fortunate to have her on their staff. And Elizabeth Yoder improved the manuscript immeasurably.

My family also gave me assistance at every turn. My daughter, Brenna Snider, took a number of photos for me, and my son, Eric, helped me identify important films. My cousins, Jacob and Marty Bodnar, also provided some key images when I needed them. And my wife, Donna, tolerated the many trips I needed to take to bring this project to completion.

INTRODUCTION

BILLY PILGRIM, KURT VONNEGUT'S FICTIONAL CHARACTER in *Slaughterhouse-Five*, never could recall exactly what happened in World War II. Pilgrim, like the man who created him, was an American veteran of the conflict who witnessed the fire-bombing of Dresden as a prisoner of war. Yet his firsthand experience in Europe had not given him total recall. On the contrary, Pilgrim struggled throughout his fictional life to remember exactly what he had been through. He did bring home "a ceremonial Luftwaffe saber," but even souvenirs could not help him remember clearly. Over time he recalled the war in fragments and in the form of troubling nightmares. When it came to the memory of World War II, Pilgrim could say only that "all this happened more or less."

The point of Vonnegut's fiction—that coherent remembrances of the war were not possible and not trustworthy—was ironically no fiction at all. Millions of people endeavored for the rest of their lives to recall, or even to forget, aspects of the frightening reality of the global struggle that was World War II. It might come as a surprise to people now living in the United States to learn that the memory and the meaning of that war was actually a matter of contention among Americans who lived through those times. Widespread celebrations of the generation that fought the war and of the nation's victory are now commonplace. Mythical images of a powerful nation and righteous citizen-soldiers command reverence. The difficulties of remembering that plagued Pilgrim and Vonnegut, his creator, are scarcely acknowledged at all.[1]

This book takes Pilgrim's problem seriously as I seek to explain how Americans struggled to craft both an understanding of World War II while it was being fought and a remembrance of the war after it ended. It is a history that argues unequivocally that the significance of the struggle was the source of a widespread political and cultural debate. Even as citizens came together to battle Germany and Japan in 1941, they expressed disagreements over why they had to fight. This is not to say that millions of Americans did not see danger and evil in the rising power of totalitarian regimes or feel that it was necessary to take up the burden of stopping Fascist aggression. They did. The point here is that such outlooks were only part of a vast public argument over how to understand what was going on and how to frame the unprecedented turbulence in the world that the war brought.

The controversy was lengthy and extensive—carried out in literary circles, movie theaters, museums, public parks, veteran organizations, and the inner recesses of private minds—because ultimately it was not so much about the war as about national identity. The cataclysm of war—like other historic events—forced Americans to consider both the virtuous and the violent sides of their nature. Various spokesmen have described Americans as morally superior, heroic, united, innately peaceful, and committed to defending human rights around the world. Others have noted racist or darker impulses that lusted for dominance over others both within and outside the nation and justified acts of excessive cruelty. At stake in the debate was, in fact, the myth of American exceptionalism with its attendant faith in the promise of individualism. In this creed it was an aggressive sense of personal freedom for all and a hatred for all forms of tyranny that made America a special place and offered its citizens and the rest of the world the best chance to create a future better than the past. In such a culture strength was favored over weakness, self-reliance over cooperation. Since liberal nations like the United States were presumed to be exemplary in their commitment to individual rights and to a just world, they faced a particular problem in conducting wars and displaying identities. Episodes of state-sponsored violence undermined their reputation for goodness by causing them to commit brutal acts and by asking some citizens to relinquish the rights they had. In wartime, the liberal hope Americans placed in human nature and the nation itself was both affirmed and shaken as democratic citizens revealed a capacity to fight for freedom but also to kill enemy combatants and civilians at will. This is why scholars have often seen war as an event that exposed the "seam" in the liberal political imagination and the darkness in the souls of even men who were free. For Americans, it underscored inconsistencies that clashed at the heart of their imagined sense of self.

This is not to say that there has never been a time for brave soldiers to save the nation and destroy evil in the world. The assault on Adolph Hitler's regime represented one of those times. But in the effort to wage wars both necessary and questionable, liberal nations had to scramble to justify the sacrifices and explain their killing sprees. They did this in part by finding ways to transform the meaning of killing and dying into virtuous acts. Proclamations of virtue, however, could never fully erase questions about national identity or personal qualms about encounters with violence and trauma. Consequently, the public memory of war in modern America was invariably contested. There were always those who could never forget the suffering war had brought, who were never completely comforted by patriotic rhetoric, and who resented the fact that they had to relinquish some of their most basic rights to liberty and life. Vonnegut took a stand in such a dispute by refusing to see World War II as inspirational and by attaching the memory of the war to a narrative of loss rather than one of victory.[2]

It should come as no surprise, moreover, to learn that the public remembering of World War II was seldom concerned with producing an objective account of what had taken place. Today we frequently hear about the unity and patriotism Americans demonstrated in World War II. There was, in fact, a general sense of oneness when it came to waging the war, especially with the outburst of shock and anger over Pearl Harbor. And there were those who proudly served their nation. At the same time, because meanings were always debated, there were noticeable discrepancies on a number of fronts, including a distinct tension between idealistic rationales for the struggle offered by Franklin Roosevelt and personal views expressed by ordinary citizens. Some of the key issues in the remembrance of the war, in fact, originated in debates that were central to these wartime disagreements. Because comprehension was never a settled matter in the 1940s and beyond, the war was not only a topic of dispute but a subject of public performances in rituals, commemorations, and various political and cultural expressions. Indeed, it became a central feature of American public memory. Kendall Phillips has suggested that public forms of remembering are highly rhetorical and performative. They provide not balanced accounts of the past but versions designed to persuade listeners of the validity of a particular point of view. And he insightfully suggests that the meanings deployed in such performances are always provisional because they contain an unsteady mix of reality and dreams. They are generally tangled versions of what actually happened and some mythical or hopeful view of what the world was like before and could become again. This fusion of the real and the mythical was driven not simply by a need to remember but also by a desire to forget.[3]

The controversial nature of public understanding and remembering meant that a total victory could not produce a picture perfect remembrance. Citizens enjoyed their success and flocked to films that relived the triumph and celebrated the grit of the enlisted man. Yet the vast trove of representations of the war in American culture ultimately told a cluttered story in which virtue was forced to share cultural and political space with streams of doubt, cynicism, and regret. Not everyone experienced or recalled the war in the same way. And because they did not, Americans were forced to create three powerful narratives to explain the event that can be labeled traditional, critical, and humanitarian. These angles of vision were never totally separate from each other, but they were fundamental to the way citizens understood the war and explain why they argued over its meaning for decades.[4]

Tradition has never been simply about the past; it has always been concerned more broadly with the task of how to use aspects of former times to move toward the future. In the twentieth century, many nations have invoked the precepts of tradition to turn violence into virtue, heal rifts created by extensive encounters with trauma and death, and restore faith in governing bodies and leaders that had called for war in the first place. America was no exception in this regard. As Jenny Edkins has argued, encounters with state-sponsored trauma serve as a "revelation" to people because they "tend to strip away" the sense of continuity that organized their lives and the faith they had that life in a home or a homeland would be safe. The trauma and fears of wartime inevitably bring feelings of powerlessness to individuals and waves of grief to combatants and those who care for them. Even in a nation that did not feel the full impact of wartime devastation, for instance, longstanding ideas of self-reliance, moral behavior, and home life were badly disrupted by mass mobilizations, long separations, and death and injury. Thus, the imperative to restore traditional ideals of individual worth, sexual restraint, and male supremacy, for instance, would become part of the process of reestablishing faith in American political traditions and sustaining a sense of American goodness. Wartime losses also raised the possibility that an excessive amount of public mourning might weaken the overall attachments people had to the state that mobilized the war effort in the first place—no matter how just the cause. Thus, nations that fight also have to engage in efforts to "encircle" the trauma, to minimize the costs of the conflict, and to console those who grieve. Citizens do this when they rely on what Jay Winter has called "traditional motifs"—often expressed in classically styled memorials or sacred rituals— which aim to honor the dead and explain why so many had to suffer.[5]

The effort to recast the war in terms of tradition was the most extensive way in which Americans tried to interpret what had taken place. This perspective saw World War II not as a human tragedy but as an opportunity for Americans to assume a position of dominance in the world and reaffirm their innate (and traditional) moral courage and bravery. No one articulated this view—both before and after the war—more strongly than Henry Luce. The founder of leading magazines such as *Time* and *Life,* Luce made it clear in his famous essay entitled "The American Century" in 1941 and in his private writings years after the victory that the war was necessary not only to stop German Fascism but to spread American values and power over the globe. In putting down his thoughts in 1965 for a book he never published, he expressed the belief that World War II was a heroic episode in American history that restored a sense of patriotism he felt was lacking in the 1930s and revealed the "greatness," courage, and endurance not only of military leaders like Dwight Eisenhower and Douglas MacArthur but of "millions of plain G.I. Joes" as well. He recalled the sense of "awe" he felt in 1945 over the victory and over the fact that Americans now controlled the atomic bomb, the seas, the skies, and the land.[6]

Not every American thinker shared Luce's jubilation or his tendency to celebrate the American character. A critic like Norman Cousins took a more sober view and raised doubt in 1945 about the capacity of the men of any nation to avoid catastrophic wars in the future. He felt the war demonstrated that there was now a fundamental need for a new form of world government to replace (competitive) sovereign nations. The noted theologian Reinhold Niebuhr—who supported the war against Fascism as did Luce—was also unwilling to be inspired by the victory and worried about the implications of the conflict's violent actions and tragic consequences. To Niebuhr the fight against Fascism was justified but troubling, because it exposed in graphic form the paradox of human nature with its potential for good and evil. Unwilling to embrace mythical and optimistic views of America and its liberal faith, Niebuhr noted in the early 1950s the "ironic" manner in which Americans talked about warfare as an "unequivocally virtuous" undertaking while being ready to "cover" or deny any suggestion of wickedness on their part. He warned Americans that, although they had carried out God's will in destroying evil forces in the world, they needed to avoid the "perils of vainglory" in reflecting on their victory.[7]

The traditionalist view of World War II and of the nation was also shaped heavily by the cultural power of what Richard Slotkin has called the "myth of the frontier." Killing and dying, of course, were issues that could call into question a righteous identity of the nation. Yet over a long period of time in America, tales of killing savages on a frontier to protect settlers and expand the nation offered powerful rationales for why some had to die. This legend also affirmed that Americans took no pleasure in the suffering of others and that their encounters with violence would be short-lived and not alter their fundamental goodness. As Slotkin has suggested, their brutal actions were seen as only a "temporary regression" to a more primitive state. The nation's defenders who inflicted horrors on others would soon revert to their normally peaceful and progressive ways once the danger to the nation ended. In this myth, Americans could fully manage the task of violence without becoming brutes themselves. They were, in other words, remarkable people who had been freed of the ordinary burden of human nature to reconcile conflicting impulses between good and evil.[8]

In all wars there are those who cannot be consoled or convinced by the authoritative language of tradition and refuse to see anything of value in the experience of mass death. Such people often adopt the role of a "moral witness" to insist that mass killings and brutal acts not be called by any other name. Their perspective is more cynical and more challenging to the aspirations of traditionalists to restate war in terms that are dignified and unambiguous. Critical accounts of war engage its brutality more fully and tend to register the moral and emotional confusion that such contests bring. Since it is not always possible to separate traditional and critical views, they frequently collide in both public and personal recollections of such events. This is in a sense what Studs Terkel found years ago in his oral histories of World War II—published as *The Good War*. The people he spoke with revealed attitudes toward the conflict that were both positive and negative. It is the writer and World War II veteran Paul Fussell, however, who has made an especially strong argument about how scornful were the views of many soldiers not only toward World War II but toward World War I as well. His work revealed a broad-based legacy of bitterness and despair on the part of men who fought and challenged attempts to consign their attitudes to virtuous images and stories. Tradition, of course, helped to mute the public expression of such resentment and the doubts many had toward the war effort. In its reliance on mythical figures, it aspired to rub out the remembrance of events and actions that threatened to undermine faith in a liberal creed or hold the political community accountable for its misdeeds. Memory without accountability and anguish fostered a heritage of innocent people who held no liability for trauma or injustice in their past. Critical memories looked to undercut such myths and keep alive a legacy of misdeeds and complaints, whether they dealt with World War II, westward expansion, slavery, or Vietnam.[9]

The human-centered approach that Americans brought to World War II was invoked extensively during the 1940s but became less noticeable in the public performance of the war as it moved past 1945. It actually had the potential to reinforce mythical perspectives because it suggested that Americans fought the war for righteous, compassionate ends. Yet it also conveyed sentiments and implications that rendered Americans simply part of a human community, an idea that bothered ardent conservatives and nationalists in the postwar era by minimizing their sense of America's distinctiveness. This more universal frame on the war was rooted in Franklin Roosevelt's argument in 1941 that the sacrifices to come would be justified not so much because they served the interests of the nation but because they would lead to a better world for all of mankind. Glimpses of this vision were already evident in the internationalism of Woodrow Wilson during the era of World War I. Roosevelt now updated Wilson with his pronouncement of the Four Freedoms and plans for an organization like the United Nations that would resolve international disputes. There was no doubt that many supported the ideal of liberal and democratic rights for men and women everywhere and international cooperation during the war and afterwards. The term "human rights," for instance, was inserted into a number of new national constitutions after 1945 throughout the world.

The problem for a human-centered version of the war and its remembrance was that—ironically—it was so human-centered. Like critical appraisals of the war, humanitarian war goals weakened the project to valorize the nation and to enhance its sense of privilege. People who might be willing to die to save their family or their country were less inclined to suffer for the sake of humanity. After the war most large nations, in fact, were reluctant to relinquish the pursuit of their national interests for the sake of international cooperation on almost any issue, including human betterment. It is for this reason that it took the U.S. Senate more than forty years to ratify the United Nations' Universal Declaration of Human Rights of 1948. When it came to remembering World War II, Americans preferred to retain a sense of how dissimilar they were from the mass of people with whom they shared the planet.[10]

Contests between traditional narratives and alternative frames also marked the public history of other nations that had fought in the war. It was, of course, easier to circulate noble sentiments about the war effort in countries that won than in nations such as Germany and Japan that carried the scars of defeat or particular responsibility for horrible atrocities. Winning provided more support for the value of sacrifice and loss and the project of healing wartime ruptures. It tended to reinforce what Terry Eagleton has called a "classical" sense of sacrifice in which the dying and suffering, especially of men, was viewed as noble and heroic. Thus, traditional sentiments gained traction in nations such as England and the Soviet Union. In the former, many movies in the 1950s were crafted in a way that allowed citizens to relive the victory. In the latter, the "Myth of the Great Patriotic War" dominated public commemoration after 1945. Traditional and highly patriotic accounts of the heroic resistance to the Nazis were also powerful for a long time after the war in France. They began to crumble, however, when

revelations about French collaboration with the German enemy and with the de-
portation of the Jews appeared more frequently in their public discourse. In the
Netherlands, the desire to reestablish the traditional power of the nation after a
period of wartime splintering forced citizens to construct a broad mythical community of Nazi victims, whether they were Jews, conscripted workers in Germany, or resistance fighters. It was much more difficult to establish a traditional
remembrance in Germany and Japan. In these nations foreign occupations made
it harder to forget the fact that the nation, or at least its leaders, had brought
about destruction and ruin. Internal debates for decades after the war centered
on questions of collective guilt and—despite considerable reluctance—a need to
accept accountability for past misdeeds.[11]

Over the course of the twentieth century—a century of incredibly destructive
wars—the United States expanded its capabilities to deliver massive forms of destruction and instigate violence. Culture, identity, and commemoration became
more militarized and centered on thousands of tales about extraordinary patriots
who protected their nation out of an inherent sense of love and duty. The land of
the free increasingly became known as the home of the brave; acts of killing and
dying were transformed into heroic deeds and cherished memories. National
identity and the remembrance of war were never issues that were completely
settled, and the trope of brave men could be inserted into tragic narratives of loss
and remorse as well. Yet over time, the defense of the nation became as important as the old dream of uplift and equality. Americans talked not only about the
pursuit of happiness but about the road to victory. In the "American Century"
towns and communities were considerably more likely to build memorials to veterans who defended the nation than to commemorate the Declaration of Independence or the Four Freedoms. Film studios made thousands of movies of
gunfighters and soldiers that suggested that our problems could be solved more
effectively through "human heroism" and military force than through political
movements. Certainly there were warriors who were courageous and battles that
had to be fought. Virtue and violence did not have to be mutually exclusive. But
to a significant extent, that is how they were cast in the great debate over the remembering of World War II that consumed the American people.[12]

The "Good War" in American Memory looks at the continual struggle to organize knowledge about World War II over the course of some seventy years after
1941. It does not attempt to cover every aspect of this incredibly pervasive discussion, such as the way the war's legacy shaped foreign policy. It does, however,
look closely at how the struggle affected ongoing discussion over the nation's
identity and at the actors who advanced distinct points of view on the matter, in-

cluding soldier-writers, veteran organizations, monument builders, filmmakers, and minorities, in hopes of explaining what was at stake. Thus, chapter 1 will trace the disputes over the meaning of the war that broke out in the early 1940s and how those divisions never disappeared entirely. Chapter 2 will then examine the highly critical writings of the war presented by veterans who questioned the brutality of the fighting and expressed resentment over the loss of their individual rights. Chapter 3 will look at the tension between tradition and fault-finding in the politics of the early Cold War, which was shaped, in part, by many of the men who served in the military in the early 1940s. In the 1950s Americans turned out to be ambivalent about just how much reverence they had for some of the war's leaders and about the need to repeat such an experience again, even as they used the legacy of World War II to justify dreams of international dominance and military supremacy. Chapters 4 and 5 show that representations of the cultural tension over understanding the war also proved highly controversial when it came to building monuments and making movies. In both instances, strains of regret and cynicism could not so easily be laid to rest as memorials were executed and films produced. The long history of how the nation treated its minorities during the conflict provoked another argument about remembrance that erupted in the later decades of the twentieth century, and is treated in chapter 6. The resolution of that controversy over human rights turned out to be contingent on the reassertion of a traditional frame on the war more than a humanitarian one. And, finally, chapter 7 suggests that the end-of-the-century celebration of the war that engulfed the nation in the 1990s and beyond served as a reminder not only of how powerful national myths could be but of how vulnerable were the echoes of sorrow and trauma. The American memory of the war was indeed contested, but like the recollections of other wars the nation had fought, the sweet sounds of valor ultimately eclipsed the painful cries of loss.

CHAPTER ONE

WARTIME

FOR THE UNITED STATES, World War II precipitated not only a military struggle but a cultural one as well. The problem revolved around the meaning of the war. President Franklin Roosevelt had already staked out the high ground of human-itarianism before Pearl Harbor when he implied that the next war would be a contest to ensure human rights throughout the world. The outlooks that ordi-nary Americans held in their homes and hometowns, however, were not so sim-ple or honorable. Certainly, many Americans affirmed the value of underwriting the political and economic rights of people everywhere. Yet most citizens did not want to go to war in 1941, and, among those that did, their motives were often based more on anger and revenge for Pearl Harbor than on the president's ideal-ism. Once the battle broke out, moreover, attitudes and feelings became even more complex. Men and women quickly realized that the war brought new opportuni-ties for work and income that had been scarce during the 1930s. Others grew con-cerned over the sudden disruptions in moral behavior and race relations activated by massive wartime mobilization of workers and soldiers. Parents and spouses fretted over the fate of loved ones sent off to fight, and soldiers now thrown into combat wondered if they would ever come home again. With so much changing at once, how could anyone presume to understand fully what it all meant? Cer-tainly, most Americans wanted to defeat their enemies. Yet public opinion polls made it clear that much confusion existed in the public's mind. As late as 1944 some 40 percent still claimed they were unsure why they were fighting.[1]

A BETTER WORLD

As Roosevelt considered how to move America into a position to challenge the expanding power of Nazi Germany, he faced not only the normal reluctance of people to fight and die but the specific memory of World War I, which still weighed heavily on the American mind. Many Americans could recall the defeat of Woodrow Wilson's plans to commit the nation to an active involvement in world affairs with his dream of a League of Nations. Ideals such as pacifism and isolationism—so strange to Americans today—actually commanded considerable support in the 1930s and were tied to the public memory of the last war. By 1940 many isolationists who wanted to keep the United States out of foreign wars had organized an America First Committee dedicated to resisting Roosevelt's efforts to confront Hitler's power. They believed that America's entry into World War I was a mistake that should not be repeated. And among African Americans there was still a bitter taste of failed expectations regarding the last war. They had presumed that their contributions and sacrifice would be rewarded with greater levels of social justice and an end to hideous practices such as lynching. Yet such improvements were not readily discernable.

Faced with political division at home and a population less than enthusiastic for another war, Roosevelt moved into the realm of propaganda and high-minded rhetoric in an effort to convince a skeptical public. In his address to Congress in 1941—nearly a full year before Pearl Harbor—he offered a rationale for why it was that citizens might be asked to forget the bitter legacies of the past and fight again. Anxious to proclaim an alternative to National Socialism that would rally public support at home and abroad, the president framed the coming struggle in terms of individual rights and guarantees that had long been part of liberal politics in America. He argued that the future could only be made more secure if a world order was built upon what he called the "four essential human freedoms." For him this meant the realization everywhere of freedom of speech; "the freedom of every person to worship God in his own way"; freedom from want, by which he meant a stable economic life for the citizens of every nation; and "freedom from fear," or military aggression by one nation toward another. Roosevelt had served in Wilson's administration and was painfully aware that the last American crusade for democracy had ended badly. He decided, however, that the time to "harp" on the failures of 1919 had passed and that it was now necessary to fight again to spread the dream of a better world for all—a sort of global New Deal. "Freedom," the president declared, "means the supremacy of human rights everywhere." To him it was worth all the dying and killing that was to come.[2]

This human-centered perspective was America's most utopian explanation of why Americans had to fight World War II, and it would be continually invoked not only during the war but for decades afterward as a frame of remembrance. It was also a vision that was promoted not only by Roosevelt but by other leading political figures of his day such as Henry Wallace and Wendell Willkie. And it would become one of the central political visions of postwar history that helped in the formation of the United Nations and the formulation of its declaration on human rights in 1948. When an amended version of Roosevelt's vision was issued in August 1941 as the Atlantic Charter, a joint communiqué with Winston Churchill, his political ideas reached an even wider audience. The charter included some additional language that spoke of the need for "all men in all lands to live out their lives in freedom from fear and want." Historian Elizabeth Borgwardt has insightfully revealed how the reference to "all men in all lands" caught the attention of those who listened not only in Western democracies but in colonial possessions where activists were intent on resisting foreign domination and repressive regimes. Nelson Mandela, for instance, claimed that he had been inspired by the Atlantic Charter and its promises. And from nations everywhere—even from those dominated by the empire Churchill represented—the question of whether the provisions of the document were meant for them as well emerged.[3]

In the United States, citizens of color were also quick to pick up on the implications of Roosevelt's dream. Leaders of the National Association for the Advancement of Colored People (NAACP) saw in the president's language the promise for an end to racial oppression and restrictions on black voting in the South. And many blacks saw in the term "freedom from fear" a critique of the practice of lynching. African American leaders such as Walter White took the Four Freedoms literally as a call to whites to end their harsh treatment of blacks in America, although historian Carol Anderson has made it clear that as war clouds approached many African Americans questioned whether they could really fight for the United States without receiving explicit guarantees of just treatment. Roy Wilkins, an NAACP official, did sense from the start, however, that the war might offer a unique opportunity for blacks to trade patriotic sacrifice for political and economic rights.[4]

Responding to the Four Freedoms in a different way, painter Norman Rockwell used his artistic talents to temper the internationalist and universal implications of the president's pronouncements and transform them into symbols of American exceptionalism and virtue. Rockwell's artistic renditions of these liberal principles began to appear in the *Saturday Evening Post* early in 1943 and won instant popularity. During the war years they helped to sell some $130,000,000 in war bonds and became iconic and highly sentimental representations of American political culture and home life. His various depictions of Roosevelt's ideals showed America at its best—a common man standing up in a town meeting exercising his freedom of speech, ordinary men and women deep in prayer, parents tucking their children safely into bed in a nation free of fear and oppression, and an extended family enjoying a bountiful meal on the American celebration of Thanksgiving. This work, as historian Rob Westbrook has observed, was popular not only because it romanticized life in America but also because it managed to connect the abstract rhetoric of Roosevelt to practical concerns most Americans had about the well-being of their families and communities. To the extent that Americans would commit to the battle at hand, they had to be convinced that the struggle involved their own safety and welfare more than it did the political dreams of the rest of the world. Rockwell elaborated on his mythical view of America with countless other artistic images that showed people living in complete harmony in their political community and essentially free of any sense of alienation. Thus, he pictured Boy Scouts helping older people, firemen serving their communities, children at play, mothers toiling in the kitchen—and, of course, civilians happy to see GIs coming home from the war.[5]

The Roosevelt administration moved quickly after Pearl Harbor to promote the war in terms of liberal dreams. The Pentagon commissioned noted Hollywood director Frank Capra to produce morale-building orientation films that celebrated the ability of ordinary Americans to defeat powerful enemies. The Office of War Information (OWI), an agency the president had created in 1942 to sell citizens on the merits of the war, worked hard to frame the struggle in terms of liberal dreams of human improvement. The OWI advanced Roosevelt's vision, for instance, by asking Hollywood producers to insert democratic images and sentimental depictions of America into its features. The administration was especially concerned that the conflict be seen as a "people's war" being fought by citizens who were innately loyal to their country and completely committed to the Four Freedoms. America was envisioned as everything the enemy nations were not. To accomplish this goal, the president staffed the OWI with progressive-minded liberals such as Archibald MacLeish, Arthur Schlesinger, and Robert Sherwood, who could write with conviction about the sterling qualities of the American people and the liberal ideals. This is in part why there was a revival of the public veneration of Abraham Lincoln in the 1940s. Images and stories of the sixteenth president appeared everywhere as a symbol of national strength and purpose and as a sign that citizens had a deep faith in the ideas of equality and democracy. Seven months after Pearl Harbor, the OWI distributed a poster showing a "resolute Lincoln" standing above a quotation from the Gettysburg Address that expressed the hope that "government of the people, by the people, and for the people shall not perish from the face of the earth."[6]

In 1942 Roosevelt reiterated the need to connect the war to a liberal agenda. He sent to Congress a report from the National Resources Planning Board that

included designs for the overall war effort and a reaffirmation of New Deal policies that had supported the right of people to a job and fair pay. And in his 1944
State of the Union message, he proclaimed the need for a "Second Bill of Rights"
as part of a larger effort to sustain support for the wartime sacrifices at a time
when no one was sure when the struggle would end. Again he noted the need to
create a world free of fear and political oppression. He elaborated on this point,
however, by arguing that the simple defense of the idea of freedom by itself was
not a sufficient war goal. He now made it clear that the problem of totalitarianism and aggression would never be solved unless people obtained stable levels of
economic security in addition to freedom from oppression. Realizing that the
war had to be about more than revenge and rhetorical calls for freedom, the president felt strongly that citizens everywhere would need specific guarantees and
benefits that included a decent home, medical care, and some protection against
unemployment and old age. Without such assurances, Roosevelt felt that economic turmoil would simply breed another wave of dictators and aggression.[7]

The high-minded liberalism of Roosevelt's arguments did not sit well with all
Americans. Official pronouncements that the war would make the world a better
place for all were routinely criticized in many newspapers. And dreams of a new
international order were debunked by many who still recalled Wilson's crusade
and now derisively referred to Roosevelt's as "globaloney." The OWI learned
from its own polls that most Americans fought for more personal reasons, such
as the "self-defense" of the nation and retribution against the Japanese. In 1942
the OWI also learned that about one-third of the people they sampled wanted to
negotiate a separate peace with Germany, a perspective Roosevelt wanted to
squelch for fear of disrupting America's alliance with the Soviet Union. One
housewife told an OWI researcher that Americans were really fighting to "save
our hides." In fact, OWI officials realized that the circulation of images like those
of Lincoln or the promotion of the rhetoric of the Four Freedoms only tended to
boost morale to a modest extent. Thus, the agency designed its radio programs
and pamphlets in ways that stressed the personal stake Americans had in seeing
that their nation emerged victorious. The agency soon realized that the most po-
tent appeal they could make was one that stressed what would happen to some
loved one if Hitler took over.[8]

Conservatives in Congress were even more of a problem for the Roosevelt administration. Many of them were vehemently opposed to the ideas embraced by
the Four Freedoms and the concept of a "people's war" because they seemed like
a simple reiteration of the New Deal. Politicians on the right feared a rise in federal power (which the war mobilization inevitably brought) and the implication

that human rights rhetoric might foster racial equality in America. In 1943 conservatives were able, in fact, to emasculate much of the organization's budget that funded domestic operations, while leaving alone funding for the liberal promotion of the war overseas. They dissolved the National Resource Planning Board as well. Roosevelt himself—now more desirous of winning the war than of starting a fight with political opponents at home—elected not to raise much of a fuss over these powerful attacks made against this liberal frame on World War II.[9]

Conservative resistance and the public's preoccupation with private matters, however, were never enough to totally derail attempts to frame the war in terms of human rights. After all, most people had a vested interest in seeing that the idea of political and economic rights were sustained at some level. But liberal viewpoints were also kept alive by prominent crusaders like Henry Wallace, who never let up on promoting a New Deal vision for the world. Serving as Roosevelt's Secretary of Agriculture in the 1930s, Wallace came from the "cooperative farm culture" of Iowa and became a staunch liberal who by the war years was moving to the left of even his president. In 1942 he gave his most famous speech, in which he laid out his own vision for the future that not only called again for political freedom but made specific pleas that people have "plenty to eat" and strong labor unions. Wallace also claimed—in a response to those who felt free men would not fight as effectively as Germans—that the goals of the "four freedoms" and the "rights of the common man" would stir Americans to fight more bravely than the forces of totalitarian regimes. He acknowledged that some American leaders, like Henry Luce, had envisioned the future as an "American Century" where the United States would use its power to dominate the course of world events. Wallace saw the future differently, however, and claimed that it must not be led by one nation but must be shaped by an ideal of international cooperation and the pursuit of economic well-being for people everywhere. "We ourselves are no more the master than the Nazi's," he reasoned. For Wallace it would be the tenets of international cooperation and economic security that would create what he called "the Century of the Common Man."[10]

Archibald MacLeish also emerged as a leading spokesman for the liberal version of the world conflict. After his military service in World War I, he had come to detest war but concluded by 1939 that Hitler had to be stopped. In an almost endless series of speeches and articles, MacLeish sounded themes familiar to anyone listening to Roosevelt or Wallace in the 1940s. In 1943 he spoke extensively about the need for internationalism in an address entitled "For This We Fight." He argued against the idea that nations should aggressively pursue only their self-interests and called upon them to work instead for "a new world" that would include all "human beings of various traditions and origins." In a long commencement address at Indiana University in the same year, he elaborated upon the idea that the war raging at the time was ultimately about democratic values. He made the point that most wars ended with the defeat of hostile forces. But this war was different, he reasoned, in that "a soldier's triumph cannot serve a people's war." Distinguishing between the military and moral objectives of the struggle, he told the Indiana graduating class that Fascists had only contempt for the idea of free men and women governing themselves and that the defeat of the enemy would be an insufficient basis for claiming victory if the principle of a "people's government" was not established everywhere after the war ended.[11]

The internationalism and liberalism of the Roosevelt administration attracted some Republican support as well. Wendell Willkie, who fought for the Republican nomination for the presidency on a platform that included a defense of the idea of "free enterprise" could also be heard making calls for guarantees of employment, social insurance against joblessness, and assistance for the elderly. Willkie, like Roosevelt and Wallace, felt that America's political calculations should be driven by an assessment of what it would take to defend freedom everywhere and not by any retreat into isolationism or the simple defense of national interests. It is now clear that Willkie was part of a large contingent of Americans in the middle decades of the twentieth century for whom, as David Hollinger has observed, "global perspectives were fashionable." Willkie set out his version of a liberal and international future in his best-selling book of 1943, *One World*. In it he offered an assessment of why he thought the allied nations were fighting. Certainly, they wanted to end the brutal expansionist tendencies of totalitarian regimes. But like MacLeish, he also suggested that the destruction of Germany and Japan was not the true end point and that the problem of totalitarianism would return unless democratic rights and economic security were established everywhere in the world. Willkie even referred to what he saw as "imperialisms" in American society in the form of racism and religious intolerance. He reminded his readers that they could not expect to fight for victory and ignore the need to expand democratic principles at home.[12]

Letters to Willkie suggested that some of his readers were not entirely convinced of his views. Most people certainly approved of the idea of internationalism and the need to discard older isolationist beliefs. They sensed that the United States could not hope to live peacefully in the world if it did not actively engage other nations and world issues. Yet many who wrote to him made it clear that while they saw value in helping people in need, they wanted no more "new deals." One man exclaimed that he was not an isolationist but that he took issue

with Willkie's dream "regarding the necessity of world-wide leveling and uplifting after the war." Charles Collins of Denver was more direct. He felt that both
Willkie and Roosevelt were "all wet about all these big things you are going to do
for people all over the world." Another reader from Idaho claimed that he was
not prepared to commit to "underwriting the peace of the entire world." Arthur
Kirk wrote from Kentucky to say that while he favored cooperation with other nations, he did not favor "the surrender of such a degree of national sovereignty"
that the "status" of the United States would be lowered.[13]

Despite conservative opposition and a good deal of public skepticism over
high ideals, liberal dreams of international cooperation and human rights definitely survived the war and became a powerful part of the legacy of the conflict.
Part of this dream was realized when delegates gathered in San Francisco in
April 1945, before the war was over, to draft a charter for the United Nations, a
new international body that would, it was hoped, resolve international tensions
and further the cause of human improvement. Roosevelt had backed plans for
the United Nations, and many delegates to the San Francisco meeting had indicated that his rhetoric about the Four Freedoms had inspired them. Nevertheless, the original charter for the world body had little to say specifically about
human rights. Thus, the organization was forced to issue a human rights declaration in 1948 that made it a point to recognize the "inherent dignity" of all
members of the "human family" and reaffirmed the belief in the rights of all
men and women to "life" and "liberty." This declaration even affirmed the need
for specific rights such as "social security," "free choice of employment," a decent
standard of living, the privilege to join a union, and access to "health care."

Importantly, the document—so much a product of the internationalism of the
1940s—failed to say anything about the need to outlaw racial discrimination.
Race was an obvious sore point for American officials negotiating the UN declaration in the first place. In 1946 government officials were upset when the National Negro Congress appealed directly to the United Nations for more racial
justice in the United States after a wave of postwar violence directed toward
blacks. The United Nations responded by saying it could not intervene in the internal affairs of a nation. Eleanor Roosevelt and other American representatives
would work to keep the subject of racial discrimination out of the 1948 document
as well, in order not to offend powerful southern politicians in Congress.[14]

More powerful than liberal dreams in generating acceptance of the war were
romantic ones. Both government officials and a wide array of culture producers
began to offer perceptions of American life in the past and present that were extraordinarily sentimental—an approach that reinforced an ideal of national in-

nocence. Stories now appeared that celebrated the matchless goodness and innate patriotism of citizens and especially the joy of living in small towns characterized by harmony and love. In this more nation-centered version of the war, Americans fought willingly to preserve a wonderful homeland and never really questioned what the effort would cost. Certainly, such noble images could reinforce government calls to support the Four Freedoms, but over time the romantic nationalism at the heart of this argument would trump many of its links to liberal humanitarianism.

The Office of War Information (OWI) was certain that such idealistic characterizations of American life were convincing. Thus, it published a booklet called *Small Town USA*, which stressed how such communities were peaceful places and outstanding exemplars of democracy at work. But the project to defend the nation (and accept the war) by seeing it in mythical terms was promoted even more heavily by filmmakers and writers. A number of film scripts were now based on the reminiscences of citizens from ordinary towns. *Human Comedy* (1943) was initially drawn from the experiences of writer William Saroyan and his life in Fresno, California. It was very much the story of a town in which everyone was treated with respect, and of a family that was willing to accept the death of loved ones with only the barest hint of emotional devastation. In the extremely popular movie *Since You Went Away* (1944) prewar domestic life was idyllic, and women did all they could to maintain a warm and loving home for the male head to return to after he had served his nation. It was based on the personal life of writer Margaret Buell Wilder, who drew on her experience in Akron, Ohio.

Mackinley Kantor's story *Happy Land*, which was a widely read novel before it became a film, constituted a model of wartime sentiment. In the novel, published in 1942, Kantor drew heavily on the memory of his boyhood in Webster City, Iowa, to craft a mythical tale that illustrated why American life was worth defending without any qualms over the tragedy that loomed ahead. His narrative was centered on the town druggist, Lew Marsh, whose store served not only as an important business establishment but as a community center where citizens could gather for ice cream and gossip. When Marsh learns that his son Rusty has been killed in a naval battle, he has trouble accepting this tragic loss. But the boy's grandfather returns from the dead in a dream sequence to explain why such a sacrifice was necessary. He reviews the past life of the Marsh family in the town and how it was marked by happiness and had a history of men willing to fight for their country. The ghostly visitor says, "If an American small town isn't a good place for young folks to grow up, then I'm suffering from delusions." In the grandfather's estimation, the small town was also the breeding ground of war heroes: "I never heard tell that MacArthur came from a big city."

Many readers seemed to accept Kantor's point that life in the American town was idyllic and therefore worth defending at all costs. A resident of Kansas told the author that the tale reminded him of how much he "treasured" his boyhood in Iowa and should convince those who are "wondering why this nation must fight for its existence and if it [the war] is worthwhile." One woman wrote the author that she had not yet lost a son in the war but that if she did the story of *Happy Land* would be of "great help" to her. Another woman from Nebraska told Kantor she was going to introduce the book to her reading club because most of the members have relatives in the service and one had already lost a son. She indicated that the story would do them all a "lot of good." A minister from Boston told Kantor that he had actually used the story in a sermon and felt the example of the Marsh family would help "all Americans" accept wartime losses. And a mother living in Massachusetts said she had sent the novel to her son who was on Guadalcanal in the hope that it would "distract his mind from what the boys are having to take out there."[15]

Popular music also helped to sustain a sentimental view of Americans during the war years. Some songs like "God Bless America" were avowedly patriotic and were used to make explicit calls to support the war and purchase war bonds. But the music that sold the best resonated less with love of country and more directly with the possibilities of loving relationships once people returned home. These songs, like Kantor's tale, expressed a longing for a world not at war and evoked images and scenes, not of battlefield valor, but of home reunions and sexual fidelity. Thus, people tended to buy records like "Sentimental Journey" by Doris Day that spoke of putting one's heart at ease by taking a "sentimental journey home." And it should come as no surprise that the most popular song of the war era was "White Christmas," which called forth a memory of family holidays in some time before Pearl Harbor where children could listen to "sleigh bells in the snow."[16]

TURMOIL ON THE HOME FRONT

A sentimental culture could not, of course, fully mask the reality of commotion on the home front. Roosevelt himself discovered that there were distinct limits to the degree to which people were willing to sacrifice when he was forced to give up his effort to set limits on wages and prices. And wartime Washington was filled with charges of "greed, fraud, and negligence in the award of defense contracts." The level of upheaval in people's lives, in fact, was enormous. Historian William Tuttle has estimated that some 30 million Americans were forced to move because of the war—with 16 million of this number going into the armed forces. Between 1940 and 1944, some 200,000 migrants moved to the region around the massive Willow Run production facility near Detroit, with many coming from the Deep South. Shipbuilder Andrew Higgins, who eventually sold some 14,000 combat boats of all types to allied nations, saw his production force rise from 400 in 1941 to 20,000 by 1944. Another 400,000 men and women moved to the Los Angeles area and its booming aircraft industry, and more than 100,000 went to San Diego, a key naval port.[17]

The sense of change was particularly powerful in these boom towns that emerged almost overnight and whose alteration was fueled by rich government contracts that led to the building of new factories and shipbuilding facilities. Social tensions were exacerbated by the sudden infusion of people from various parts of the country seeking jobs and living space. Along with this economic growth came a booming night life. In 1942 adult night clubs in New York such as the Copacabana and the Latin Quarter saw unprecedented profits as people seemed to have "money to burn." "Honky-tonk districts" sprang up near military bases everywhere. In the red-light district of Albany, Georgia, "whores had their names displayed in neon signs." The moral situation in Fort Worth, Texas, seemed so bad that one advertisement for an apartment carried the warning that "no street-walkers, home wreckers, and drunks" were wanted. And in some cases, married couples who sought an apartment for rent were asked to supply a copy of their marriage license.[18]

Citizens of Orange, Texas, a major shipbuilding center near Beaumont, recalled the war years not as a time of military struggle but as a time of upheaval in the moral life of their community. Thousands of former sharecroppers from Arkansas, Texas, and Louisiana moved to the town as the population tripled during the first year of the conflict. One resident recalled that before the war everyone seemed to know everyone else, and that helped to "keep everyone else in line." The vast inflow of strangers, however, disrupted the sense for many that the town was a friendly and orderly place. Moral behavior appeared to be on the decline. Many newcomers, flush with cash and liberated from the older constraints of families and locale, now flocked to downtown Orange almost daily to have a good time. Tensions rose between sailors, war workers, and many older residents who resented the newcomers and their constant rounds of drinking and fighting. Julia Bacon, an Orange native, claimed that it became much less safe for girls to go into the downtown during the war than it had been earlier. Tensions also emerged with more women working outside the home. One resident claimed that the presence of women on the production lines now constituted a distinct threat to family stability and raised the possibility of more sexual affairs. "They'd work together three or four months," he remembered, "and the first thing you know they'd be quitting their wife or husband and . . . shacking up with somebody else." Another citizen of Orange agreed with the idea of moral disruption but said that "there was nothing you could do about it because that's what they wanted to do." A number of residents recalled an increase in racial tension as well. In one case, a man told of how local police would exploit blacks by simply taking beer and cigars without paying from establishments run by African Americans because they knew they were in no position to fight back.[19]

Concerns over the disintegration of community life were at times matched by anxiety over the fate of the traditional American family. The root problem was that both mothers and fathers were being asked to leave their homes in unprecedented numbers. One common fear was that now children would be less likely to receive the care they needed—especially, fatherly discipline. In a study of families in Iowa, investigators learned that when the government announced that fathers would become subject to the draft, many families were in shock. Some women expressed the fear that they would be unable to cope with the demands of generating an income and caring for offspring. The same report also indicated, however, that some females looked forward to the prospect of being free of male domination and control. And in a few cases both men and women looked forward to a government-induced separation in order to free them from "intolerable" marriage situations. Children, too, were affected by all of the coming and going. The Iowa study reported on one young girl who felt "badly frightened" and unloved when her father went into the service and her mother entered the workforce. Throughout the United States, in fact, there was an extensive discussion about the harm children might receive if they lost "motherly attention." Critics raised alarms about "latchkey" children, who spent the day at home without any parental control. One journalist traveling through boom towns reported on what she felt was a sense of "chaos" because of cases of "child neglect," although by 1944 the government was able to reduce some of this worry by creating more day-care facilities.[20]

The call to women to enter wartime jobs was never meant to signal a permanent change in traditional gender roles. Yet the scale of female employment was substantial. The percentage of women in the workforce increased by some 50 percent in the five years after 1940. And although many working women were forced to return to home duties in 1946, the percentage of females working outside the home began to rise again in 1947 and moved steadily upward through-out the next decade. Indeed, the typical "Rosie the Riveter" was not a newcomer to the workforce. She was likely to be a lower-class individual who needed a job before the war in order to supplement the income of the "breadwinner." War work was particularly attractive to these women because it offered them access to industrial wages that were usually much higher than they were able to earn be-fore 1941. This was true for both white and black "Rosies." In a study conducted by the Ford Motor Company at the time, it was found that 77 percent of the women employed in production had worked at least once before Pearl Harbor. For black women the new wages were especially valued, because so many of them had been consigned to poorly paid work as domestics.[21]

The upheaval in gender relations on the home front was matched as well by a rising level of mistrust between women at home and men away in the service. Sometimes the prospect of such separations caused couples to rush into hastily arranged marriages. But whether married or not, long-term separations often led to suspicions and break-ups. Servicemen a long way from home had access to a good deal of sex near military bases and overseas. John Costello, a scholar who has looked at such sexual tension in the war era, concluded that virtue itself was a casualty of the war experience and that the increase in separations led to count-less "wartime love affairs." The armed forces were even forced to conduct educa-tional campaigns designed to educate men on the dangers of syphilis and gonor-rhea. And numerous surveys conducted by army officials revealed that GIs generally distrusted their girlfriends back home. Scholars of wartime literature have also noted that fiction produced during the war era registered themes of a rising pattern of misogyny and hostility among men who felt that women could no longer be trusted. This was certainly true of literature authored by women. In novels written by men there was a tendency to talk now more about the role pros-titutes and foreign-born women played in their lives, for they were seen as more compliant or reliable than the women who remained at home.[22]

Domestic turmoil was grounded not only in concerns over family and moral stability but over racial issues as well. Various racial and cultural groups were thrown into close proximity after Pearl Harbor in ways that they had not been before the war. Sometimes the meeting of different people caused strains but did not lead to enormous levels of violence. Thus, "Okies" from Arkansas, Okla-homa, and Texas who flooded shipbuilding centers like Oakland or Mobile were often treated with derision. A teacher in the Alabama port expressed the hope that the "poor whites" would leave her community as soon as possible once the war was over. Because so many rural whites had moved northward to plants in Indiana during the struggle, people joked that there were now only forty-five states in the union instead of forty-eight, since Kentucky and Tennessee had moved to Indiana, and Indiana had gone to hell.[23]

There was little humor to be found, however, in the wartime clashes between blacks and whites. In Oakland, southern whites talked a great deal of how they had kept blacks in their place in the South and would do so again in California even if it meant raising again the threat of lynching. Indeed, throughout America the wartime legacy of racial conflict and violence was astounding. In Harlem and Detroit major race riots erupted in 1943, with the latter resulting in the death of some twenty-five African Americans and nine whites. In southern cities flooded with war workers and military inductees, the situation was no less explosive. In one incident in Mobile, white workers attacked twelve blacks because they were angry that some recent job promotions had gone to minorities. In Beaumont, allegations that a black man had raped a white woman caused several thousand war workers to march into black residential districts and wreak havoc for hours. Two blacks and one white were killed in this outburst, and thousands of blacks fled the city despite the fact that medical examinations showed the alleged victim had no sexual activity during a twenty-four-hour period around the time of the alleged incident. In Alexandria, Louisiana, in January 1942, just weeks after Pearl Harbor, an arrest of a black soldier in an African American entertainment district touched off a full-scale riot in which white military police and state troopers exchanged shots with African Americans. When the turmoil subsided, the War Department claimed that a number of blacks had been wounded but that none had been killed. In the remembrance of the event—discussed later in this book— African Americans would argue for decades that the government had covered up the reality of many black deaths and the full extent of the mistreatment of minority GIs in the community. In the same town in another incident, a Louisiana state trooper shot and killed a black soldier, but a grand jury refused to indict the alleged perpetrator. In Los Angeles, Mexican American youths, identified by the flamboyant "zoot suits" they wore, were badly beaten for several days by white sailors who often visited their neighborhoods looking for "women of color."[24]

Clearly, millions of citizens were more preoccupied with new work opportunities, moral qualms, changes in domestic arrangements, and even hatred than they were with high-minded liberal visions. While working and surveying wartime attitudes in the Oakland shipyards, Katherine Archibald noted that the attachment most people felt to the nation was real but weak. The citizens she met wanted the United States to win, hated the Germans and the Japanese, and were willing to pledge a percentage of their paychecks to the war effort, but that was about as far as it went. She found that many men of draft age in the shipyards did all they could to stay out of the service and keep jobs that were considered "essential." Many told her that they definitely hoped to escape induction, and one said that no shipyard worker he knew willingly left his job to enlist. Archibald detected a fair amount of "indifference" to the war and cynicism over speeches that said the war was being fought for "high ideals and splendid goals." To the people she met, the Four Freedoms and the Atlantic Charter were "passed over as so much pious patter from a Sunday school." Many workers told her that they were even skeptical of claims that the United States had only honorable intentions in the struggle and felt that only the wealthy would benefit from the entire war effort. A few even thought that a small group of businessmen and politicians had arranged the attack on Pearl Harbor in the first place. Archibald coined the term "shipyard patriotism" to describe the sarcasm she found in the Oakland yards.[25]

Of course, some Americans could not remain indifferent to the national endeavor to win the war no matter what their circumstances were. People with loved ones fighting abroad worried incessantly. Local newspapers carried a steady stream of news of men who were leaving for the service or who were missing or killed. The fate of those held dear and of neighbors was a topic of wide discussion in nearly every town. In Orange, Texas, Marion Tilley recalled how her husband thought about their son who was overseas so much that one day he told her that he had had a vision that the young man was standing next to him as he sat on his bed. The troubled father wrote down the date of his dream on a calendar, only to learn several weeks later that the boy had been killed on that very same date— November 8, 1942. Forty-five years later Marion Tilley still recalled the date of the vision and her son's death and the day her family received news of the tragedy. In Rice County, Minnesota, Albert Quie revealed that there was always a "great deal of talk" about the men who were in the armed forces and what they were doing. When news of a war death arrived, he claimed that "grief came upon the whole town." Vivian McMorrow of Howard Lake, Minnesota, remembered that when she learned of her husband's death at Normandy she asked her mother, "Are you sure this is not hell we are living in now? What did I do to deserve this hell?" And many parents were thrown into periods of agony for days and weeks, trying to learn something of the fate a child after receiving a telegram saying that he was missing in action.[26]

MEN AT WAR

Soldiers serving in the military found the war years to be as confusing as everyone else did. Certainly, there were those who felt a deep desire to help their country and accepted the need to uphold the Four Freedoms. Over 40,000 men
affirmed their opposition to all war and became conscience objectors. Many
more, however, were intent on repaying the Japanese for their attack, and thousands concluded that they had little choice in the matter and presumed that they
would have to join the fight sooner or later. Peter Kindsvatter, who studied the attitudes of some of the soldiers, told the story of a young man from Mississippi
who went to war because he realized that people in his hometown would never
tolerate the idea of an able-bodied fellow taking an essential war job as a way of
escaping the draft and because most of his friends on the local high school foot-
ball team had already expressed an interest in becoming marines or fighter pilots. A chaplain who had sailed to Europe in both world wars recalled that GIs in
the 1940s seemed more somber and not nearly as eager to fight. And while most
complied with the call to arms, the military in the 1940s still felt the need to station MPs armed with submachine guns at several ports of embarkation to deter
men from fleeing as they stood in line to board a ship.[27]

Most examinations of why men fight in wars stress the primacy of private
goals over public ones. This did not mean that broad political and ideological visions had no meaning to soldiers in World War II. Many of the men noted such
ideas in letters they wrote home and made comments such as "Germany must
be stopped" or a fight must be made for the "freedom and the life of a united
people." Generally, however, their letters dwelt on private affairs. This may seem
inevitable and may even be attributed to the fact that their correspondence was
censored. But the key in understanding their preoccupation with "home" and ordinary events such as family life was also to be found in the symbolic implications of what "home" meant in the early 1940s. In a time of turmoil, it was imagined to be a place where—unlike in the military—individual men counted for
something and life was not so vulnerable and regulated. Thus, most letters were
filled with questions and accounts of parents and siblings, of the whereabouts of
friends who were now working or serving somewhere else as well, of births,
deaths, and other routine occurrences. And such correspondence also allowed
soldiers to express intimate feelings of love and caring when the lives they were
now living often seemed to be so much more impersonal.[28]

Letters written home also offered a glimpse of how the men saw actual combat and reported on it to their loved ones. In a sense, much of what they wrote

countered the more ideological frames on the war that circulated through wartime propaganda. Edgar Shepard, a marine on Guadalcanal, wrote his parents
about how a friend sacrificed his life to save him by fighting off Japanese attackers in hand-to-hand combat. Shepard described how his buddy killed two enemy
soldiers with his knife as he was trained and then was killed by a bayonet to his
back. He said the event had given him a new reason to fight: to avenge the death
of the "best pal I ever had." Paul Curtis, who was fighting in Italy, wrote home to
his brother about his experience at Anzio. He explained how he had felt fear, anger,
hunger, thirst, exhaustion, loneliness, and homesickness and said that the "cries of
the wounded are pitiful." Others wrote of seeing "hundreds of dead and wounded"
and of blowing up the enemy on bombing runs. Some even told of the racial discrimination and poor treatment accorded black soldiers by American forces. A soldier from Nebraska told his parents of seeing the destruction at Nagasaki and Japanese people walking around a "dead city." He surmised that these victims must
have thought "What manner of people would do such a thing to us?"[29]

Glimpses inside the mind of GIs can be obtained not only from their letters
but from the results of numerous opinion surveys conducted during the 1940s.
These polls indicated that the war was essentially ill-defined in the minds of the
GIs who fought in it. They confirmed that there was, in fact, wide disagreement
over why the nation was fighting. Samuel Stouffer, who helped direct one of the
largest surveys of soldier opinion, concluded that there was, indeed, a "basic unanimity" that the war could not be avoided but that there appeared to be "an absence of thinking about the meaning of the war." From a 1942 sample of opinions of 6,000 troops, Stouffer found that some 91 percent agreed with the
statement that "we have to fight now if we are to survive." Moreover, one year
later, he discovered that only about 13 percent of the men could name at least
three of the Four Freedoms. And about one-third of this sample failed to give any
response to the question of why the nation was waging the war. One-quarter of
the 1943 groups did say they were in a struggle to defend the nation—which
most likely inferred that they saw their homes threatened as well. When it came
to political goals, only 16 percent of the 1943 group said they were fighting for
"freedom" or "democracy," and some 15 percent noted the need to rid the world
of Fascism.[30]

There is even evidence that some men found the prospect of war attractive because it seemed like an opportunity to experience a unique sense of
adventure—at least before one entered actual combat. Men sent to the Pacific
sometimes saw it as a chance to see "exotic places" and looked upon a trip to the
Far East as a stroke of good fortune. Quite a few American soldiers had never

seen an ocean and looked forward to doing so. And many were attracted to the idea of actually going to the South Pacific, which had often been pictured by Hollywood as a paradise filled with strange landscapes and exotic women. In his study of the First Marine Division, Craig Cameron discovered that many soldiers collected photographic images of native women as they moved through the area. Peter Schrijvers concluded that for some men the "craving for seeing new exotic places" like the South Pacific was so strong that it even survived the horrible experience of jungle combat itself. Many men not only took to the region mythical images of women but also fantasies of warrior heroes doing battle against savage enemies that they had gleaned from Hollywood features and from marine training itself. Thus, senior officers on Guadalcanal told their troops to think of frontiersmen in the American past who were able to enter "Indian Country" and track and kill a brutal enemy. Marine training also fostered ideas of strong men and virile warriors who had the capacity to vanquish all who stood in their way.[31]

The first encounter with the war came, of course, not in some exotic paradise but in boot camp. The camp was a transition zone between home and the military, and it produced not only trained soldiers but also a good deal of resentment. Part of the problem was that military training by nature sought to erode the strong sense of individualism that many Americans felt. Military thinking was not like the liberal progressivism of the political culture and was not designed to respect the dignity of the singular person. On the contrary, it stressed the need for regimentation and for individuals to subordinate their own interests to the demands of a larger group. Most recruits understood this to a point as well as the fact that military discipline was necessary to the basic operation of the armed forces. Military recruiters in the 1940s were also aware, however, that there was a fundamental level of antagonism to their approach. Authorities, consequently, had to devise recruitment strategies that presented the various branches of the service as somewhat respectful of the "individuality and autonomy" of each serviceman. The Army would frequently focus recruitment messages on the notion that military training sought to achieve a balance between personal accomplishments and the type of teamwork that many men had experienced in playing various sports. This tension between independence and submission lingered throughout the war and accounted for some bitter feeling among veterans after the conflict as well as for some of the opposition Americans would display toward calls for Universal Military Training after 1945.[32]

Enlisted men resented not only the loss of personal freedom but a military class system that privileged officers to a significant extent. Soldiers were frequently upset that officers tended to have better food and liquor—and certainly better quarters. That is why, in part, GIs revered leaders who seemed to have their best interests at heart. GIs also suspected that some officers were promoted for their "ruthlessness in battle," a perspective that in their minds led to an excessive number of casualties. Many men were also incensed by what they felt was a tendency for officers to make them perform a whole series of meaningless tasks or jobs that they called "chickenshit." Such assignments were perceived to be not only irrelevant to winning the war but a form of "petty harassment of the weak by the strong." Kitchen duty especially bothered them, as did standing for long periods of time for weapons to be inspected. Paul Fussell, who served in the Army, said that the men recognized "chickenshit" instantly and always resented it.[33]

Aware of some of the discontent within the enlisted ranks, military officers tried to provide an outlet. One answer they had was to authorize the publication of *Yank,* a War Department newspaper given free to servicemen. Its popularity was partially due to the fact that it printed "pinup pictures" of gorgeous women and stories by GIs who were stationed in war zones all over the globe. But it was also widely appreciated because it allowed the men a chance to express their own dissatisfaction with a number of aspects of military life. Thus, letters to the paper often complained about unfair treatment from officers. A comic strip entitled "Sad Sack" furthered the effort to expose GI discontent. The pages of *Yank* made it clear that the officers who earned respect were those who diligently tried to minimize the distance between themselves and enlisted men and were willing to sleep in the mud instead of looking for special quarters and privileges.[34]

In combat, individual grievances and a desire for personal autonomy generally gave way to a deep attachment to comrades-in-arms. Men bonded closely in battle as a way to protect each other. Although only about one million men out of some sixteen million who served in World War II actually experienced extended combat, the bonds among actual combatants were powerful. This process of coalescing usually began in basic training, where some men arrived with the romantic idea that the war would be a test of individual strength and bravery. In the wartime military, however, the plan was not to make men think they would become heroes by single-handedly charging ahead with bayonets fixed (as some recruits thought) but in integrating them into an effective fighting unit that was part of a much larger organization. It was true that massive amounts of technology and equipment often counted for much more than individual acts of courage and best explained the ultimate American victory. But on the ground men had to come together rather than stand alone if they were going to succeed. S. L. A. Mar-

shall, who studied American troops in combat during the war, concluded that
"battle morale comes from unity" and that it rose or fell depending on how much
the sense of solidarity was "felt by the ranks." In a 1944 survey of some 500
American infantrymen, the respondents said that they were able to keep fighting, not because of leadership, discipline, or political idealism, but because of the
"solidarity" they felt with their battle group and "thoughts of loved ones." Historian Gerald Linderman concluded that the impact of comradeship was pivotal
and "visceral" and was at times felt more powerfully than any attachment to
home. In fact, soldiers often felt estranged from home when they were fighting
not only because they were being pulled into the battle unit but because they resented the privileges people back home had and the comparably peaceful lives
they lived, while they had to suffer and die. In dire emergencies men thought
very little of home or political dreams. William Manchester remembered that
when he fought in Okinawa the men he knew thought not of flag or country or
even the Marine Corps but only of "one another."[35]

Despite the commonality of battlefield unity, the experience of war also produced a new set of emotional problems for the GIs. Combat led to conflicting attitudes. There were those who could not bring themselves to fire their weapons
in the face of enemy fire, and others, like Joe Kennedy, who craved opportunities
to become a war hero and upstage his brother, who would eventually become
president. Some felt elation over seeing an enemy plane go down and were awed
by the spectacle of the "dazzling lights of a firefight at night." A few found the
sight of tracer bullets darting through the sky erotic. And yet feelings of elation
could be short-lived and quickly followed by a pervasive sense of vulnerability.
Men in battle could also feel demoralized, an attitude captured in the wartime
saying that there was a bullet somewhere with their name on it. Feelings of powerlessness sometimes pushed some men to commit atrocities that allowed them
to feel that some sense of potency had been restored in their lives. Thus, men on
both sides killed unarmed prisoners and desecrated the bodies of enemy dead.
Certainly, there were GIs who felt uncomfortable with such acts, but they generally tolerated them. Evidence suggests that American troops were more likely to
commit such acts against the Japanese than against the Germans—a fact that
was partially explained by attitudes of racism and revenge that dominated combat in the Pacific. Japanese weapons and body parts were often collected and sent
home as souvenirs. Yet such deeds were committed in Europe as well. In 1943
soldiers from the American 45th Division created controversy when they claimed
that they were merely following orders when they gunned down unarmed German and Italian prisoners in a number of separate incidents in Sicily.[36]

Men far from home often sought sexual gratification wherever they could find it. There were, of course, GIs who remained faithful to their wives and girlfriends back home, but others struggled with such commitments. Hyman Samuelson, a white officer in a largely African American engineer battalion in New Guinea, recorded in his diary the conflict he felt between feelings he had for his wife in Louisiana and the lust he felt for an Australian nurse. He actually wrote home to tell his spouse of the joy he experienced from his affair with the nurse. Thousands of GIs found wives overseas and brought them back to America. Yet it appears that most of the sex the men had was more utilitarian. Prostitutes were one outlet. Economically desperate women in places such as war-torn Italy provided another opportunity for a physical relationship. Thus, it is not surprising to learn that the arrival of a large number of GIs in a European city inevitably brought a dramatic rise in the incidence of venereal disease. In Manila, after Douglas Mac-Arthur's forces returned, it was estimated that some 8,000 "native" females offered prostitution services to American forces. An army survey in 1945 on sexual behavior revealed that the "level of promiscuity" rose the longer a man remained overseas, that some 80 percent of the men acknowledged having sex with women they met abroad, and that many felt women back home were unfaithful. Rape by American troops at times became an issue, as it did on Okinawa and in Germany in 1945. Rates of venereal disease tended to decline when men were involved in combat but rose dramatically when there was a lull in the fighting. Army officials warned the troops incessantly about the health dangers of many of their sexual practices and issued condoms. Yet wartime conditions were unpredictable, and it was not uncommon for officials to conclude that the war had led to "unbelievable degeneracy" when it came to sex.[37]

Some of the suffering and chaos the men faced in the war was duly reported to the home front by acclaimed correspondents such as Ernie Pyle and Bill Mauldin. Traveling with the GIs to fighting zones, these writers risked their lives to sustain a critical perspective on the war and affirm some level of respect for men who were feeling increasingly insignificant in the midst of a vast military machine fixed on winning. Pyle wrote in 1944 that "everyone by now knows how I feel about the infantry. I am a rabid one-man movement bent on tracking down and stamping out everybody who doesn't fully appreciate the common front-line soldier." Mauldin felt the same way. He affirmed that he had real "affection" for the "old battered outfits" that had slogged through the war over a period of several years and fought numerous campaigns in Europe and Asia. He claimed that he truly admired these men, whom he felt had given so much of themselves and received so little in return. His cartoons captured the encounter of the men he called "dogfaces" with the war and the feelings and attitudes they held. For Mauldin the ordinary GIs had "nobility" and "dignity" because they risked their own lives to help each other.[38]

Mauldin was not only empathetic toward the common soldier's plight but willing to give voice to his discontents, especially their gripes about officer privilege. In some of his cartoons, officers appeared indifferent to the downtrodden lives that many of their men spent in harsh circumstances and seemed more interested in their own needs. In one drawing his fictitious characters, Willie and Joe, are seen after a battle in Italy pondering a remark made to them by another soldier who envied them because he thought they would now get the "first pick o' wimmen an licker" as they entered a liberated town. Willie and Joe, of course, knew well that such fruits of victory would go to their superiors. Mauldin, a mid-century champion of the common man, seldom treated members of the officer corps well in his depictions and tended to respect only those leaders who were admired by the rank and file themselves. Thus, he brought Joe and Willie to life again after the war to honor George C. Marshall on the occasion of his death in 1959 and Omar Bradley when he passed away in 1981. Ironically, however, Mauldin did not address the death of the ordinary soldiers represented by his characters during the war. He found such a subject difficult to talk about and said, "I don't describe dead guys being buried in bloody bed sacks because I can't imagine anyone who has become adjusted to it."[39]

The compassion shown by Pyle and Mauldin toward the men was understandable, but at times it actually undermined the very critical perspective they were seeking to preserve. Although both correspondents certainly raised the issue of the tragic costs of the war in terms of the suffering of American men and the idea that GIs were victims of forces beyond their control, they also reinforced larger efforts in the culture of the early 1940s to mythologize the American people as virtuous and devoid of dangerous impulses. Censorship had some role in explaining this. Yet the concern these observers demonstrated toward the welfare of the GIs, the extent to which they talked of their being innocents thrust into a horrible situation, and their tendency to stress the victimization of the men at the expense of their agency, tended to reinforce the image of American goodness and determination. In his various portraits of the men, Pyle would frequently stress their strong connection to their prewar worlds by informing his readers of the hometowns where their families lived and worked. Alienation or inequality, for instance, never seemed to be part of the lives they had lived prior to the war—a point that simply was not true.

In the midst of remaking these men into sympathetic figures and raising

questions about the war, the correspondents also participated in the larger project to mythologize America as a place and the generation of Americans who were
doing the fighting. Because they were portrayed as raised in loving families and
congenial hometowns and as willing to soldier on despite the hardships, it
was easy to accept the notion that these men were virtuous and that in no way
could any of them be natural-born killers. It is interesting, in fact, to observe Pyle
treading carefully around the issue of American-driven violence in the war. He
stressed that the men he knew were quite capable of being good warriors and
killing the enemy and admitted they had become "wise in animal-like ways of
self-preservation," and he affirmed that they "knew how to take care of themselves and how to lead others." About one soldier from Iowa he wrote that the
man was a "great soldier" and so good-natured that it was hard to imagine that
he could kill anyone. Mauldin also admitted that many of the men he met in Europe were not the same "clean-cut" men many knew at home. He reasoned that
they had to kill or be killed but reassured his readers that "you don't become a
killer in war." Both Pyle and Mauldin seemed to be accepting a central point of
the frontier myth that the aggression American troops demonstrated was only
temporary.

The figures described by these war correspondents not only lacked natural instincts to commit violent acts but also had no political dreams. Willie and Joe had
little to say about the Four Freedoms or patriotism, a portrayal that was consistent with the wartime surveys of GI attitudes. Mauldin admitted that he had refrained from trying to picture the war "in a big broad-minded way" in order to
focus on their personal struggles. The characters in the work of Pyle and Mauldin,
in fact, bore little resemblance to those in John Hersey's 1944 Pulitzer Prize–
winning novel, A Bell for Adano. In Hersey's book, set in a liberated town in Italy
during the war, an American officer is dedicated to bringing New Deal–type reforms to the community, which had suffered under Fascist rule. Ultimately, the
figures created by Pyle and Mauldin were meant to serve as players in a moral
drama. Their war was not a worthwhile endeavor to save the nation or even to
promote a better world. It was a drama in which the actors were stripped of their
individuality and pushed into the depths of a moral vacuum. Yet Pyle and Mauldin
brought to the cultural debate over what the war meant not only a critical perspective but a mythical one as well when they downplayed the aggressive actions
and instincts of many of the men they described. Their characters were both real
and fictive, and in a sense they served as props in a performance that revealed the
widespread debates and viewpoints that circulated through the public mind during a period of sudden rupture and change.[40]

The mental landscape of wartime America was an uneven one, marked by various fractures and fissures. Doubts and confusion over the social and moral changes that marked the period were pervasive, and public attitudes toward the world struggle were varied and often confused. It was for this reason that the government worked hard to promote sentimental and high-minded images of Americans and the battle they fought. In the aftermath of the war, many of the controversies of wartime would, in fact, persist and continue to stand at the center of the long debate over the meaning of World War II.

CHAPTER TWO

SOLDIERS WRITE THE WAR

SOME SOLDIERS STARTED TO fashion memories of the war soon after it ended by writing extensive accounts of what they saw and felt. Less accepting of Roosevelt's optimism about creating a better world, and deeply suspicious of the sentimental language of the war years that characterized the motivations and attitudes of men like themselves, these literary-minded veterans were ultimately responsible for producing the most critical remembrance of the American experience in World War II ever offered to the public. The writings and recollections of these soldiers were not always explicit antiwar statements, and at times they supported traditional perspectives on the conflict. Overall, however, they provided substantial testimony that was designed to refute the widespread layer of patriotic virtue that had marked their times—or what soldier/author Paul Fussell called "moral simplification"—and insisted that many of the men who served their nation now felt more like victims than heroes.[1]

Like literary-minded veterans from other nations who served in the wars of the twentieth century, these writers were generally disillusioned by their encounters with military authority and mechanized warfare and troubled by a moral outlook that sanctioned indiscriminate killing. The most successful of them also recognized that there was a market for their views. After analyzing novels authored by soldiers from both world wars, a critic like Malcolm Cowley noticed that both generations provided accounts that were "painfully honest." He thought he noticed, however, that men writing after 1945 were also "more disheartened." That is to say, they expressed little hope that the problem of war and violence would ever go away and that people would sufficiently question mythical images of national innocence that helped to sustain a martial spirit. Thus, the stories they told—in novels, memoirs, and fact-based reports—not only stressed the tragic costs of the war more than the gains but to a surprising extent rendered a harsh judgment on the character of the Americans themselves and their political and military leadership. Their version of the war seemed haunted more by dark forces in the veterans' homeland than in evil regimes abroad. With many public spaces resistant to such an ironic version of the war, these veterans turned to the relatively open terrain of literature to fashion stories that were more pessimistic than cheerful.[2]

Certainly, there were books and articles that took pride in the war effort and that praised the extensive military planning and civilian production that went into the victory—books such as Dwight Eisenhower's *Crusade in Europe* and Henry Luce's *Life's Picture History of World War II*, which referred to the American victory as a "tremendous feat." Such writings tended to offer what James Dawes has referred to as a "therapeutic narration" of the event and served to expunge from public memory the convoluted and idiosyncratic nature of personal experience. The efforts of these soldiers turned authors, however, did what modern literature has done best—probe the twisted reality of individual experience in ways that subverted attempts to mythologize it. The fact that their subjects tended to be GIs plagued by feelings of confusion, anger, bitterness, and hatred was no invention. They carried to the public the real feelings of millions of enlisted men who had found military life repressive and demeaning. Most of the characters fashioned by literary veterans emerged from the war with an uneasy feeling that the future would be driven not by individuals in charge of their own destiny but by large-scale organizations and massive bureaucracies—much like the military organizations they had just served. Seldom did the figures in these stories think about grand political ideas or national destiny. Their public role was centered more on the critical effort to insist that the war be recalled less as an American victory and more as a warning that hopes for a more democratic America and for a better world for all men and women everywhere were fragile at best.[3]

THE ASSAULT ON VIRTUE

Just three years after the surrender of Japan, Norman Mailer published his probing novel of the American personality, *The Naked and the Dead*. A veteran of the Pacific war who felt a tremendous sense of relief when he heard the news of the atomic bombings and realized it would remove the need for men like him to invade the Japanese homeland, Mailer still managed to fashion a highly critical appraisal of the American war effort. He was impressed less by the virtue of the American victory and more by the level of brutality the United States was able to muster to defeat its foes. He saw the American show of force not as a temporary regression into a savage state but as a true reflection of an antidemocratic streak within the American soul. The fact that the story was set on a Pacific island was also important, because Mailer believed that, unlike the fight against Fascism in Europe, the struggle in the Pacific was basically an "imperialist" struggle on the part of the United States. Guided by the "long symbolic arm of MacArthur," it was more about the recovery of the Philippines than about the Four Freedoms. Mailer wrote to one of the readers of his book that the Pacific war revealed "all the cancerous tendencies of American life." The novel makes it clear that this American drive for dominance over others was already manifested every day in the ruthless competitive struggle that marked American capitalism and that moved easily into the theater of war. Many of his characters actually find satisfaction in fighting the Japanese and inflicting as much pain as they can. For these men the war is not an unwanted intrusion into their lives thrust upon them by Pearl Harbor but a welcome opportunity to let go of the anger and frustration many of them had accumulated in struggling to forge a home and work life in America itself. In 1957 Mailer further expanded his discussion of American violence, connecting it to the existence of racial oppression in the United States in his essay "The White Negro." For him the war had "presented a mirror to the human condition which blinded anyone who looked at it." That nations used atom bombs and "concentration camps" proved that all men were dangerous and that any nation could bring "psychic havoc" to its own citizens.[4]

The Naked and the Dead is marked not only by a disparaging outlook on the nation's war effort but by a sensitivity to life in the working class, a suggestion that Mailer was working partially within the political frame of the Popular Front, with its tendency to see war and modern society as exploitive of lower-class individuals. His effort to offer a history of working-class life in America in the 1930s and 40s is to be found mostly in background sketches he created for a number of the GIs who fight. For instance, Sam Croft, a soldier from West Texas, is a man fixated on killing Japanese troops. In the masculine culture in which he was raised, he hunted deer with his father and listened to countless conversations between ranch hands in bunkhouses—conversations that were heavily racist and misogynist. These men were fond of hard drinking, taking whores to bed and beating them, and talking about wives who could not be trusted. Life was equally unsettling for Red Valen, who was raised in the rough culture of a Montana mining town. When his father was killed in the mines, he expected that he would help support his mother. Yet he soon tired of the prospect of replicating his father's life, which included long bouts with alcohol and frequent marital quarrels. Pearl Harbor represented for him not an unwarranted attack on the nation but a chance to get away from traditional work and family routines that he had come to despise. Another GI recalled a past where hard times had forced him to work as a bellhop for tips. He made little money, Mailer wrote, but "there was always women and liquor" to be had. The Army at first represented a chance for him to be a "free man," but he was eventually disillusioned by the vast amount of inequality and injustice he saw in the service.[5]

Mailer's men share not only a troubled past but a dim view of the future. There are a few who truly see the struggle as a "people's war" and accept the high-minded liberalism of the Roosevelt administration and the idea that all of the suffering would lead to a better life for men and women everywhere. But most of his soldiers are more cynical than that. Croft, for instance, is so intent on defeating his enemy and besting his own rivals in the Army that he pays little attention to liberal visions of postwar life. And General Edward Cummings (who probably represents MacArthur) explicitly rejects any talk that the time to come would represent a "Century of the Common Man" and the idea of liberal humanitarianism. For Cummings, it would be a century of the "Right," led by powerful and "omnipotent" men like himself. Inequality and exploitation were here to stay. In the general's estimation, Americans were driven, ultimately, not by dreams of justice but by the pursuit of power and wealth and by the drive to climb over anyone who stood in their way.

The reaction of readers and reviewers to Mailer's book supported the idea that many Americans in the postwar era shared his sense of despair. Their gloom was tied to two strands of thought that were prominent in the work of Mailer and other soldier-writers. First, the war's massive slaughter suggested that all men—including Americans—had such a capacity for evil that optimistic hopes of a better world were fragile at best. Second, the experience with mechanized warfare and army mobilizations had left many veterans feeling that individuals no longer counted for much. One reader wrote that the novel exposed the "faults and frailties" of human beings and that some of Mailer's characters showed that even American men could act only with "one dominant instinct—the urge to kill." Another reader from New York City told Mailer that he had exposed the "decay and putrefaction of our so-called moral codes" and that it was troubling that "our civilized behavior finds its greatest expression in war." A woman from Fresno, California, concluded that "the world can't be that evil" but said, "I know it is true word for word." She urged the young author to keep up the task of writing more "terrible books" and "terrible words" as a way to counter all the "nice" ones. Others complained that his story was simply too negative and were disappointed that the "fascist" Cummings crushed more liberal thinkers among the GIs, insisting that some soldiers fought in the real war because they found fascism abhorrent. But most comments in letters and reviews found the book to be a more honest rendition of the brutality of war and the warriors than was normally found in the nation at this time and accepted the premise that whatever else it was, World War II was to a substantial extent a "war without dignity."[6]

James Jones was another army veteran who worked from the perspective of the political Left and devoted a considerable part of his literary efforts to a remembrance of his experience. In his 1951 novel *From Here to Eternity*, which is set in Hawaii on the eve of the Pearl Harbor attack, Americans struggle mightily with their relationships to the military and to each other. His portrait of American life, like Mailer's, is far from flattering. Mythical takes on the men who serve are explicitly rejected. Near the end of the story a woman named Lorene, who had worked as a prostitute in Honolulu but is forced to return to the safety of the mainland now that war has broken out, tells a friend about a former lover who was killed in fighting off the Japanese attack and who earned a medal for his efforts. Readers of the novel know, however, that that the man (Robert Prewitt) actually hated army life and was drunk and AWOL on the morning of December 7, 1941. In reality, he was shot by military police for resisting arrest. Not all stories of wartime valor were to be believed.[7]

Prewitt, like many other characters in the tales soldiers wrote, was more than a representation of a GI. He was also another in a line of working-class men who had suffered from the poor economy of the prewar decade. Raised in the mountains of Kentucky near the West Virginia border, Prewitt was an American victim. His father beat him from time to time, and his mother died of consumption when he was in the seventh grade. He had an uncle who was killed in labor conflicts that erupted in Harlan County during the 1930s, and his entire family struggled endlessly with poverty. Prewitt did think for a time that the military might offer a way out of this troublesome life, but in the end he found it to be a place where the oppression of the ordinary man simply continued.

Despite the fact that his mother had begged the young man to refrain from acts of violence—a rejection of his father's behavior—he enlisted in the Army when he was seventeen. Sent to Schofield Barracks near Pearl Harbor, Prewitt found military life unsatisfying and punctuated with enormous pressures to conform and with a vast array of privileges for officers. His captain, who believed strongly that "good athletes make for good soldiering," forced the new recruit to go against his mother's pleas by joining a boxing team. With no war going on at the time, boxing competitions provided officers a chance to advance their careers—a point that resonated with many in the 1940s who felt some officers put their own interests above those of their men. Feeling frustrated and fearful that "we are livin' in a world blowing itself to hell as fast as five hundred million people can arrange it," he decided to go AWOL and into the arms of Lorene. Rejecting any call to patriotic service, he exclaimed that the only thing a man can do is "find something that's his."[8]

Jones uses Prewitt to articulate some Popular Front sensibilities as well—impressions that would gradually fade from the public remembrance of the war. Prewitt claimed that he had learned of the need to resist capitalist and racist exploitation in the 1930s from the movies, not from the labor movement. He especially liked films like *The Grapes of Wrath* and actors like John Garfield. From Hollywood he claimed that he learned the value of "fighting for the underdog against the top dog." He asserted that he would definitely fight for Jews in Germany but not for the ones who run Wall Street or even Hollywood itself. "And if the Capitalists were the top dog in America and the proletariat the underdog," he said that he would fight the Capitalists and would stand for "Negroes against Whites everywhere." Prewitt finds a kindred spirit named Angelo Maggio, a shipping clerk from New York City. But Maggio is also beaten down and is eventually killed in a fight in the service. Both men are grim reminders of how Jones— in typical left-wing fashion—saw the war not only as a contest against totalitarianism but as another example of how powerful institutions exploit ordinary people.[9]

From Here to Eternity takes the rare step in a soldier's version of the war of letting women speak extensively. They too contend with conflicting emotions and troubling relationships. Karen Holmes, the wife of Prewitt's captain, is highly critical of her husband's ideal of devotion to military service and embarks on a series of affairs in a desperate search for happiness. She wonders aloud if women might follow alternative paths through adult life that involve more than a forced march from virginity to marriage to becoming a grandmother. Lorene, on the other hand, would prefer marriage to her life as a prostitute. If she cannot find a husband, she would at least like to have a degree of respectability in her life. Toward that end she earnestly saves her money in the hope that someday she will be able to build a home for herself and her mother and join a country club. She reasons that if she could attain middle-class status she would be in a better position to attract "proper men with the proper position" and build a traditional marriage with a home and children.

Jones himself had been stationed at Schofield Barracks when the Japanese planes arrived and in the aftermath of the attack felt strongly that the world he knew would be changing dramatically and that he might not live much longer. His personal fears of going into combat were not explored in the first volume of his wartime trilogy, but they were treated in the second one, *The Thin Red Line*, published in 1962. In this story, enlisted men now move slowly and figuratively into a brutal encounter with the Japanese on Guadalcanal. His fictional soldiers are thinking less about creating a better world and more about their manhood and whether they could hold up under fire. They thought long and hard about whether they would be able to cross the "thin red line" between sanity and madness and about whether it would be possible to cross back again.

Traditional interpretations of World War II come under severe attack in this novel. In the first instance, the myth of individualism, or the idea that the singular person will be able to determine their own future as an American citizen, is completely undermined. Some are killed, but few gain any sense of redemption or honor from their participation in the fight against the enemy. Old-line soldiers in this portrait of the Army are surly and disdainful of war, and they look upon new recruits as "cannon fodder." Newcomers—represented by two privates named Doll and Fife—are presented as fresh-faced youth with considerable naïveté who embrace the myth that the war will offer them a chance to test their courage though man-to-man combat. Indeed, Jones portrays the young recruits as imaging the war as something to be settled by one-on-one bayonet fights and individual deeds. Thus, on his voyage to Guadalcanal, Doll scours the ship for a pistol that he can strap to his waist before meeting the Japanese. Once in battle, the men quickly see the falsity of many of their prewar beliefs. Everything is determined not by personal heroics but by a random and chaotic set of events. As Fife concludes, there is simply too much to watch out for and it is as easy to get killed by accident as by enemy fire. Men soon realize that their fates are no longer in their hands and that they are now merely being offered up for sacrifice.

GIs on Guadalcanal come to see that they are now not only highly vulnerable, no matter what type of gun they carry, but just as brutal as their foes. Guadalcanal proved to the characters in this story—and to many real Americans in the early 1940s—that they certainly could perform as competent soldiers against what was perceived to be a savage-like enemy. But this knowledge was tempered by the realization that they themselves had little qualms about killing. An American colonel in Jones's remembrance—who happened to carry a revolver in a low-slung holster—remarked after an encounter with the enemy that his men had now been "bloodied," or initiated into the culture of war. They would now see that they were driven to fight not by high ideals but by the "savage happiness" or "joyous feeling" many of them derived by killing those that threatened them. Sergeant John Bell saw this when he watched a fellow GI pull the body of a Japanese soldier from a mass grave with brute strength just to get a souvenir. And in another moment in the story, an American fighter who had already knocked a

Japanese soldier unconscious continued to emit an "animal scream" as he kicked the man, clawed at him, bayoneted him, and shot him over and over again. It was scenes like this that made Bell think that once the war was over such men would gather at a local American Legion hall and tell stories that failed to acknowledge that "once they had seen something animal within themselves that terrified them." In fact, Bell thought the process of denial was already underway on Guadalcanal. He noticed that the guilt some carried from taking the life of another was outweighed by the excitement many now felt over defeating their enemies. In the war novels of both Mailer and Jones, American men kill not only because they have to but because they want to. Some do so to survive; others are driven by rage and revenge. Bell even says that he was aroused sexually after assaulting a Japanese position and that the prospect of such excitement caused him to volunteer for another patrol.[10]

The last volume in the Jones trilogy, Whistle (1978), placed the GI back home in a military hospital after the war, replicating the author's own postwar return. A release from the stress of battle did not bring peace of mind, however, and his characters are now haunted by their memory of war and the physical and emotional scars it brought. The transition of leaving the war now appears as difficult as that required to enter it in the first place. Men plunge into an endless rounds of drinking and sex not only to forget what they have just endured but to recapture some of what they thought they missed when they were away. There are no homecoming celebrations for these men, no rejoicing over GI benefits, and no sense of satisfaction that they have served their country. They are too preoccupied with their war wounds, and they are actually reluctant to cut the ties to comrades they had formed in battle. As they assess their military experience, they conclude that the war was won not by any exceptional performance of duty on their part but by the workings of massive bureaucracies that orchestrated the use of men and machines. If they happened to survive, they were convinced it was due simply to pure luck. And if the past was contingent upon good fortune and large-scale organizations, then who was to say these same forces would not shape the future and again leave them at the mercy of powers beyond their control? One GI exclaimed that the "wins and losses of this war" were governed by "industrial percentages," and certainly not by acts of "individual heroism."[11]

A memory of the war that downgraded the potential of the individual and tarnished the promise that men could derive honor and redemption for their deeds was encapsulated in the story of Bobby Prell, a wounded veteran in Jones's fictitious hospital ward. Prell won the Congressional Medal of Honor but paid for this award with a pair of mangled legs. Army doctors recommended amputation, but the young soldier had learned from the war and from serving in the military not to trust authority. Thus, he insisted that any operation be delayed. His buddies rallied to his side as well and pleaded with hospital officials to try to save his legs. Marion Landers, a GI from Indiana, passionately supported Prell's resistance to amputation, not because he wanted to save humanity, but simply to help his friend. "We don't give a shit about humanity," Landers exclaimed. The men in the hospital even raised the idea of circulating a petition to see that the man's legs were saved—an act of defiance to military authority that would have seemed preposterous in the wartime Army. Yet, it was the type of action that some men had dreamed about in the real military, where many had concluded that officials had often issued orders that resulted in unnecessary deaths and injuries. In the end, Prell's delaying tactics actually help to save his limbs.

The men in *Whistle* find no solace in being home again and certainly little consolation from medals. Landers goes AWOL from the hospital and returns to his hometown, only to find that he does not feel comfortable there anymore. Other men are upset to find that their wives had cheated on them and return to more rounds of alcohol and parties. In the end, Landers takes his own life and Prell is killed in a barroom brawl while on a tour to sell war bonds. *Whistle* insists that the soldier's view of the war as tragic not be forgotten. One GI near the end of the book even gives a speech in a public square, calling upon all soldiers and veterans to unite into a political movement that would insist that wars be ended for all time. But no one is listening to the speaker, and one bystander calls him a communist. In such a moment, fictional space mirrored closely the actual public culture of the postwar era.[12]

The most famous novel to critique the American war effort, *Catch-22*, was written by Joseph Heller and appeared in 1961. Since *Catch-22* appeared as a film in 1970, many have tied its antiwar message to the realities of Vietnam. Although the fallout from Vietnam definitely helped to sell more copies of the book and more movie tickets, it must be noted that Heller flew some sixty missions for the Army Air Corps in Italy in the early 1940s and began his writing project in 1953. Like many literary veterans who served in the war, the author chose to focus his story not on the grandeur of an American victory but on the madness of the contest and the potential danger the very idea of war held for all human beings. In a work of dark satire, Heller—like Mailer and Jones—not only saw World War II as a reason to be pessimistic about the human future but also suggested that life in America itself—with its militaristic and material power—was indifferent to the welfare of the individual.

Heller's "hero" is Captain Yossarian, a bombardier in Italy like he was. Yossarian is consumed not by a quest for victory but by an overpowering sense of paranoia and a desire to stay alive. He distrusts all the men who give him orders and especially those who keep increasing the magic number of bombing runs a man must make before he can be decommissioned. Heller explains Yossarian's predicament well: "There are many dangers for Yossarian to keep track of. There was Hitler and Mussolini, for example, and they were out to kill him. There was Lieutenant Scheisskof with his fanaticism for parades and there was the bloated colonel with his big fat mustache and his fanaticism for retribution, and they wanted to kill him too. . . . There were lymph glands that might do him in. . . . There were tumors on the brain."[13]

Yossarian expended enormous amounts of energy to get out of the military and to avoid combat. He frequently tried to convince his superiors that his paranoia and fear was a sign of insanity. But of course the "catch" was that they told him such fears were rational. A better proof of insanity would come if a man volunteered for more bombing runs, something he was loath to do. Thus, he was left only with the diagnosis of his psychiatrist that he suffered from "survival anxieties" and was probably also fearful of "being robbed, exploited, degraded, humiliated, and deceived." Doctors told him he was also the type of person who would find violence and misery depressing—but he already knew that.[14]

Eddie Slovik was a real-life soldier who shared Yossarian's reluctance to fight. Unfortunately for him, he served in the actual conflict and was put to death for insubordination in January of 1945. Slovik became, in fact, the only American soldier executed for desertion in the face of enemy fire in the eighty years after the Civil War. News of his death was spread throughout his division in Europe as a warning to others that they could not leave the line of fire. However, the story was completely unknown to most Americans until it was published as a nonfiction book by William Bradford Huie, a naval veteran of the war, in 1954—the year the Iwo Jima memorial to American courage and bravery was dedicated in Washington, D.C.

The Execution of Private Slovik introduced a critical edge into the cultural remembrance of World War II at a time when such expressions were viewed with scorn. Huie argued that with 40,000 deserters in the war, Slovik was singled out for execution not for his refusal to fight but because he was simply a poor "dead-end" kid from the Detroit working class and therefore lacked any standing in American society. For this author, he was more of a victim than a coward. Although most reviewers actually accepted Huie's critique, the chief army historian of World War II, S. L. A. Marshall, felt the book rendered a disservice to the many men who stood and fought. He concluded his review in the *New York Times* by

suggesting that it should not have been published. A *Times* reader quickly countered that Huie's story was more about a man who abhorred killing than about
an individual who was a coward and asked, "What has happened to love in our
world when he who would rather love than kill must die?" Other commentators
accepted Huie's arguments and raised questions about the entire episode and
the overall exercise of military authority—a theme that was quite prevalent in
postwar America. One reviewer called the book "brilliant journalism" and felt it
truly made Slovik a "sympathetic figure." Other commentators felt Huie had
raised questions that deserved the attention of all Americans and that spoke to
the relationship between citizens and the nation itself.

Like many of the men in novels by Mailer and Jones, Slovik's life on the home
front and in the military was marked by suffering. Huie detailed, with a fair
amount of empathy, the turbulent life Slovik led in a working-class family in the
Polish neighborhoods of Detroit. His father had labored only sporadically during
the 1930s, and both of his parents drank to excess. Hard times pushed Slovik
into a life of petty crime, and soon he ended up in a Michigan reformatory. Upon
his release he married a woman from the Polish community, and the couple
worked and saved in hopes of getting a better apartment and new furniture.
Slovik appeared to be in love, content, and under the impression that he would
never be drafted because of his criminal record. A change of heart by his draft
board disrupted the life plans of these newlyweds, however, and the young man
was soon writing letters home every day from an army base. Indeed, Huie de-
votes a good portion of his story to excerpts from these letters as a way to temper
Slovik's reputation as a deserter with other human qualities he possessed.[15]

Huie also explained that he recalled that the government faced a fairly significant problem in recruiting an armed force during the war years. He remarked
that, in fact, the war had been "particularly cruel on the individual" who was
asked to serve, because many did not believe it was conducted for the best of reasons. It was Huie's firm conviction that no one should be asked to fight in a conflict that was not waged for noble goals. He also explained that there had been a
considerable amount of "belly-tightening cynicism" at the time, because a few
were being asked to sacrifice everything, while most citizens were able to enjoy
the war years and get "richer and more comfortable." He insisted that there were
so many "reluctant youths" in America that some of them were eventually discharged from the service or hospitalized for psychiatric reasons. He even charged
that there was rampant discrimination in the way men were distributed throughout the armed services. Those with an education and some status received ap-
pointments as officers; individuals with talent were normally sent to the Air

Force or the Navy, where there was danger but also more comfortable conditions. For Huie, the ranks of the infantry were filled mostly with men from the lower rungs of the social scale—in a process he referred to as "barrel-scraping." To the author, men like Slovik simply did not get a fair shake in America, and some of his reluctance to fight and die was understandable.

On the field of battle Slovik never masked his intentions. After being unable to fight and leave his foxhole after his first foray into combat, Slovik actually drafted a statement that said he refused to follow orders to return. Obviously, such a document helped to convict him at his court marshal. But Huie, holding onto strains of antiwar and humanitarian sentiment, was not so ready to condemn his subject. He questioned the very premise that nations had a right to turn citizens into killers against their will.[16]

Huie was also critical of Dwight Eisenhower, who ordered the condemned man to his death. He felt that Eisenhower did not review the case as carefully as he should have and simply relied on briefings from some of his attending officers. In the second edition of his book, published in 1970 when antiwar sentiment was stronger in American society, Huie recollected a televised 1963 interview with "Ike" by historian Bruce Catton. Their conversation had turned to the issue of death sentences for military crimes, and the wartime hero recalled that only one American man had been executed for such crimes since the 1860s and that he had been the one who authorized it. What galled Huie was that Eisenhower never mentioned the man's name and that he said that he went to the gallows for his offence instead of recalling that Slovik was actually shot by a firing squad. This convinced Huie that the general "never gave much thought to the execution in 1945 or since" and that the common man simply did not matter in the war effort.

Huie and others were also convinced that it took twenty years to make a movie of his story of Slovik because the Pentagon frowned on the idea and no one wanted to embarrass Eisenhower. Frank Sinatra, who played a common-man soldier in the movie version of *From Here to Eternity*, at one time owned the movie rights. Sinatra most likely saw another opportunity to perform the role of a lower-class man who was victimized by society and by the military, although he did say that Slovik should be punished. The famed actor and singer had to give up his quest for the role, however, because he had hired a screenwriter (Albert Maltz) who had been blacklisted by Hollywood and because, in the early 1960s, the controversy might prove harmful to the political career of his friend John F. Kennedy.[17]

Huie took up problems created by the war experience again a decade later when he published a book on the experience of Claude Eatherly, a man who had piloted a reconnaissance plane over Hiroshima and reported to the crew of the Enola Gay that weather conditions were suitable to drop the first atomic bomb. After the war Eatherly's life had taken a turn for the worse. Published reports indicated a bizarre pattern in which the former airmen was now suffering from extremes pangs of guilt over the death of innocent civilians, having troubling nightmares, and even facing court trials for armed robberies. Eatherly, in fact, became a symbol of support for an anti-nuclear movement that was emerging in the late 1950s and early 1960s not only in the United States but in Europe and Japan as well. His status as a symbol against the use of such weapons and even for pacifism reached a crescendo of sorts in 1961, when Gunther Anders, an anti-nuclear activist and Austrian moral philosopher, published an exchange of letters he had had with the former pilot. In the book, entitled *Burning Conscience,* the American flyer was presented as remorseful over the bombings and hopeful that the production of such weapons could be ended. What attracted Huie's attention, ironically, was not so much the moral issues raised by the atomic bombs but his concern that much of what was being published about Eatherly was simply not true. In his book *The Hiroshima Pilot,* Huie set out, not to explore any lingering sense of guilt over how World War II ended, but to set the record straight on Eatherly and to defuse the mythical status he had attained as symbol of regret over Hiroshima and the need to oppose nuclear proliferation. Huie took exception to a number of articles that had reported that Eatherly had actually led the attack on Hiroshima and received the Distinguished Flying Cross. He showed that both claims were false and stressed that Eatherly was only assigned to the non-heroic task of checking weather conditions over the target area. He even questioned psychiatric reports that the former pilot "suffered an emotional wound for Hiroshima" and that he harbored a misgivings over his actions, although it was clear to all that Eatherly's life was in considerable disarray after 1945. Huie did admit that he could never prove one way or the other that the war had left Eatherly with mental problems or a deep sense of culpability. But he argued that the idea of guilt being associated with Hiroshima was coming more from an incipient anti-nuclear movement than from Eatherly, although some of the airman's published letters certainly affirmed a need to see that such bombings never took place again. A staunch anti-communist, Huie wanted to blunt any criticism of either America's past actions or its Cold War military build-up. Yet he still managed to give wide exposure to the more critical legacy of Hiroshima and to the reality that the war in the 1940s had left many men in various states of emotional disarray.[18]

Critical literary accounts authored by veterans were focused not only on the problems associated with combat but on a host of domestic difficulties that plagued the wartime military as well. James Gould Cozzens, who spent much of his time in the Army writing training manuals, set his novel on an air base in Florida. *Guard of Honor,* which won the Pulitzer prize for fiction in 1949, paid little attention to the ferocious fighting that took place in the Pacific or the struggle against the Germans in Europe. Based on a diary he kept and notes he took while he served, Cozzens reported that many people in the military remained largely unaffected by the most severe form of pressure that the war brought. Told from the perspective of officers rather than enlisted men, the book painted a more sober portrait of the men stationed in bases in the United States, contending that they were preoccupied mostly with furthering their own personal agendas, which included more promotions, sex, or nonthreatening tasks like writing training manuals.

A major part of the story was devoted to an exposé of the racial attitudes that pervaded the armed forces of the time. When the Army Air Corps tries to organize a bomber group consisting entirely of African American flyers (something, of course, that actually took place in the war), angry white airmen actually assault blacks on their base. An officer in charge of the operation even tells black airmen that they should be proud of being selected for such a prestigious unit but then sees to it that they are barred from the all-white officer's club—a facility that consumed a great deal of time and expense to construct while many fought and died abroad. Cozzens gives voice to black servicemen in his novel, revealing how angry and resentful they are over the way they are treated by their commander and by many of the other men. The African Americans finally mount their own civil rights march in an effort to integrate the club so that they can socialize with other officers. Cozzens also allows some women in the service to speak, and readers learn that they too have grievances over their secondary status in the service—specifically, over the fact a few doctors were perceived to take "liberties" with them during physical examinations. There was really no ending to *Guard of Honor* as there was to the war, because the problems that it addressed were not resolved by the defeat of the Japanese or the Germans. Like other veterans who wrote about the war, Cozzens was unwilling to let sentimental and traditional views of Americans and their war effort prevail in the contested culture of the times.[19]

Richard Brooks, a former Marine, also looked at military life among men stationed on domestic bases. As with other veterans who narrated the conflict, Brooks was unwilling to accept wartime rhetoric about American innocence and preferred to see the war as another example of the cruelty that lurked in the souls of men everywhere. The fictional GIs in his novel *The Brick Foxhole* (1945), are discontented with military life and the mundane tasks they are asked to perform at a camp located not far from the nation's capital. They do not dream of a better world but spend a good deal of time imagining what it would be like to kill another man. Indeed, the soldiers in this story are filled with rage and contempt for many in their own nation, especially blacks, gays—and, at times, women. One soldier in the novel even challenges conventional explanations of how the war began by dismissing Pearl Harbor or Hitler's rise to power as casual events and claiming that the true origins of the conflict were to be found in "some distant swamp with some unpronounceable name." A woman in his novel was convinced that the war came not from other nations but from forces located "inside" men and women which would never go away until people "cured themselves."

The central figure in *The Brick Foxhole* reveals no clear understanding of what the war was about and is adrift emotionally while in the service. Corporal Jeff Mitchell worries constantly that his wife back in California is cheating on him and thinks about how he might punish her. The experience of serving his country does not transform Mitchell into a virtuous man but merely makes him more angry, hateful, and disillusioned with authority in America. He can find no good reason to believe all the talk he hears about the need to kill more Japanese or to turn the nation's military forces against the Russians once the war is over. He is further alienated by the racial prejudice of his colleagues, some of whom hate "niggers" and even murder a gay man because they detest his sexual preferences. To Mitchell, wartime is not about defending the homeland or remaking the world but simply an excuse to allow men of all nations to vent their violent rage. Thus, he spends most of his free time looking for comfort and love in the arms of a prostitute who has fled to the Washington area to put behind her a life of impoverishment and frustration in the coal fields of Pennsylvania.[20]

A SEMBLANCE OF HEALING

A few of the stories told by veterans moved some distance from broad assessments of the war and the character of American society. In these instances, veterans focused on placing their war experiences into a narrative of their own lives. These memoirs did not shirk from presenting critical appraisals of the war experience and bearing witness to the suffering the men saw everywhere. And they certainly did not offer a massive dose of hope that the world could be made better. But on a limited basis they suggested that individuals traumatized by combat and terror could eventually return to some semblance of a stable life and, by implication, matter again. In the memoirs of men like Paul Fussell, William Manchester, Audie Murphy, and E. B. Sledge, citizens could not only see how destructive the war was but also catch a glimpse of the possibility that there was life after death.

Audie Murphy had become an American hero as the most decorated GI of World War II even before he published *To Hell and Back* in 1949. This infantryman's view of the war as he slogged his way through campaigns in Italy, France, and Germany drew considerable public attention despite the fact that it refused to see the war in terms that were glorious and mythical. Murphy did not raise larger issues about the American character and military authority as had Mailer and Jones, but he did offer an unadorned depiction of the ceaseless struggles he and his comrades faced in fighting the Germans. His remembrance of the war centered on the view that the soldiers felt they were in a state of "constant peril." The men in this story are both courageous and crude and only want to survive. Some charge enemy gun emplacements and face adversity without complaining, traits that Murphy admires. Others fight because they can see no way out and desire only to return to a world of drinking and sex. Generally, the battlefield is a hellish place where death is seen at nearly every turn. At times, Murphy even seems like a natural-born killer, who compares shooting Germans to shooting "skeet" as a boy in Texas. And when a close personal friend dies, he guns down scores of enemy soldiers in a fit of rage and recalls that his "whole being" was "concentrated on killing" at the time. Indeed, his skill as a warrior and this indifference to killing Germans constitute the key traits he manifests in battle until the very end of the book, when he expresses some remorse over the deaths of several comrades and the horror of recalling dead bodies and "burning flesh." He even praises his nation for fighting for what it thought was "right and decent." Ironically, the weight of this story is really about the brutality of battle and the ability of one gunfighter to master its enormous challenges.[21]

In his 1979 chronicle of his Pacific war experiences, *Goodbye Darkness*, William Manchester walked a finer line between critical and traditional perspectives than most of the men who wrote. He was not averse to recalling the savagery he encountered in the Pacific as a young Marine, but he also makes a plea for the restitution of faith in the traditional values he felt had shaped his life as a boy before 1941. Heroic and cynical threads fight for space in his masterful book. Tied less to the political sentiments of the 1930s and 40s, as were Mailer and Jones, he wrote in the 1970s after a time of much domestic turmoil in America and tried to use his memory of World War II as a moral guidepost to indicate what he thought the nation had lost. He called the three decades after 1945 a period of moral decline and was troubled by the youth rebellions of the 1960s, the tragedy of Vietnam, and the assassinations of John Kennedy and Martin Luther King. He also regretted what he saw as the erosion of a virile sense of masculinity among the individuals of his generation who had eagerly gone to war in the 1940s but now had been reduced to "docile old men who greedily follow Dow-Jones averages" and follow their wives on European tours. He claimed that he had expected a "nobler" America by now but found instead that the character of the nation was much less satisfying.

Manchester's effort to use the memory of war to address problems in the post-war era was not unusual. Cozzens and Heller did as much when they extracted from the war lessons that challenged white supremacy or Cold War militarism. But Manchester revealed greater support for a patriotic remembrance of World War II than they did. His book was a sign that veterans differed a great deal over what they thought they had encountered in the early 1940s. Manchester found much less fault with the nation—and with the military, for that matter—and talked more about the "patriotic identification" of his generation and the belief that America was—at least before the 1960s—an exceptional nation. Like the depictions of Ernie Pyle, the personal interests of citizens in his time flowed easily into the interests and needs of the nation. Individualism and communal responsibility were perfectly compatible. He wrote that the United States was a different country in the 1940s, "with half of today's population, a lordly figure in the White House, and a tightly disciplined society." He noted that the idea of the "counterculture" did not exist in the world of that time and that if it had he was convinced that it would have been "dismissed as absurd." The foundation of that ideal nation and the "bastion of social stability" was for him the traditional family, where children were guided not by "radar beams" but by "parental discipline."[22]

It was the idea of discipline—and the obedient individual—that figured prominently in Manchester's view of wartime America. He revered his father, who served in the Marines in World War I, and the position of authority he commanded in the writer's life. Despite his pride in the U.S. Marine Corps, however, Manchester's father told him that he would be reluctant to see his son go off to war. Indeed, his mother felt the same way and always stressed the need for the boy to become a "gentleman." As the 1930s gave way to the 40s, however, Manchester increasingly came to question the value of being a gentleman. He recalled that the pacifism of the 1930s "maddened him" and that he "yearned for the stern discipline" he eventually encountered in the military. At the beginning of World War II he and his friends realized that they knew nothing of real combat but noted that they were still ready to "fight for our country"—a desire he felt was lacking in the 1970s when he wrote. He lamented, in fact, the loss of what he termed a "blazing sense of patriotism" and the pride he and his peers felt in serving his nation in the 1940s. Maturation for him meant becoming more like his father than his mother, and especially that part of his father that was embedded in the warrior ethos. No modern man in pursuit of his self-interests, Manchester contributed to the larger rhetorical project of crafting a meaning of World War II by presenting himself as bearer of tradition, willing "to surrender my individuality" to the Marines, where his father had "learned discipline a quarter-century before."[23]

Despite his eagerness to serve, Manchester became conflicted about his experiences in World War II. He felt that his sense of discipline and loyalty not only enabled him and many in his generation to serve their nation but also to accept death and injury. Yet he admitted that the encounters with dying and killing were difficult, especially when he "slew" his first man. And he concluded that when he and his comrades were in battle they all became "psychotic inmates of the greatest madhouse in history." Like many who fought in the war, he also criticized officers who needlessly ordered men into risky situations. Of course, he experienced unprecedented bouts of fear, but he insisted that the men he knew rose above the chaos and demonstrated an inspiring degree of valor and brotherhood. He recalled the heroic actions of comrades such as William "Hawk" Hawkins, who knocked out machine guns by standing in full view of the enemy and firing into their positions. And he recalled a man named Jim Crowe, who charged toward Japanese lines shouting, "You'll never get the Purple Heart a-laying in those foxholes, men!" It was the bond he felt with his buddies that caused him to ignore orders and jump from a hospital bed on Okinawa and return to the front. He described his move as an "act of love," for he felt "the men in the line were my family, my home. . . . They would never let me down." It was out of respect for these men that he now castigated the government for letting some of the memorials he saw in the Pacific in the 1970s fall into disrepair. In fact, he made it clear that he did not like any war memorial that obliterated the legacy of horror and suffering that they had known so well. What moved him were not "counterfeit" memorials but "souvenirs of anguish" like rusted planes, tanks, shells, gas masks, and guns that were grim reminders of the actual pain and loss he and his friends had known. It was because of the feelings these men had for each other that in the end he claimed they fought not only for the nation but mostly for each other.[24]

E. B. Sledge was another veteran of the Pacific war who sought to reflect upon his personal experience. Like Manchester, he certainly did not glorify the war itself but claimed that he remembered certain ideals that were manifested in the struggle that needed to be preserved. Manchester's story called for a revival of traditional authority and a sense of self-restraint. Sledge invoked a traditional memory as well, one that expressed a sense of reverence for old-line officers he met in the Marines and for the degree of professionalism they brought to their military duty. In his tales from the Pacific, his veneration of traditional authorities actually serves to contest the more frightening recollections of savage behavior on the part of both Americans and their enemies. For instance, he does not hesitate to describe atrocities committed by men on his side. But he makes it clear that the brutal behavior GIs manifested was not, in his opinion, ingrained and was not driven by basic instincts but only by the exigencies of war. For him savage impulses ended when the war ended.

Sledge's book *With the Old Breed: At Peleliu and Okinawa* (1981) honored the professional soldiers who served long before the attack on Pearl Harbor. He was impressed by how much they approached the tasks of war with a sense of "professional detachment" and how much their calm outlook differed from the "high spirits" that new recruits like Sledge—a young man from Alabama—and his friends carried into the Marines when the war broke out. The seasoned veterans took the eager newcomers into the corps and instilled in them the confidence they would need to survive the bloody horrors of Peleliu and Okinawa. These mentors told the new men that, as Marines, they should "relax, work hard, and do your job right and you won't have any trouble." They imparted to the men a belief that they could actually survive the fight that was to come. It was their ability to normalize the war and the terror that ultimately gave Sledge the assurance he felt he needed. His description of his mortar instructor, for instance, comes close to the idealization of a prototypical American hero as one might ever expect to read: "His bearing oozed with self-confidence. There was no arrogance or bluster about him, yet he was obviously a man who knew himself and his job and would put up with no nonsense from anybody. He had an intangible air of subdued, quiet detachment, a quality possessed by so many of the combat veterans of the Pacific campaign I met at this time."[25]

Sledge grew to love some of the "old breed" officers he met. He admired a gunnery sergeant who appeared to live in a world totally preoccupied with his weapons and "obsessed with wanting to bayonet the enemy." He inspired "youngsters" like Sledge and made him feel that he had a "direct link" to the "Old Corps." Sledge felt that his commander, Captain Andrew Hacker, was "the finest Marine officer" he ever knew. The young soldier was in awe of men like him who repulsed repeated Japanese bayonet charges at Cape Glouster. When Hacker was killed at Peleliu, Sledge "sobbed quietly," such was his respect for this model member of the "old breed." "Our company commander represented stability and direction in a world of violence, death and destruction," Sledge wrote. "He was human, but he commanded our individual destiny under the most trying conditions. We knew he could never be replaced." With these words the Alabama Marine captured—as did Manchester—the bonds that men in battle fused and suggested one powerful source of inspirational memories long after the war ended.[26]

Sledge also revealed that he was overjoyed to feel that he was part of U.S. Marine Corps history. He was especially excited about being selected to serve with the First Marine Division and claimed that had it been left up to him, it would have been the unit he would have selected. He was fully aware that it had been the division that had initiated the fight against the Japanese at Guadalcanal—a place where many of the "old breed" had already acquired valuable battlefield expertise. He was eager to embrace its culture of professionalism, its links to the "old corps," and its "passionate hatred for the Japanese." Sledge did not mention anything about other "traditions" the Marines had brought from Guadalcanal. According to Craig Cameron, the fighting on the island had helped to destroy the image of the Japanese as "super-human" warriors and led to a racist view that this enemy lacked normal human qualities, a conclusion that allowed Americans to kill them at will.[27]

Sledge's faith in the professional approach to battle was tested time and time again in his story. He admitted that from the war he took the notion that leaders could not always be trusted. He remembered that some American officers had ordered marine landings that were not necessary to the final defeat of Japan and had resulted in high numbers of casualties. And he was amazed from time to time at just how savage some American troops could be. His retelling of American atrocities at Peleliu is one of the most compelling parts of his entire book. He too disclosed a sense of estrangement from the home front and felt that many noncombatants both in the military and at home could not begin to appreciate the "world of horror from which escape seemed less and less likely." To him time and life itself came to have no meaning, and the "fierce struggle for survival in the abyss of Peleliu eroded the veneer of civilization and made savages of us all." He vividly recalled watching another Marine pry a gold tooth from the mouth of a Japanese prisoner with his knife while the man was still alive. When that did not work, he cut the man's mouth from cheek to cheek as the enemy soldier was "thrashing about," so intent was he to get a souvenir. Soon other Marines simply shot the man to put him out of his misery. In another incident he watched as a comrade casually tossed pebbles into the open skull of an enemy soldier. At first Sledge was repulsed by such behavior, but over time he came to accept some of it himself because he had seen American bodies mutilated as well.[28]

There were times when Sledge lost not only any attachments he had to civilized behavior but his faith in the power of discipline and expertise that he had acquired in basic training. On Peleliu he quickly felt a sense of "utter helplessness," and during one episode of heavy shelling he felt "a wild, inexorable urge to scream, to sob, to cry." He began to think that he would eventually lose all control and that his mind would be "shattered." One night, while sitting in the dark, he came to a realization that he and his comrades were "expendable." This was a difficult point for him to accept because he felt Americans had always valued life and the well-being of the individual. He called the moment a "humbling experience," and it left him with a powerful sense of loneliness.[29]

Near the end of Sledge's conflicted memoir, he portrays his final battle on Okinawa. By this point in the war, the American command was relying more on massive levels of troops and arms in a war of attrition than on the professional standards of old-line soldiers. Sledge saw the fight on the island as "brutish" and "inglorious." But these horrors did not turn him into a pacifist or even a critic of American culture and leadership as it had Mailer and Jones. Instead, he thought back on how he managed to survive it all and concluded that it had something to do with the values he learned from the "old breed" and the way they helped newcomers to manifest "incredible bravery" and "devotion" to others. On Okinawa he felt compelled to live up to the standards that his professional mentors had taught him, to surmount the huge sense of vulnerability he felt, and even, in turn, to offer some reassurance to another young recruit.

At the end of his book, Sledge again proclaimed a traditional remembrance of the war, but one that was only able to hold back his grief by the thinnest of margins. He wrote that we would always need men like the ones he fought with to take responsibility and be willing to make sacrifices for the nation. He said the troops he knew used to say that "if a country is good enough to live in, it's good enough to fight for." But he also had to conclude that war was a "terrible waste" and that its only redeeming qualities were the bravery of his comrades and the devotion they felt to one another. Sledge's literary effort to contain the sense of trauma and loss by upholding traditional military values also failed to divulge the reality of personal traumas he carried home. He does not tell readers in his book what a friend of his, Katherine Phillips, disclosed many years later in the final episode of *The War*, a 2007 television film by Ken Burns. In talking of life after the men came home, she revealed that Sledge was haunted by nightmares for years after coming back to Alabama and was unable to "throw off the war." Possibly there were things the "old breed" had not adequately prepared him to face. Interestingly, other writers, like Audie Murphy and James Jones, also concealed the realities of their own postwar traumas even as they wrote about the horrors of war.[30]

The efforts of Manchester and Sledge to elevate virtue over violence were not replicated in a memoir by Paul Fussell, another sign that discordant notes reverberated through the memory of the war among the generation that fought it. When he released *Doing Battle* in 1996, Fussell had already gained a reputation as a leading scholar who had published insightful accounts of how the men who fought in World War I and World War II held highly cynical views toward their experience. Fussells's boyhood was somewhat like Manchester's. He had been raised in the pleasant surroundings of Pasadena, California, where Los Angeles commuters raised their families in "gentility and peace" and where the streets were "immaculate" and the weather "benign." He noted how his parents had imparted to him a strict sense of moral values that included regular church attendance at a local Presbyterian church that offered pious sermons and "father-son" dinners. He was constantly admonished against "lying, cruelty, and damaging property." The son of a man who had served America in World War I, Fussell recalled playing war games in a vacant lot with his childhood friends. When he entered Pomona College in 1941, however, he was not thinking much of war and admitted to feeling quite optimistic about his future.[31]

Like many of his peers, Fussell found that Pearl Harbor triggered in him a wish to fight. He recalled that most of the students at Pomona shared Franklin Roosevelt's argument that no matter how long it took, Americans would avenge the "premeditated invasion" by the Japanese and win an absolute victory. He felt that most of his fellow students quickly came to hate the Japanese and felt same the urge to destroy them that he did. Privately, Fussell even admitted to being "exhilarated" by the sudden turn of events, for he was confident that no harm would come to him since he felt he had been fortunate throughout his entire life.

Fussell found army life and basic training jarring and sensed he was losing some of the feelings of confidence and security he had. He was certainly not happy about endless rounds of cleaning up the parade ground and emptying trash cans. He came to feel that the dog tags issued to him and the other men were simply signs of how they were treated. And because he was an ROTC-trained second lieutenant, he felt contempt for the "old breed" regulars he met. He also believed that most soldiers held almost no interest in the ideological discussion that permeated the political climate of his times. The men he knew, as he tells it, fought not out any deep conviction for the "allied cause and the Four Freedoms" but from a sense of duty to their comrades-in-arms. Of far more interest than the politics of the war was the date at which things would be finished or how one could get promoted. "My boyish illusion, largely intact to that moment of awakening, fell away all at once," he observed, and "suddenly I knew that I would never be in a world that was reasonable and just." Mailer and Jones could not have expressed such disillusionment more aptly.[32]

Doing battle in Europe only caused Fussell's cynicism to grow. It was not long before he, like others, realized that the ordinary individual was expendable. He did meet men who were courageous and effective in combat, and he paid tribute to officers he knew who could remain calm under fire and gain the respect of their men. He revealed that he had been capable of working himself into a high state of excitement when he and his comrades were "violently attacking." But to him it was regrettable that to reach such a state of courage and bravery it was necessary to suppress "normal human sympathy so that you can look dry-eyed and undisturbed at the most appalling things." Ultimately, he felt he had to report on American atrocities he witnessed, including instances when GIs laughed, howled, and engaged in "good-ole boy yelling" as they gunned down German prisoners. He explained how some men derived "deep satisfaction" from shooting an enemy soldier whose body was already "twitching." When some of the colleagues laughed about such episodes over campfires, Fussell felt a sense of revulsion that he was expected to keep to himself.[33]

After the war was over, this veteran claimed that he was cleansed of any sense of optimism or American innocence. He framed the ground war and the experience of the infantry as nothing more than an "unintended form of eugenics, clearing the population of the dumbest, the least skilled, and the least promising of all young American males." He also noted that some American combat units, like the 28th division (Private Slovik's unit) were so ineffective during the Battle of the Bulge that the Germans selected their position as a point to attack. The war also left him tired of all the calls he heard to become a team player. "I became irrationally angry at any attempt to coerce me into group behavior or to treat me as if human beings are sane," he wrote. In fact, he was now rejecting the aspirations of traditionalists like Manchester and Sledge to a restore a faith in self-sacrifice and an older set of moral values, because he had come to resent how they could be placed into the service of warfare. When he listened to government reports of "body counts" during the Vietnam War, it reminded him of the revulsion he felt over the inhuman attitudes he had observed in World War II.[34]

HUMAN IMPROVEMENT

The powerful contest between critical and traditional interpretations of the war in the writing of veterans nearly obliterated the frame of high-minded liberalism that Franklin Roosevelt had identified before the war began. Yet a few of the veterans who elected to write were determined to keep alive a human-centered view of the struggle and its possibilities. One of those who thought about the war in this way was John Horne Burns, a man who had held the rank of 2nd lieutenant in military intelligence and who had served in North Africa and Italy. In his novel *The Gallery*, originally published in 1947, Burns looked at the war, not through the prism of combat, but through a cast of characters, both soldiers and civilians, struggling to find peace and happiness in the chaotic and unpredictable world of wartime Naples. No individual in Burns's parade of humanity is heroic or beyond reproach as they enter the Galleria Umberto Primo in Naples just after the allies have gained control of the city. Rather, everyone is seen to be struggling—and often drinking heavily—in a place where moral values are in shambles and futures are unpredictable. Actually, Burns is quite sympathetic to the people who come to the galleria, realizing that war has pushed all of them into desperate quests for happiness. Thus, the book documents the reality of GIs trading their food and clothing supplies for sex from desperate Italian women and even of American men seeking gratification from homosexual relationships. There is no traditional world or proper way to serve as a guide through life in this book and little hope that the human future will be better than its past.[35]

By far the most popular writer linking the sacrifices of wartime to the need for human betterment was James Michener. Back from his tour of duty in the Pacific, Michener was certainly more optimistic than Burns that human beings could learn to treat each other with respect and improve their life conditions. His 1946 book *Tales of the South Pacific* offered a variety of perspectives on the meaning of the war, but none was more central than his argument that all of the trauma and chaos demanded not that people celebrate heroes but that they work to craft a world marked by tolerance and human understanding. He further reinforced this liberal and democratic frame on the war and moved away from a soldier-centered remembrance by giving a greater voice, as did Burns, to characters who were women or noncombatants.

One way that Michener worked to promote his politicized remembrance and erase the wartime divide between enemies and heroes was to build stories around interracial love. Consider the tale of Nellie Forbush, a navy nurse raised in the segregated South. Forbush had made a promise to her boyfriend in Arkansas that she would return to him after the war and become his wife, although she did tell him she wanted to meet other people and see the world before she settled down. Stationed on a remote Pacific island, she finds, ironically, that her most dangerous enemies are not Japanese but American soldiers with lust in their hearts. When one of her nursing friends is raped by a GI, she and other women are forced to date men who carry loaded weapons to protect them. Forbush is challenged not only by the sexual drives of some of her fellow countrymen but also by the love she feels for a French planter who lives on the island, a civilized and wealthy man who is also a "De Gaullist." She finds the prospect of marrying him and not returning to Arkansas to be appealing, save for one problem. The planter once lived with a woman of color on the islands and fathered some of her children. Michener wrote that "her entire upbringing made it impossible for her to deny the teachings of her youth." She wondered how she could accept "nigger-children" who would become her step-children. Her first response was to think that she will need to return to the South and marry the man she had left behind. In the end, however, she is converted to the attractions of the South Pacific and the idea of casting aside her racial prejudices in order to help raise a family with a man she loves.

Racial issues also confront another character, Joe Cable. The young Marine falls into a torrid romance with a young native woman named Liat. Scholarship on the subject of such liaisons has suggested that most Marines in the South Pacific actually had very little opportunity to develop relationships with native women and were more likely to think about having sex with women back home. Nevertheless, Cable is smitten by a "lovely statue in brown marble." When Liat's mother confronts him about his intentions, Cable has to face the issue of marriage as well. Although initially he felt that their love was strong enough to overcome any racial barriers, upon further reflection, he concludes that he could never take her home to America because of the color of her skin. The matter of their love becomes moot, in the end, when Cable dies in an assault on another island. But the import of this story and that of the navy nurse was clear. The way people could earn the sacrifice of World War II was not simply to honor the soldiers or cover over horrors perpetrated by all sides but through renewed commitment to the ideals of human tolerance.[36]

At the end of these tales one can read of an American officer walking among the graves of hundreds of his comrades. Appalled by the slaughter the war has brought, he tries to think of something positive that can be taken from this global tragedy. His mind turns to a naval commander he had known who is buried where he now stands. He recalls that the man was a staunch defender and "champion of the Negro," that although upper class he befriended the "meanest enlisted man," and that he was a gentile who placed Jews in position of responsibility. In this rare moment of postwar fiction and memory, humanitarianism found a life.[37]

Soldiers wrote about the war in order to sustain a memory of its tragic dimensions and the tortuous experience many of them endured. As a group, they often had varying interpretations of what it all meant, but they generally agreed that it degraded individuals and could not be reduced to heroic stories and myths. Generally, they refused to celebrate the victory because they had witnessed too much violence, racism, and indifference to their fate—even from their fellow citizens. To them the entire episode had not ratified hopes that liberal dreams could be realized on earth but concerns that they could not.

CHAPTER THREE

"NO PLACE FOR WEAKLINGS"

THE AFTER-EFFECTS OF World War II left the United States on a permanent state of alert. Despite the victory over Germany and Japan, the nation remained on the lookout for enemies and dangers. After visiting the ruins of Berlin, President Harry Truman told his fellow citizens that he was grateful that "this land of ours had been spared." He was quick to note, however, that the future safety and security of the nation now depended on a heightened ability to defend itself and to deploy its military forces throughout the world. Thus, even as the size of the American armed forces shrank dramatically after 1945 and civilians lobbied to bring the men home as soon as possible, the United States continued to spend heavily on national defense. In the late 1940s the defense budget, which had accounted for only about 15 percent of federal expenditures before Pearl Harbor, now consumed nearly one-third of the budget. More than ever the exercise of military power was viewed as a fundamental way to resolve disputes in a world that appeared to be permanently divided between the forces of good and evil. Michael Sherry, who has studied this "militarization" of America, has argued insightfully that the "impulse to apply wartime reflexes to postwar problems" was a central feature of the political culture of the United States after 1945.[1]

The preoccupation with national security and military supremacy—goals vigorously supported by powerful veteran groups—was not the only way the war experience reverberated through the postwar years. There were also those Americans who saw in the forceful calls for national defense and power a retreat from the liberal dreams articulated by Franklin Roosevelt and the spirit of the Four Freedoms. Some, like Henry Wallace, sought to honor the sacrifices of the war by sustaining a dream of human improvement and cooperation—a vision that looked beyond a divided world of heroes and villains. A yearning for human collaboration and uplift also helped to explain the popularity of Edward Steichen's

1955 photo exhibit, "The Family of Man." Steichen, who had served in the Navy as a photographer, mounted an exhibit that implicitly challenged the very idea of war and national power with photographs that depicted the commonality of the human experience. His work featured people in all nations loving, marrying, working, and grieving. Its human-centeredness was appreciated so much that it toured the world under the sponsorship of the U.S. Information Agency for seven years. Militarization was also questioned by millions of veterans and their families who were now forced to struggle day to day with the emotional and personal scars of the war experience and who certainly did not relish the prospect of mobilizing resources for another war.[2]

COLD WAR MILITARISM

The postwar years were marked not only by a sense of relief that the war had ended favorably but also by a feeling of dread that evil still lurked in the world and would threaten the nation again. The anticommunist impulse that helped to justify militarization was the strongest manifestation of this fear. Communism now appeared to represent the same type of threat that Fascism had in the early 1940s. Congressional investigations led by the House Un-American Activities Committee and Senator Joseph McCarthy not only reflected the nation's anxiety but demonstrated that anticommunism could attract substantial political support. Apprehension over new threats was also seen in the discussions concerning the return of millions of veterans to American life. Numerous articles and news features admonished women to show understanding toward returned soldiers and accept the fact that some of them might be emotionally "wounded" by the war and still not be ready to put their violent ways behind them. This theme was, in fact, a staple of many postwar films.

Historian Paul Boyer has documented strong cultural currents of "anxiety and apprehension" that something terrible might happen in the postwar years. Thus, even comic books featured tales of how the world might end, and mainstream news outlets offered stories of what might happen if an atomic bomb hit a large American city. The government fueled the general sense of unease by calling upon citizens to take measures to protect themselves in case of an atomic attack. In the early 1950s the Federal Civil Defense Administration, for instance, suggested how citizens could join in an effort to defend America by building shelters in their backyards. Families were given precise details of how this could be done as well as useful tips on how to keep their homes clean, since it was assumed that a well-kept home was less likely to burn in a nuclear blast than one filled with clutter. Very few Americans actually built such shelters, but most were quite aware that the world now seemed more dangerous than it had ever been before.[3]

Militarization and anticommunism, powerful ideals that drove a traditionalist remembrance of the war and a retreat from Roosevelt internationalism, led not only to a larger defense establishment than had existed before Pearl Harbor but to attempts to reinvigorate traditional morals and beliefs. This could be seen in the ideas of conservative spokesmen like Russell Kirk and Billy Graham. Fearful of the growing power of the state over personal life—a fear directly tied to the mobilizations and sacrifices of World War II—intellectuals such as Kirk argued strongly for a political outlook that was at once patriotic, individualistic, and religious. The future, that is to say, would not be shaped by Roosevelt-type reforms or liberal dreams but by military power and moral individuals who placed their faith in God. Fearful of a third world war, conservatives supported the need to arm the nation but wanted government mostly for the sake of protection and not as a force that interfered with domestic or economic life. Thus, in the early years of the Cold War, an evangelical preacher like Graham gained a significant following by articulating a message that combined "conventional morality with fervid Americanism." The growing links between military power, anticommunism, and longstanding moral beliefs were coming together as a consequence of the militarization of society and its defensive posture that sought not to enlighten the world but to dig in and defend America and its interests at all costs.[4]

Even liberals were moving in a more conservative direction and preparing to fight again. Arthur Schlesinger's 1949 book *The Vital Center* expressed concern over the rising power of states to control individual lives and the expanding power of corporations as well. Less willing to cast off state regulation of economic life than conservatives, liberals like Schlesinger staked out a middle ground where some state control of the marketplace remained but where the need for men and nations to be ready to fight again was fully accepted. It was this agreement on the need for virile men, national preparedness, and the use of military power in the future that revealed the extent to which many conservatives and liberals moved away from any ideal view of the goodness of human nature or the dream that it could be reformed. The violent legacy of World War II had mitigated such dreams for many; it became harder to speak about a century ahead as one that would benefit the "common man."[5]

Veterans who now ran for political office were quick to pick up on these cultural reverberations of the war and postwar era, even if they did not do so in the same way. Both John Kennedy and Richard Nixon ran for Congress in 1946 and invoked their wartime records and sacrifices to win support. Kennedy, of course, had gained a significant amount of public attention and status as a war hero from accounts of his actions to help save his crew after his PT boat was demolished by a Japanese destroyer. John Hersey's 1944 account of the incident in the *New Yorker* offered readers a riveting story of JFK pulling a wounded comrade through the sea to safety. It is no wonder his father spent hundreds of thousands of dollars to distribute copies of the article in Boston as part of his campaign effort. Kennedy was also not averse to reminding audiences, as he sought election, that his mother was a Gold Star mother who had lost a son in a wartime plane crash. Kennedy exploited patriotic sentiments even further by setting up a local Veterans of Foreign War post in his district named after his dead brother. Nixon too used his war record to help attract support. One advertisement used by his campaign organization in the Los Angeles area referred to him as "Your Veteran Candidate" and spoke of how he had learned to serve his fellowman by "sleeping in fox holes" and "sweating out air raids." Importantly, their common experience in war did not translate into similar political attitudes. Kennedy offered voters a blend of militarism and traditional liberalism, with calls for expanded Social Security and a rise in the minimum wage. Nixon joined his pro-military outlook to a politics that was more conservative and critical of government intervention in the personal and economic life of Americans.[6]

No organization embraced the ideas of military strength, national defense, and a devout faith more than the American Legion. Erle Cocke, the Legion's national commander and a veteran of World War II, declared in 1950 that America this year was "no place for weaklings" because the nation now faced an "unrelenting battle" against its enemies. At the time he was referring to the Korean War, but he was also reiterating the established policy of the Legion to offer unquestioned support for American military activities and for efforts to secure the nation from "internal subversion" and "external aggression." Indeed, World War II had contributed mightily to the Legion's brand of Americanism by infusing its membership rolls with more than one million veterans. Before the war the organization had already established itself as an ardent opponent of communism and even militant labor unionism in the United States, although it had expressed some caution over entering another global war before Pearl Harbor. World War II removed any sense of caution when it came to fighting again, however, and pushed the Legion to make calls for a stronger military and a vigilant stand against the nation's enemies. In statements and articles in the Legion's magazine, officials worried that even after Pearl Harbor and Bataan, many Americans still did not hold an "adequate conception of what we were up against" and an appreciation of the fact that national defense now needed to be an utmost priority. As early as 1943, the Legion criticized politicians who "make us skip over the actual winning of the war and focus thought and work upon some utopian future." Instead of worrying about remaking the "post-war world" into a better place for all humanity, Legion officials argued that it would be better to concentrate on the "slaughter" and "black times" that now permeated the globe and confront the reality that Americans had to do whatever was necessary to defeat their enemies and save "all that we hold dear." Not surprisingly, thousands of members of the Legion cooperated with the Federal Bureau of Investigation (FBI) in the 1940s and 50s in a covert operation to look for dangerous enemies at home and report any "subversive" activities to authorities. This secret program, referred to as the American Legion Contact Program, continued into the 1960s despite the fact the FBI's own records showed the legionnaires supplied very little of actual value regarding national defense.[7]

Patriotism in America has always been an ideal forged from several strands of thought. A Progressive variant of national loyalty affirmed the idea that citizen loyalty was contingent upon expectations that the nation would ensure justice and economic security for all. Others, however, saw their attachment to the nation in terms of power and expected that their devotion would be rewarded with a newfound status of superiority over those less powerful at home or those considered inferior or dangerous abroad. These variations were never mutually exclusive, but American history is replete with examples of how men and women in wartime often rallied to what Jonathan Hansen has called the "prospect of a fight" and a celebration of national loyalty based in a dream of victory and strength. Certainly, the American Legion tended to present itself as the patriotic defender of a powerful nation. This is not to say that no one in the Legion believed in the ideals of equality and justice, but such notions were not central to the public image the organization displayed. During the war itself, the Legion gave evidence of a growing impatience, for instance, with the liberal rationale for the war, which rested on government action and the ideals of the Four Freedoms. Their problem was rooted in a growing fear of government control over individual life, a fundamental tenet of conservative thought and one partially rooted in the experience of wartime sacrifices and mobilizations. The Legion acknowledged that "centralized controls in the interest of the war effort" were necessary but ultimately felt that "government is best that governs least." In 1943 the Legion magazine stated unequivocally that "freedom of individual enterprise is of importance equal to the Four Freedoms and the Atlantic Charter." And it made vigorous calls for an end to wartime controls once the conflict was resolved. Indeed, Legion messages argued strongly that GIs were fighting mostly for "liberty and individual freedom" and the preservation of the "free enterprise system," points that suggested a deep faith in the power of individualism and an inherent dislike of the New Deal and Roosevelt liberalism. It was for a society based on an ideal of people of "ability" and "merit" competing to get ahead, according to the Legion, that men were willing to die on the "slithery slopes of the Apennines and in the steaming jungles of the Solomons."[8]

Legion publications offered readers tales of mythical American men, at once powerful individuals and true patriots, who had little trouble relinquishing their personal interests for the sake of the nation. In 1944 the Legion published a story of Nathan Van Noy, a "mild mannered" young man assigned to an engineering brigade in the Pacific. This short story described how Van Noy refused an order to move to the rear and insisted on manning a machine gun on a beach while his comrades retreated inland. When Japanese forces landed one night, he silently held his position until they approached to within a few feet and then opened fire, sending tracers "streaming across the beach." He kept firing even when Japanese grenades tore his legs off. When his comrades finally came back to him, they found blood oozing from his head but his hands still holding the trigger firmly. They concluded that he continued to fire his weapon "even after his heart stopped beating." Several years later readers of the Legion magazine could also read of Otto Erler of Dallas. Captured at Corregidor, the young Texan grew angry as he saw the American flag lowered and as he was forced to submit to the rule of every "buck-toothed runt" at the Cabanatuan prison camp. One day he found an old U.S. flag in a closet that reminded him of home. He carried the emblem with him secretly as he was transferred to various Japanese prisons and would display it to honor fellow prisoners who died. Eventually a Japanese officer discovered his secret and took the flag from him, promising to return it if he were ever freed. Once liberated in 1945, the soldier proudly carried the flag while marching before his superiors in Yokohama. When he returned home to Texas, he donated it to the Dallas Historical Society and told a reporter that he wanted it preserved as a sign of the deep sense of honor he felt from having fought in the war and of how grateful he felt to have survived the torture and death of the prison camps.[9]

The ideal GI was presumed to be loyal to his country and morally upright. Many assumed that victory was the result not only of a well-trained military machine and powerful weapons but of a fundamental religious faith that made America stand out as a nation blessed by God. In the postwar period, the fusion of patriotism and traditional moral behavior served not only to enhance America's struggle against communism but also to reverse much of the moral decline that many felt the war had brought. During the early 1940s soldiers could enter into all kinds of sexual relationships—including homosexual ones—that would not have been tolerated had they remained under the close scrutiny of their families and hometowns. In fact, the lenient nature of wartime life and the mobility of the population actually precipitated the flourishing of gay and lesbian communities in many areas. Thus, the crusade against communism sought to purge not only communist sympathizers from American public life but also gay men, who were now considered too feeble to join the fight against America's enemies and infected with a proclivity for traitorous behavior.

As groups such as the Legion joined the Cold War struggle against the Soviet Union, they demanded not only that Americans line up behind this new political crusade but that they undertake efforts at "Moral Re-Armament" as well. The Legion's "Back to God" program specifically called upon members to attend church regularly and encouraged their families to pray together daily. Stories in the Legion's magazine made reference to the faith of the fighting men. It told of one man who wrote a letter before his ship went down in the Pacific in 1943 urging his surviving son not only to take care of his mother and be a good American but to be a "good Catholic" as well. In "Faith Under Fire," another piece that appeared in the same journal the following year, a navy chaplain told a story of serving on a ship in the Solomon Islands. He expressed amazement at the display of power exhibited by American vessels that fired "salvo after salvo" before his own ship was hit by the Japanese. This man of God admitted that during the heat of battle he experienced conflicting emotions—being repelled by all the killing going on around him and also feeling a desire for revenge against a hated enemy. As he saw Japanese ships hit he cried aloud, "Good, good, let'em burn." Yet he also talked of how painful it was for some American men to die and noted that, "unlike a Hollywood movie," many "screamed their way into eternity." But his drift into reality ultimately convinced him not that war was evil but that it could be transformative and lead men to accept God. At the end of his tale he stressed how he had met many men who drew from their encounter with battle only a deep desire to return to their "fundamental instincts" and to find God and have faith in their lives. God and country mattered most. They were ideals that would sustain the wartime spirit of unity after 1945 and the notion of America's superior virtue.[10]

At times the veneration of military service was so great that the Legion could suspend its general antipathy toward government influence and work assiduously for veteran benefits. In order to generate enthusiasm for such an agenda, the Legion regularly supplied lawmakers with information during the war on the problems men faced once they came home. This was quite apparent in a 1943 report to Congress entitled "Forgotten Battalion," which described the many physical and emotional wounds men brought home from battle and their need for proper medical assistance. Actually, veteran's compensation had been a prominent issue for the Legion since World War I. National leaders like Woodrow Wilson and Herbert Hoover had indicated a degree of skepticism over the idea of publicly funded benefits for returned soldiers because they saw military service as a civic duty and because such programs tended to be quite expensive. Historian Jennifer Keene has shown that it was the resentment many veterans from World War I felt over Hoover's stance and his repression of the Bonus Marchers of 1932 that helped to fuel a desire on the part of that generation to secure benefits for the men who now fought in World War II. These older veterans—many of whom now held influential positions in Congress—and the lobbying of the American Legion ultimately accounted for the passage of the Veterans Readjustment Act of 1944, generally known as the GI Bill. Modern scholarship has made it clear that this legislation was of monumental significance to the men who took advantage of it. Historian Lisabeth Cohen, for instance, has revealed that access to the bill's educational and health provisions and low-cost mortgages helped World War II veterans as a group acquire a higher medium income and rate of home ownership than non-veterans of a comparable age. Keene argues that the bill helped many returned soldiers leverage their military service into upward mobility, although racial minorities and women who served their nation did not share in the fruits of the program to the same extent as white men did. By 1948 expenditures under the bill represented 15 percent of the federal budget, and veterans constituted nearly half of the students at American colleges.[11]

The Legion's militant brand of national identity and patriotism did not cause it to oppose completely new visions of liberal internationalism that emerged in the aftermath of World War II, but it did serve to moderate considerably the group's commitment to them. The Legion—as did many other groups—concluded that a new approach to world affairs would be needed after 1945, and consequently it offered a general form of support for the newly created United Nations. The United States, it argued, had a "high and solemn responsibility" toward the world organization and an obligation to sustain the "spirit of unity" that emerged from the war and keep it alive as a "force for world peace and security." It had little desire to return to prewar isolationism. Yet it was forthright in its belief that the United States should never relinquish its right to remain strong and use its power to pursue national objectives. Legion spokesmen argued that they expected that China, Great Britain, and the Soviet Union would do the same. They indicated that those nations would not "stand up for American rights," and thus America should not be "ashamed to insist on our own rights too." The Legion's outlook on international relations was evident at its 1950 convention. Legion members passed a motion calling for the United Nations to amend its charter by removing the veto power of key member nations in matters of aggression. Such a move would remove a potential obstacle in cases where the United States deemed it in its best interests to act unilaterally. In the same motion the Legion also affirmed the right of the United States to use any means possible to retaliate against future Soviet aggression, including the "release of atomic weapons." During the war in Korea, Erle Cocke, who had survived a Nazi "firing squad," even declared that the United States would be better served if the running of the war were placed entirely in the hands of U.S. military authorities and taken out of the control of politicians in Washington and the United Nations. In a similar vein, the Veterans of Foreign Wars started an "American Sovereignty Campaign" in the early 1950s that sought to oppose any legislation that would inhibit the ability of the United States to pursue its own interests.[12]

The conservative stance of the Legion in the postwar era—with its veneration of national power, fighting-men, free-market capitalism, anticommunism, and religion—was essentially unfriendly to liberal causes such as unionization and civil rights. This did not mean that all of its members held strong anti-liberal views, although the national image of the organization was seen as reactionary. The national office was able to retain the support of its members, regardless of what views they held, partly because it exercised considerable power in Washington when it came to veteran's affairs and had been authorized by the federal government to assist veterans in signing up for federal benefits in their local halls. Thus there was little challenge to the organization's leadership from the inside. This also meant that some locals were left to pursue whatever politics they chose. In the South, black veterans were still confined to segregated posts in the late 1940s, despite their wartime service and national movements to integrate the armed services at the time. In fact, no black youth could be part of the Legion's popular Junior Baseball program south of the Mason-Dixon Line, despite the fact that the intent of the program was to build character among young men. When a Legion official in charge of the program was asked if he thought such segregation was really the best way to build "good citizenship" and character, the man explained that "people's prejudices" had to be respected and that, if the "color line" was not accepted, there would be no Junior Baseball program at all in the South. In fact, partially because the Legion did not push for an end to white supremacy, black veterans could not gather all the information they needed to secure the GI benefits that whites got.[13]

In the early years of the Cold War, veterans not only tried to shape national politics but sometimes took to the streets to perform again their roles as defenders of the nation as they imagined it should be. Members of the Legion, along with Catholic and Jewish veterans groups, organized in 1948 to disrupt rallies held for Henry Wallace, the most liberal of all the presidential candidates that year. In 1949 veterans in Peekskill, New York, stormed a crowd of concert-goers who had come to hear Paul Robeson, a prominent African American singer and political activist who was supportive of socialism and better relations with the Soviet Union. The anti-liberal nature of the "riot" was exacerbated by the fact that a good number of those attending the concert were Jewish Americans who vacationed in the area during the summertime. A local paper printed a letter from a Peekskill veteran who argued that the last war was fought to destroy the type of totalitarianism that, he charged, Robeson supported. During the melee in the streets, some veterans hurled rocks and racial and anti-Semitic epithets and threw punches at those in attendance. After the turmoil subsided, local veterans claimed that their actions had served notice that "pinks" and Robeson were not welcome in the town. A historian who has studied the incident concluded that the national press was generally supportive of the "veteran's cause."[14]

THE LIMITS OF MILITARIZATION

The aggressive defense of the nation that marked the outlook of major veterans organizations and many leaders after the war was by no means a true reflection of how all Americans saw the lessons of the last war. There were strong efforts in the late 1940s to temper the obsession with national defense with an insistence that wartime sacrifices demanded a powerful effort to fashion a more democratic society in America. This was certainly central to the thinking of the American Veterans Committee (AVC). Although it never generated the large membership base enjoyed by the American Legion or the Veterans of Foreign Wars, the AVC kept alive the idea that World War II had been fought primarily for the realization of human rights everywhere. Founded in a small apartment in New York City near the end of the war under the leadership of Charles Bolte, the AVC argued forcefully that veterans needed to seek more than just government benefits. Bolte, an ex-soldier who had lost a leg in battle, insisted that once home from the service men also had to think of themselves as "citizens" interested in human betterment as well. Although the AVC certainly supported all measures designed to ensure the security of the nation, Bolte also insisted that the group focus on more than "national survival alone" and said that it was now a "political necessity" to work toward the creation of a "better world."[15]

In its earliest years the AVC promoted a program of "Peace, Jobs, and Freedom." Appealing directly to women and racial minorities as well as to white males, the organization declared that veterans from World War I had dreamed of similar goals but had been disillusioned by economic hard times and a call to arms again in 1941. The AVC now asserted that "American men and women, regardless of race, creed, or color," must work together to secure a New Deal–type agenda that included "adequate financial, medical, vocational, and social security." It also called for free speech, the right to worship as one pleased, and the disarmament of Germany and Japan. And in a nod to internationalism (rather than unilateralism), the AVC made a plea for a world council of veterans that would work for peace and justice among all nations. In a rebuke to the more militant outlook of the American Legion, the AVC declared that, although they could fight well when "aroused," Americans were not "militaristic people" and that "the Army was not the American way." One notable war hero, Colonel Evans F. Carlson, (a marine leader from Guadalcanal) wrote to the AVC to reinforce their position and argued that the war had been about "our conception of democracy" in which political power resided in the "people" and where all races and creeds were treated with "dignity and nobility."[16]

Bolte thought that the American Legion was "dangerous" and was simply too conservative for the good of a democratic society. He recalled the anti-radicalism of the organization in the 1930s and felt it was "unduly" patriotic. When he came home from the war, he did join a Legion post to please his father and found that the men he met were not the "fascist" types he recalled marching in uniforms in the 1930s. Most seemed to be "good-hearted businessmen" who were disinterested in national and international issues. From this experience he concluded that the Legion's leadership was simply not in touch with the rank and file and was run mostly as a "top-down" organization with traces of militaristic and racist thinking among its membership. Bolte surmised that the Legion continually invoked the specter of the nation's enemies as a way to keep in line members who, in his view, were mostly "prosperous" and middle class. Subsequent leaders of the AVC generally retained Bolte's perception of the major veteran organizations. In 1947 Chat Paterson, the national commander of the AVC at the time, wrote to civil rights leader Walter White to tell him that he felt the VFW had done very little to end discrimination against veterans of color. Bill Mauldin, who served for a brief time as the leader of the AVC in the early 1950s, critiqued the

Legion and the VFW, claiming they relied too much on a politics of fear rooted in a staunch anticommunism and did not pay sufficient attention to matters of justice and equality.[17]

The AVC worked especially hard to recruit black members to its ranks. Bolte cultivated a relationship with White and the NAACP, and on occasion they dined together. At their 1946 convention in Des Moines, Iowa, the organization adopted a platform that included a statement of opposition to any form of discrimination on the basis of race, religion, color, or sex. At the same meeting, when it was learned that two black delegates had been refused service at a café near the convention hall, AVC delegates set up picket lines in front of the establishment and called local police to report the incident. In 1947 a New York City chapter of the AVC formed a group called "America's Team," which assumed responsibility for fighting "mongers of hate." The "team" consisted of "a Negro, a Catholic, a Jew, and a Protestant." In 1954 the organization even filed an amicus curiae brief in support of the NAACP in a number of school desegregation cases, including *Brown vs. the Board of Education*.[18]

The NAACP itself also worked to improve the situation for black veterans. It complained publicly that blacks had difficulty joining Legion posts and therefore acquiring information they needed to receive GI benefits. The civil rights group was also concerned over the segregation of black veterans in military hospitals and discovered that in some southern states, such as Alabama and Louisiana, black veterans had even been refused a Legion charter to set up a segregated post. In 1944 the national office of the Legion reported that it had no way of knowing how many posts might be "non-segregated" and that it was up to each individual unit to decide whether to accept "colored members."[19]

Militarization was tempered not only by the goals of a more progressive politics but also by the weariness and bitterness millions now felt after four years of mobilizations and sacrifice. Most Americans at the time looked forward, not to defending the nation or preparing for another war, but simply to going home. Both civilians and GIs expressed their displeasure with the slow pace of separating men from the service, and in several cases troops organized public protests in hopes of accelerating the process. One observer of a mass demonstration of American forces in Manila over the issue of demobilization wrote in 1946 that the men were simply anxious to get home and "be done with the Army." There was also widespread anger over the regimentation many encountered in the service and the status system that was so central to military life. Many even complained that the military had not improved the character of men but had simply encouraged them to smoke, drink, and abandon restraints on sexual activity.

Some vets—like Fred Gole of Euclid, Ohio—were also upset when they came home and learned that there were men in their hometown who never served. The postwar press was often filled with controversies over the poor treatment and racism encountered in veterans hospitals and the "abuse" that many suffered in such institutions when suffering from "neuropsychiatric" disorders.[20]

Homecomings not only brought huge parades of welcome as they did in Haverhill, Massachusetts, in June of 1946, but brought insurmountable difficulties to individuals and families as well. Although the transition to civilian life went well for most soldiers, the number who encountered serious bouts of depression and anxiety or endured troubled relationships after 1945 was substantial and will never be known. Studies have demonstrated that during the first decade after the war veterans were more likely to get divorced than non-vets, in part because of their personal battles with depression and "intrusive memories of battle scenes." People could see with their own eyes the damage war had wrought. Men walked around with missing limbs and all sorts of war-related injuries. Al Schmid, who gained stature as a Marine hero during the war for killing hundreds of Japanese on Guadalcanal, was frustrated for years because battle had cost him his eyesight. He did not like having to depend so much upon his wife, and he eventually retreated from public events completely because he felt his heroic image was simply too far removed from the everyday struggles he faced with his disability. Thomas Childers wrote of his parent's postwar lives and said that his mother could only recall the war as a time that changed his father—in her opinion, for the worse—and brought much tension into their marriage. In Crotonville, New York, Richie Garrett recalled that as a young boy he met men who carried plates in their heads and who seemed "genuinely disturbed." On one occasion he witnessed a veteran beating his wife in an open lot.

Other young men recalled how their fathers came home from World War II with a strong penchant for heavy drinking. Tom Matthews of Helper, Utah, remembered that his father—who fought in Italy—experienced mood swings and bouts with alcohol to the point that he was frightened by him. Red Ditterline, who won a Purple Heart in Europe, returned to Griffith, Indiana, to spend many evenings drinking with buddies and yelling in the middle of the night that "you're not gonna fucking do that to me" as he bashed his fists into walls. He also would often beat his sons "until their backs were striped with welts and blood." It is no wonder that Alcoholics Anonymous experienced significant growth just after the war as the men came home. And even if they were not in distress, surveys revealed that many felt their wartime service constituted wasted years and could have been better spent in pursuit of a career. Critical attitudes toward military service, in fact, helped explain why enlistments lagged in the late 1940s and why the armed forces were forced to offer better benefits and take steps to moderate the deep division between officers and enlisted men that characterized the war years.[21]

Strains of liberal idealism and critical appraisals of the war years eventually made it difficult for staunch militarists to win public approval for Universal Military Training (UMT). The American Legion, for instance, felt military-type training was as an essential component of the education of young men if they were to defend the nation again. The organization made a UMT bill their chief legislative goal in 1945 and argued that there was no good reason to teach young people topics like reading and math and never give them an "inkling of self-defense or the defense of the nation itself." The Legion compared UMT to the need for American youth in the Early Republic to learn to shoot a rifle. It argued that such skills have been lost in much of modern civilization and that adolescents today lack not only the ability "to shoot" but the "discipline" necessary to fight.[22] Legion leaders even argued that UMT would strengthen the "spiritual and moral training" of young men and thus make them better citizens. In the Legion's conception of UMT, recruits would not only learn how to fire a rifle but would spend time with chaplains to discuss "citizenship and religious faith." They even claimed UMT would foster an ideal of democracy because it would include people from all classes and backgrounds. Yet the ultimate goal was not a more democratic America but one dependent on the rule and power of strong men who could fight off threats at home and abroad. Furthermore, the Legion was quite clear that such training would help prevent a return to prewar pacifism and what they referred to as "the old indifference to all things military." "Perpetual peace mongers" had no place in their vision of postwar America, which they hoped would never be "without a large, trained army." The outbreak of war in Korea only confirmed this lesson that the Legion felt it had learned from World War II. In the end, however, UMT was never approved by Congress for many reasons, including its high costs and an argument from many that it would make America "a more warlike" nation.[23]

A DIVIDED NATION

The debate over UMT suggested again that not all Americans looked back at World War II in the same way. Some saw it as an example of the need to be ready to fight again. Others held grave reservations over the very idea of militarization and were reluctant to embark upon another quest for total victory. This point was made clear in 1951 when General Douglas MacArthur, an American hero from the last war, wanted to earn a triumph again by extending the conflict in Korea into China. The ensuing contest between the popular general, who sought total victory, and President Harry Truman, who was willing to settle for a stalemate in this bitter struggle, revealed a great deal not only about public opinion in the early Cold War but also about the conflicted way World War II still reverberated through the American consciousness.

When the general challenged his constitutional authority by voicing disapproval of his policies in public, President Truman elected to remove MacArthur as his commander in Korea for insubordination. In the spring of 1951 the Truman administration decided to withdraw from Korea and leave the northern part of the peninsula to communist forces. Truman and his advisors were fully intent on enhancing America's military capabilities to fight a global Cold War overall, but they saw Korea only as a "limited" conflict not warranting any dramatic expansion. In fact, the Truman administration had trouble generating public support for the venture and was able to do so only by stressing its restricted nature. Truman as well as a good deal of the American citizenry abhorred the possibility of initiating a third world war. However, MacArthur, who saw no substitute for victory, feared that any concessions would encourage communists to expand elsewhere in the world. The firing of the World War II hero provoked a firestorm of controversy in the United States, with millions of citizens siding with the war hero and directing their anger toward a president who chose to stop fighting before the enemy was vanquished. Senator Joseph McCarthy, a staunch warrior in the battle against communism and a World War II veteran who had falsely claimed a war wound from his days in the Pacific theater in order to attract votes, called Truman "a son of a bitch who should be impeached." The subsequent dispute turned into a highly public controversy when Americans ultimately revealed that while many (but not all) admired MacArthur's accomplishments in World War II, they were reluctant to embark upon a crusade to earn a victory again at any cost.[24]

Most of the major veterans organizations moved quickly to MacArthur's defense. "A storm of protest" over the president's actions arrived in the form of letters and calls to the national headquarters of the American Legion. Erle Cocke, who had recently made a tour of the Korean battlefront, came out strongly for the general and his plans. He supported the bombing of Chinese bases across the Yalu River in Manchuria and called for the rearming of Japan and for the blocking of Chinese ports. Addressing a Legion meeting in Florida at the time, Cocke said he accepted the idea of civilian control of the military, but he complained bitterly that putting "stupid handicaps" on military leaders was no way to fight or win a war. "Military decisions" must govern the waging of war and not the views of "swivel-chair politicians," he proclaimed. The Legion commander felt that "soldiers have always fought wars, and they should fight this war and the wars of the future." Cocke expressed shock when informed that the American Veterans Committee had sided with Truman in the matter and indicated that even Mac-Arthur's successor, Matthew B. Ridgeway, could not succeed without the freedom to act as he saw fit.[25]

Ordinary citizens also had strong views on the Truman-MacArthur issue and expressed them in thousands of letters to the White House. During the first five weeks after the president fired the general, more than 84,000 Americans wrote the chief executive to tell him what they thought. An analysis of this correspondence in 1966 concluded that about 55 percent of the mail found fault with Truman, and the rest supported his decision. The important point here, however, was that the numbers revealed a deep division within the population over issues pertaining to the conduct of the last war and a substantial level of disapproval toward a prominent World War II hero.

MacArthur's supporters valued the man as a highly skilled soldier and seemed to desire a wartime victory again in Korea. In a sense they wanted a replay of World War II and felt MacArthur could provide it. Many could not imagine the nation moving forward or being safe without men like him. And they inferred that the sacrifices of war were only justified if the nation won. Joseph Campbell of Flushing, New York, called MacArthur "America's greatest general and statesman" and felt his dismissal was "an insult to every American" and to "every soldier, sailor, and marine both in this war and in World War II" who served in the Pacific theater and to those who made the "supreme sacrifice." A veteran from Delaware wrote to say that he admired MacArthur a great deal after serving under him and that if Truman did not at least appoint him secretary of state he should vacate the office of president. Another writer from Wisconsin compared the firing of MacArthur to Munich and saw it as an act of appeasement toward a treacherous enemy. A woman from Michigan also invoked the idea of appeasement in her letter and argued that Truman's dismissal implied that he recognized the communists as the rightful government of China and that he was now as guilty of "mass murder of our American soldiers as if he had stabbed each one in the heart." Mary Langevin of Springfield, Massachusetts, wrote that MacArthur's role in making the Japanese a "conquered people" won for him the respect and admiration not only of Americans but of the Japanese as well. She felt that his leadership qualities were indispensable in Korea because he was the finest soldier America ever produced and always had the best interests of the American fighting man at heart.[26]

MacArthur's supporters not only celebrated the ideals of leadership and victory but felt he was emblematic of true patriotism because he was driven to destroy the nation's enemies—now envisioned as communists. Helen Cook of New Jersey asked the president if "pro-communist" sympathizers had blinded him to the "great wisdom and one-hundred percent Americanism" of MacArthur. Others charged Truman for failing to realize that America was in a real war with "Red China" and that it made no sense to have MacArthur "gagged, bound and then fired." Another World War II veteran, J. J. Carey of Denver, told the president that the dismissal of the general constituted a greater victory for "Russia" than if the United States had been pushed out of Korea. A woman from Pennsylvania argued that MacArthur was the "greatest foe" of communism in the world and that along with Franklin Roosevelt was the greatest man who had ever lived. Others asserted that MacArthur was the one who was upholding "truly American ideals" in the Cold War and that everything that can be done should be done to win this contest.[27]

Echoes of wartime anger and cynicism could still be detected in the views of many who wrote in support of Truman's position. Despite his popularity with much of the public, McArthur had always been derided by many of the men who served under his command in the Pacific during the war. Some veterans felt his losses in early Pacific campaigns such as Guadalcanal were unacceptably high. And thousands of troops recalled that he had been unable to deliver on his promise of reinforcements to the defenders of Bataan and that he had spent nearly all of his time during the siege in relative safety on Corregidor—a decision that earned him the nickname "Dugout Doug." John F. Kennedy, serving as a PT boat commander in the Pacific, for instance, indicated that he and many of the men who served with him detested the general's military strategies as unnecessarily prolonging the war (and therefore insensitive to the welfare of the men). The residue of this criticism was expressed again in letters to the White House in the early 1950s. A woman from Alabama wrote Truman to tell him that she felt better now that MacArthur was removed from Korea because she had a brother who was fighting there and felt the general would have only put him in further danger by extending the war for the sake of his personal glory. She claimed that she "didn't like [MacArthur] in World War II" either because she had worried constantly over the fate of her husband, who served in the Pacific. Another citizen from Houston wrote that he thought MacArthur was a "terrible man, an egomaniac, and I believe a war monger." Seven people from Cambridge, Massachusetts, joined together to compose a letter that backed the president and charged that the general was more dictatorial than democratic and that "his adventurous

policies had brought the world hard to the brink of a general war that could have
ended only with the destruction of modern civilization." Harriet Ray of California asserted that "only the military wants wars—which are an utter waste to all
common people." Philip Adams of San Francisco congratulated Truman for removing "a despotic and super-arrogant militarist" from power. Others raised objections to any more killing and argued that there could be no honor in war and
that the "death of our boys is aimless and tragic." And another citizen wrote that
most people "loathe the idea of war more than they desire a victory, which on
MacArthur's turn would be rather a holocaust."[28]

In a good number of instances, letter writers who supported Truman and articulated critical attitudes toward war identified themselves as veterans of the last
conflict. Charles Marriott of Cincinnati told Truman that the "greatest thing" the
president could do was to keep the nation out of another conflict. "War never
settled anything," he wrote, and he urged the president to do all he could to avoid
a "third world war." Edward Cibel of Los Angeles, who had fought in the Pacific,
wrote that every mother of a son will be thankful for Truman's actions in dismissing MacArthur and every GI will be grateful for such a "wonderful deed." A man
who served in the Army from "March 1941 to November 21, 1945," asked the
president to do nothing that would help spread the war in Korea. "I wonder if
the chaos and misery of warfare were visited upon the supporters of General
MacArthur here at home would they still be so ardent in their support of him?"
he asked. And Joseph Adaline of Allen Park, Michigan, noted that he was a World
War II veteran who counted himself very fortunate to have returned home "all in
one piece thanks to God." From his military service Adaline surmised that he
would rather pay higher taxes to introduce freedom and liberty to people of the
world through the Marshall Plan than through military actions that spilled "good
American blood in World War III."[29]

MacArthur received a thunderous reception when he finally came home in
1951 after serving in Asia for some fifteen years during World War II, the reconstruction of Japan, and the struggle in Korea. In many ways he was seen at the
time of his return as emblematic of the ideology of militarism that ran through
the postwar culture of the late 1940s and early 1950s with its reverence for brave
warriors, military power, and the victory in World War II. MacArthur, of course,
was partly responsible for his heroic image. During the 1940s his staff
had worked diligently to craft his public profile by staging photographs and film
footage of his wartime exploits and postwar duties in Japan. Moreover, he was
well known for claiming considerable credit for victory in the Pacific in conversations that tended to diminish the contributions made by the Navy and the Ma-

rines. As he paraded down the main streets of American cities in the spring of 1951, millions of citizens cheered wildly for the man who helped to bring them victory in 1945, suggesting that they felt the values he stood for were still necessary in the present. In a world filled with anxiety and uncertainty, MacArthur evoked a sense of the timelessness of the virtues of loyalty and sacrifice that were deemed to explain how World War II was won and a rebuke to those who would look upon any American war with cynicism and dread. It was the defenders of this virtuous view of America and its wars who cheered for the general, dominated the public opinion polls that seemed to favor him over Truman for a brief time, and in some instances were even moved to burn the president in effigy.[30]

MacArthur performed virtue at every turn. In his first public appearance on his way home from Asia at the Punchbowl National Cemetery in Hawaii, he placed a wreath of honor at the graves of the "heroic dead." News reports stressed the fact that the five-star general stood for a full minute in silent tribute. MacArthur remarked to reporters that he did "not know the dignity of their birth" but he did know the "glory of their death." World War II sacrifices were recalled again during a massive parade in Chicago, when his motorcade stopped for a ceremony at the Bataan-Corregidor Bridge, where he placed another wreath in honor of the "American boys" who died in the defense of the Philippines. Many also remarked how the sight of him in his "five-starred trench coat" and his "famous upswept cap with the faded gold braid" reminded them of the many times they saw these images in photos and films during World War II. The parades and events now centered on him were frequently compared to V-J Day just six years earlier. In an address to Congress, which was widely covered by the press and was interrupted repeatedly by applause, the war hero took advantage of the moment to assail the idea of "appeasement" and argued that victory in the Pacific in 1945 had provided the nation with a "vast moat" that would protect it as long as we held it and that removed any need to make unnecessary concessions to "Red China."[31]

Until his death in 1964, MacArthur remained a symbol of the traditional remembrance of World War II that celebrated honor over tragedy, the idea of total victory, and personal devotion to the defense of the nation. Organizations that wanted to promote these values always found a rich source of words and stories surrounding the general that reinforced their views. In 1952 the Heritage Foundation, for instance, published some 400,000 copies of a book entitled *Revitalizing the Nation: A Statement of Beliefs, Opinions and Policies Embodied in the Public Pronouncements of General of the Army Douglas MacArthur.* The introduction to the volume was written by a prominent American religious leader, Norman Vincent Peale, who said that "no man in our time is more authentically the voice of the real America" than MacArthur. Peale felt that the war hero now helped to renew faith in the "land of Washington, Jefferson, and Lincoln" and demonstrated that faith still lived in the "hearts of the people." In fact, viewed in its entirety, the book was not just about the thoughts of the general but was really a ringing defense of a national identity that was thoroughly conservative and patriotic—one that drew from its past the idea that the nation's destiny was grounded in religious and patriotic faith more than in any liberal or humanitarian creed. MacArthur stated clearly in the book that the path to the future would be built on timeless values such as "our Christian faith" and the readiness to fight again. "Our greatest hope and faith," he proclaimed, "rests upon two mighty symbols—The Cross and the Flag." These were symbols that pointed out how America would remain strong and free, for they would encourage a sense of personal morality and confidence that would allow citizens to face death if the need arose. And religious faith and patriotic ardor would help Americans "regain the faith of our fathers."[32]

In 1961, after MacArthur had made a sentimental journey back to the Philippines, Senator Thomas Dodd delivered a speech in Congress indicating just how much MacArthur's trip had reminded him of victory in the Pacific and the failure to secure such a triumph in Korea. Dodd's words are worth quoting at length:

> The sight of General Mac Arthur in uniform . . . receiving the plaudits of admiring millions recalls vividly to our minds the picture of our Nation as we would always hope to see it, a nation that kept its promises, a nation victorious on all fronts, a nation at the pinnacle of worldly power and esteem, a nation triumphantly dedicated to the cause of freedom. The name of Douglas MacArthur causes to flash through the mind unforgettable images which are an essential part of the American story: the gallant, magnificent defense of Bataan and Corregidor against hopeless odds; the promise of return and depth of conviction that made men believe the promise would be kept, the vast, brilliant island-hopping campaign. . . . the incomparable battleship *Missouri* where General Mac Arthur accepted the surrender of our enemy.[33]

Completely separated from any home by a lifetime of service in the military, MacArthur and his wife lived a rather lonely existence in a suite at the Waldorf-Astoria Hotel in New York City in his final years. With his death in April 1964, however, public attention turned again to his military exploits and the ideals that were attached to him. News and magazine articles summarized his long and illustrious military career that included combat service in World War I and his leadership in the Pacific war. Readers again could relive the story of how he was ordered by Franklin Roosevelt to escape the Philippines, how he regrouped his forces in Australia, how he returned to liberate the islands, and his acceptance of the Japanese surrender on the deck of the USS *Missouri*. No one argued that MacArthur was anything less than an American hero of World War II. *Time* called him a "great warrior" who was "larger than life." To the editors of *Time* he was one of the "most brilliant soldiers of all time," who used creative battle plans that included a reliance on air and naval power to support army troops and a clever scheme to leapfrog from island to island that frequently left Japanese forces isolated. More importantly, this moment of remembrance served to remind all Americans of his well-known values and beliefs, especially his firm conviction that there "could be no substitute for victory." In a letter to *Time*, one veteran who served with him commented that the general inspired devotion among his men because of his "greatness." Another called him "one of the most brilliant military commanders since Napoleon" and claimed "true greatness lay in his absolute devotion to his country." The press also gave considerable attention again to the 1962 speech he gave to West Point cadets in which he told young soldiers to focus on "duty, honor, and country." He exclaimed—in an indirect reference to the controversy surrounding his removal from Korea—that the cadets must realize that it is not for them to engage in politics. Their mission was to "win wars." "The duty of the American soldier is to achieve victories," the war hero noted, "and there is no substitute for victory."[34]

As Americans moved into the era after the Vietnam War, individuals would continue to summon up the memory of MacArthur from time to time. In 1978 William Manchester wrote an opinion piece in the *New York Times* in which he explained that MacArthur could be egotistical and melodramatic. But the noted author of a biography of MacArthur also praised what he felt was his "excellence" and "manliness" and lamented what he felt was the "timid nature" of America in the 1970s (just after the retreat from Vietnam) and the "flight from eminence" on the part of the entire nation. President Ronald Reagan picked up some of this argument when he spoke at the dedication of a "memorial corridor" at the Pentagon honoring MacArthur. Admirals and generals had called for such a memorial for years after corridors had already been dedicated to Dwight Eisenhower and George Marshall. In his speech Reagan pointed out that MacArthur had warned Congress in the 1930s that they needed to be ready militarily for the possibility of war and that he had believed in the principle that there can be no substitute for victory. Three years later in a discussion involving Vietnam, Reagan said, "Maybe General MacArthur was right; there is no substitute for victory."[35]

MacArthur, of course, did not stand alone as a heroic leader of World War II. His fame was matched by that of Dwight Eisenhower, the leader of the victory in Europe. The differences between the two, however, resided not only in their respective theaters of operation but in the symbolic weight each carried in the overall remembrance of the war. Eisenhower came to represent the idea that it was acceptable to hold deep reservations about American military power and about the very idea of war. In fact, when he ran for the presidency in 1952, he was adamant about seeking a peace settlement in Korea instead of a complete conquest of the enemy—a position that helped him get elected. Americans have always had an ambiguous relationship to militarization and the use of force itself. Their commitment to civilian rule over the armed services is longstanding and stems in part from a historic distrust of standing armies. Yet time and again they have supported (or not strongly opposed) presidents who have led them into war and have honored those who have fought and died for the nation.

In the 1952 election—despite the cheers for MacArthur the year before—most voters demonstrated strong support for a man who promised to do just the opposite of what MacArthur wanted to do. Eisenhower's election, in part, represented a victory not only for more moderate forces in the Cold War against communism but for those who came away from the experience of World War II with a sense of caution regarding the need to fight again. Robert Griffith, who has studied Eisenhower's career, concluded that "Ike" did not really "share the feeling of vulnerability that pervaded so much of the military during the early postwar era" and that he supported calls for military preparedness but "only in moderation." His promise that if elected he would go to Korea and bring the troops home attracted enthusiastic support. Eisenhower's backers correctly surmised, however, that voters did not want a mythical figure in the White House but someone who seemed more like them—firmly entrenched in the civilian world, friendly, and approachable. To most people, Eisenhower seemed to have really put the war behind him. Many had a more difficult time imagining MacArthur out of uniform and therefore in the White House.[36]

During the campaign itself, a number of observers made explicit references to the different qualities each man was thought to possess. In a lengthy discussion in the *New York Times*, Hanson Baldwin cited the long and distinguished careers both men had enjoyed in the service of their nation. But he was quick to stress their different personalities. On the eve of the Republican convention in Chicago in the summer of 1952, Baldwin indicated that MacArthur would be backing the more conservative candidate, Robert Taft of Ohio, and not the more moderate and popular "Ike." Baldwin referred to MacArthur as a "twentieth-century Caesar" who had been raised for military greatness by a father who had won the Congressional Medal of Honor himself and a mother who was domineering and had made him "egocentric" and flamboyant. The writer pointed out how Eisenhower, in contrast, had been raised in a large family of humble circumstance, had never been surrounded by the "aura of glory," and was able quite naturally to "rub shoulders with the multitudes." Baldwin argued that MacArthur was a man of legend—"grandiose, detached, aloof, and Olympian." "There will never be myths around Eisenhower," he concluded, for "his philosophy is less imposing" and "his feet are in the mud of today." In the same year, historian T. Harry Williams wrote that MacArthur would never become the hero to ordinary soldiers and civilians that Eisenhower had been. For him "Ike" represented more of a "democratic" military tradition in which civilians retained control and in which a stronger sense of connection prevailed between the people in the service and those at home. He said people felt "safe" with Eisenhower and trusted him not to lead them into military adventures. For Williams, MacArthur appeared to be part of an older "aristocratic society" in which men proved their worth not at home but on the field of battle and seemed to have a feeling of superiority to ordinary citizens—a belief that made it easier for him to order men to their death.[37]

After his public career, Eisenhower, like MacArthur, continued to stand for certain values that had long been associated with the remembrance of World War II. Both men surely reinforced the legacy of patriotic service in American life. The president, however, represented a set of traditions different from the general's. Instead of total victory, Eisenhower became associated with an ideal of peace and a lingering skepticism of all things military. And it became quite clear during the quarter century after the war until his death in 1969 that "Ike" was also able to come home and resume something of domestic life, playing golf and lavishing attention on grandchildren. While MacArthur remained in the upper floors of a New York hotel, Eisenhower tended to his farm in Pennsylvania. When he died five years after MacArthur, a *Time* essay referred to him as a "Soldier of Peace." In a sense, he was seen as an antihero and a man who had not abandoned his ties to home, to family, and to the humble people from which he came. *Time* called him the "storybook American" (similar to the types crafted by Ernie Pyle) because he was "a hero who despised heroics" and a man "of high ideals and down-to-earth speech." "Ike" was praised for his embrace of "co-existence" with the Russians during the 1950s rather than seeking confrontation and his warning of the dangerous power of the "military-industrial complex" in America. "A soldier-President in a time of peace," the magazine pointed out, "Eisenhower personified the respect of the nation for its military after the war." But it was quick to point out that "some of his most eloquent words" were directed against the vast expenditures of funds for military power. And many news outlets commented on his humble beginnings in Abilene, Kansas, his sense of modesty, and his ability to relate to enlisted men and ordinary citizens. Some reprinted excerpts from the speech he gave in 1945 as he returned to Abilene to accept the plaudits of thousands of citizens. In this moment of victory, he told his audience: "I am no hero" but only the representative of the "heroic men" the United States had sent to war. In a sense he represented the ideal of American virtue in World War II better than anyone else.[38]

At the time of Eisenhower's death, Louis Harris, sampling public opinion, wrote that despite the fact that "Ike" had spent most of his life in the military, most Americans felt he was not only a "great general" but a "good man" who had helped keep intact the separation between military and civilian power while he was president. Harris argued that the public saw him in stark contrast to MacArthur, who seemed to represent the "forbidding austerity of the high-ranking military." In a eulogy to a man he once served as vice-president, Richard Nixon made a point similar to Harris's. He claimed that despite his military honors and triumphs, Eisenhower's popularity rested ultimately on his character and his ability to capture the "trust and faith" of many citizens. Nixon stressed how the late general and president was really a family man who told his loved ones, as he lay dying, that he had always cared for his wife, children, and grandchildren and "my country." Several years later, when American political passions were inflamed by Vietnam, George McGovern, then a candidate for the presidency, indicated that he had always admired Eisenhower because he showed "restraint" and settled "for less than total victory" in Korea and for his realization that much of the money spent on defense was wasted. In the same year a young history professor, Blanche Wiesen Cook, writing in the Los Angeles Times in criticism of the "bellicosity" of Nixon, evoked the memory of Eisenhower as a leader who "feared militarism" and refrained from going to war in Korea. And in 1983 David Broder, a news columnist, made public a letter "Ike" had written in 1956 in which he said that after years of dealing with issues of war and armaments mankind was getting to the point where no war could really be won anymore.[39]

Today visitors to the final resting places of these two war heroes can still see evidence of their differences and the varying ways in which they are recalled. Heroic statues of both men in military dress stand near their burial sites. Eisenhower and his wife are buried in a simple chapel across the street from his boyhood home in Abilene. Several of the inscriptions of Eisenhower's words near the tomb continue to work against any effort to see war as glorious. One from a speech in 1945 says that "humility must always be the portion of any man who receives acclaim earned in blood of his followers and sacrifices of his friends." Another from a 1953 address of the president exclaims that "every gun made, every warship launched, every rocket fired signifies, in the final sense, a theft from those who hunger and are not fed, those who are cold and are not clothed."

General and Mrs. MacArthur are buried in what was once the city hall of Norfolk, Virginia. They lie under a monumental rotunda in a building whose aesthetics resemble a classical temple more than a chapel. Inscriptions near the tombs draw from the words of the general as well, and one of them speaks of the hope that a "better world" might come from "the blood and carnage of the past." But the emphasis is more on MacArthur's career, including his flight from the Philippines and his promise to return to liberate the islands. And another—from his address to Congress upon his return in 1951—proclaims that "war's very object is victory. Not prolonged indecision. In war there can be no substitute for victory." Millions of Americans who had experienced the war years of the early 1940s had already indicated that they were not so sure he was right.

The need to arm and remain on the lookout for enemies was a central lesson many Americans drew from the experience of World War II. It was this powerful frame of remembrance, in fact, that helped to shape the American response to the spread of Soviet power in the postwar world, drove the politics of many leading veteran groups after 1945, and explained the veneration of powerful leaders like Douglas MacArthur. Despite the calls of veterans and anticommunist crusaders for a continuation of a strong military and a restoration of traditional values, however, all Americans did not reflect upon World War II in the same way. Organizations like the American Veterans Committee struggled mightily to keep alive the flame of humanitarianism, and critics of MacArthur's war record and of the value of military training were not hard to find. Many individuals returned from the war preoccupied with their personal problems and anxious to put the idea of war—the last one and the next one—out of their minds. Ultimately, when the war generation elected a war hero to the presidency, they turned to a man who reaffirmed their dream that Americans need not be obsessed with victory marches and the cant of being ready to fight again. It may also have been more than a coincidence that when they chose their president in 1952 they turned to the man who led the European war rather than the one who commanded the fight for revenge in the Pacific.

Victory Arch, World War II Memorial, Washington, D.C. Dedicated 2004. The aesthetics of such arches aspire to recall the glory of a victory and to erase considerations of the costs of warfare. Credit: Brenna Snider.

Victory Arch, National D-Day Memorial, Bedford, Virginia. Dedicated 2001.
Credit: Edwina Dickson, Sabyron Industries, Roanoke, Virginia.

Four Freedoms Memorial, Evansville, Indiana. Dedicated 1976. Each of the columns contained the name of one freedom. However, the memorial builders of Evansville revised Franklin Roosevelt's words so that "freedom from want," a direct link to the New Deal welfare state, did not appear and was replaced by "freedom from oppression." Credit: Adryan Dillon.

Opposite, Four Freedoms Memorial, Troy, Michigan. Dedicated 1948. The memorial is topped by a symbolic stone figure of Earth with representations of human beings. All of this is supported by figures of American fighting men. Credit: Marty and Jacob Bodnar.

Scenes from dedication of Bataan Memorial, Janesville, Wisconsin, 1948. Note
the mix of symbols: a tank, the names of the local men who died and those who
returned, and wreaths of mourning. Credit: The Rock County Historical Society,
Janesville, Wisconsin.

Bataan Memorial, Harrodsburg, Kentucky. Dedicated 1961. The tank reflected the
idea of the brave stand local men made on Bataan against a superior enemy force.
Next to the tank, not depicted in the photo, is a list of the men who returned home
and those who did not. Credit: author.

Bataan Memorial, Las Cruces, New Mexico. Dedicated 2002. The aesthetics of this monument refuse to depict the war in inspirational terms and retain the legacy of suffering endured by local men. Credit: Erin Michelle Photography, Tucson, Arizona.

"Tayabas Trenches." Artistic rendition from memory of American prisoner suffering in the Philippines by former POW Ben Steele. Used with permission of Ben Steele.

Heroic image of a Tuskegee Airman at the Tuskegee Airmen Memorial,
United States Air Force Academy, Colorado Springs, Colorado. A plaque
on the base of the memorial notes that these African American flyers
"rose from adversity" to "set a standard few will transcend." Credit: Blue
Fox Photography, Colorado Springs.

Opposite, Grieving parents hold folded American flag in aftermath of
losing a son in World War II. This image is part of the 50th Anniversary
World War II Memorial, Omaha. Dedicated 1995. Credit: Photo courtesy
of John Lajba, sculptor.

Etta Compton's memorial wreath to the African American dead in the Lee Street riots of 1942, Alexandria, Louisiana. Photo, 2007. Credit: author.

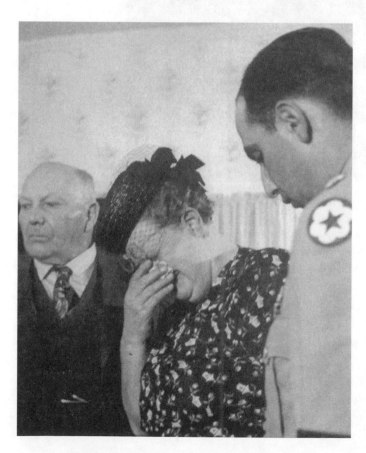

Gunda Borgstrom weeps as she recalls her four sons during their reburial in 1948 in Tremonton, Utah. Credit: Photo from *Life Magazine*, licensed for use by Getty Images to author (50774295).

CHAPTER FOUR

MONUMENTS AND MOURNING

DISAGREEMENTS OVER THE MEANING of the war led to political squabbles as well as widespread controversies over how to memorialize the dead. In local places and private spaces where unrelenting strains of bitterness and sadness festered, neither the traditional language of patriotism and honor nor the dreams of humanitarianism could fully console those who regretted the war's costs. As a result, a surprisingly strong debate erupted over the type of monuments that would best serve local needs to remember or to forget. There was certainly a strong effort to impart a legacy of virtue and respect for the war dead in traditional memorials, and there were extensive efforts to focus commemorations on the needs of the "living" at the expense of recalling the dead at all. Yet in countless localities, there were also those who appeared reluctant to cede the landscape of memory to those who wanted to simplify the remembrance of the war by invoking abstract images or living memorials. Local citizens who insisted that the loss of those whom Avishai Margalit has called "the near and the dear" be recalled were not prepared to accept the war as simply just or necessary, because they remained haunted by the pain it brought them for the rest of their lives.[1]

TRADITIONAL MEMORIALS

Traditionalism and its abstract images remained prominent in World War II monuments and memorials throughout the postwar era. At American military cemeteries overseas, at the Marine Corps War Memorial, the USS Arizona Memorial, and the World War II Memorial in Washington, D.C., the veneration of national sacrifice stood above reminders of personal loss. These highly visible national memorials performed well the cultural work of turning the tragic aspects of war into honor and heroism and diminishing the reality of suffering. Virtue and strength stood above violence and death.[2]

As it had after World War I, the American Battle Monuments Commission took responsibility for designing and building overseas cemeteries and memorials after 1945. These commemorative sites were constructed in various locations, including Europe, Honolulu, Manila, and North Africa. Designed by officials to be "inviolable shrines," these commemorative projects surrounded thousands of graves and lists of those missing in action with pieces of symbolic sculpture, chapels, battle maps, and even narratives of victorious campaigns from the war. The reality of death could not be masked, but efforts to justify and honor it were substantial. A key difference in the design of these memorials after 1945 when compared to World War I was noted by Ron Robin, who observed that the later sites relied more on symbols and designs that were "modern." Classical or traditional symbols evoking religious sentiments and the ideal of redemptive sacrifice were still to be found, however. Thus, the cemetery at Normandy contained walkways laid out in the shape of a "Latin cross" as well as customary headstones containing Christian crosses or the Star of David—a far cry from the helmet placed on top of a rifle stuck into the ground that was often used by soldiers in the field of battle to mark the dead. In the aftermath of 1945, however, symbols such as battle maps, narratives of victory campaigns, eagles, and dramatic sculpture indicated that there was now a felt need to center remembrance on actions mounted by the nation itself and on the newfound sense of power that victory brought. Whether the symbols were traditional or modern, the goal was still to transform tragedy into honor and mass death into national pride. At the cemetery near Florence, Italy, an inscription placed into a wall asked that visitors "not mourn with the parents of the dead who are with us. . . . Rather, comfort them. Let their burden be lightened by the glory of the dead, the love of honor." And at Normandy, in a modernist turn, a sculpture erected to the "Spirit of American Youth Rising from the Waves" transformed the legacy of the slaughter at Omaha Beach into the figure of a muscular American youth rising upward into the heavens and transcending the idea of tragedy completely.[3]

Left out of these colossal memorials to the dead were the countless traces of private recollections that many visitors brought to these sites. Consider the lingering thoughts and nightmares that Raymond Halloran carried home after flying bombing runs over Japan and being tortured as a prisoner of war. Decades after the war, Halloran felt compelled to fly to Hawaii to visit the National Memorial Cemetery of the Pacific and find the graves of some of the men from his bomber crew. The former B-29 navigator wanted to "talk" with his former comrades and tell them that they were "great guys" and that he was glad they had served together. For him such a visit helped to temper the effects of troubling nightmares that still plagued him more than four decades after he came home. In his dreams he would relive the terror of being shot down and suffering beatings and confinement as a prisoner of war. Having been on the ground when American forces fire-bombed Tokyo in March 1945, he would also visualize that his house was on fire as he slept. And frequently he would scream and put his hands over his face in a reenactment of being hit by the rifle butts of his captors.[4]

The Marine Corps War Memorial near the nation's capital took a photograph from an incredibly gruesome battle in the Pacific and turned it into another symbol of national unity and triumph that effaced traumatic memories almost completely. The memorial, based on the iconic photograph of Marines raising an American flag on Iwo Jima in 1945, was dedicated in 1954 and served for decades as the most popular image of the war. Although it was designed to enhance the reputation of the Marine Corps and to recall one of its greatest battles rather than to celebrate national unity, this image was reproduced in art, on school textbooks, and even in Hollywood films as a victory monument to World War II. In 2006 its central image of thrusting the flag upward in victory was evoked again in the design of the new National Museum of the Marine Corps in Virginia. National power was represented here in the form of six masculine figures, some thirty feet tall, fused together in bronze and evocative of a nation that was united and triumphant. This massive work of public art was also notable for the way it depicted one of the bloodiest battles of the war without any hint that there was tremendous loss of life. One-third of all Marines who died in World War II succumbed on the island. There are no names of any casualties on this memorial, however, but only the names of major marine battles throughout history and words etched in granite that refer to the "uncommon valor" demonstrated by the men who fought.

It is well known by now that the image on the memorial of the men raising the flag was based on a famous photograph by Joe Rosenthal that was widely circulated in the American press while the battle still raged in the Pacific. The image appears to suggest that the men raised the flag in the aftermath of victory, but in reality it was put up well before the contest was settled. Three of the six men depicted in the monument, in fact, never left the island alive. President Dwight Eisenhower was so upset by the failure of the memorial to recognize the full horror of this encounter with the Japanese that he cut short his attendance at the dedication ceremonies. Today the National Park Service has moderated some of the abstract symbolism at the site by erecting panels nearby that offer more details, such as the names of the six men commemorated in bronze. But the overall sense of male heroism and national unity still dominate the site. After the war the Marine Corps saw the value of Rosenthal's photo. At the time they not only wanted to reinforce their image as a group of patriotic and skilled warriors but worried that in the postwar era more government support might go to the Air Force and the Navy, which had been so instrumental in the American victory. The corps hired the public relations firm of J. Walter Thompson to help promote the idea of a memorial and raise the funds necessary to built it. Their efforts eventually paid off, and this monument to the victory at Iwo Jima became, in the words of Karl Ann Marling, "the definitive collective memory of the war."[5]

As the Marine Corps War Memorial presented images of national victory and male valor, it concealed not only the reality of the carnage on Iwo Jima but also the fact that many of the men depicted on the statue and their families suffered long after the war was over. In his best-selling book *Flags of Our Fathers*, James Bradley described how his father, part of the flag-raising team, never talked about the war once home in Wisconsin. In part this was because he still mourned the loss of a good friend from Milwaukee whose mutilated body he had seen on the island. Another flag raiser, Ira Hayes, a Pima Indian from Arizona who had volunteered for the Marines because he wanted to represent his people in a positive way, grieved for the rest of his life for buddies who were not able to leave the island alive. Hayes also remained frustrated that the service record of Native Americans had not translated into measurable improvements in their living conditions. In 1955, just three months after he had attended the dedication ceremonies of the Marine Corps War Memorial, Hayes died alone and almost penniless in the desert near his home, a victim of alcoholism. The racial divide that had bothered him was still evident in his funeral ceremonies. A public event, attended mostly by whites, was held at the state capital in Phoenix. Native Americans gathered separately at a small church at Sacaton to honor one of their own.[6]

Another Marine who helped to raise the flag and was immortalized on the Iwo Jima monument was Michael Strank, the son of a Slovak American coal miner from Franklin, Pennsylvania. In the public commemoration of Iwo Jima and in the stories told by men who knew him, Strank is repeatedly portrayed as a heroic warrior and ferocious fighter. When he was interred at Arlington National Cemetery in 1949, his family attended along with many residents of his hometown on a bus chartered by the Sgt. Michael Strank Post of the Veterans of Foreign Wars from Franklin. At a ceremony in nearby Johnstown commemorating the fortieth anniversary of the flag raising on Iwo Jima, an officer from a local Marine reserve unit referred to Strank as a "rough, tough, hard-nosed Marine" and the "kind of person everyone wished they could become." The following year the Pennsylvania Historical and Museum Commission dedicated a historical marker in honor of Strank. At the dedication ceremonies a local state representative noted that he was only six years old when he heard the news of Strank's death, and he wanted to keep alive his legacy of "bravery and ultimate sacrifice." A man who had served under Strank in the battle on Iwo Jima, Joe Rodriquez, remembered Strank as a "hero" and a "shining mentor" whom he viewed with great admiration. Later, in a news interview, Rodriquez told a reporter that he recalled seeing Strank's "mangled body" at his feet during the battle on the island. The text of the state marker, however, did not mention any "mangled body" but noted only that the young soldier was killed on Iwo Jima and that he took part in the flag raising that was the subject of Rosenthal's famous photo.[7]

Not surprisingly, the public depiction of Strank as a hero and model soldier also hid from public view the sadness that remained within his family long after 1945. Relatives shared some of the honor many saw in his sacrifice. Yet his sister, Mary Strank Pero, said in a phone interview in 2006 that it was always hard for her parents to accept his death. She indicated that it was especially difficult for her mother because Michael was "her firstborn" and because she had been so proud of the career he had established for himself in the Marines, having joined the corps in 1939. Living in a household supported by the modest wages of an immigrant miner, both Michael and his mother had seen military service as a way to improve upon their working-class status. His death not only shattered the family but destroyed many of his mother's aspirations. Mary Pero herself still keeps an album of the various news clippings about her famous brother and a copy of the telegram that arrived in 1945 announcing his death. Strank also had a brother whose ship was torpedoed in the South Pacific and who was plagued by war injuries for years afterward. Michael's parents and other family members attended the Iwo Jima memorial dedication in 1954, but eventually they declined to attend reunions of Iwo Jima survivors because they found such events too painful.[8]

The USS Arizona Memorial was dedicated just eight years after the monument to Iwo Jima. A memorial at Pearl Harbor could not mask entirely the legacy of death and loss that marked the first American battle of the war because the ruined hulk of the great battleship was visible just below the surface of the water where the memorial stood, and visitors generally knew that the remains of dead sailors were entombed within the ship itself. The aesthetics of the memorial were designed to portray the American nation as inherently pacifistic and a victim of the surprise Japanese attack. Thus the elongated white structure over the remains of the battleship "sags in the center"—as did the nation after the Pearl

Harbor attack—but "stands strong and vigorous" at its ends as America did after the war. This sense of victory and national power has since been reinforced by the placement of the USS *Missouri*, the ship on which the Japanese surrender took place, near the site of the *Arizona* in 1998. This tourist attraction was designed to foster a sense of "respect" for the generation that fought the war and the sacrifices they made. Victory and innocence here have always "encircled" the reality of the American dead at the site. Names of the men lost on the *Arizona* are inscribed inside the memorial, and during the war itself the crews of passing ships in Pearl Harbor would stand at attention and salute fallen comrades. Indeed, it was the presence of the dead in the harbor that caused many visitors to the site even in the early 1950s to express concern that the final resting place of these Americans was not yet properly commemorated. Already in 1949 a Pacific War Memorial Commission was created to consider ways to create a "living memorial commemorating the sacrifices of our heroic dead." And in 1958 a group of American veterans organized the Pearl Harbor Survivors Association, which consisted of men who had been in Hawaii at the time of the attack and who wanted to devote their energies to "honor and shield from neglect" the graves of their comrades who died to "protect the United States from its enemies." Over time, a few surviving sailors even elected to take an option granted to them by the Navy to have their ashes buried with comrades in the hulk of the *Arizona* instead of near their family plots at home.[9]

Before the final design for the *Arizona* memorial was accepted, however, the memorial commission did consider a number of alternative plans that allowed more direct access to the burial site itself. One idea submitted in 1950 called for a floating "eternal flame" with a submerged viewing chamber where visitors could view through portholes the twisted wreck where the fallen men remained. Another plan, which would be built in cooperation with the citizens of Japan, called for a remembrance of the war that transcended the nation-centeredness of the memorial. It proposed a "Hall of Humanities" in which the corpses now lying under the sea would be re-interred alongside an "Unknown Soldier from Japan." This plan even called for the destruction of the sunken battleship into small pieces that would be auctioned in order to raise funds to pay for the hall itself. Historian Edward Linenthal revealed that many saw this idea as "an intrusion on American sacred space." More specifically, it also threatened to weaken the myth of exceptional virtue that pervaded American culture and to turn the American dead into ordinary human beings. This was something many found difficult to accept in the aftermath of Pearl Harbor and the nation's victory.[10]

By the 1990s there was some evidence that commemoration at the site was shifting slowly from the traditionalism of the early 1960s. A new orientation film was provided for visitors in 1992, revising an older account that had used an "authoritative male voice" to recall the patriotic sacrifice and the lessons of unpreparedness at Pearl Harbor. In the new film a female voice now spoke and, instead of raising the possibility that the nation would have to be defended again in the future, asked visitors to reflect on what their own interpretations of the war were and why all of the sacrifice had taken place. Geoffrey White has explained how the new film seemed to reflect a more "mournful reflection" of the war's losses than the earlier one. In the first film, there were triumphant shots of big guns firing, and the names of the dead were merely whispered as the audiences viewed underwater shots of the remains of the *Arizona*. In the new film, audiences could see clearly the names of the dead carved in marble in the memorial and more film footage of the realities of battle and wounded soldiers lying on a beachhead.[11]

The strongest and most recent assertion of the war as the triumph of a strong and virtuous nation is to be seen at the World War II Memorial dedicated in 2004. Standing on the Washington Mall between the Lincoln Memorial and the Washington Monument, this classically designed structure celebrates victory in war and works against the aesthetics of the nearby memorials to conflicts in Korea and Vietnam. Yet the new memorial not only counters the idea of loss but represents an effort to forget much of what it ostensibly seems to commemorate—the experience of America in World War II. It contains no images of soldiers moving cautiously through a field of battle as can be seen at the Korean Memorial, and certainly no list of the names of the dead. The tremendous loss of American lives in World War II—some 400,000 individuals—is represented only by 4,000 gold stars. Its classical pillars and arches effectively substitute a sense of national harmony and grandeur for the sordid reality that was the war itself. This memorial contributes to the process of myth making by simplifying the history of the war and concealing the complex set of attitudes and emotions that haunted the wartime generation. Its aim is to uphold myths of national power and innocence that have long been central to America's collective identity.

The idea for the memorial came from a veteran, Roger Durbin, who worked as a mail carrier after coming home. On a visit to Washington in 1962, Durbin was struck by the fact that there was no national monument to the war. Subsequent travels to Europe had convinced him that American participation in the war was better commemorated abroad than at home and that most of his fellow servicemen would probably die before the nation properly recognized them. In 1987, just five years after the dedication of the Vietnam Veterans Memorial,

Durbin told his congresswoman about his ideas and pointed out that the Iwo Jima monument was designed to recognize only the Marines. Joined eventually by prominent figures such as Senator Bob Dole and Hollywood stars like Tom Hanks, an organizing committee raised some $190,000,000 to build the new memorial. Hanks, of course, attracted much attention to the fund-raising effort because he had starred in the 1998 movie on the D-Day landing, *Saving Private Ryan*. Dole used many of his connections with corporate leaders such as Fred Smith, the CEO of Federal Express. Smith, a veteran of the war himself, had served along with five of his uncles. Walmart donated $14,000,000 to the drive, and national veterans organizations such as the American Legion and the Veterans of Foreign Wars contributed several million dollars each. Unlike the memorial itself, a film produced to further the fund-raising campaign actually did discuss some of the traumatic experiences soldiers encountered. Dole talked about his "near-death experience" when wounded by Germans in Italy and how he had struggled after the war to rehabilitate himself. In another scene Luther Smith, an African American veteran and member of the Tuskegee Airmen, reminded viewers not only of black patriotism during the war but of the fight blacks made to integrate the armed services after 1945. And a Japanese American veteran described the brave deeds of men like himself who fought despite the fact that the government had imprisoned their relatives.[12]

Memorial designers and planners consciously opted for classical aesthetics in building the memorial rather than more realistic ones. One plan they rejected was simply too authentic. It involved a museum being placed in a "bunker" underneath the Mall where wartime newsreels would be replayed, a statue of a grieving mother would stand, and copies of Norman Rockwell's paintings of the "Four Freedoms" would be displayed. The winning design by Friedrich St. Florian mostly ignored or downplayed wartime realities, however. From the beginning he saw the project as only about the American victory. His memorial is dominated by a series of fifty-six granite pillars representing the forty-eight states, seven territories, and the District of Columbia that constituted the nation in the early 1940s and suggesting the idea that Americans were united in their fight against their enemies. At each end of the columns stand "victory arches," one for the Pacific theater and one for the Atlantic. St. Florian explained that his classical plan conveyed a sense of "timelessness" and that his overall design celebrated the "essence" of the American victory, which he believed was that "it allowed the free world to continue to be free." There are a few bits of "realism" in the memorial: small panels carved into the sides of the structure depict wartime events such as the attack on Pearl Harbor, the D-Day landing with the figure of a dead body on a beach, women working in a war plant, and a war bond parade. Names of specific military operations are also to be found. But ultimately all of the words and images are dominated by the large classical pillars and arches and the idea of national victory.[13]

At the opening of the new memorial in May of 2004, thousands of World War II veterans and their families came to Washington to embrace the honor and the accolades that younger generations gave them and recall the war years of their youth. The general tenor of the public festivities surrounding the dedication and the overall impression of the memorial itself left little room for the expression of attitudes critical of war or evocative of the chaos and distress the war had brought to many. Yet such outlooks were not forgotten. Dennis Wolfe, who was born after the war ended, traveled from Red Oak, Iowa, to see the new memorial. He certainly realized that it conveyed a sense of dignity and respect for the individuals who served their nation in the early 1940s, and he appreciated such a point. Yet he also carried with him a more critical perspective from the memory of his personal life.

The dominant war story in Red Oak involved the capture of national guardsmen from southwest Iowa. In March 1943, the local telegraph office received a torrent of bad news, as messages arrived announcing that some twenty-seven men from the guard unit at Red Oak were missing in action in North Africa. The news came as a shock to the town, although there was some relief when it was learned several weeks later that many of the men had become German prisoners and were at least still alive. One of the POWs, Wolfe's father, Darrell, came home in 1945 after spending more than two years in German prison camps and remained embittered by the experience for the rest of his life. He was especially angry that another prisoner from Red Oak, Dean Halbert, had been killed by the Germans. The elder Wolfe and other veterans in the town never believed a German account that Halbert was shot while trying to escape. They believed the Germans killed the man for no good reason at all. Moreover, upon his arrival home, the veteran learned that his wife had taken up with another man, a fact that embarrassed him greatly because some of his letters home expressing his wish to see his spouse again had been published in the local newspaper. Dennis recalled one moment in the early 1950s when his father's bitterness exploded. He had taken his children to see the movie *Stalag 17*, which depicted a rather cynical outlook toward the war on the part of the imprisoned GIs. What really bothered Darrell Wolfe, however, was a scene in which two Americans were killed trying to escape, and their bodies were left lying in the mud for the other prisoners to see. At that point in the film, the veteran stood up, slammed his seat back, and stormed out of the theater, leaving his children to watch the film by themselves. Subsequent arguments with the Veterans Administration over requests for more benefits due to his incarceration only heightened his sense of anger over his war experience. Another POW from Red Oak, Elwin Diehl, who spent time in the same camp as Darrell Wolfe, also recalled his ordeal with some disdain. He said he had "wasted fifteen years of my life" serving as a POW and struggling to make a living as a farmer once he came home. In fact, he held a dim view of Dwight Eisenhower for two reasons. He felt that as a general in Africa he could have done more to get men like him out of the area near the Faid Pass where he was captured, and he thought Ike's policies as president did not help his prospects as a farmer. Diehl finally gave up on farming and took a steady job with the railroad in the mid-1950s.

Driven by his knowledge of private grievances involving individuals who were "near and dear" to him, Dennis Wolfe taped a photo of his father and a list of some ninety men from the Red Oak area who died in World War II to a pillar in the new memorial that recognized the contributions from Iowa. He appreciated the honors veterans like his father were receiving, but in his own way he challenged the effort of this traditionally designed structure to erase from memory the sorrows and sufferings the war had brought to people he knew.[14]

LIFE OVER DEATH

Despite the American victory and the prominence of the traditional memorials—invariably located in public places that also served as tourist destinations—there was actually substantial criticism voiced just after the war toward classic designs. James Mayo has pointed out that by the time of World War II many American communities already had their fair share of traditional statues of brave soldiers from the Civil War and World War I. In hundreds of towns after 1918, for instance, statues were erected to honor the "American Doughboy," idealizing the common soldier by showing him charging into battle with a rifle in one hand and a grenade in another. Panels containing the names of the dead were often attached to the base of such statues, of course, but the thrust of the commemoration focused more on victory and martial valor than on the carnage that had just taken place. Ernest Viquesney of Spencer, Indiana, who designed and sold one very popular version of this statue called the "Spirit of the American Doughboy," advertised his creation as a tribute to "democracy's greatest sons." Variations on the theme were plentiful. In Wausau, Wisconsin, the doughboy carried a gas mask and was coupled with the figure of an "angel of winged victory." In Ft. Wayne, Indiana, he was joined by another statue of a sailor in front of a victory arch.[15]

The supreme expression of national sacrifice and of forgetting the messiness of the war was unveiled in November 1921, when Warren G. Harding dedicated the Tomb of the Unknown Soldier at the nation's capital. Inside the tomb were the remains of an American soldier from the "Great War" who was "known but to God." At the dedication ceremonies, Harding mythologized the American fighting man by claiming that he went forward with no hatred for any people in the world but only disdain for war itself. He now proclaimed that this "dead man" would be gathered to the "nation's breast within the shadow of the Capitol," and he made a specific appeal to all mankind to move to a "higher plane" that would bar tragedies such as war from the "stage of righteous civilization."[16]

Protests against remembering only the American victory or the fighting spirit of American soldiers were evident as well in the years just after 1918. In Orange, Massachusetts, a long debate took place over how best to memorialize the eleven local men who died in the war. The American Legion mounted a display of photos of the men in 1929, but Orange's chapter of the Veterans of Foreign Wars decided to celebrate the victory by placing a cannon in the town's Memorial Park the very next year. Yet the major memorial to the war, dedicated finally in 1934, presented the figure of a soldier without any weapon who was seated, not charging, and was talking to a young boy. A plaque on the base of the monument contained a "shrouded figure" crushing military weapons under her feet and an inscription that represented a distinct victory for local pacifists: "It shall not happen again." In New York City, the debate over how to commemorate the war was so contentious that no permanent memorial was ever erected. A temporary victory arch modeled after the Arch of Constantine in Rome did appear for a time. It was roundly attacked, however, by artists like Alexander Calder, who thought its aesthetic ties to a "Roman imperial arch" were antidemocratic and insufficiently evocative of what he thought was the real purpose of the war—the creation of a new international order of peace under the aegis of the League of Nations. Calder felt that his "liberal internationalist" views and dreams of international reconciliation were undermined by victory celebrations because they tended to humiliate defeated peoples.[17]

The memorial debate after 1945 did not return to ideas about pacifism and internationalism to much of an extent. The thrust of commemoration was now centered more on a need to forget and repair the ruptures the war had brought to people's lives. Thus, many called not only for traditional images to console but for "living memorials" such as auditoriums and civic centers that were intended to improve the quality of life for those who survived. However, both forms worked to erase memory of the slaughter and, for that matter, the past as well. Some living memorials incorporated historical details like the names of the dead, but the prevalence of such structures was ultimately a sign that many citizens simply wanted to disregard much of what the war had brought to their lives. Even the American Legion at one time suggested that citizens "not erect victory arches" but build Legion halls that could also serve a community's needs for meeting rooms and gymnasiums. An article in the *Christian Century* in 1946 noted that many American towns were busy discussing how to memorialize the struggle but doing so in a "far different" way than they did after other wars. The magazine predicted that there would be fewer traditional monuments built after World War II because "there was a general revulsion against the very idea of war" and "many feel the streets of our cities already contain enough bronze warriors."

Sometimes the concept of a "living memorial" was tied to the strains of internationalism that pervaded the 1940s. One veteran was quoted in the *Christian Century* as suggesting that there should be more spending on "scholarships for Negroes" rather than for monuments. And a story was told of a Marine on Iwo Jima who left a note just before he died indicating that 40 percent of his estate should be used to foster peace between labor and management. Senator J. William Fulbright pushed through Congress in 1946 his own commemorative idea to launch a program of student and teacher exchanges across national borders as a way to use the memory of the war to advance the cause of international peace. Fulbright was particularly concerned by the bombings of Hiroshima and Nagasaki and the overall explosion of violence in the war, and he hoped that programs like his would promote human understanding. More typical of the "living" format, however, were projects like one in Fort Wayne, Indiana, to build a field house (dedicated in 1952) with names of the local dead placed in tablets inside the large structure where citizens could enjoy sporting events.[18]

Milwaukee was the site of a huge public campaign to build a living memorial to the war that promised both to "honor the dead and serve the living." Led by a group of prominent citizens called Metropolitan Milwaukee War Memorial Incorporated, residents were asked whether they would prefer a "cold, granite shaft" or a "warm, throbbing living community center." Leaders of the drive to build the center claimed that the city would never fully recover from the "ache" of the loss of 2,035 residents of Milwaukee County but insisted that those still alive "deserve the finest facilities on earth" to listen to music or view "art masterpieces." Promotional literature for the fund drive also made it clear that leaders were intent on competing with rival cities such as Baltimore and Kansas City, which had already built large auditoriums after World War I, and were concerned that "for years Milwaukee County had been a laggard in properly memorializing its war dead." They now felt a new memorial center would enrich the lives of the living and allow them to enjoy things such as music and art that are an "affirmation of our common human emotions." The dead would not be forgotten, and their names would be listed in a "Memorial Arcade." And civic leaders were confident that the funds could be raised because they said life savings and earnings were rising in the 1940s and "we should be able to afford it." The center, which was finally completed and dedicated in 1957, promised "To Honor the Dead by Serving the Living" through a variety of artistic and cultural activities.[19]

In 1944 the Los Angeles Times asked its readers to make suggestions for "fitting memorials to honor the heroes of World War II," reminding citizens that the building of the Los Angeles Memorial Coliseum was an outstanding example of a living memorial erected to commemorate World War I. Responses from the public were varied. James Mayo has argued that the highest social purpose that such commemorations can serve is "humanitarianism," or the idea that society should not allow such suffering or "inhumanity" to repeat itself." Some of the newspaper's readers were clearly thinking in this direction. One respondent called for the creation of a national peace college. Another woman wrote to describe her idea for a "center for democracy" that would direct "the enormous energy of veterans and their families" into "peacetime channels" and foster "interracial friendship" with other nations. Other ideas were focused less on world peace and more on the everyday needs of the survivors, such as a memorial park with "subtropical flora and fauna" that would be two miles long, the creation of a forest in the San Fernando Valley, and a hospital with a large "V" for victory carved on its front entrance.[20]

Not everyone supported the idea of living memorials. James Fraser, a prominent American sculptor, made a plea for the traditional memorial. He argued that such structures were indispensable because they made "men remember," while stadiums, libraries, and swimming pools do not "properly honor our boys who died fighting" and fail "to inspire us to be worthy of the sacrifices." For Fraser the living memorial simply did not show the respect for the dead that the "traditional type" did. The quintessential war memorial for him was something like the Arc de Triomphe in Paris; he recommended that at the very least American towns erect panels of "enduring granite or marble" bearing some "symbolic figures" and "great words" such as Thomas Jefferson's "I have sworn upon the altar of God eternal hostility against every form of tyranny over the mind of man." Other critics lamented survey data that showed that many American communities were simply not interested in "honor rolls, plaques, or monuments" and that thousands of citizens had been willing to put welcome home signs in their windows but seemed to be uninterested in "monumental sculpture." A few defenders of tradition made specific calls for a return of statues like the doughboys that had been popular after World War I or even like the Statue of Liberty so that Americans could remain aware that evil forces still threaten the world and that the nation had come together in the past to defeat them. As a writer in the *New York Times* claimed, living memorials were all well and good, but ultimately they failed to recall the sacrifices that marked the war effort and to generate a "spirit of reverence and love" for those who died.[21]

THE RETURN OF THE DEAD

Public debates over memorials to the war were actually dominated by the many ways the dead—and the tragic aspects of the war—could be overlooked. Yet the private sense of sorrow and bereavement that many felt after 1945 could never be erased entirely from public memory. Indeed, to a surprising extent, especially in local places where smaller communities of memory survived, mourning the dead proved to be a central feature of public remembrance. Even if the home front had been spared devastation, the bodies of dead soldiers were scattered around the world, and decisions had to be made about how to collect their remains and where they would be buried. This would involve not only a substantial effort by the government but decisions by next of kin as to where they wanted their loved ones interred—if they could be found at all. In the several years after the war, most Americans could read in their newspapers accounts of ships arriving from overseas with thousands of bodies, of public ceremonies centered on displays of flag-draped coffins, and of services at local churches or cemeteries where local men were buried.

The same nation that had claimed the bodies of the soldiers for the war effort now sought to pay them respect by searching the world for their remains. As part of the overall demobilization efforts after the war, plans were formulated by the Army's Office of the Quartermaster General for the "final disposition of the overseas dead." Search and recovery teams were sent to Asia, Europe, and wherever Americans had fought and died. Remains were exhumed, and "identification teams" closely examined "fleshy parts" and clothing for any clues as to the dead soldier's identity. Dental records were often crucial, and fingerprints were used "if the flesh permitted." Families were asked whether they wanted the remains of loved ones returned or placed in an overseas cemetery next to the men with whom they had served. Some seven out of ten American families elected to have the remains of their kin brought home.[22]

To help families decide on the issue of reburial, the Office of the Quartermaster General published a pamphlet called *Tell Me About My Boy,* which explained to citizens the process by which dead soldiers would be repatriated. During the war most of the "honored dead" were buried in temporary military cemeteries. The government now declared, however, that it was the right of next of kin to decide "where these valiant dead shall rest." Generally speaking, if a soldier was married, the decision was left to his widow; if he was single, the decision was first left to his father and then to his mother. Relatives were also told that the process of recovery was long and difficult. But the government did promise that it intended to find the remains of every one they could and to cover all burial expenses, whether a decision was to bring the body home or to leave it in an American cemetery abroad. Bodies delivered to hometowns would also be accompanied by a military escort in order to "dignify" the deceased.[23]

Dead bodies have symbolic and political power. Encased in traditional images and patriotic slogans, they can help sustain the authority of states. Given over to their families and placed in local graveyards, they can remind people as well of how wars can bring tragedy and diminish the symbolic promise of the nation itself.[24] Just as the wartime generation argued over proper forms of commemoration, they also debated where to bury their dead. The issue of the final resting place centered on two key points. There were voices that argued that the soldiers themselves would choose—if they could—to be buried with their comrades near the place they fell. And there were those that claimed that the men wanted to come home. An editorial in *Life* in June of 1945 insisted that if the decision were in the hands of the fighting men, they would prefer to remain with their fellow warriors near the places their deaths had now "made sacred." Interestingly, the magazine published next to the editorial Archibald MacLeish's poem "Young Dead Soldiers," with its lines about the fallen soldiers not being able to speak and about the need for the living to determine the meaning of their deaths. Harold Martin, a Marine lieutenant, also wrote a piece in *Readers Digest* in 1946 reaffirming the desire of the fallen men to be left where they "now slept." He claimed that most of the troops he had talked with during the war said that they wanted to be buried near their comrades. He also remarked that the bonds between the men in combat were so strong that survivors often commemorated their fallen friends on the field of battle itself. Usually these markers were devoid of explicit patriotic images and took simple forms like a pile of stones or plain words carved on wood, such as "God bless Bill." The *Washington Post* joined the call for leaving the men overseas with an argument in 1947 that the current program to allow families to bring their loved ones back home was the result of a bill "rushed through Congress largely at the insistence of selfish interests waging a campaign of "hypersentimentalism" and said that reburials back in the United States would only "open a new chapter of grief for the next of kin." The newspaper argued that it was difficult to understand how comfort can be derived from the "mere physical presence of artificially transplanted remains of men whose greatest glory was in what they did for their country." One set of parents, who tragically lost four sons in battle, told the War Department that, despite the "catastrophe" they had suffered, they now had time to "meditate over what has happened on different battlefields and ask why our losses should be four-fold." They concluded that they wanted their boys left "unmolested" where they fell. Another grieving mother said, "I wish to say that our dear boy will never be dead" and "not for one minute would it lighten my heart to have him moved" home.[25]

President Truman announced the program of repatriation in 1946 and said that the nation held a "deep and everlasting appreciation of the heroic efforts" of those who made the "supreme sacrifice," and that the United States was dedicated to "disposing of the mortal remains of those honored dead in a manner consistent with the wishes of the next of kin." His announcement resulted in hundreds of letters being sent to the White House seeking information on the fate of loved ones or commenting on the program of reburials. Few criticized the program as did a group of Catholic clergymen from Boston, who warned that the public program to bring back the dead seemed like a form of "organized paganism" that would elevate secular ideals over religious ones. They also felt that leaving the dead where they fell would serve as a reminder that the world is "truly one." If they had spilled their blood in Asia and Europe, these religious men felt, their remains in foreign lands would serve to remind all that the struggle for justice, peace, and equality was global in nature. Funds for reburial would better be spent, in their view, to help alleviate the suffering of humanity, a goal for which these prelates felt the war was fought.[26]

Most citizens did not seem to connect the sacrifices of the dead to the ideal of human improvement. They were more intent upon healing the deep wounds that wartime losses had brought. One mother who wrote the government pleaded for the return of her son's body because he was her "only son and we feel that his remains should be here so that we can console ourselves with frequent visitations to his grave." The widow of a naval officer killed in the line of duty wanted her husband's body returned so that the father her children never knew would seem less like a "stranger." A mother from Greenfield, Indiana, asked the president rather caustically why it was taking so long to bring the bodies home "when it took such a short time to take them." She wanted the remains of her son close by so that she could at least "visit his grave and place flowers." She explained that when "one has lost their only child and are up in years life takes on such a sad picture knowing he will never come home again." She even took note of the fact that Truman seemed to be fond of visiting his own mother and wondered if he ever thought that women like her "would like to be able to see our dead son's remains once more on good U.S. soil." Another mother complained that the president should expend less effort in ordering Liberty Ships to bring refugees to this country and more time on bringing home the fallen soldiers. At the request of "a grief stricken father," a Catholic priest from Fordham University wrote to Truman to see if he could speed up the return of the man's son from Guam. The cleric said the father was "very much affected by his son's death" and was also interested in visiting the place where the young man was killed. A man from Baltimore told the president that he not only wanted his son's body returned but desired to be buried next to the soldier—"or in the same grave"—when he died and that he did not think he will "bear the grief much longer." One parent wrote about the "grief in my heart" over the death of a son in Germany and believed that there were other families who suffered from the pain and sense of loss they felt over the war death of a loved one. One man reported to the White House that the mother of a soldier named Donald Hathaway suffered "a nervous breakdown and great mental anguish" over his death in the South Pacific and "went to pieces, fainting several times and going into a total collapse" at services for him at Arlington National Cemetery.[27]

Some people even questioned government announcements that their loved ones had died. They wrote to the White House asking for more "authentic" information than a War Department telegram. Others asked the president to launch an "investigation" into events surrounding the death of a serviceman. In the White House files on these matters is a legal brief filed on behalf of one distraught mother whose son was apparently killed in France in December of 1944. Udya Podoloff of Connecticut had received a notice informing her that her son, Stephan Lautenbach, had been killed in action. The following April, however, the woman saw a man she was sure was her son in a photo of liberated American prisoners in the New York Times of April 8, 1945. Friends and relatives also noticed the photo and were equally sure it was Stephan. Mrs. Podoloff pursued the matter for several years by writing to army officials, finally getting them to agree to exhume the body they claimed was her son. In February 1946, she went to France to see if she could learn more and discuss the results of the exhumation. She was not pleased with what she found. When the body was removed from the ground, she learned that no "scientific tests" such as a careful comparison with dental records were made. Her son's dog tags were in the grave, but the body that was examined was clothed in a spotless military uniform, which tended to discredit information that her son had been shot in the chest and had died in battle. "Sick at heart and in body," the woman returned to the United States after spending six months in France and asked for a second exhumation. This time an examination of the body produced even more confusion. Officials now noticed that the body in the grave was nearly three inches taller than her son and had black hair instead of brown. Two years after the war, this grieving mother was still not sure of the fate of her son.[28]

Other citizens who suffered immense personal losses wrote their president to see if the government would help them visit the graves of loved ones abroad or send them a photo of the site. While the government would not fund overseas travel to such sites, the existence of such requests implied how much those that grieved cared little for victory celebrations and longed for some form of reunion with those they lost. Frances Gagliardi of Youngstown, Ohio, wrote to the White House that her son was killed in France in 1944 and that she felt she was entitled to have her way paid to visit his final resting place if he was not brought home. The mayor of Ventnor, New Jersey, wrote on behalf of one mother whose son was shot down over Italy in 1943 to ask if the government would send her to visit the "last resting place" of the man. Abraham Eiser of Toledo, Ohio, the father of a dead soldier, said that he grieved "day and night over the loss of the boy" and sought assistance in traveling to Kamchatka, where his son had been shot down flying bombing missions over Alaska with five other airmen. In fact, the man wanted to locate the remains of all six flyers that were killed and arrange for their shipment back to the United States, a task that was made difficult in 1946, apparently, because the area was now under Soviet control.[29]

The handling of the remains was done according to a strict protocol. Transport ships were unloaded in New York or San Francisco, and coffins were sent to distribution points across the United States. At these points a military escort was assigned to take each casket to next of kin in some hometown. All men who undertook such duty were required to watch a film called *Your Proudest Day*, which instructed them in how to help and comfort the bereaved. Sometimes the local reburials were private affairs, but many times they turned into public or communal events where people came to comfort those in distress. At such occasions traditional expressions of patriotism were evident, but so were vivid reminders that powerful strains of sadness and grief remained and could not easily be put away. In New York City in October 1947, some 400,000 people gathered to watch a parade and attend a service in Central Park to commemorate the arrival of the first shipment of 6,200 coffins from Europe. One casket was selected to be put on a caisson and paraded through city streets to muffled drum beats. As the coffin was unloaded from a ship, reporters noticed that "women who saw this wept openly and men turned away," so raw was the sorrow of the wartime generation. Later, at the service, chaplains from three faiths—Catholic, Jewish, and Protestant—prayed for the dead, and the *New York Times* reported that "their words" and the sound of taps "evoked women's sobs" and caused men to choke up. In a front row seat, a woman was reported to have "started up" by stretching out her arms and screaming, "Johnny!" After a pause, she was reported to have screamed again, "There's my boy, there's my boy," as she shook with emotion.[30]

The often troubled relationship between tradition and grief commanded so much commemorative attention that hardly anyone seemed to have thought about erecting monuments to the more transnational ideal of universal human rights. Thus, few structures were designed to evoke the memory of the Four Freedoms. One that did was dedicated at Troy, Michigan, in August of 1948, when 115 caskets of dead soldiers were placed in a field in White Chapel Cemetery on the occasion of the unveiling of a new Four Freedoms Memorial. Pleas that the sacrifices of wartime be used as an inspiration to help all of humanity were represented in the memorial at Troy by the very name given the structure and by the replica of the planet Earth that stood atop the monument holding several human figures. One could view this memorial and hope that no harm would come to the innocent figures that stood at its apex again. But a sense of national power and victory was evident here as well, for holding up the planet and its people in peace were two figures of American fighting men—a soldier and a sailor— with guns in their hands. The men were clearly not dead; in this rendition of the war they had fought for the improvement of all of mankind. This was a rare instance where a public memorial linked the sacrifice of the American troops to the international dream of human rights articulated in the Atlantic Charter, although the government did execute a "Victory Medal" in 1946 with a list of the "Four Freedoms" on one side.

One reason for the relative inattention to the political idealism of human rights was quite evident at the ceremonies at Troy attended by thousands. Reports noted how much the spectators, who formed a giant ring around the caskets, "wept for the boys whose dreams would never come true." Planners had wanted to bring home the "boys" so that "those who loved them would feel the nearness of the sleeping ones and would be able to visit the last resting place as has been mankind's habit through many centuries." In fact, as many in the crowd stood "sad-faced," the memorial itself was unveiled by the children of a dead soldier who had never met their father. Inevitably, loved ones grieved and patriotic symbols were mobilized to assuage their sorrows and explain the loss. But in this intricate cultural process of remembering the dead, little space was left to contemplate the high-mindedness of internationalist dreams.[31]

Ceremonies in smaller towns also provided an occasion for important community rituals of mourning and honoring. In Tremonton, Utah, for instance, four caskets were delivered in June of 1948 that contained the bodies of the sons of Alben and Gunda Borgstrom. All four men had been killed within a six-month period during 1944. Upon learning of the death of the four brothers, the military discharged a fifth son (Boyd) from Marine duty in the South Pacific. On June 26 a large ceremony was held in the small Utah town, where businesses closed for the day and where flags and bronze stars were presented to the grieving parents. Words of consolation were offered by officials of the Church of Jesus Christ of Latter Day Saints and by Army General Mark W. Clark. One religious leader told the large crowd that the grieving parents took consolation from the fact that "God lives" and that all people—including the dead boys—have had the chance to prepare for "eternal life." Clark added that the Borgstrom brothers "achieved what very few of us dare hope will be our fortune—"a share in the shaping of destiny." Clark affirmed his own interpretation of the war by saying that he continued to pray every day that "our American way of life" will be maintained and that in the future Americans would be ready again to "meet every call for whatever sacrifice might be demanded with the same uplifting loyalty and selfless purpose" as did the men from Utah.

The remembrance of the men's parents and the local citizens was more personal and less tied to precepts of national destiny. This is not to say that local people would not be ready to defend their nation, but that was not the first thing they thought of when recalling the sacrifice of the brothers. Some recalled the men as "tall and husky lads with a reputation for working hard and living clean." And some inferred courage when they said the men would rather go to war than "hide behind cows." As their parents walked from the mortuary before the start of the public events, heads bowed, their father recalled how his sons had turned over every cent they made to their mother and how they had loved to hunt, fish, and roam the "open spaces" of Utah. Through "tear-reddened eyes" their mother remembered discrete events from their childhood like the time one boy broke his hip while skiing. She painfully proclaimed that it "was hard to bear her boys coming home" in caskets. During the ceremonies, reporters described her as "near collapse" and said that she had to be attended to continuously by an army medical detachment. For herself, she claimed she could not have endured the ritual if it had not been for the support she received from the "priesthood" of the Mormon Church. Photos published in *Life* on July 19, 1948, showed the Borgstroms sitting stoically in their home awaiting the services for their sons, the four caskets lined in a row during the religious services, and an image of Mrs. Borgstrom breaking down completely and crying with her hand covering her eyes.[32]

Dead soldiers drew an enormous amount of attention in Hurly, Missouri, as well, when the remains of Henry Wright's sons were returned by the government in 1948. All three men—Frank, Elton, and Harold—had been killed in Europe in a four-month period following Christmas Day 1944. Their grieving father—described by a reporter as "a gray haired man, stooped and broken with suffering"—had requested specifically that the boys not only be brought back to their hometown but that their caskets be placed in the bedroom in which they had been born. He wanted the "boys" to be in his house "one more time." Throughout the day of November 4, friends and relatives called at the house and laid floral tributes on the floor in front of the remains. After paying their respects, neighbors gathered in small groups in front of the Wright house, as described in one report, "not knowing quite what to say but reluctant to leave." They recalled the boys as "average farm boys" who had attended local schools, helped their father with farm chores, and "kept themselves out of trouble." A community ceremony was also held in the local school gymnasium, where a chaplain read the Twenty-third Psalm, a prayer that offered comfort and solace to the mourners in terms more religious than patriotic: "The Lord is my shepherd; I shall not want. . . . Yea, though I walk through the valley of the shadow of death, I will fear no evil: for thou art with me, thy rod and thy staff comfort me."[33]

Public ceremonies were short-lived, but family members would carry the memory of the dead men for years after 1948. In 1980 Louella Dulin, Harold Wright's widow, decided to write a short history that focused on the war years and the deaths of the brothers. Her narrative had almost nothing to say about the value of defeating totalitarian regimes but was essentially the story of a family whose life was severely ruptured by death. Dulin called her story a "tragedy" and a "nightmarish experience" and wrote of how she met and married Harold, how they had a son, and how she saw her husband off to war. Lovingly, she told of how as a high school student she started dating Harold in the summer of 1940 and married him the following year. The young couple lived in a small structure that had served as a smokehouse where meats were prepared on the farm owned by Harold's father. She recalled the special celebration friends and relatives gave the young couple when they were married and at the birth of their only child, Stephen, in their modest home in 1943. She particularly recalled how Henry Wright loved to hold his newborn grandson on his lap and feed him.[34]

Married life was disrupted in the summer of 1944 when Harold and his brother Elton were taken into the Army. An older brother was already in the service, but Harold's entry had been deferred because he was married and because he had been helping his father on the farm. The last time Louella saw her husband was at Christmastime in 1944, when Harold held his wife and child as long as he could before he had to board a train on a trip that would take him to battle in Europe. Six months later she would learn of his death. It came as a shock because she felt he would come back to her and their son, but as Louella wrote, "Believing just didn't make it so."

Louella's son, Stephen, also thought of the death of a father he never knew with regret. He has clear recollections of the time the brothers were brought back to Hurley and of the burial ceremonies. He remembered himself as a five-year-old, playing in his grandfather's yard at the time the men were brought home and looking into a room where the caskets were displayed and seeing his grandfather standing alone by his dead sons. He also recalled asking which coffin was his father's. For years after the reburials, he always felt awkward when people would come up to him and tell him they had been at the 1948 ceremonies; he was never sure how he should react. Today he feels mostly "sadness" and "anger" over the fact that he could never know his father. The sound of "Taps" still makes him cry, and he says he is instinctively drawn to visit national cemeteries with their rows of war dead. For her part, his mother, Louella, keeps a scrapbook that details the war years in Stone County, Missouri, and the list of the thirteen men from the county who were killed in the war. She also has kept telegrams informing her that her husband was missing and another that he was dead.[35]

After the war Louella remarried, but she never stopped thinking of Harold. In 1981 she wrote a poem to her deceased spouse, asking him not to shy away from talking to her even though she now had another husband:

> Although I held you close to me for one fleeting minute
> I awakened to find my day without you in it,
> Somehow, someway I must press on
> My days aren't "totally whole" since you are gone
> My darling, it was so long ago since God took you from my side
> In that "hell hole" a prisoner of war you died
> Why did it prove to be like this?

After all this time—you I so sadly miss
And I remember and become very sad
And wonder what we might have had . . . ."[36]

THE NAMES OF THE DEAD

The sentiments of national victory and patriotic honor that marked national memorials were evident in local commemorations but were also more likely to be
joined by the names of the dead. This was quite evident in large war memorials
built just after the war in Richmond and Omaha. A huge memorial was dedicated in the Virginia capital in 1956 to "revere the memory of the heroic dead"
from both World War II and Korea. In fact, a remembrance of death was the
central feature of this memorial, which listed the names of more than 10,000
soldiers from Virginia who did not return. Overlooking the rows of panels that
contained the names was a large white statue of an allegorical figure called
"Memory," which was meant to stand vigil over the names of those "who died in
battle." An eternal flame was also placed at this site to symbolize "the spirit of
liberty and patriotism of every Virginian who served." Inside the structure arti-
facts of the war were buried, including a Japanese rifle, parts of a B-52 bomber,
and a German cannon.[37]

In Omaha the central public memorial to the war also tempered the spirit of
national victory with a deep sense of loss. In June of 1948, President Harry Truman traveled to the Nebraska city to dedicate the large Memorial Park that contained a white colonnade situated on high ground overlooking a tranquil scene
of grass, trees, and flowers. Again the local dead took center stage, as the names
of 900 people from Douglas County who did not come home were placed in
plaques on the walls of the colonnade. Small images of real wartime events were
carved into the side structure, showing workers in a war plant, a wounded soldier
receiving a transfusion, and the flag raising at Iwo Jima. In a dedication speech,
Truman tried to assuage the local sense of sadness with references to some of the
liberal visions that formed part of the nation's wartime rhetoric of why the war
was fought and why some had to die. He told the assembled group that the fight
had been for the ideal of world peace and the cause of the United Nations. He
urged the living to continue the effort to make the United Nations a "going
concern." The intent of the local planners of the memorial, however, had been
narrower—to provide a "peaceful setting" for the "heroic Omahans" who gave
their lives.[38]

The original idea for the Omaha memorial came not from a veteran or political leader but from a woman who ran a tea shop in the city. She thought of it one

day during the war as she drove by the site that at the time was an old golf course. For her a marker for the dead within a park would constitute a "living memorial" that could be enjoyed by those who survived; town leaders quickly picked up on the notion and raised the necessary funds. A local newspaper helped fund raising immensely by publishing the names of donors and reporting when the funds came from relatives of deceased soldiers. Competing ideas were expressed at the time. Some wanted a stadium or civic auditorium; others debated the merits of using weapons such as tanks or planes as memorials. In the end, however, Omaha was unwilling to forget much of what the war had cost and preserved the names of the local dead.[39]

Fifty years later, as anniversary celebrations of World War II were held throughout the world, Omaha invested again in the site and refurbished the memorial and rededicated its park. Hundreds of new trees were planted, and deteriorating plaques with the names of the war dead were cleaned. The rededication ceremony itself turned out to be a major event and mostly reaffirmed the idea of national power and might, as National Guard planes flew overhead and paratroopers from the 101st Airborne Division landed in the park. Combat veterans from each branch of the service placed wreaths at the colonnade. And speeches now paid more attention to the survivors—the men and women who "returned fifty years ago from the European theater, the Pacific theater, and anywhere else in the world wartime service took them" and contributed to the growth of the city.[40]

Despite the public focus on national power and on the living in 1998, traces of the private sadness that had shaped much commemoration just after the war could still be found. Reporter James Martin Davis wrote of the experience of the family of James Laferla, whose name was placed on the colonnade in 1948. The newsman learned that the tribute of being listed with the other dead did not fully comfort the family or remove the deep distress they felt when they saw other men come home in 1945. Angie Laferla, the mother of the fallen soldier and the grandmother of the reporter, never fully recovered from the loss of her son and wept openly over his death many times for the rest of her life. The dead man's sister attended daily mass and lit a candle for her deceased brother for years after the war. And Davis recalled that each time she would drive by Memorial Park, his grandmother would look toward the memorial "with tears on her cheeks" and point out with a "quivering voice" that the site was "Jimmy's Memorial." Another article told of Jimmy Ziemba and the remorse he continued to feel over the death of his two brothers who were lost in the war. In 1998 he still talked of the fun he had shared with his older siblings and of the moment in 1942 when a telegram came while his father was at work. One of his sisters accepted it but withheld the news from their mother until her father came home that night and could convey the devastating information to her with the entire family present. His sister had told him she did not want her mother to be alone when she first heard of her son's death. The family followed the same routine when a second son was killed in Italy. Again his father broke the news to his mother "in Polish" as he had the first time. Jimmy, too, claimed that his mother never "accepted" the deaths of her sons; and when she died of a "stroke" in 1950, everyone in the family believed that the real cause of her death was, in fact, "a broken heart."[41]

By the 1990s the city had expanded its efforts to commemorate World War II. John Lajba, a local artist, was commissioned to create a memorial on the occasion of the fiftieth anniversary of the war in Heartland of America Park. Lajba drew upon his own family history—his mother had toiled as riveter in a bomber plant and his father had won the Purple Heart in the war—and tried to create a monument that would "honor everyone who worked and sacrificed during that historic time." Lajba noted that he had often heard stories of the wartime experiences of his relatives and that their contributions were foremost in his mind as he executed his design. Like many in the generation that had not experienced the war and its losses directly, he felt that the war was a prime example of national unity and collective effort when "every American patriotically set aside his or her own concerns to support our troops and accomplish a greater goal." He believed that the ability of Americans "to pull together and sacrifice as a nation" was the key to victory and the reason "our loved ones" could come home. Completed in 1997, his sculpture attempts to visualize these themes with a group of human figures facing each other. In the center and elevated above the others is the statue of a father/soldier just home from the war who is embracing his children. Facing the returned veteran are figures representing a female plant worker, a young boy pulling a wagon of scrap iron and saluting the soldier, and an elderly couple holding a folded American flag and grieving for the child they have lost. This memorial evoked both the living and the dead, but the dead—and their names—are now erased and are represented only by the flag. Freed from the need to contain the sorrows and regrets of wartime that marked the 1940s, this modern memorial was able to link the memory of the war to raging debates in the 1990s over patriotism, "family values," and national unity. The man who channeled his loyalty into fighting in the 1940s is now depicted as resuming the task of leading a traditional household and being a father in a society that now wondered if his form of fatherly and patriotic behavior would continue.[42]

Local commemorations reworked the national focus on loyalty and unity again in Waterloo, Iowa, the hometown of the five Sullivan brothers who were killed when their ship was sunk near the Solomon Islands in 1942. The Navy had been reluctant to assign all five men to the same ship, but they had insisted that they be allowed to serve together. The news that the sons of Tom and Aletta Sullivan were missing reached the community in January of 1943 and drew considerable attention not only locally but nationally as well. Drawing on the sentimental culture of wartime and the tendency of wartime Americans to see the war as a disruption of normal family life, news stories immediately focused less on the traumatic impact of what had just taken place and more on the way the Sullivan family had always been steeped in traditional American values of solidarity, religious faith, and patriotism. They were seen as particularly proud of their Catholic faith and Irish American heritage. Readers learned that all of the boys left high school early to work in a local meatpacking plant, a pattern typical of young men tied to a working-class family economy of the time. They apparently had idyllic boyhoods hunting, fishing, and playing in a typical American hometown. It was a desire to seek revenge for the death of a friend at Pearl Harbor that caused the men to enlist in the war in the first place.[43]

The traditional language used to report the death of the Sullivans was also used to frame conceptions of how they should be commemorated. One month after it reported the men missing, the local newspaper launched a campaign to build a "Fighting Sullivan Memorial" and "perpetuate the memory" of the men who "believed it was their war." Local editors felt the memorial would constitute a "lasting tribute to the gallant spirit and heroic sacrifice" they were thought to exemplify. Two years later, while the war still raged, their story was told again by Hollywood in the film *The Fighting Sullivans*. This wartime drama did more than blunt the trauma of their loss; it essentially removed it from view. Only a few minutes of the picture were devoted to showing the sinking of their ship. Most of the movie focused on their prewar lives, their idyllic childhood, and the loving family life they enjoyed in Iowa. Family members were shown as intensely devoted to each other, a bond that led to their wanting to serve together on the same ship. Upon learning of the loss of their sons, the parents do not really grieve or suffer any emotional collapse in this story. Rather, they accept their losses and move on. Their father returns to work on the railroad to continue his part in the war effort. At the end audiences see not the image of men lying at the bottom of the sea, but only the five sailors appearing as apparitions walking through the clouds on their way to some form of heavenly reward.[44]

Despite the patriotic frames of wartime, the actual commemoration of the Sullivans took on a variety of forms in the years after the war. In 1956, a memorial to the brothers was dedicated on the lawn of the parochial school they had attended as children. Here the dominant symbol was not a tank or flag but a statue of the Virgin Mary, entitled "Our Lady of Peace" and set on a stone. Etched into the base of the memorial were the names of the dead men and a brief statement that they were lost in a naval battle during the war. In 1959, a small park in Waterloo was dedicated to the brothers, and five years later an even larger park was named for them as a living memorial. In 1988, Waterloo decided to name its civic center after the brothers because of a suggestion by retired Rear Admiral James D. Ramage, a Waterloo native, that the "Sullivan loss" should be recalled again because it represented the sacrifices that all veterans have made for the nation. Ramage claimed the idea came to him upon a return trip to Waterloo for his fiftieth high school reunion in 1984 and felt that the center should be named after "exceptional men" whose deeds were heroic. In 1997, members of the Sullivan family and other Waterloo residents received another opportunity to honor the men when they traveled to New York City to attend the dedication of a new naval vessel named for the brothers that replaced one Franklin Roosevelt dedicated in 1943. A naval commander speaking at the ceremony asserted that the brothers defined "what is right in America today" and that they were "living proof" that ordinary Americans, "no matter where they came from and where they went to school can still accomplish extraordinary things."[45]

Public commemorations and virtuous talk almost never mentioned the private pain endured by the parents of the men. Although there was some resentment in Waterloo over the fact that the focus on the Sullivans had overshadowed losses suffered by other local families, some citizens were quite aware that Tom and Aletta were badly shaken by the entire ordeal. The couple found it almost too much to bear in 1945 when they saw many other men returning home. Over time Aletta grew despondent and Tom increasingly turned to drink. Aletta did manage to mask some of her grief in the numerous public appearances she undertook during the war to raise morale and sell bonds. In 1943 she told mothers in "America, England, Russia and all our allied nations" to "keep your chin up" and that "our boys did not die in vain." Yet as late as 1964, it was reported that she was visibly "broken-up" and crying at one ceremony, and her grandson recalled in 1988 that she would often "break down" when talking about the boys. It certainly bothered her to learn before she died in 1965 that the park named for the men had fallen into disrepair.[46]

By now it should be clear that traditional commemorations of war grounded in words and images that evoked honor and national greatness, while popular, effaced deep layers of regret that festered in private lives. This point was underscored in remembrances of the war that took place in the community of Bedford,

Virginia. Set in the bucolic foothills of the Blue Ridge Mountains, Bedford seemed far away from the brutal battlefields of World War II in the 1940s and from the great public celebrations of the war in our own times. Yet it turned out to be a center for the celebration of the American victory. The story starts on D-Day, June 6, 1944, when sixteen men from the town were killed in the first wave of American forces that hit Omaha Beach. Three more local men died in the subsequent Normandy campaign. Unfortunately, by the summer of 1944 Bedford had grown somewhat familiar with bad news from the war, with more than 1,500 men from the area serving in the military and gold stars already appearing in as many as two dozen local homes. Yet all that had come before had not fully prepared the citizens of Bedford for D-Day and the news that so many local men had just been killed. As author Alex Kershaw has written, "In a matter of minutes a couple of German machine gunners had broken the town's heart."[47]

As was the case in Waterloo, Iowa, initial public responses to the news of the deaths at Omaha Beach, which came in bits and pieces over the course of the summer of 1944, tended to frame the tragedy in terms that were noble and abstract. The *Bedford Bulletin* talked of how the men had died for the high ideals of "liberty and justice toward which mankind has been struggling since the dawn of time." A mother who lost two sons in the invasion force published a piece in the local press that minimized the sense that her losses were tragic and asked others not to say that her sons died but that "they only sleepest" and had merely "crossed into the great beyond." She told other Gold Star mothers, "Weep not" because "your sons are happy and free."[48]

Private distress and emotional pain, however, could not be easily concealed. Relatives of the dead published a number of memorial letters in the local press and left inscriptions at local cemeteries that actually questioned the war and the need for these men to die. Consider the following statement placed in the local newspaper that explicitly raises doubts about the entire war effort:

> I can't even see your grave except in a dream. Now my mind wanders thousands of miles across the mighty deep. To a lonely little mount in a foreign land where the body of my dear soldier boy might be lain away. . . . His dear body was laid to rest in a blood-soaked uniform. Maybe it was in an American flag. There will not be any more cruel wars where you have gone. . . . For our religious freedom they say. A dear price to pay.[49]

The "parents, sisters and brothers" of another dead soldier wrote to the local paper as well. They talked of a "long year of the deepest sorrow" and of "lonesome hours of grief and pain" and "a wound that can never be healed until the day we meet again."[50]

Other signs of the damage caused by the war could be seen as one walked around the town. Kershaw reported that when he returned from the war Roy Stevens, whose brother was killed in the service, found it very difficult to readjust to postwar life and tried to "wash the memories away" by drinking heavily. He also noted that Dickie Overstreet could not forget the sight of "young GIs being mangled" in battle and would jump out of bed at night whenever a loud wind would blow. Some in the town harbored resentment toward General Eisenhower for ordering the invasion when he knew that weather conditions were not as good as they should have been. A grieving father was quoted as saying that he would like to "blow Franklin D. Roosevelt's brains out."

Local historian James Morrison has found additional expressions of regret on gravestones. The family of John Allen, who was killed in 1944, placed the following words at his burial site: "Sleep dear son and take your rest. Our hearts are broken but God knows best." The mother of Henry White suffered a "major, coma inducing stroke" on the day his casket was returned from Europe in 1948. Today, in the Bedford Christian Church, stained glass windows contain the names of John Dean and Frank Draper Jr., local men killed in action. In fact, in 2006 one could visit a Web site devoted to the memory of Draper, who was killed at D-Day. The site informs the reader that his death "devastated his family" and that his father built a large stone monument at his grave in Bedford with an inscription indicating that nothing could be said to repair the rupture the family had experienced in their lives. The inscription read: "Our precious son from us is gone. His voice we loved is still. His place is vacant in our home which can never be filled. We loved you, Juney, dearly loved you, but God loved you best."[51]

The high point of the local commemoration of the D-Day dead took place on June 6, 1954, when some 5,000 citizens crowded into the relatively small space in front of the Bedford County Court House to dedicate a "memorial stone." The Bulletin noted that the gathering "recalled the tragedy that stunned the town ten years ago today." On a granite stone brought from Normandy a plaque was attached that contained the names of those killed at Omaha Beach. The paper's editorial linked the tragic deaths at Normandy not to the ideals of the Four Freedoms but to the legacy of the Civil War and the Confederacy, claiming that the dead were "lineal descendants of the men in gray who followed Lee, Jackson, and Stuart and the courage and fortitude and patriotism of their forebears." While the local editors expressed "sorrow over the deaths of so many fine young men," they claimed the memorial stone would now "stand forever as a memorial of the courage of the men who died there" and will serve as "an inspiration to greatness yet unborn and keep alive the will to serve." The stone itself was actually placed directly in front of a column that contained no names of individuals but was dedicated to the "Confederate soldiers and sailors of Bedford Country" who manifested "patriotism, courage, fortitude, and virtue" and were "devoted sons."[52]

The dedication of the memorial stone in 1954 settled matters of public recognition of the World War II dead in Bedford for the next several decades. As in Waterloo, however, a renewed effort was noticeable in the late 1980s (not long after the dedication of the Vietnam Veterans Memorial) to honor not only the local men who fought on D-Day but the battle itself and its part in fashioning the nation's victory, a perspective that had received very little attention in 1954. In 1988 a Normandy veteran who was part of the third wave on Omaha Beach, Bob Slaughter, decided to campaign for greater public recognition of D-Day and the men who fought there. He and several other veterans from Roanoke formed a committee to see if a memorial or statue of some sort could be erected because they felt the event had never received the public recognition it deserved. Driven by a strong sense of obligation to the men with whom he served and to "buddies" who were "lying over there in a grave," Slaughter worked for a time almost single-handedly to keep the idea alive. In 1994, after Roanoke failed to find the land needed for a memorial, the town of Bedford offered him a site on a hilltop with a magnificent view of the Blue Ridge Mountains—a sight many of the local men who died in the war surely saw many times. In fact, one of the Bedford officials backing the plan was the sister of a local man who had been killed on Omaha Beach. Eventually, major donors such as movie director Steven Spielberg and cartoonist Charles Schultz supported the project. John Warner, a senator from Virginia, got Congress to pass legislation designating Bedford as the official site for what was to be known as the National D-Day Memorial, and the project to celebrate the national triumph was moved closer to reality.[53]

The D-Day memorial was dedicated in June of 2001 in an event that favored mythical remembrances of the battle over more critical ones. Dwight Eisenhower's order to the men on D-Day that they were about to embark upon a "great crusade" was not read at the Bedford commemoration in 1954, but now, at the beginning of a new century, it was inscribed on a plaque at the new memorial site itself. The governor of Virginia, James Gilmore, called the men who landed on D-Day "sons of democracy" who were "willing to make the supreme sacrifice." President George W. Bush came to the ceremony with Bob Slaughter walking by his side. The president stood in front of a large sculpture that depicted American rangers climbing a steep bluff at Pointe Du Hoc in order to destroy large German guns during D-Day itself. Bush called the men who went ashore on June 6, 1944, "among the bravest ever to wear a uniform." He offered details of how they "overran" machine gun nests and "overtook bunkers." And he elevated the ideal of sacrifice in battle to the highest level of citizenship when he said that "whatever it is about America that has given us such citizens it is the greatest quality we have and may it never leave us." Near the end of the ceremony the audience was reminded of the nation's military might as jets flew overhead and explosives were set off to simulate a bombing run. Despite the heavy use of traditional language and symbols of power, some of the residue from the years of Bedford's grief remained, however. Bush himself paid tribute to Raymond and Bedford Hoback, brothers from Bedford who died on Omaha Beach. Raymond had carried a Bible into battle, and it was later found on the beach and eventually returned to his mother. In the new memorial there is a bronze figure of a GI on a simulated beach with a Bible as a reminder of Raymond Hoback's ordeal. What is not noted at the memorial site or in the president's remarks was that for the rest of her life the mother of the dead men often woke up at night asking where her boys were.[54]

The aesthetics of the new memorial are complex rather than simple and abstract, mostly because they insist on celebrating the elements of a national victory. Driving up a long and winding road to the entrance, one sees a view dominated by a huge "Victory Arch" inscribed with the word "Overlord" (the military code word for the invasion). Later one learns that the arch stands exactly 44 feet and 6 inches high to symbolize June 6, 1944, the date of the Normandy landing. Driving around the other side of the memorial, one can see a seven-and-a-half-foot statue of Eisenhower (added in 2006) looking toward the arch and overseeing the battle as it is replicated before him. Necrology plaques containing the names of the dead from the invasion are still being erected as donations from both the United States and its allies become available to mount them, and death is represented as well by the sculpture of a dead soldier on a beach with the sounds of gunfire hitting the water quite evident. Although the memorial does not erase the reality of death, its overall aim is to enshroud allied losses (and erase enemy ones) within the images of victory and courage.

This modern memorial really tries to tell much more of a story than most traditional war memorials. The architect, Byron Dickson of Roanoke, told an interviewer in 2001 that he was attracted to the project because he had always been interested in the subject of World War II and because, professionally, he had long been fascinated with "monumental architecture," which he felt was "architecture that has a spirit to it." A visit to Normandy convinced him that he did not want to recreate the "cemetery-type environment" he found in France, and he was more interested in having the Virginia memorial "entertain" people in the sense that they would linger on their visit. It would give them more to look at and think about and cause them to revere the spirit of sacrifice. Thus, he was willing to insert the figure of a dead body, names of the dead, and—under the arch—a rifle stuck into the ground with the helmet of a fallen soldier and his dog tags on it in order to reaffirm the "sense of intense sacrifice soldiers made during World War II." The site also manages to show this with its central piece of sculpture, a nineteen-foot bronze statue of four American rangers called "Scaling the Wall," which represents the assault at Pointe du Hoc. Despite the fact that flags of allied nations can be seen around the perimeter of the site and the names of dead soldiers from nations allied with the United States will appear on the walls, the site is clearly an American memorial dominated by Eisenhower and the images of American rangers—and one that is willing to reveal some of the brutality of the invasion only to surround it with a huge overlay of reverence for the nation's soldiers and their leaders. That the war was fought as well for the Four Freedoms and that it produced a legacy of regret in thousands and thousands of American families are not subjects that attract attention at this particular site.[55]

BATAAN

The lingering realities of private anguish and local memories proved particularly resistant to public efforts at consolation and inspiration when it came to the experience of Bataan. To be sure, successful attempts were made to transform the experience of a military defeat in the Philippines and a staunch defense against Japanese forces into a tale of honor and heroism. Yet a careful look at the way this encounter with the Japanese was recalled by various survivors and communities over a long period of time suggests that virtuous images could never fully soothe many of the men who returned or the families of the dead. Like Pearl Harbor, the surrender of a combined force of some 77,000 American and Filipino troops at Bataan on April 9, 1942, was an unmitigated disaster and a distinct military setback. When Bataan fell and a remaining force of Americans on the nearby island of Corregidor under the command of Jonathan Wainwright gave up the fight one month later, Japanese forces acquired control of the Philippines. American prospects in the Pacific war looked bleak.

The surrender on Bataan was followed by the notorious "death march," in which thousands of captured soldiers were forced to walk miles without adequate food or water and endure atrocities at the hands of their Japanese captors. Many GIs and Filipinos were killed or beaten by enemy troops. Those that survived often died later in horrible conditions in prisoner-of-war camps. When the government finally revealed details of the march in January 1944, Americans reacted with outrage and anger. Many called immediately for revenge; the chairman of the House Military Affairs Committee, Andrew May, demanded that "the fleet be sent at once to blow Tokyo off the map." And a dramatic spike in war bond sales was noticeable. After the war, a tribunal held the Japanese commander of the Philippines, General Homma Masaharu, responsible for the atrocities and executed him.[56]

The public memory of Bataan was immediately portrayed as a tale of American heroism and bravery. *Life Magazine* proclaimed that in resisting the Japanese the men had proven that they were "fighters, clever, and more resolute than their enemies." In fact, the popular journal compared their defense to the heroic stand of the Greeks against the Persians at Thermopylae, long a symbol of courage in the face of overwhelming odds. Wainwright, who was held as a prisoner of war until 1945, was honored at numerous dinners and ceremonies once he returned from Asia and was awarded the Medal of Honor for his leadership in the defense of the Philippines. "Bataan Day" became a time of celebration in numerous American communities even while the war was still going on. In Maywood, Illinois, a town that saw a large number of local men captured at Bataan, large festivals begun while the war still raged lasted for years afterward. In 1943 Maywood dedicated an honor roll listing some 2,400 names of individuals who were serving in the armed forces at the time. Reporters noted that some women were weeping during the ceremonies because the fate of many of the men on Bataan and elsewhere was still uncertain. Yet the keynote address at the ceremony framed the surrender in mythical terms and claimed that the "heroes of Maywood" who fought on Bataan were the "spark that set American military might aflame." Interestingly, eleven years later at the 1954 Bataan Day event, with public memories of the defeat and the suffering fading, ceremonies centered not on the warriors but on a living memorial—the dedication of a street named Bataan Drive. Citizens also enjoyed a giant parade with floats that included one that replicated the flag raising on Iwo Jima, a fireworks display, and a "street dance." When a Chicago reporter visited the town in 1985, he noticed that few of the younger generation even knew of Bataan, and those that recalled war at all were more preoccupied with Vietnam.[57]

Hollywood was also quick to see Bataan as a valiant stand and to tone down its tragic dimensions. The 1943 film *Bataan* portrayed the Americans as stout defenders who supported the war effort without question. Unlike the barbaric enemy they faced, the GIs in this feature film were inherently tolerant and able to overcome ethnic and racial differences to cohere into an effective fighting force. At the end of the film the war is cast in ideological and not sorrowful terms when a narrator exclaims, "It doesn't matter where a man dies as long as he dies for freedom!" The patriotic courage of the men is mirrored by women serving in the Philippines in two 1943 features, *So Proudly We Hail* and *Cry Havoc*. In these films army nurses do not regret that they are trapped in places like Corregidor and do whatever they can to help their male comrades. By 1945, with victory in sight, Bataan was recast almost completely as part of a larger story of American heroism that left unanswered questions of military preparedness for the Pacific war and, once again, soldier suffering. In *Back to Bataan* and *They Were Expendable*, actor John Wayne represented American bravery and skill. In *Back to Bataan* he led Filipinos from jungle hideouts in a guerrilla campaign against the Japanese after the Bataan surrender. The film actually begins with a reenactment of the liberation of American POWs in the Philippines by their fellow soldiers and with shots of the faces of real survivors. In *They Were Expendable*, Wayne plays a dedicated PT boat commander who leads daring raids against the Japanese naval vessels in waters off the Philippines. This heroic version of Bataan was repeated in the 2005 feature *The Great Raid*. The opening of the film refers to Bataan as the "largest single defeat in American military history." But the story quickly incorporates the setback into a larger narrative of the American victory as the POWs are liberated in what the film calls the "most successful" rescue mission in American history.[58]

Images of brave men and stout defenders were powerful and widely accepted as key ways of understanding what happened on Bataan. Yet many who survived could not be comforted by such talk and felt a sense of obligation to former comrades to keep alive the story of abuse and death they had experienced. Many Bataan veterans expressed for years the belief that "Uncle Sam" and the military had let them down by not sending help while they fought the Japanese. Not surprisingly, it was a veterans organization called the "The Battling Bastards of Bataan" that sustained a remembrance of loss by erecting a memorial containing the names of the men who died at Camp O'Donnell in the Philippines.

The capture of the men, moreover, had an unusually powerful impact on a number of hometowns. Many of the soldiers stationed in the Philippines were part of federalized National Guard units that had been activated before Pearl Harbor. Most did not even suspect that there would be a war with Japan as they sailed across the Pacific. They had simply joined the guard as a way to make some extra money during the hard times of the late 1930s and went off to the service with a large contingent of friends they had known most of their lives. Thus, when the surrender occurred, a community like Janesville, Wisconsin, suddenly learned that 97 of their fellow citizens were now hostages. The figures were 87 men for Maywood, Illinois; 66 for Harrodsburg, Kentucky; and 62 for Brainerd, Minnesota. The capitulation hit New Mexico particularly hard because some 1,800 troops from the state had been sent to the Philippines, and no one knew for sure how many were dead or alive.

Life, always quick to see a good story, sent a reporter to Harrodsburg in July 1942. He portrayed the townsfolk in highly virtuous terms, describing the town as an ideal community "where neighbors call each other by their first names and have watched each other's boys grow up." Photos show local people praying in church and mounting displays of pictures of the missing men in a storefront window. The essay gave a nod to the traumatic effects of the sudden loss when it admitted that "the swallowing of sixty-six of its young men in a single day is hard to bear," but it noted that citizens were standing in firm support of the men and the war and that the dedication of a new armory was now planned to which the men would someday return. The men's innate patriotism was suggested when it was reported that they had enjoyed learning how to operate tanks as guardsmen before the war and running them "proudly up and down Main Street."[59]

Soon after the surrender in June 1942, Harrodsburg held the annual commemoration of its founding. Speakers inserted references to what had just transpired in Asia into their traditional historical orations. The hostages from Company D, 192nd Tank Battalion were compared to "Mercer County boys" who had defended settlers on the Kentucky frontier in the eighteenth century. Both groups of men were seen as heroic defenders of their homes, a formulation designed to mitigate private feelings of concern that circulated among many families. Without knowing the details, the *Harrodsburg Herald* claimed that the men in the Philippines "demonstrated that young American manhood is as good today as it was 150 years ago" and were carrying out a tradition that began with the "winning of the West." The paper proclaimed that the sacrifices they now made would eventually lead to the "winning of the Far East." Local editors also refused to accept any suggestion that the men were anything less than brave warriors, saying that they would still be fighting if they had not run out of ammunition. A reporter from *Life* did say that there was some sadness in the community "over the fate of the men" but that mostly people talked about the "valor, bravery, and sacrifice" the tank battalion manifested just as "the pioneers" before them had done.[60]

Timeless values rather than wartime realities were invoked continually during the celebration, and a large parade was held to honor "heroes in the past and in the present war." A line of tanks from Fort Knox brought a fighting spirit to the streets—at a time when the men could no longer fight—and young girls placed flowers at a federal monument to George Rogers Clark and other Kentucky pioneers "who died in the wilderness." The local historical society staged a program "in grateful recognition of the heroic soldiers of Mercer Country" in front of a large honor roll that listed the names of local residents who now served in the nation's armed forces. In fact, a reporter from the *New York Times* discovered that most people had heard absolutely nothing from any of the captured men but that nonetheless several expressed the opinion that some of them must certainly be waging guerrilla operations against the Japanese, so strong was the ideal of courageous resistance. One local man with two sons in the service said that no father wanted to see his boys go off to war but that he also did not want a "slacker" in his family and that it was "right" that these men should fight. He added that "all the farmers around here feel that way."[61]

During the remainder of the war, scattered reports on the fate of the men dribbled into the town. In the fall of 1942, one local mother reported that she had tried to send a cake to her son but that it was returned with the marking "suspended service." The parents of James Shewmaker told the local newspaper that they had written the War Department seeking news of their son who was on Bataan, only to learn that his name did not appear on any casualty list. It was 1943 before the International Red Cross, which collected information on prisoners of war, sent word to local families that some of their loved ones were held by the Japanese. In January 1944, the mother of one captive said that she had received several messages from shortwave operators in the United States telling her that they had picked up the voice and name of her son and that he was "well" but in a Japanese camp. By the end of the war many residents were receiving postcards from the prisoners, and a few learned that their loved ones had been liberated by MacArthur in the Philippines.[62]

As the pressures of wartime ebbed and people learned more about the details of Bataan, public expressions of sorrow in Harrodsburg became more noticeable. At the annual festival of the town's founding in 1946, the *Herald* published the names of all local dead from the war and reported that many citizens stood with tears in their eyes as the list was read aloud. At the same time, grieving family members placed memorial statements in the paper. The parents of one Bataan prisoner—the one who never received the cake his mother sent him—placed the following note in the *Herald*:

> In loving memory of our dear son, Sgt. Jennings B. Scanlon, who died in the Philippine Islands, July 8, 1942, four years ago. Dear Son, four years ago today, God called you away to live in Heaven above. Where all is peace in love. No more wars to win.

You have left this world of sin. But our hearts our sad within. When we think of the lonely grave so many miles away.

The family of Herbert Steele also recalled the loss of their son with a public statement:

> In loving memory of our son and brother, Sgt. Herbert Steele, who died in a prison camp in the Philippine Islands on June 14, 1942. Oh hear my prayer tonight for my son who was taken away from me. So far away to fight. I loved my son, dear Father. And wanted him by my side. It was four years ago today that my dear son passed away. In that far-off land he fought so brave. For us, dear God, our lives to save."[63]

The language of personal loss and references to a "world of sin" and a son "taken away" did not constitute a complete rejection of the war effort, but it questioned the sacrifice and moderated significantly the rhetoric of courage and honor that had surrounded so much of the public framing of Bataan during the war itself. The tension between the celebration of the last stand at Bataan and a refusal to erase the memory of loss was still evident in 1961 when Harrodsburg veterans erected a memorial to Bataan. Today, driving into the town from the north, one can see traces of the patriotic memory of the war by viewing a World War II–era tank and an American flag. At the memorial site, the idea of a heroic last stand is noted in an inscription on a plaque that says that the defense of Bataan and Corregidor "was one of the greatest battles of the world in the long-protracted struggle to save the Pacific and Australia from enemy hands while the United States gathered the strength to resist." But there is also a plaque that insists that the local dead be recalled by listing the names of the thirty-seven men who came home from the prison camps and the twenty-nine who did not.

A driving force behind the creation of the local memorial was Maurice Wilson, a Bataan survivor. Wilson and other men who made it home were often interviewed after the war and usually told stories that tempered images of a heroic defense with tales of how they suffered at the hands of their captors. Wilson himself recounted how at times he had only the heads of fish to eat; others explained that they withstood the rigors of the camps not by brave deeds but by creating a mutual support system in which the men helped each other.[64] Historian Studs Terkel visited Wilson for an interview for his 1984 book, *The Good War,* and found him to be consumed with the Bataan experience. Terkel reported that his home was filled with books, photos, and other forms of memorabilia concerning Bataan. In his interview, Wilson invoked the language of patriotism and asserted that he was no "draft-dodger" and would be ready to defend his nation again. Yet he also expressed anger toward the government for not adequately compensating him for his injuries.[65]

A large group of men captured on Bataan also came from the town of Janesville, Wisconsin. For a long time local residents knew very little of what had happened to them. When the survivors returned home, however, the celebrations were joyous and heartfelt, and the men were treated as heroes. Captions under photographs of the homecoming in the local press described the return of "My Hero" and ""Bataan Heroes Given Welcome Home." In 1947 Janesville dedicated a memorial to the men near the local National Guard armory. A campaign for funds was quickly oversubscribed, and there was enough money left over to furnish a room at the local hospital "in memory of our boys" after the monument was built. Images evoking thoughts of the brave defense shared space on the memorial with reminders of the community's loss. On top of the monument stood a replica of the tank commemorating the courage of the men of Company A, 192nd Tank Battalion. Under the tank, on the wall of the memorial, a tablet was placed listing the names of the men who lived and those who died. Thousands filled the streets for the 1947 dedication, but as time went on crowds at various commemorations became smaller. In 1964 only about forty citizens showed up for a wreath laying ceremony.[66]

As they waited for news of the missing men during the war, the citizens of Janesville turned instinctively to patriotic ideals and rituals, as did their fellow countrymen in Harrodsburg. A group of wives, mothers, and sisters in the town formed a "tank battalion auxiliary" whose by-laws stated that the aim of the group was to "foster patriotism" and "render aid and comfort to our men in the military service and their families." It was also true that some women in the town were angry at Franklin Roosevelt for not doing more to help the men while they resisted the Japanese. At monthly meetings the group would attempt to minimize the massive disruption the war had brought to their lives by reading letters sent to families from servicemen in various parts of the globe, attending memorial services as a group for local men reported killed in action, and reciting the "Pledge of Allegiance" and singing the "Star Spangled Banner." In February 1944, they gathered to hear a shortwave broadcast from Forrest Knox, a local man now held in captivity by the Japanese, and were gratified to hear him read a list of names of local men who were imprisoned with him. After the war the auxiliary group continued to meet and undertake projects designed to help the returned veteran such as giving the men savings bonds. One was eventually presented to Knox. Not surprisingly, the group was at the forefront of efforts to raise money to build the local Bataan memorial and hold services at the site in the postwar era.[67]

In Harrodsburg and Janesville, the aesthetics of the local memorials worked very hard to screen undercurrents of remorse and pain from view. As is often the case, the language and appeal of patriotic images and rhetoric proved to be a powerful way to understand what was happening to the hostages and why this tragedy had befallen their community. Yet local memorials in both communities could never entirely erase the fact that some local men had to die, and that is why in these towns and others the names of the dead frequently appeared. The local sense of loss was simply too palpable to be ignored completely, even as it was cast within the language of tradition. Local people knew the victims and their families. They passed by homes on a daily basis where some of them had lived and were sometimes aware of the suffering that went on within their walls.

In Janesville as in Harrodsburg, some of the returned men did seem able to put the war behind them. Dale Lawton suffered from malnutrition as a POW but prospered after the war and was proud of the fact that he was eventually able to purchase a home and send his son to college. In an interview in 1967 he told of how he had been liberated by the American raid on Cabanatuan, but he said he no longer held any hatred for the Japanese and did not even think much about the war at all. Yet the widow of another resident who never came home explained how she had wondered about the fate of her spouse for years after the war while she attended meetings of the "tank auxiliary" group and stressed that "it was not something you forget."[68] Forrest Knox also recalled that once back in Janesville he kept returning to thoughts of the dead bodies and acts of torture he had witnessed in the Japanese prison camps. For years after the war Knox would suffer from nightmares. The slightest noise would wake him in the night, and suddenly he would find himself standing shivering by his bed, not knowing where he was. He was especially troubled by his recollection of an experience inside a Japanese ship where some American prisoners actually strangled several fellow GIs who had "gone mad" and whose screams had brought threats from enemy guards that air supplies to the lower depths of the vessel would be closed if the screaming did not stop. He was also angry that doctors at a military hospital in 1946 kept telling him that there was really nothing wrong with him, even when he told them he had frequent hallucinations of "dead men walking down the street." Knox concluded that army doctors were not really interested in offering long-term care for such emotional distress, and soon after the war he felt many in Janesville really did not care what happened to men like him.[69]

Historian Donald Knox interviewed many Bataan survivors like Forrest Knox in the 1980s. After talking to the men—often at reunions of the Defenders of Bataan and Corregidor—he concluded that they had "entered a wilderness that had no rules" and felt that the men who made it home were not really heroes but victims. Forrest Knox told the oral historian that he knew well how others like him suffered in Janesville. He recounted the story of Red Lawrence, who spoke to a "big city hall meeting" after the war and told citizens how much the men had to endure and that the "war department never told mothers" the real truth about the trauma of incarceration. Lawrence's own torment actually prevented him from leaving his home most of the time after the war was over because he grew tired of people asking him to retell his war story, and he remained "a prisoner in his own house." Forrest Knox also talked of another local Bataan survivor who drank constantly "to kill the headaches," and he related with some disgust that the Veteran's Administration had told the man that his medical problems had developed only after he returned from the war. When the man died at a relatively early age from a stroke, Knox was certain his death was due more to the failure of the government to provide him with adequate care. He recalled the plight of another Bataan veteran who stumbled a great deal when he walked because he had lost feeling in his legs while a prisoner. Not realizing the extent of his injuries, neighbors thought that the man was drunk most of the time. Knox himself harbored a great deal of resentment over the fact that the local General Motors plant was reluctant to hire him after the war because they felt he was an "emotional wreck" and refused to favor him in any way because he was a veteran. In public, Forrest Knox kept his feelings to himself. In fact, he frequently attended civic ceremonies at the local Bataan memorial, "regularly met with gold star mothers," and served as a pallbearer "for every casket that came home." He said he realized that some of the coffins were probably empty but that "mothers wanted a grave and marker to mourn over." He also noted that "he closed his mind at those times" so as not to give an indication of the anger and regret he carried inside.[70]

In Brainerd as well, men from Bataan continued to suffer long after a large parade welcomed them home in October 1945. The celebration itself was an especially difficult event to witness for those whose loved ones remained buried overseas. Don Samuelson, whose father died as a prisoner of war, recalled that when men came home from the war he wanted to go to the local train station to look for his father, but his mother kept cautioning him that he "won't be there." Samuelson said he realized on one level that she was right but still hoped that his father might someday "come walking off the train." One of the thirty-two men who did come back to Brainerd from Bataan, Ken Porowoll, revealed that for decades after the war he felt uncomfortable around relatives of fallen comrades who did not return. He remembered the father of one dead soldier asking him what sort of knowledge he had that had allowed him to survive and why he had not passed it on to his son who was now dead. Another man once accused him of not fighting hard enough against the enemy. The accuser felt that had he put up a better fight the surrender on Bataan would never have taken place. Porowoll also claimed that others in the town were reluctant to ask him about the war experience for fear that they would "trigger some bad memory" and cause him to lose control of his emotions.[71]

Ben Steele was another Bataan survivor who struggled for decades with the aftermath of his war experience. Raised on a ranch in Montana, he and his family knew nothing but hardship in the 1930s. At one time his father was forced to sell bootleg whiskey just to make ends meet. Steele joined the Army Air Corps in 1940 and, like other men, was sent to Asia before the actual war broke out. In the spring of 1942 he was on the front lines in the fight against the Japanese to defend Bataan, but he was forced to lay down his weapons along with his comrades and embark on the forced march to a Japanese prison camp. Already weakened by malnutrition, Steele had to march for six days without much food or water. At one point, when trying to help a friend, he was bayoneted by a Japanese guard, although the resulting wound was minor. Eventually, he was assigned to a road detail that involved excessively hard labor under intolerable conditions and caused the deaths of many soldiers. Steele survived the rigors of working on the Tayabas Road but did contract dysentery, pneumonia, and malaria. He spent the next eighteen months in Bilibid Prison, where he began to pass the time by creating drawings of the men and events he saw around him. His depictions of how the prisoners lived and suffered had to be done without the knowledge of his captors and involved considerable risk for the Montana soldier. In 1944, while a prisoner in Japan, Steele entrusted his artwork to a Catholic chaplain, John Duffy, in the hope that the prelate had a better chance of seeing that they might survive the war. Unfortunately Duffy lost them at sea when his ship was destroyed. Amazingly, after he returned to the United States, Steele was able to recreate his many drawings from memory. They have served as one excellent source of what conditions for Bataan prisoners were like.[72]

The restoration of his art work was therapeutic for Steele. He had never been trained as an artist, but the experience of making the drawings in the camps convinced him to attend art school in Cleveland after the war. Steele also claimed that the effort to go back and reconstruct his POW experience in a realistic (and not abstract) way helped him to forget the terrible nightmares he suffered for years after 1945, which included imagined fights with Japanese guards. He admitted also in a 2001 interview that he was hospitalized for "psychological problems" at a military hospital after the war. The significance of his commemorative work—something that he claimed was possible because he had a "photographic memory"—is that it left a critical record of the war experience and one resistant by its very nature to easy assumptions that the men were simply heroes or that, as some thought during the war, they must still be waging some sort of resistance effort to the Japanese even after they were captured.[73] His drawings "Tayabas Trenches" and "Burial on Tayabas" both picture gaunt American prisoners suffering horribly. In the former, weakened men are being forced to crawl into trenches in the Philippines that served as latrines. Some are so ill from tropical diseases that they fall dead in the slits in the earth. In "Burial on Tayabas," we see POWs burying their dead comrades in hastily dug graves with dog tags tied to crossed sticks as markers.

New Mexico was especially affected by the surrender at Bataan and the subsequent death and imprisonment of so many men. Some 1,800 troops from various National Guard units in the state were taken prisoner, and about one-half that number never came home alive. When these men traveled to Asia before Pearl Harbor, most of them thought that if war did break out it would be in Europe and that they would be home relatively soon. News of the capitulation caused them and their loved ones back home to adjust to shocking new realities in the spring of 1942, however, when the news arrived that guardsmen from the 200th and 515th Coast Artillery Regiments were now in the hands of the enemy.

Traditional patriotic responses appeared in New Mexico in response to Bataan as they did elsewhere and continued to explain to many what had happened during the war. Upon learning of the surrender, the mayor of Deming called the men's defense of Bataan "heroic." A local woman talked in 1943 about how the men had fought "in valor's name." Overall, however, a legacy of loss and suffering tended to predominate in New Mexico when it came to the surrender in Asia. In 1991 a memorial dedicated in Deming—a town that recorded thirty-eight deaths from Bataan—reflected a more realistic remembrance of what the local men endured. The aesthetics of the memorial turned away from traditional images and were centered completely on the idea of the "buddy system" or the story returning men told of how they survived the war not through courage but through an extensive effort of mutual assistance in the prison camps. At the center of the memorial is an image of two prisoners standing behind barbed wire and looking emaciated. Behind them are drawings of a watch tower, and below them are the words "Bataan-Corregidor," both reminders of the defeat they had suffered. Prisoners are also seen helping each other survive in a monument dedicated in Las Cruces in 2002.[74]

The actions of one survivor of the "death march," Manuel Armijo, further reveal how difficult it was for many to simply accept the language of patriotic honor or forget the war. On the first anniversary of the surrender after the war ended in April 1946, Armijo went to the state capital building in Santa Fe, lowered the American flag, and hoisted a "white flag of surrender." He would repeat this ritual every year until he died in 2004. By 1975, in fact, this ceremony had expanded into a major public event that included the attendance of other veterans, the playing of music, and the lighting of symbolic candles for the men who did not return home. A memorial text was read at the ceremony. Entitled "The Voice of an American Boy," it reflected a mix of regret and approval for the nation's war effort. A speaker would explain that many of the American boys of New Mexico had lived happy lives before the war, playing sports and living in warm families, but they were now dead and missing. Armijo said he hoped the celebration would help "keep history alive," which in this case meant a record of the suffering the POWs endured. Today in the Bataan Museum in Santa Fe, a piece of sculpture depicts men walking on the "death march," with one prisoner lying on the ground and a Japanese guard following the group with a rifle. The inscription reads "Lest We Forget."[75]

Armijo knew from personal experience just how traumatic memories of Bataan could be. He had not only endured the brutal march but had been pistol whipped by a Japanese guard. In a documentary film *Colors of Courage: Sons of New Mexico/Prisoners of Japan*, Armijo's daughter related how her father felt despondent for years after the war and believed that "God had abandoned him." In the same video the veteran is pictured returning to the Philippines and crying in front of a memorial to the prisoners at Camp O'Donnell upon viewing the names of friends who never returned. Armijo explained that as a prisoner he felt both "helplessness" and "hopefulness." His wife also revealed that for many years he would scream during the night. In 2004 Armijo told a reporter that he still had dreams of "prison guards" and would wake up "screaming" and "dreaming." "It just hasn't gone away. It just never goes away!" he exclaimed.[76]

Many other Bataan survivors in New Mexico were haunted by traumatic memories. Hank Lovato was unable to sleep for years after his experience as a prisoner and claimed that he "just wandered around at night and slept on the floor." Don Harris endured recurring visions of bombs falling on him. James Gunther claimed that he went to work each day only so he would not be tempted to start drinking. Other Bataan veterans said they found it difficult to face the relatives of men who died in Asia. Gerald Greenman of Deming found his hometown to be a "depressing" place after the war because so many of his old friends were now gone. Many other vets were so shaken by the experience of captivity that they could find little solace in the widespread belief that they had exhibited patriotism and courage in helping to slow the Japanese advance in Asia before they were captured. They needed more than virtuous images, and they indicated as much when hundreds of them clogged the highways around the sacred chapel at Chimayo, about thirty miles north of Santa Fe, in 1946 as they made a pilgrimage on foot at Easter time to a shrine that promised to relieve people in distress. They said they did not feel heroic but simply felt lucky to be alive and wanted to thank God. In 1946 local papers even reported on one veteran, Conrado Vigil of Belen, New Mexico, who walked for several days to get to Chimayo because he had made a promise to God at Camp O'Donnell that if he lived he would offer his gratitude.[77]

The survivors not only continued to bear witness to the painful experience of Bataan and to withstand traumatic memories, but from time to time they revealed that they harbored deep anger toward their captors. In Colors of Courage, Armijo told a story of meeting Harry Truman after the war and telling him that he appreciated very much the decision to drop the atomic bombs. He reported that Truman hugged him and said that he never regretted using the deadly weapon. In 1999 several Bataan survivors expressed outrage when the Santa Fe town council passed a resolution to erect a historical marker noting the site of a former Japanese American internment camp near the city. One man stated that the decision "just kicked the Bataan veterans in the teeth in the twilight of their years." Armijio himself asked why the council could not have just waited until he was dead before commemorating the camp. And he claimed it now "opens old wounds" and "hurts." Some veterans, however, were more forgiving. One survivor said that when he returned from the war and noticed the guard towers at the local site it reminded him of his own imprisonment at Camp O'Donnell, but he was willing to let the new marker stand.[78]

Patriotic rhetoric and heroic images certainly predominated in many memorials and monuments erected to commemorate the war and were often accepted by citizens as explanation of why so many had to suffer and die. To a surprising extent, however, these words and symbols were often challenged by veterans and other citizens in communities throughout the nation. Close to home, citizens sometimes chose to ignore patriotic sentiments and forget much of the war completely by constructing memorials for the living. Moreover, to a considerable extent they managed to hold on to an artifact that was generally expunged from the

great public monuments to the war—the names of the dead. Those that continued to grieve suggested that talk of victory and a "good war" could never compen-
sate them for what they felt they had lost. That is why, when given a choice in the
late 1940s, most parents and relatives preferred that the dead be returned to
them and that their service to the nation be ended.

CHAPTER FIVE

THE SPLIT SCREEN

HOLLYWOOD PLAYED AN IMPORTANT ROLE in interpreting the war as it was fought as well as a vital role in the long debate over its remembrance. As the battles raged and for years afterward, numerous movies produced images of loyal Americans and gritty GIs who persevered in the face of danger. Films, of course, were no substitute for the actual horrors of the conflict, and they often reaffirmed a noble view that many in the audiences longed to see. Contrary to popular opinion, however, the full record of the cinema's retrospective on World War II was actually rather twisted and saturated with many of the arguments that filtered through the larger culture. Countless movies did inspire and remind Americans that the war had provided them with some of the best years of their lives. Thus, when he was in the White House fighting another conflict, Richard Nixon frequently ordered viewings of John Wayne films or drew encouragement from actor George C. Scott's speech in *Patton* (1970) that claimed, "Americans play to win all the time." Yet numerous characters and plot lines also challenged the storybook take on the war with a wide array of images and narratives that registered various forms of disapproval of the entire experience. At times films even undermined the idea that the men who fought were always resolute and gallant. As moviegoers entered this land of cinematic fiction, far removed from battles on the ground, they were actually presented with the reality of another contest—over how the war was to be recalled.[1]

World War II had an almost unprecedented impact on cultural production in the United States. Film studios expended considerable efforts to endorse the war and to reinforce sentimental views of the Americans in the early 1940s. Ironically, they also found ways to project more critical and pessimistic attitudes that swept through the culture as well. Disparaging takes on the war and the warriors were not so visible as the war was waged. Thus, the most prominent wartime movies were unabashedly patriotic, and depictions of violence were moderated.

Yet, even in the early 1940s, as Sheri Biesen has insightfully suggested, movie producers began to take note of the rising tide of violence in their world. At times this effort indicted the war indirectly, with features like *Double Indemnity* and *Murder, My Sweet* that reflected deep-seated anxieties about the potential for evil that resided in the hearts of Americans themselves. On a few occasions, such as in the 1944 film *I'll Be Seeing You,* the damaging effects of combat on the psyche of American veterans was revealed as well. After 1945 the spotlight on cruelty and aggression was intensified by an entirely new set of fears connected to emergence of nuclear weapons and the outlook of many left-wing filmmakers opposed to Cold War militarism. Films now turned to the hard-boiled side of American life, with gangsters serving as surrogates for capitalists, and delved deeper into the realm of deviancy and sexual perversion. During the postwar era psychopaths and serial killers moved across the screen as much as resolute soldiers. Representations of violent acts abounded—and in fact were more accepted—as a less-than-virtuous outcome of the total war experience. And because they were so widespread, the brutality of the war was just as likely to be evoked to criticize what had happened in the early 1940s as it was to reinforce the ideal of courage and bravery that some assumed to be uniquely American.[2]

The braided memory of the war offered by Hollywood was rooted not only in larger cultural debates over the violent temperament of the American personality and Cold War politics but in critical attitudes brought home by influential moviemakers who had served their nation in the conflict. The personal outlooks of men like John Ford, Carl Foreman, Samuel Fuller, George Stevens, and William Wyler were not part of war's commemoration in the 1940s but—like the work of their literary counterparts—began to seep into their cultural productions in order to interrogate concepts of American innocence. Most of these men were certainly antifascist and supported the goal of destroying Hitler's regime. Yet they were disheartened by the level of human cruelty they saw all around them and the high cost of the struggle. The war had shaken their confidence in a liberal future, and they managed to express such sentiments in their artistic work.[3]

Film also proved to be dangerous terrain for mythical views because it was frequently crafted within the conventions of melodrama. Unlike traditional frames on reality, melodramas lacked the self-assurance that reality could be represented in terms that were unambiguous, that moral truth was clear, and that male authority could always be trusted. It recognized the unpredictability of life and the emotional conflicts that resided in the human soul. Not all films about the war were melodramas, but those that were tended to portray Americans who were victims as well as heroes and frequently raised questions about authority figures. Because they dreamed about the way the world ought to be instead of how it was, these melodramas often attached a love story to a war story.[4]

THE FIGHTING MEN

The "combat genre," as Jeanine Basinger has explained, was one of the dominant ways the war was performed for decades after Pearl Harbor. The focus in these stories tended to be more on the men who fought than on people at home, and the goal—at least during the early years of the war—was to foster the idea that the ordinary American soldier had an innate potential for bravery and that the sacrifices to come were completely acceptable. These features kept ironic and critical perspectives to a minimum. American warriors in these films were generally devoid of sarcasm, willing to fight, patriotic, and deeply attached to women in their lives and to their hometowns. Even when some of these movies dealt with American defeats—such as *Bataan* (1943)—they still managed to preserve unreal images and impressions and conceal the full range of emotional reactions that permeated the population. And during the dark days of the early war with the news of setbacks in the Pacific theater, they also conveyed a sense of American virtuousness by depicting GIs as innately averse to killing and willing to fight only because they had no choice.[5]

Hollywood, of course, was already pushing for entry into World War II even before Pearl Harbor. Filmmakers, many of whom had fled Germany as the Nazis rose to power, were among the first to sound the warnings about Hitler in features such as *Confessions of a Nazi Spy* (1939). And they worked assiduously to erase pacifist leanings from the last war in movies such as *Sergeant York* (1941), which told the story of a World War I hero who decided to put aside his objections to killing and join the fight. Once America entered the war, the Roosevelt administration, fully aware of the power of film to persuade, had the Office of War Information (OWI) review, but not censor, film scripts to see that they backed the war effort and stressed the goodness and loyalty of Americans. Historian Lary May, who has studied wartime movie plots, found that most characters willingly sacrificed personal ambition to the needs of large organizations such as the military. He also noticed that domestic tension between men and women was muted and that citizens generally loved their country. In instances where some doubt was expressed about the war, May found that characters would frequently undergo a "conversion" experience that allowed them to realize that all of the sacrifice was necessary.[6]

Although the early war films were consumed primarily with mobilizing sentiment for the struggle ahead, they also made strenuous efforts to sell it as a "people's war" that would bring about more democracy and tolerance. "Melting-pot" platoons were featured in which American soldiers transcended ethnic and racial barriers and fought together as a cohesive unit. Such images not only muted contemporary domestic tensions that might weaken the war effort but raised the possibility of what postwar society would be like. The high-minded liberalism of the Four Freedoms was featured in *Air Force* (1943) when a reference to the Gettysburg Address reminded audiences that "it is for us the living" to remain dedicated to the idea that "this nation under God, shall have a new birth of freedom and that government of the people, by the people, and for the people shall not perish from the earth." The movie even backed up Lincoln's words with music from "The Battle Hymn of the Republic." During a mail call scene from *Guadalcanal Diary* (1943), a soldier received a book entitled *The Battle of Gettysburg*. And a sergeant in *Bataan* (1943) wrote a letter to the mother of a dead comrade to explain that the man died to save the whole world and that "it don't matter where a man dies as long as he dies for freedom."

In order to strengthen the view that Americans not only fought out of a commitment to high ideals but were also free of original sin, these films also insisted that ultimately the GIs wanted a traditional home life, downplaying the possibility that they may have harbored sinister impulses. Again, film messages spoke to distinct problems. If the dream of democracy for all was meant to partially quell domestic racial and ethnic tensions as well as raise visions of a better world to come, commitments to an exemplary home life spoke to tensions emerging between men and women who were separated. After the war, Hollywood would be willing to reveal more about these pressures, but for now they were minimized in narratives that featured constant references to a longing for domestic life. In *Guadalcanal Diary* (1943) a former taxi driver explained that he was not a hero but "just a guy" who was disinterested in medals and only fought because "somebody" had to take up the task and that he longed to "go back home" as soon as he could. Sacrifice was normalized. A Polish American character in the same film dreamed of a postwar in which he could taste his mother's homemade soup again. And troops on a ship taking them into battle in the same picture often thought about seeing their wives and girlfriends and playing baseball again. They endorsed the glories of domestic bliss when they sang together, "I want a girl just like the girl that married dear old dad." They were, in this rendition, not warriors but unblemished souls—the "pure of heart," as a black soldier referred to his comrades in *Bataan*—whose encounter with killing and dying was only a temporary retreat from their everyday pursuits of rendering love and kindness.

Early combat movies walked a fine line between their desires to cast America and its citizens as wholesome on the one the hand and as revengeful on the other. Everyone who watched *Bataan* knew that the men who gunned down wave after wave of Japanese attackers were doomed, but they could also see that they had no remorse in killings thousands of enemy soldiers. In *Guadalcanal Diary* the GIs actually reveal a desire to retaliate when they see their comrades killed and elect to "go for blood" and bayonet a Japanese soldier even after he is dead. And they sometimes appear as racist, referring to the Japanese as "no-tail baboons." After shooting one enemy sniper, a GI exclaims that he could now "scratch one squint-eye."

By the later stages of the war, when victory appeared to be a distinct reality, Hollywood moderated its sentimentality. Images of soldiers committed to traditional moral and marital values persisted. In *The Story of GI Joe* (1945), the encounter with the enemy is even stopped for a moment to allow one of the men to marry a nurse in the ruins of a church in Italy and recite vows about cherishing one another until death. And in the same story another man volunteers for a patrol at Christmas time, reasoning that every step taken toward defeating the enemy "is a step forward to home." Combat films, however, were now increasingly dominated by stories that had less to say about the men's commitment to democratic or traditional ideals and more to say about their suffering and determination to push forward in difficult circumstances. There was now a dual recognition of both their courage and their victimhood. Innate support for the war effort and for a new world seem much less apparent. The war was now seen as more of an endurance test and a brush with death than a cause to rally around. Hopes that individuals could continue to shape their own futures in the modern era were countered by suggestions that their fate was no longer in their hands.

In *The Story of GI Joe* the point was made that there was little that was noble about war and that the soldiers faced mostly pain and death. The film, based on the experiences of the war correspondent Ernie Pyle, used fewer mythical figures. Americans win and lose various skirmishes with the Germans and fight from house to house in Europe. Through it all, we see Pyle conversing with the men and trying to sustain their spirits as he writes about the experience from their perspective. In a sense, Pyle serves as a witness to the pain of the infantrymen and conveys what he sees as their emotional turmoil rather than reaffirming the need for the war or the political benefits it might bring. He notes that in the Air Force one could die "clean shaven," but on the ground the GI lives "so miserably and dies so miserably." His image of suffering men is reinforced by another image of enlisted men who could only revere officers who respected their individuality and saw them as more than mere cannon fodder. Pyle even makes an appeal near the end of the story for a future of no more wars. He pleads that "out of the memory of our anguish" people must "reassemble our broken world into a pattern so firm and so fair that another great war can never again be possible." At this point, Pyle is hardly ready to buy into tales of war breeding virtue.

Lewis Milestone, a director who had offered portraits of death in war as random and non-heroic in *All Quiet on the Western Front* (1930) and *A Walk in the Sun* (1945), also raised questions about World War II in *Purple Heart* (1945). The film does not question the crusade against Fascism but does challenge certain military strategies. Here the battlefront is not a landing beach or jungle but a courtroom where audiences can consider not only the valor of American men but the moral ambiguity of American tactics. In a Japanese court a melting-pot platoon is put on trial for violating international law by bombing innocent women and children. The men defend themselves by arguing that they only attacked military targets. There is a suggestion here that evidence used against them may have been manufactured by the enemy, but the picture also offers a hint that all Americans may not be "pure of heart." Eventually, the men are threatened with death unless they reveal the secret location from which their bombers took off to attack the Japanese homeland. But they adhere to strict orders not to divulge such sensitive information. And in a dramatic moment that forcefully suspends any pretense that American men are above suspicion, one GI tells a Japanese court that if these American soldiers are killed, more will come and "bomb you" and "blacken your skies and burn your cities to the ground and make you get down on your knees and beg for mercy." Unmoved, the Japanese tribunal condemns the men to death, but they remain defiant and march from the courtroom to the music of the "Air Force Hymn."

Postwar films generally offered positive images of the men who fought but did not shy away from raising questions about the entire experience and the need to resort to violence to resolve disputes. After a brief lull in the late 1940s, Hollywood resumed the production of stories about the fighting men in 1949 with vigor in features such as *Battleground* and *The Sands of Iwo Jima*. Again these movies cast the war experience into the ambiguous frame of melodrama by restating the determination and courage of the American soldier and simultaneously widening the effort to review the war from a greater variety of perspectives. The reaffirmation of virtue in the light of victory was not hard to explain. The contest had, after all, been a hard-fought triumph over evil political regimes that had brought an inordinate amount of death and destruction to the world. It is important to stress, moreover, that such positive images were reinforced by the direct contributions that branches of the armed services made to the actual production of the movies themselves. The military often provided troops, tanks, planes, ships, and strategic locations to studios desiring to restage the war. In his extensive study of the ties between Hollywood and the military, Lawrence Suid demonstrated the importance of such assistance. The alliance gave the armed forces a chance to enhance their reputation, attract recruits, and even boost the morale of those already in uniform. For the studios, the arrangements resulted in substantial cost savings and brought a degree of "visual accuracy" to their final products. The Marines, for instance, who worried that their role in the postwar military might be diminished by the rise of air power, provided a considerable amount of material for the production of *The Sands of Iwo Jima*. In the making of *From Here to Eternity* (1953) filmmakers toned down the depiction of brutality within the service in order not to jeopardize support from the Army. Suid indicated that this alliance did not begin to decline until the 1960s, when a new wave of directors and producers, less emotionally involved with the experience of World War II, emerged.[7]

Courage and steadfastness abounded in many of the postwar combat films, as one might expect. The war had already fostered the idea that the continued security of the nation would rest on the ability and authority of its fighting men and military leaders. This was clear in *Battleground,* where GIs persevered in a bitter contest with the Germans at the Battle of the Bulge. Surrounded by the enemy at Bastogne, these "battling bastards" stood strong against superior German firepower and refused to concede, despite the fact that their situation looked bleak. Enlisted men—symbolized by actors James Whitmore and Van Johnson—appeared as resolute as they ever had in many wartime features and seemingly unconcerned about larger political dreams. They are, in fact, disdainful toward ideas that suggest that a more tolerant world awaits them or even that the home front is solidly behind them. To a certain extent they are shown as victims or men who miss home and who carry photos of wives and children. But mostly they reinforce the notion that most GIs saw the war as just another job that had to be done. This makes warfare a routine experience, their courage innate, and the idea that they may carry dangerous impulses only a remote possibility.

Despite these reassuring portrayals of American soldiers and the war itself, a stronger tendency to make more disparaging assessments of some of the men who fought and of the idea of going to war itself was also becoming noticeable after 1945. And to a surprising extent, some of these films featured the actor-hero John Wayne. At issue were not only traces of regret over the losses of the last war but the nature of male authority in postwar America. If Wayne and the men he represented could defeat the nation's enemies and not become savage themselves, their authority in the Cold War 1950s might be more acceptable. If such men were portrayed as incapable of managing both the art of war and relations at home, however, it might mean that their rule and plans for a military build-up in the period after the late 1940s were open to discussion. To a surprising extent, visions of virtue collided with fears of male aggression and insensitivity in many of these postwar films. Indeed, judging from the movies, the fears and anxieties of Americans in the early Cold War era were not only about Russians and bombs but about the makeup of the men who had just won the last conflict. Gary Wills has explained that Wayne emerged as a star at a time when America took up the "imperial burden" of leading the free world against communism. He argued that Wayne became the ultimate symbol of self-discipline and manly virtue as he fended off the nation's enemies. But Wayne became popular when such images were also challenged time and time again. In such a light, he may not have been a simple reflection of American power in the world but a weapon in a domestic cultural battle to quiet deep concerns about powerful men who now held the nation's fate in their hands.[8]

Although he did not actually serve in World War II, Wayne was able to establish his reputation as a warrior and a patriot in several wartime features. In 1944 he starred in *The Fighting Seabees* as a civilian contractor skilled in the martial arts. As Wedge Donovan, he led an effort to build airstrips in the South Pacific. It was enemy air strikes against his construction crews that convinced him that he and his men needed military training to defend themselves properly. Quickly they are transformed into Navy Seabees, capable of putting down runways and killing the "bug-eyed monkeys" from Japan that attack them. The film certainly promotes a heroic image of a dedicated American willing to do whatever it takes to help win the war. At the end Wayne, as Donovan, dies while driving a bull-dozer loaded with explosives into a group of Japanese soldiers. The next year in *Back to Bataan*, he helped to diminish the legacy of an American defeat and surrender by leading a group of Filipino guerillas in a daring raid against the Japanese to free allied prisoners. Heroism and bravery dominate this feature; Filipinos themselves are also presented as true believers in American political ideals, especially in their hatred for authoritarianism. The Japanese are again evil-doers and barbarians, who commit atrocities such as the hanging of a Filipino man in front of school children because he tried to prevent them from lowering the American flag.

John Ford, who would collaborate with Wayne in many films, directed him in the wartime feature *They Were Expendable* (1945). This story was part of a series of films that looked more at American military leaders and less at the exploits of common soldiers. In this feature Ford took a reverential look at two naval officers, played by Wayne and Robert Montgomery, who captained PT boats in dangerous waters off the coast of the Philippines in the days just after Pearl Harbor. The Navy had suffered catastrophic losses in Hawaii, and the nation was in dire need of time to rebuild and mobilize resources for the fight that was to come. Wayne's character is eager for battle, and he makes a spirited defense of the value of PT boats to his superiors as vital to disrupting Japanese shipping. He has a few minor encounters with women in this drama, but the movie is ultimately too much of a patriotic piece to be considered melodrama. These naval officers are instinctively loyal and courageous and are devoid of cynicism and complexity. They are more than ready to obey a command and help in the evacuation of Douglas MacArthur from the Philippines across enemy lines so that he can flee to Australia and plan a counterattack. The men in this movie—and John Ford himself—worship MacArthur. When he is actually represented on the screen, audiences hear "The Battle Hymn of the Republic" and witness the raising of an American flag. The PT boat captains, moreover, are eager to shake his hand. Near the end of the story, Wayne hears a radio broadcast about the surrender of Bataan, and things look bleak for the Americans. He too is ordered to Australia to join in MacArthur's mobilization effort, but everyone watching knows how it all turns out. And both the reality of victory and veneration of MacArthur seem to make the tragic losses in the Philippines more acceptable—or forgettable.

With pressures to win the war removed after 1945, Ford started to use Wayne in roles that offered a more serious look at the men who fought and the idea of war as a way to resolve conflict. Wayne appeared again as an emblem of patriotic valor and manly virtue but also as someone who held reservations about martial combat as well. This cultural work—the work of both ratifying and questioning war and warriors—was performed after World War II in both combat movies and westerns, which acquired a new level of popularity after 1945, as Richard Slotkin has demonstrated. Wounded while filming his documentary on the Battle of Midway, Ford was extremely proud of his wartime service but not averse to reconsidering the value of resorting to massive violence as a solution to anything. Slotkin noted how many of Ford's postwar westerns, for instance, managed to not only affirm "the patriotic solidarity" that helped Americans win the war but also offered a "moral critique" of the victory itself. To do this Ford returned to stories set on the mythical American frontier and centered on the debate that had long marked American mass culture over whether American men could expect to destroy enemies and savages on some distant "frontier" and still remain devoid of barbaric impulses themselves. A heroic view of the nation's past, of course, tended to affirm that they could. A more critical—and melodramatic—point of view acknowledged that Americans also carried dangerous drives as they moved through history—a point that made them unexceptional.[9]

What Slotkin called the "crisis of postwar ideology," or the inability of myths to completely dehistoricize the past, was clearly evident in some of Ford's postwar work such as *Fort Apache* (1948) and *She Wore a Yellow Ribbon* (1949). In both movies the esteemed director crafted a story that raised doubts about the need to resort to aggression as a way to solve problems. In the former, Wayne plays a cavalry officer skeptical of the entire process of killing and dying and more interested in the peaceful resolution of conflict. In the latter, he performs the role of an army leader who opts to negotiate with the Indians rather than fight them. He tells his Native American counterpart that "war is a bad thing," a point with which his adversary is in complete agreement.

Wayne achieved major box-office stardom in the postwar years not only as a cavalry officer who fought Indians but as a Marine leading men into battle against the Japanese. In *The Sands of Iwo Jima* (1949), he played Sergeant John Stryker, a dedicated soldier who knew how to turn innocent recruits into warriors capable of killing the nation's enemies. This film has often been cited as an inspiration by young Americans who volunteered to fight in Vietnam in the 1960s and is singled out for its depiction of patriotic valor. But such moral clarity is not so evident when the film is closely scrutinized, and the heroic qualities that Stryker displays are often challenged. Clearly, America could not have won World War II without men like Stryker who gave themselves over completely to the military task at hand. Yet this hero pays a high personal price for his devotion to duty—and is not attached to home in the way many of the men described by Ernie Pyle were. His long absences from home, in fact, have damaged his relationship with his wife and children. A friend tells him that women need a "regular guy to come home on time every day." Stryker's remorse over the rupture with his family hits him particularly hard when he sees other men get mail from loved ones and receives nothing himself. Saddened and dejected, he goes into a town in New Zealand where his men are training and gets "blind, staggering, stinking fall-down drunk." A young officer (John Agar) also expresses serious reservations about the "gung-ho" attitudes of some Marines and tells Stryker that someday his son will read Shakespeare but not the Marine manual. Some have interpreted Stryker's death in battle as a sign that postwar society was growing disenchanted with men who wanted to fight more than love. Yet as others have suggested, Stryker stood for values and attitudes that were still considered essential for the nation's survival.[10]

REVIEWING THE OFFICER CORPS

Some of the growing debate over the nature of American fighting men—and therefore national identity itself—was also directed toward a reconsideration of the war's leaders. Many citizens emerged from World War II not only with a feeling that they did not want to repeat such a horrible experience but with a deep sense of resentment toward many in the officer corps. Some officers were thought to have placed personal ambitions over the welfare of their men. Thus, it made sense that one of the serious features of the postwar retrospective was a reconsideration of the commanders who held the fate of many in their hands—and someday might do so again.[11]

The turn to leading men was evident in *Task Force*, a 1949 story that celebrated a naval commander as well as the power of American technology—in this case, an aircraft carrier—that helped win the war. In this feature, actor Gary Cooper played a patriotic man who loved his wife and his ship and recalled his wartime exploits with fondness. Audiences learn that before World War II naval officials were slow to realize the value of ships that could launch planes, an idea that Cooper's character avidly endorsed as an instructor at the Naval Academy. Luckily, he was at sea on a carrier when the Japanese attacked Pearl Harbor and was now more than ready to enter the fight and extract revenge. Scenes that replay the American victory at Midway reminded viewers of the key role carriers played in the war and the foresight of men like this naval officer. As in many postwar movies, audiences were also exposed to actual combat footage along with staged reenactments. At the end of this story, Cooper's character steps down from a distinguished career as squadrons of jets fly overhead to show their respect for the wartime leader. It is not hard to see the point that the nation can continue to feel safe because of the existence of such dedicated men and powerful weapons.

Effective leadership in battle is performed again in *Twelve O'Clock High* (1949). The American victory is restaged through the frame of strong authority and effective technology—in this case, the alleged effectiveness of precision bombing. This drama opens, not with any reference to the Gettysburg Address, but to the brave deeds of American flyers. Gregory Peck plays an air force major who visits an abandoned airfield in England after the war and recalls with nostalgia the sounds of the men and the planes taking off. Peck's character ran a bomber group that was charged with conducting raids over Germany and was proud that he had brought to this task a willingness to make a "maximum effort" and take many risks to accomplish his mission. In this case, however, as his losses mounted, he came to feel a great deal of stress. Here audiences learn that even leading men could weaken under the burdens of war and that extreme efforts can also result in high losses. In a similar fashion, in *Command Decision* (1949) an air force general is questioned about taking an aggressive approach to initiating bombing runs over Germany that lead to an unacceptably high rate of American casualties. The officer is removed from his post, but his successor soon learns that costs will always be high to defeat powerful enemies.

There were even moments in postwar films when American commanders were put on trial for not having the best interests of their men at heart. Dana Holmes, a character in *From Here to Eternity* (1953), is an army officer who possesses few redeeming qualities. In a story authored by an enlisted man who basically saw the military as an oppressor of a person's independence rather than as an organization that nurtured their best instincts, Holmes cheats on his wife, drinks to excess, and favors GIs who are willing to join his boxing team. Boxing, in this feature, is something like the moral equivalent of war, for it can turn men into good soldiers and bring rewards and advancement to their commander. Eventually, GIs are beaten down in this movie, and Holmes has to face a court martial on charges that he was cruel to his troops. The picture ends, as does the novel, with the American entry into World War II in 1941. Yet it makes no assurances that the American leaders from the war era could serve as models of behavior.

The Caine Mutiny (1954) and *Mister Roberts* (1955) expanded the debate over the character of the officer corps and therefore over the legitimacy of male authority in the nation's past and present. Although a statement at the beginning of *The Caine Mutiny* affirmed that there had never been an actual mutiny on a ship of the U.S. Navy, one is staged on the *Caine,* an old minesweeper ruled by a dictatorial and unstable captain played by Humphrey Bogart. Bogart's character has been ordered to take over the ship to replace an officer who was considered too lenient and thus too popular with his subordinates. Any chance that men would respect the new leaders is soon undermined, however, by his inclination to act erratically and insensitively. On one occasion he even appears to exhibit a degree of cowardice. When the ship is threatened by a severe storm and Bogart is unable to order the maneuvers that will save them all, the seamen, led by a junior officer played by Van Johnson, take over. Johnson has to face a court martial for his actions, but the trial actually reveals, not that the men were insubordinate, but that Bogart's long tenure in the war had led to emotional stress and paranoia. In the end he is a victim more than a coward. This formulation tends to exonerate him somewhat, but it also makes clear that not all American officers could deal with the challenges before them.

There was a right way to lead men in war, and it did not include the extreme authoritarianism performed by James Cagney in Mister Roberts (1955). Set on a Navy cargo ship that managed to escape the brunt of the fighting in the Pacific, this film suggested again that some American officers had been consumed with quests for personal glory and were disinterested in the well-being of the men who served under them. Henry Fonda portrayed the prototypical leader of men as Lieutenant Doug Roberts, who stands up against the repressive captain when he denies the sailors a shore leave they have earned. When the crew learns that Roberts relinquished his desire to transfer to another ship to join the real fight in order to get the men some of the benefits they deserved, they not only admire his selflessness but find a way to falsify documents that ultimately get him the transfer he wants. The departure of the one officer who helps the captain to maintain control and who is also a model leader capable of putting the interests of others above his own inspires the rest of the crew. One ensign is motivated enough to stand up to the unjust captain himself. And when the men learn that Roberts is eventually killed, they all realize they have lost a good man.

At times the reconsideration of leaders put aside harsh judgments and succumbed to a wave of deep nostalgia for the men who led Americans in the early 1940s—an outlook that served the cause of mythologizing the war and reinforced the acceptance of Cold War leadership. This was noticeable in White Christmas (1954). The plot featured Bing Crosby and Danny Kaye as two former GIs who had entered show business after serving their country. When the men learn that a former commander they had held in high regard is struggling financially to run an old inn in Vermont, the singers quickly organize a show designed to revive his business and, at the same time, honor his military legacy. Actor Dean Jagger played the "old man" whose memories of the war were so pleasing that he kept an army jeep. He is elated to see some of his former soldiers again and to watch Crosby don his old uniform and sing about a wish to be back in the service again. When the popular singer performed "White Christmas"—a song that the wartime generation had linked to a yearning for peace and home—World War II and the men who fought it were suddenly seen in the most romantic of lights. Historian Christian Appy has insightfully remarked how such sentimentalism offered a "blanket of moral certitude and nostalgia under which Cold War militarization could be hidden." He is surely correct, but it is also true that a broad effort to sentimentalize the American experience of war had already emerged with vigor during World War II.[12]

Fond memories of the war and its leading men also took center stage in the 1955 feature *Strategic Air Command*. The veteran officer in this film, played by James Stewart, enjoyed the fruits of postwar prosperity in the 1950s and the support of loving wife, played by actress June Allyson. As a former bomber commander from World War II, a role similar to his own war task of flying bombing runs over Germany, Stewart's character recalls his war years with affection and is thrilled when he has a chance to enter the Air Force again and test the more sophisticated planes of the Cold War era. Impressed rather than concerned by the destructive power of the new weapons that can inflict as much damage as a thousand World War II bombers, Stewart tells Allyson that they are the "most wonderful things that you can ever imagine." A preamble had already alerted audiences to the idea that this story was about the need to defend the skies of the 1950s to preserve the peace. After bearing the couple's child, however, Allyson comes to regret the fact that Stewart is away so much testing planes. For his part, he becomes so enamored enough with his new job that he signs on for another tour of duty without telling her. She angrily asks him, "Wasn't one war enough for you?" It is a medical condition that finally forces him to leave the Air Force again, however, and not his wife. His general praises him for putting duty over family and career, and even his spouse expresses pride in the service he has rendered. As he comes home for good, the camera lingers almost lovingly on the new weapons of mass destruction that seem to float effortlessly in the sky, and one is left to wonder if this World War II vet can ever be happy again in a world at peace.

The veneration of leading men and commanding figures reached an apotheosis in the early 1960s with *The Longest Day* (1962). In this story of the D-Day invasion of June 1944, American and allied leaders are devoid of complex human qualities and remembered as legendary. Based on the best-selling book by Cornelius Ryan, who conducted interviews with hundreds of American, British, French, and German combatants, the film treats the allied effort on this day—"the longest day in history"—with reverence and awe. The entire project would not have been realized without the efforts of producer Darryl Zanuck, who was moved by reading Ryan's book. Zanuck had already established a major reputation in film making with such features as *The Grapes of Wrath* (1940) and *Gentlemen's Agreement* (1947). He now wanted to fashion this highly laudatory tale in part because he thought it would attract a very large audience—a sign that he had detected the sentimental longings of some of his audience. For him the war had been essentially a contest between good and evil; he wanted the film to reaffirm the need for allies to stand against evil in the present as they had in the past. This was a message that also helped him to get a substantial amount of military hardware and government assistance not only from the United States but from England and France as well. Filmed in black and white because Zanuck thought this would enhance the movie's "authenticity," *The Longest Day* became the highest-grossing black-and-white film ever until the appearance of *Schindler's List* in 1993.[13]

The stars of the film were mostly American officers who directed the Normandy landing. There is absolutely no questioning of war or the military or the men who led the Allied troops into battle in this picture. They are portrayed as competent and completely dedicated to the task at hand. Their German counterparts are seen as lax and not sufficiently vigilant in preparing to resist the invasion. Zanuck claimed that he used so many major stars in this feature that audiences had a hard time trying to keep track of all the key figures. It is the stars/officers, however, who are portrayed as most responsible for the success of the invasion. John Wayne, as Colonel Ben Vandervoot, appears as a tireless leader who trains his airborne troops incessantly in England, worries over tactics that may prove harmful to them, jumps into battle himself, and even continues to fight after sustaining a broken leg. He cannot be stopped. Neither can his colleague, General Norman Cota, played by Robert Mitchum, who refused to consider an order to retreat from Omaha Beach when pinned down by German fire and who orchestrated a daring assault on a German wall. Henry Fonda as General Theodore Roosevelt made it clear that he did not want the fact that he was the son of a famous president to keep him from leading his men onto Utah Beach. Dwight Eisenhower and Omar Bradley are represented as respected figures who are more than capable of dealing with the stress of preparing and executing the battle plan. Their power is matched only by the muscle of the massed military might of the allies that day. As is fitting for a story about supremacy, victory, and glory, there is little display of blood or even blood lust.

There are other dedicated fighters in the film. French resistance forces carry out raids against Nazi positions. Enlisted men also appear ready to fight, although overall they do not appear as fearless or as capable as the officers. A number of reviewers, in fact, noted how the men "who kill, are wounded, and die" appear to be treated in a second-rate fashion. And one reviewer noted the absence of African American faces. Enlisted men may be good soldiers in this version of the war, but in this story they lack the qualities of leadership that are held by their superiors. Moreover, this veneration of military authority came at a point in the postwar era when a critique of such power was actually growing. Just two years after this movie, Stanley Kubrick produced *Dr. Strangelove, or How I Learned to Stop Worrying and Love the Bomb.* Most critics noted how well Kubrick mocked military authority in America and the "assertive masculinity" that had been popular during the Cold War era when the nation's security was ensured by the mass production of highly destructive weapons. Margot Henrickson has explained how this movie helped to undermine "the sacred Cold War institution of the bomb" and the reputation of the military. She claims that it even helped to "reinvigorate a dynamic tension between the forces of cultural dissent" and those of the "political and technological status quo." Yet it should be clear by now that a critique of war and the men who made it even in America had predated the 1960s and could be found in many quarters of American culture.[14]

In 1970 *Patton* sustained the celebration of American military leaders at a time when they endured harsh criticism over Vietnam. This was the story of a true warrior, who discovered that the path to his own self-realization moved through the field of combat. War was not an experience that destroyed individuals or even led to a better world but an opportunity for men to realize basic masculine qualities. George Patton was an American general who was no innocent but a rabid fan of martial valor. When actor George C. Scott declared that all Americans love the "sting of battle" and that "no bastard ever won a war by dying for his country; he won it by making the other dumb bastard die for his country," sentimental views of Americans were cast aside. Patton represented longing for the chance to prove one's worth by standing and facing an enemy; he was the embodiment of the rugged individualist and the lone gunfighter. In real life, Patton did not really like modern wars with their massive armies and powerful technologies, for he felt they diminished the opportunity for individuals to earn honor through their own deeds. For him the fate of his men was not nearly as important as the chance to find glory and respect on the field of battle. He revered men who fought and died for him and detested those that appeared weak and traumatized by the terror they faced. He was especially fond of leading his men into a liberated city or town in a victory parade where the inhabitants lavished them with adulation and praise.

MacArthur (1977), which appeared in the same decade as *Patton,* just after the nation's armed forces had fled from Vietnam, staged again the ideal of brave and virtuous American leaders. The film followed the career of Douglas MacArthur as he fought American enemies in Asia from the time Franklin Roosevelt ordered him to leave the Philippines to his campaign against communist forces in Korea. Always on the offensive, he is pictured planning his return to the Philippines, accepting the surrender of the Japanese in Tokyo Bay, and being removed by President Truman in a dispute that involved civilian control of military authority. In this narrative MacArthur is nearly mythical, free of emotional turmoil, and certainly a righteous figure as he defends the nation and addresses the cadets at West Point on the merits of a life dedicated to duty, honor, and country.

WOMEN IN WAR

It may appear to be normal that most films about the war dealt with the experience and nature of men. Yet the home front—and the women who waited there—could not be ignored in either the real war mobilizations or theater audiences. Hollywood had built part of its success on its ability to speak to women's issues and remind them of the way men could dominate and control their lives. During the war, however, it needed to send women a number of messages that were often contradictory. Females were told to maintain traditional domestic roles, to keep their families intact as best they could, and to remain supportive and loyal to the men who were away. Some were also encouraged to leave home and find work in wartime industries to contribute to the ultimate victory. During the Cold War a number of war-related features portrayed them in highly traditional roles as well, although in both the 1940s and 50s one could always find women on the screen who were discontented with domestication and homes that were in turmoil. There was never a shortage of filmic calls for women to remain attached to their marital responsibilities and for men and women—above all else—to love each other. There was constant cant about the value of home life and the family as a site of love and stability in a world of turmoil and danger. Yet, as Dana Polan noticed, much of the wartime and postwar cinema also "staged" the impossibility that such ideals could be fully realized in America—such was the divided nature of melodrama and the public memory of the war.[15]

The ideal of faithful women and traditional home life was venerated in *Tender Comrade* (1943). The main character of Jo Jones, played by Ginger Rogers, worked tirelessly to uphold her marital vows even as she labored in an aircraft factory. Jones and her girlfriends pool their resources to rent a house and help build bombers as they wait for a postwar of marital happiness. They also pay heed to democracy by allowing everyone in their group to participate in the running of a household, but they see the war mostly as an interruption in their pursuit of private dreams centered on marriage and family. Jones frequently recalls the words her husband offered before he left for the fight when he said that someday they would have a "little place" at the edge of town, sleep late on Sundays, and host backyard barbeques. One woman who does start to stray by dating other men is quickly "punished" because she learns that her spouse's ship was hit by the enemy. When she eventually finds out that he has survived, she is quick to declare that she will "knuckle down to him" when he comes home.[16]

The ending of *Tender Comrade* again reveals the effort wartime films made to generate acceptance of the conflict and the losses it brought. Jones receives the dreaded news that her spouse will never return but decides that she will take this blow "on the chin" like a "good guy" and soldier on with a newborn son. She embraces death and tells the baby (and the audiences that watch) that his father sacrificed his life to create the "best world a boy could ever grow up in." After seeing this film, James Agee observed that such Hollywood productions had failed to fully confront the horror and trauma of war. The critic, in fact, looked unfavorably on the countless features that showed citizens merely accepting the death of loved ones as necessary or being comforted by the idea that it is noble to die for your country. For him *Tender Comrade* offered a "comfortable realism" but not a true picture of the enormous complexity of the human response to war and its devastation.[17]

In *Since You Went Away* (1944), a film noted earlier as an example of how mythical views of Americans were produced during the war, the idea of the American home as a site of masculine privilege and domesticity is celebrated. Here the home is both the center of the American past and future and the symbol of American goodness in a world punctuated by moral confusion and violence. The final scene of *Since You Went Away* projects one of the most romantic images ever of this wartime ideal when the camera lingers on a classic Cape Cod house with snow falling slowly to the ground on the outside and warm lights shining from within. In the mass culture of the 1940s this was, indeed, meant to be a powerful symbol of what men would return to and of why most Americans fought.[18]

In this picture women again must fend for themselves in a world without a breadwinner. Anne Hilton, played by Claudette Colbert, is more than up to the task of managing the household while her husband is in the service and raising two daughters. Audiences never see Hilton's spouse but only the women of the household dreaming of his return and doing all they can to help the war effort. The dutiful and patriotic wife is completely devoted to her task and makes a promise to "keep the past alive like a warm room" until he can get back. Men do enter her life. An elderly man joins this domestic space as a boarder able to help with household expenses. And actor Joseph Cotton plays a naval officer and old friend who tries unsuccessfully to strike up a sexual relationship with her. But nothing can deter this female hero from the exercise of her love and loyalty.

Anne's greatest test comes when she receives a telegram indicating that her husband is missing in action in the South Pacific. The family joins together in prayer and sheds tears to the background music of "Ave Maria." Anne responds to this setback, however, with determination and finds the confidence she previously lacked to leave the confines of her home to enter a shipyard and work as a "lady welder," a task she finds exhilarating. But work outside the home will not last because the good news arrives that the head of the household will, indeed, be coming home. The joy experienced by the women is overwhelming; a life of love and peace in the traditional home is at hand.

Traditional moral values also dominate visions of the future in *The Clock* (1945), starring Judy Garland and Robert Walker. A prototypical GI from a small town in Indiana, the soldier falls for Garland while on leave in New York City and, with little time left before he must leave for war, the couple soon discuss marital plans. They both agree to remain virtuous until they can exchange their vows. Friends caution Garland about getting involved with a soldier on such short notice, but the man paints a picture for her of a postwar in which he will run his own business building homes for others while she cares for their children in his hometown. It comes as no surprise that they marry just before he leaves to fight and that she tells him that she will love him until the day he dies.

Sometimes women went off to war as well. *So Proudly We Hail* (1943) told the story of three army nurses—including Claudette Colbert as Janet Davidson—who were trapped with American men on Bataan and Corregidor. Colbert is completely dedicated to her wartime task of caring for the wounded because "she had a job to do." She does eventually give in to sexual pleasure one night in a foxhole, but talk quickly turns to marriage with her lover and a future dream of a life on a family farm with children. Yet she does not let daydreams of another life interfere with the pressing need to fight the enemy. In a moment when she is trapped with other nurses by the Japanese, Davidson is able to remain cool under fire and crawl over the body of a dead enemy soldier in order to lead her fellow nurses to safety. Another nurse even sacrifices her life in the ordeal to help in the escape. It is clear that during the heat of battle the women never waiver in their task to help the wounded; individual goals are simply secondary here, as they are in most wartime films. One caregiver, after witnessing her son's death, even affirms that the war must go on and claims that she derives satisfaction that "like his father he died for what he knew was right." These women wear pants, endure hardships like men, hate the enemy, and exhibit valor and courage. Men do promise to protect them, but they never ask for such help and do not seek any special privileges.

Women also taste battle in *Cry Havoc* (1943). Coming from different backgrounds—a fashion writer, a garment worker, an art student, and a burlesque dancer—these women are pressed into active duty as army nurses as the Japanese invade the Philippines. The group is able to function under the command of a dedicated nurse called "Smitty" (Margaret Sullivan) who is able to exert her leadership despite being afflicted by a case of malaria and concerned over the fate of her husband to whom she is secretly married and who is stationed nearby. She warns the new recruits that they will now face enormous hardships but learns quickly that these civilians believe fully in the war effort. One exclaims that she feels it is a war "to the death," and another claims that they are all fighting for their lives or to escape the possibility of becoming "slaves." A few of the women are visibly disturbed by their first encounter with bombs and wounded men, but most adjust quickly and are able to render comfort to the wounded. As the Japanese close in on them, they are given the option of fleeing to the relative safety of Corregidor, but their brush with violence has created only a new sense of determination to stand and fight with the men on Bataan. Dreams of the future are kept to a minimum in this rendition of the war, where women are more focused on holding off the Japanese as long as they can.

COMING HOME

Postwar depictions of men and women were less idealized. Everyone was not completely committed to the war effort as it was replayed in some of the postwar features and not entirely patriotic. Romantic images of what Americans were or could be were still evident on the screen, and women were called upon again to serve their country by doing all they could to attend to the various needs of veterans. There were even continued expressions of the belief that the restoration of traditional home life would be the key to rebuilding the sense of male authority and social stability that many felt the war had taken away. Yet it was becoming harder to keep a sentimental lid on depictions of American life after 1945. Certainly, the removal of pressures to win the war explained this trend to some extent. However, it was also due to the appearance of countless news article reporting the return of large shipments of dead bodies and soldier remains and to the appearance in many towns of men who were visibly injured and emotionally scarred their war service. It has been estimated that some 1.3 million men returned with some form of neuropsychiatric disorder. Films were made that suggested that war-related injuries might be healed, of course, especially through the love of a woman. *Pride of the Marines* (1945) told exactly such a tale about Al Schmid's return to Philadelphia, which, as we have already seen, was a gross distortion of the personal struggle he actually endured in his postwar life. It was becoming clear, in fact, that no one knew for sure what the future would be for so many who were damaged by their war experience.

World War II actually helped to effect a change in attitudes about the emotional harm war could bring. Before the 1940s there was a general assumption on the part of psychiatrists that individuals who broke down in battle had a particular predisposition toward such stress. The massive scale of such injuries in the war, however, made it clear that "all men have a breaking point" and that the problem was rooted not in personal failings but in the pressures of war itself and the level of vulnerability and stress it could bring. In fact, there was less stigma attached to men traumatized by war after 1945 than there had been before that time and a greater recognition overall that mental illness required more professional and sympathetic treatment than had previously been the case. Such a position was not easily won, however, and both Hollywood and military officials were slow to accept graphic depictions of the psychiatric problems war brought. Director John Huston saw his gritty documentary film of psychologically damaged veterans, *Let There Be Light,* confiscated by armed guards from the War Department just before it was to be seen in 1946 at the Museum of Modern Art in New York and kept from public view for over thirty years. Huston's assignment in the Army was to produce documentaries, but his up-close view of battle and death in Italy had caused him to become cynical about heroic views of war. In fact, he carried some degree of nervousness back to the United States himself, and he recalled carrying a pistol on walks through Central Park in New York, just hoping "some hapless bastard would try to jump me." His documentary, filmed in an army hospital on Long Island, included startling footage of African American as well as white veterans plagued by a variety of emotional disorders. The war had done nothing to inspire them, and many grieved visibly from the loss of comrades in battle. Others were simply sullen, could not recall their own names, or tearfully explained that they could no longer go on with life. Huston's film referred to the patients as "casualties of the spirit."[19]

The Best Years of Our Lives (1946) was the most powerful postwar drama to reject mythical views of the war and expose the harm it brought to real lives. Based on MacKinley Kantor's 1945 novel *Glory for Me,* the story showed how much the author had moved away from the sentimental portrayal of the war he had offered in *Happy Land* (1942). His changing attitudes were derived from what he called the "highly emotional experience" he had of visiting the relatives of GIs he had known who were never able to return home. This time, unlike the reaction to *Happy Land,* his fan mail reflected this more critical attitude as well. One writer expressed satisfaction that Kantor had exposed some of the "thoughtless reactions" of many who had spent the war safe on the home front. And a man from Chicago, who lost a son in a plane crash, thanked Kantor for his story, which he felt was a "diatribe against war" and a "plea for a lasting peace." Kantor's reaction to the suffering and damage war brought was shared by the film's director, William Wyler. Having seen the horrors of war up close, Wyler came home a "changed man," painfully aware that he now lived in comparative luxury in California, while millions were still suffering and struggling in the postwar world. Thus, he was attracted to a story that was sensitive to the lingering pain from the war and one that tempered sentimentality with elements of cynicism and bitterness.

The movie, which generated twice the box office of popular combat films from 1949 such as *Battleground* and *The Sands of Iwo Jima*, centered on three veterans who need to be helped back to a normal life by women who care for them. All three experience difficulties in readjustment, although the task of Harold Russell, a real-life veteran who lost both of his hands in the war, was probably the most difficult. Russell, a figure selected by Wyler, requires the complete support of a loving girlfriend who accepts his disability and still proclaims her willingness to serve his needs. In one crucial scene she has to help him dress for bed. He laments that he is now as "dependent" as a baby, but the woman is undaunted and willingly does all that she can to assist him.

Russell's fictional buddies also find love and understanding, although not always from the women they left behind to go to war. Fred, who is haunted by nightmares from his many bombing runs over Germany, discovers that his wife lost interest in their marriage while he was away. After a night of heavy drinking, he falls asleep and has a disturbing dream of his wartime experience that causes him to scream aloud. At this moment, he is comforted by the daughter of one of his buddies, who rushes into his room and cradles him in her arms. During production of the movie, film censors worried over Fred's attraction to a woman that was not his wife, but the cultural need to repair the damage of war took precedence over qualms about adultery. Another character, Al, also struggles with a drinking problem once home but is able to rely on the love and support of his wife, played by Myrna Loy, and his children, who are overjoyed with his return. The female support these men receive is crucial to allowing them to eventually return to work and become "self-reliant" again.[20]

The tragic aspects of war and the wounds it brings are again recalled in *The Men* (1950). The script was authored by Carl Foreman, a war veteran, screenwriter, and director who was forced to flee to London during the height of the attacks on the Hollywood Left in the early 1950s. Foreman had already worked on a script that exposed the injury that war—and racism—brought to soldiers in *Home of the Brave* (1949) and would interrogate the war experience again in 1963 when he directed *The Victors*. As in *The Best Years of Our Lives,* there is no reliving of the victory in this postwar drama, which is focused on the message that war is harmful and that the future is contingent not on capitalist abundance but on the reconstruction of loving relationships—a subtle way of critiquing war and capitalism itself. Much of the story is set in a hospital ward filled with battered veterans—some of them real—in a hospital in Birmingham, Alabama. Physicians conduct a question and answer session with women who are now forced to deal with men who have been seriously injured both physically and emotionally. The scene in some respects amounts to an instructional video on how to respond to the needs of the disabled soldier. The women ask questions such as whether paraplegics can have children or how much their love and care actually temper the emotional confusion some men face. Medical professionals—and the story— make it abundantly clear that no matter how severe the problem, women can bring these men back to health through understanding and the reconstruction of traditional marital relationships.[21]

The main character in *The Men* is Bud Wilcheck, played by Marlon Brando, a man whose war wounds have taken away his ability to walk. Not surprisingly, like Al Schmid, he is haunted by the thought that he may never be able to assume the roles of provider and lover, and he sinks into a deep despondency when a doctor tells him that his legs "are gone" and that he will have to allow his head "to take over." His girlfriend (actress Teresa Wright) is actually more willing to make the relationship work than he is. Over time she convinces him to stay with his physical rehabilitation program and eventually marry. Wilcheck experiences much anger and frustration once he leaves the hospital for a home, however, and quickly returns to the sick ward and the company of other men with whom he had fought and suffered. The medical staff tells him he can never have "peace of mind" if he does not accept his disabilities—something Wright has already done. Eventually, he follows their advice and allows Wright to take him home. Although the exact nature of the couple's future can only be guessed at, the timelessness of the film's message about love and female devotion is quite clear.

Female support is again mythologized in *An Apartment for Peggy,* a story that featured a young American wife who was filled with enthusiasm at the prospect of helping her veteran-husband earn a college degree and start a family after the war. Actress Jeanne Crane played a woman of nineteen who was more than ready to have a large number of children and even help change the world by teaching people to be fair and good. Unlike most of the other films that asked women to assist men after life in the military, this feature did make an attempt to keep alive the idea that the war was also fought for human improvement. Her faith in education as a means of uplift is shared fully by her spouse, who decided after nearly being killed in battle that he would become a teacher to fight human ignorance, which he felt was the root cause of such murderous conflicts in the first place. The couple struggles to pay their bills, and this bothers the male, who feels the need to be a breadwinner. At one point he quits college in order to sell used cars. But his supportive wife tells him that "she has everything she wants" in life even as they struggle on the modest benefits of the GI Bill.[22]

The discussion about entrusting the restoration of men to the caring instincts of women and the need to rebuild traditional home life was not only a way of domesticating female desire but also a reaction to a particular memory of the war as a time of moral laxity. The public discontent over this aspect of the conflict was evident in a number of feature films that saw the war years as a moral holiday where customary ethical values were grossly disregarded. Mass culture had always revealed a capacity to challenge mythical views of a nation and the tenets of moral certainty, and the postwar cinema proved no exception. Romantic visions of the nation as a place of virtuous people who were loving, loyal, and beyond reproach could always be found. These images served to make it easier to repeat calls for continued sacrifice. But such frames of remembrance were constantly contested by suggestions that wartime led to a suspension of ethical behavior. Thus, a movie like A Foreign Affair (1948) focused a good deal of attention on the continued inclination of GIs to engage in immoral behavior in Germany. Opening scenes show footage of the tremendous destruction that was inflicted on the Nazi capital. But buildings are not the only things that lie in ruin in the story. An American congressional delegation has come to Europe to investigate charges of moral laxity on the part of the American troops. Reports had apparently reached Washington that GIs were suffering from "moral malaria" by running around with "blonde fräuleins" and engaging in black market activities. Dramatic tension revolves around an American captain, played by John Lund; a congresswoman from Iowa, played by Jean Arthur; and a female survivor of the Nazi regime, played by Marlene Dietrich. In this telling of a postwar story, the captain is more interested in romancing Dietrich's character than in going home to resume a traditional family life. He is enjoying his fling in Berlin and even takes steps to forge some papers for the German woman that would supposedly protect her from any allied investigation into her past.

The congresswoman is a moral crusader intent upon restoring a higher level of ethical behavior among the troops. She is so outraged by some of the actions she finds among the men that she is moved to call them "barbarians." Eventually, she also finds some information that proves that Dietrich's character had ties to high-ranking Nazi officials and had met Hitler himself. The story does not recognize the fact that German women were also victimized by the war when they were assaulted by Russian forces and left to fend for themselves in the chaos of postwar Berlin. In the plot Dietrich's character is arrested and a former German boyfriend is shot—a sign that former Nazis need to be punished. But the moral rehabilitation of American soldiers remains far from complete. To accomplish that task—at least for the wayward captain—the congresswoman adopts some of the sexual aggressiveness of Dietrich in order to capture his affections and convince him to go back to a traditional married life in Iowa. He seems interested in that prospect near the end, but this narrative still suggested an alternative legacy to World War II that questioned assertions that it was simply a crucible of American bravery and goodness.[23]

Other films in 1948 also recalled the war as a time of moral instability. *All My Sons* looked back at some of the corruption that took place on the home front. It told the story of a manufacturer who cut corners in building bombers in order to enhance profits. When it was learned that his greed had led to the production of faulty plane parts that caused the death of some American troops, he could no longer stand the public ostracism and took his own life. *Homecoming* looked at an ethical lapse on the part of a surgeon who recalled that while serving abroad he had betrayed the loyalty and trust of his wife. The character played by Clark Gable tended to the wounded in Europe but also became involved romantically with one of his nurses. While his spouse spent the war keeping his home warm, this Harvard-trained physician spent his off-duty hours with a nurse, played by Lana Turner, whom he had grown to love. She dies in the war and does not make it home, but the surgeon still has difficulty trying to readjust to married life even after his wife pleads with him to let her be close to him again.

This film, like *An Apartment for Peggy*, also evoked some of the democratic dreams and rhetoric of wartime that many in the 1940s felt explained why the nation had to fight. Prior to entering military service, Gable's character was portrayed as a self-centered, upper-class doctor little concerned with the fate of those less fortunate than he was. In one instance, he had ignored the medical needs of a poor patient in order to take his wife dancing. In a staged reenactment of the war as a struggle for human rights, he runs into his former patient again and sees him die in an army hospital, not from combat wounds but from the effects of an illness that he had failed to treat years ago. His nurse/lover, moved by the sight of the man's passing, exclaims that Americans "just don't care enough" about the medical problems of the poor. For his part, the experience causes the doctor to affirm that he will "never forget that boy" and that when he returns home he will be more sympathetic to the needs of others. Thus, the doubts about his future relationships are mitigated by a hope that veterans might turn the memory of the war into a call for a better society.

The consequences of war also lead to domestic turmoil in both *My Foolish Heart* (1950) and *The Man in the Grey Flannel Suit* (1955). In the former, a veteran returns from the war bereft of any feelings for his wife and soon moves in with another woman. The jilted spouse (played by Susan Hayward) starts to drink heavily not only because she is rejected but because she grieves for another man who did not return from combat but had left her pregnant. The consequences of war in this melodrama are difficult and hard to deal with, and happiness for men and women seems elusive. They also present daunting problems for Gregory Peck as Tom Rath in *The Man in the Grey Flannel Suit*. Struggling to climb the corporate ladder and fulfill the ambitions of his wife for a larger house in the suburbs, Rath recalls the war as a time of moral instability because he killed a German soldier and fathered a child with an Italian lover. Eventually, he comes to terms with his past and restores a source of virtue in his life by electing to send support payments to the mother of the child in Italy and by deciding that the climb to a high corporate office in America must be balanced by a commitment to his family.

THE DARK SIDE OF AMERICA

Sometimes the returned veteran appeared to be nothing but a brute and a danger to others. Such images were the complete reversal of wartime myths and extended the longstanding critique of American violence that permeated many films. It is seldom noticed, for instance, that Stanley Kowalski—the character portrayed by Marlon Brando in *A Streetcar Named Desire* (1951)—was a decorated master sergeant from World War II who kept a photo of himself in uniform on a mantle in his shabby apartment in New Orleans. Kowalski, of course, is known not for his wartime heroics but for beating his wife and raping his sister-in-law. The film's director, Elia Kazan, was quite deliberate in letting Brando's character perform the figure of a cruel man detached completely from traditional moral values. Tennessee Williams, the author of the play on which the film was built, in fact, saw his story as one that would expose the "ravishment of the tender, the sensitive, and the delicate by the savage and brutal forces of modern society," a view that reinforced feelings many had drawn from the experience of World War II.[24]

Kowalski directed his violent ways toward women in his own household. In a few postwar features, the returned vet actually became a danger to society. In *Suddenly* (1954), Frank Sinatra played a former soldier who was proud of the fact that he had been responsible for the deaths of twenty-seven Germans in the war. Once home, however, he had become a hired gun who took an assignment to assassinate the president of the United States. He is stopped in his tracks by a woman who kills him after he takes over her house as a site from which to kill the chief executive. It is quite clear that the legacy of the war in this telling was a highly menacing one. *No Down Payment* (1957) also exposed a darker memory of the war and some of the men who fought it. In this narrative, Troy Boone, played by Cameron Mitchell, appears as a veteran now living in a middle-class suburb. Boone is unable to put the war behind him and adapt to the niceties of backyard picnics and refined living. He finds suburban life unfulfilling because it cannot give him the sense of self-respect and worth he felt when fighting the Japanese, a feeling strikingly revealed in the large collection of war souvenirs he keeps in his garage. He does attempt to put his military training to good use by applying for the job of police chief in the fictitious community of Sunset Hills. But he is turned down for the position because he lacks the proper educational credentials. Indeed, he fairs poorly overall when compared to another veteran named Dave Martin, who managed to escape the rigors of combat during the war while working at Los Alamos. Martin is more educated, more sophisticated, and better able to leave the war behind. In the end, a frustrated Boone rapes Martin's wife but is then killed by his own spouse. Like John Wayne's Sergeant Stryker, Boone finds no place in the postwar world for men who want to continue the fighting.

The image of the dangerous veteran was, of course, only one variant of a much wider film discussion in the immediate postwar years over how brutal some men and women in America could be. Many film noir features in the late 1940s were in fact immersed in the other side of American life—the side that lacked integrity and that was riddled with episodes of decadence, sexual violence, betrayal, and even psychological disorder.[25] Thus, in noir films homecomings are anything but pleasant. In *The Blue Dahlia* (1946), several men just back from the Pacific stop in a bar for a few "bourbon chasers." One man, played by William Bendix, carries a plate in his head from a battle wound and quickly gets into a scuffle in the barroom. His buddy, performed by Alan Ladd, finds his wife throwing a party and kissing another man when he goes to his old house—so much for home front loyalty. The wayward spouse quickly asks her guests to leave, but she does express a concern that her husband might "beat" her because a war hero "can get away with anything." It turns out that the woman spent some tumultuous years on the home front partying at night clubs and even, while under the influence of alcohol, causing a car accident that resulted in the death of the couple's child. Eventually, she drifts into the arms of another man, but the veteran develops a relationship of his own with a woman (played by Veronica Lake) who asks him a question highly pertinent to the postwar years: "Where do we go from here?"

No one's future is certain either in *Dead Reckoning*, a 1946 noir feature starring Humphrey Bogart. Bogart's character comes home from the war determined to see that a former comrade is recommended for the Congressional Medal of Honor. What he finds on his return, however, is a "sick world" where women betray even the men who fought. First, he has to work to clear the name of his friend in a murder case that occurred before the war if he hopes to put his name forward to receive a high honor. In pursuit of "truth" in the case, he learns that a woman who had an affair with his friend was also responsible for seeing that he unfairly took the blame for a killing she herself had committed. At one point she even tries to kill him, despite the fact that he had developed some affection for her. The former paratrooper quickly concludes that he had trusted his comrades in the service more than he could trust a woman like her. He finally achieves his goal of gaining recognition for his wartime friend, but he is concerned as well by returning to a society marked less by innocence and love and more by treachery and deceit.[26]

NO MORE WAR

The extent to which postwar films about World War II moved beyond the project of reliving and reviewing the victory to articulating powerful antiwar sentiments has never really been fully appreciated. Elements of this critique were evident in the many narratives that contested the sentimental images of wartime that had been deployed to serve the war effort, that exposed the damage war did to many of the men who fought, and that revealed the moral ruptures of the 1940s. A few feature films, however, went even further by rejecting assumptions that war was the best way to solve disputes and that Americans would have to be prepared to fight again. In *Our Vines Have Tender Grapes* (1945), a story set in an idyllic community in the upper Midwest, a symbolic call was made for the peaceful resolution to human conflict. The story centers attention on a young girl who learns the value of love and cooperation. A friend tells her one day as they stroll through a country field that he hopes to become a soldier and carry a gun when he matures. She reacts by claiming that girls can fight just as well as boys, and she instinctively picks up a stone and hurls it at a squirrel, killing the animal instantly. But this cruel act saddens both children. Upon seeing a newborn calf, the girl expresses the hope that it will somehow make up for the life that has just been lost. Later, when she sees men from her community go off to war and hears about bombs falling somewhere far away, she tells her father that she does not think there will ever be "peace on earth, good will toward men." Her father tries to convince her that some things must be defended at all cost, but this is a point she never fully accepts. In a similar vein, *The Boy with Green Hair* (1948) looked at the postwar world through the eyes of a war orphan. Knowing that his parents were killed in World War II, a young boy encourages other orphans he meets in a dream to spread the message that war is bad for children. Many of them did not accept his message, however, because it came from someone who was different—not by virtue of his race or background but because he happened to have green hair.

The 1958 attraction *The Young Lions* challenged the effort to find anything noble in World War II. Dean Martin appeared in the film as a young singer who is more interested in finding ways to avoid the draft than in serving his country. He confides to a girlfriend that he is actually "against war" and the "super-patriotic atmosphere" of America. Martin's character also reveals that in the war-time Army there was considerable favoritism and some men were able to get cushy assignments well away from the horrors of the front. Eventually, he comes to feel guilt over the fact that some men are dying while he is relatively safe, and he decides to join the fight. There is another American soldier in this story, played by Montgomery Clift, who goes AWOL, and a German officer, played by Marlon Brando, who detests the war policies of his nation. As the Americans enter Germany, Martin's and Clift's characters find themselves in a position where they kill Brando's character, but none of the soldiers in this reenactment are enamored by the prospect of fighting for their countries.

Antiwar sentiment in films reached an apex during the early 1960s. Growing levels of dissent from powerful calls for militarization and Cold War orthodoxy served to explain part of this trend in films such as *Dr. Strangelove,* in novels such as *Catch-22* (1961), in political manifestos such as the "Port Huron Statement," and even in the early albums of Bob Dylan. Yet this thread of criticism had already been firmly established in World War II films for more than a decade. They were now intensified in features such as *The War Lover* (1962), *The Victors* (1963), and *The Americanization of Emily* (1964). In *The War Lover,* Steve McQueen as Buzz Rickson was a devotee of war and a bomber pilot whose emotional make-up challenged sentimental perspectives on the ordinary American soldier from the war. Rickson was an American individualist completely detached from any moral values and impatient with higher authority. He was interested basically in vanquishing whatever enemy was put before him. Not surprisingly, he sought to conquer women as well as Germans. He remarked that he actually liked "hunting" woman and that one of the Four Freedoms was the right to take "free" French girls in London. His superiors did not look with favor on his penchant for insubordination and breaking rules, but they realized he did get results.

This story called into question the myth that American warriors could actually inflict brutality, wage war, and still remain unsullied. By implication, Rickson was so consumed with the dark side of his nature that he could never consider settling down in loving postwar home. The good American man in this story was not Rickson but his colleague Ed Bolland, played by actor Robert Wagner. Bolland represents the noble defender of the nation who can follow orders, fly bombing runs over Europe, and still retain a capacity for tenderheartedness. Both men compete for the affections of an English woman who tells Rickson that he is "twisted" and capable of only "hate." As expected, it is Rickson—like Sergeant Stryker—who is eventually killed in the drama as Bolland gets to go off with the girl in Cambridge.

The Victors followed American troops through Europe not to relive the victory but to offer a critical perspective on the nature of war and of men who waged it. Ironically, although the film exposed many of the sordid details of the struggle, it offered very few scenes of actual combat. GIs load dead comrades onto a truck in Italy, get drunk, and even commit a hate crime against an African American soldier. These men are also able to show compassion. One consoles a frightened female as a battle rages, and some express a sense of revulsion over the cold-blooded killing of German soldiers by French resistance fighters. They are particularly upset when forced to witness the execution of an American deserter, a scene that seems to mimic the actual execution of Eddie Slovik.

Disparaging perspectives are continued in *The Americanization of Emily*. In this feature an American officer, acted by James Garner, enjoys a life of privilege in England during the war, tending the personal needs of admirals and generals, who are represented as self-indulgent and inclined to sacrifice the welfare of their men for the sake of their own advancement or the reputation of their branch of the service. The cynical Garner makes the point that millions have been "butchered" in this war and that in the next war we will have to "destroy all of man to preserve his dignity." He reasons that "as long as valor remains a virtue, we will have soldiers," so he has decided to preach the merits of being a coward.

Garner is attracted to an English woman, played by Julie Andrews, who has already lost a husband in the war and resents the favored status he enjoys. Her sympathies lie with the men who do the actual fighting. In time, however, she is "Americanized" and comes to accept Garner's doubts over the nobility of sacrifice. Garner becomes a fighter himself, however, when he is ordered to join a film crew that is landing on Omaha Beach to shoot combat footage. His naval superiors actually like the fact that he might be killed, for it would earn the Navy valuable publicity by being able to claim that it offered up the first American casualty on the beachhead. For a time we are led to believe that he does, indeed, die. But when he manages to turn up in England again, the Navy cynically launches a different sort of public relations effort that honors the return of one of the first men to hit the bloody beach.

A mythical view of World War II is shattered completely in director Samuel Fuller's 1980 film *The Big Red One*. Fuller was another combat veteran who attempted to use his artistic talents to bring a soldier's perspective to the larger cultural discussion over the meaning of the war. He had landed in the third wave on Omaha Beach and recalled seeing dead bodies everywhere. When it came to remembering the war, Fuller strongly resisted any attempt to see it as ennobling and argued that the men who fought only wanted to survive—and nothing more. In his autobiography he claimed that he had, in fact, declined an offer to direct *The Longest Day* because he felt it was too "overblown" and did not pay sufficient attention to the suffering of the soldiers. He carried his thoughts directly into *The Big Red One*, a film narrative that was marked by antiheroic views and a project that caused him to suffer "terrible nightmares" as it was produced. In the story, which follows an American rifle squad through Europe, religious symbols are employed to suggest that war, far from being a necessary political crusade, was mostly a transgression of basic Christian principles. Some GIs think that what they are doing is basically murder and therefore debatable. Older soldiers look mockingly upon new recruits as essentially innocents being led to a slaughter. "Death camps" are liberated and officers are seen as capable and responsible, but in the end the movie suggests mostly that war is insane—a point reinforced when inmates in an asylum react to a shoot-out between Americans and Germans with excitement and glee.[27]

A PEOPLE'S WAR

Hollywood's review of the war focused a good deal of attention on the temperament of the Americans. Character issues and moral actions had always been central to the Hollywood melodrama, but the war heightened that cultural discussion because it exposed the degree to which Americans—and, for that matter, all people—could flout moral conventions and engage in brutal acts.[28] This preoccupation with the character and identity of Americans themselves, however, took attention away from the idea that the war has also been fought for the realization of more liberal and human-centered society in America and throughout the world. Thus, a number of late-1940s films raised the issue of intolerance in the United States. The issue was a sensitive one because, despite the rhetoric of the Four Freedoms, racial turmoil still pervaded the military and the home front. Sometimes the depiction of bigotry was inserted into a particular scene or two. This was the case in *Till the End of Time* (1946), where two former Marines and their paraplegic comrade start a barroom brawl with men who want to form a hate club that would exclude Jews, Catholics, and blacks. One of the Marines, who had experienced on Guadalcanal the loss of a close friend who was Jewish, was furious that such prejudice could still flourish in America.

Films like *Crossfire* and *Gentlemen's Agreement*, both released in 1947, confronted the issue of injustice and hatred more fully. *Crossfire* actually reminded viewers not only that the struggle was about creating a more tolerant world but also that life in the military could lead to continued violent ways once men returned home. Breaking from sentimental wartime views, actor Robert Ryan performed the role of a drunken soldier who beat a Jewish man to death. Ryan's character mistakenly assumed that the "Jew-boy" had somehow avoided military service and profited from the war effort. In reality, the victim had fought on Okinawa along with members of many minority groups. Before he died, the man had even worried that some men would bring home brutal and hateful impulses. Not surprisingly, this story (as well as *Till the End of Time* and *The Caine Mutiny*) was directed by a staunch liberal, Edward Dmytryk, whose political views caused him to be blacklisted during the Hollywood purges of the early 1950s.[29]

Perhaps the most explicit connection in postwar film between the ideals of wartime rhetoric and the nation's racial problems was *Home of the Brave*. Starting in 1944, military recruits were made to watch a government-sponsored film called *The Negro Soldier*, which acknowledged America's legacy of racial strife but also focused more on the progress in race relations that had been made over time. *Home of the Brave* hit harder at the issue, however, by making an explicit connection between the trauma black men face in war and the pain they encountered in society. A black GI, played by James Edwards, suffers survivor guilt in the story because he returned from a fight with the Japanese when some of his white comrades did not. He is also haunted by the fact that some of his fellow soldiers did not trust him in battle and by a memory of discrimination he suffered at home in years before the war began. It takes an army psychologist to explain to him that the experiences he encountered at home and in the service both devalued him as a human being and led to what was now termed a "crackup." There is a suggestion at the conclusion of the story that race relations will get better in America as Edwards's character hooks up with a white vet, and the men go off to open a bar of their own. But there is no real assurance that all of the sacrifices the nation has just made will really end the racial divide in the immediate future. It would be decades, in fact, before the plight of black soldiers would attract major attention in a feature film again. In 2008, *Miracle at St. Anna* offered a story of how black men were also a vital part of the American combat effort and were treated better by Italians than by some of their white officers as they fought the Germans in Europe.

The war continued to be linked to a need for racial justice in the fiction of James Michener, who had served in the Navy in the Pacific theater. In two films based on Michener's writings—*Sayonara* (1957) and *South Pacific* (1958)—calls were made to citizens to use the memory of the war to promote racial harmony. These melodramas challenge any fixed notion that Americans were simply people of high character. They did not say, as most films did not, that World War II was not worth the effort. They simply stated that the effort would not be completely justified if intolerance and injustice were allowed to remain and fester in the American mind. By the mid-1950s, when these films were being formulated, there was, as Naoko Shibusawa has suggested, a greater willingness on the part of the population to "humanize" the Japanese—now a Cold War ally—and accept interracial relationships. *Sayonara* certainly helped Americans move away from the legacy of wartime hatred and racism that had driven much of their destructive assault on the nation that attacked Pearl Harbor. This film suggested at least that an American soldier and a Japanese woman could actually establish a loving relationship. Marlon Brando and Red Buttons play two American servicemen stationed in Japan in the 1950s who fall in love with Japanese women. In Brando's relationship, the woman (played by Mikko Taka) needs to repress the anger she carries toward Americans because they killed her father and her brother during the war. A larger problem for Brando is that a marriage to a Japanese woman would clearly threaten his chances for advancement in the Air Force. In this tale, his superiors actually expend considerable energy to end the relationship. Racial barriers to their relationship lead to despondency for Buttons and his lover, who take their own lives when they feel there is no hope for their union. Brando and his girlfriend are more defiant of racist conventions, however, and allow their love to grow.[30]

Michener's insistence that Americans fought in the 1940s for a more tolerant world is repeated in *South Pacific*. Instead of battles, this story is centered mostly on characters who live outside the battle zones and out of the way of the most direct danger, a situation that replicated what Michener himself experienced when he served in the Navy. A naval officer named Joseph Cable in the film is assigned to monitor Japanese ship movements. He is also drawn to a young native woman called Liat who causes him to forget his "blue-eyed" girlfriend in Philadelphia. Cable starts to think less of ever going home and more about a future in the Pacific islands with a woman of a different race. His death eventually solves the dilemma of an interracial marriage. But another character, a navy nurse from Arkansas played by Mitzi Gaynor, does live to overcome racist thinking and stay in the islands. In her case, she has doubts about marrying the owner of a French plantation partially because he had previously fathered several children with a native woman. Her upbringing in Arkansas had made her think twice about the possibility of trying to serve as a mother for children of color. Eventually, she come to terms with her racist past, however, and concludes that tolerance and understanding are preferable to hatred.

The imprisonment of some 120,000 Japanese American citizens during the war also raised questions about the nation's racial outlooks and, in a modest way, intruded into the Hollywood remembrance of the struggle. There was no evidence of any treason on the part of these American citizens in the 1940s; their only crime was that they were of Japanese descent. Twice in early 1950s Hollywood paid heed to his episode of wartime life, although the expulsion of these Japanese Americans from their homes would not receive a full treatment until some four decades after the war. In *Go for Broke* (1951) the film industry celebrated the fighting qualities of Japanese American soldiers who fought the Germans while many of their relatives sat in internment camps in the West. A preamble to the story commented that audiences were about to see a "heroic story" of an outfit that had earned thousands of individual decorations. Led by a white lieutenant who had initially held doubts about the ability of these men to be effective soldiers, this movie constituted a persuasive attack not only on the intolerant beliefs most Americans held toward Japanese Americans during the war but on the viability of such outlooks in the postwar era. The soldiers in this story command admiration as they fight courageously while receiving letters from home telling of how their loved ones are losing their property and being treated poorly. It is no wonder that President Truman is shown awarding many of them medals as they come home once the war was over.

Bad Day at Black Rock (1954) turned the camera more directly on the hatred Americans directed toward their neighbors of Japanese descent on the home front. Set in the mythic landscape of the American West where men were often shown as testing their courage and bravery, this picture portrays average (white) American citizens during the war as being consumed with hatred and meanness. Actor Spencer Tracy plays a veteran who comes to a remote town to find the father of a Japanese American soldier who saved his life in Italy. He plans to give the man a medal earned by his son. He soon discovers, however, that the town is run by a man named Reno Smith (Robert Ryan) who had killed his friend's father in a drunken rage just after Pearl Harbor. The veteran sees that the rule of law no longer applies to this community and that "guerillas have taken over" and are trying to cover up Smith's crime. Eventually, he is able to end Smith's power over the local population, but no guarantees are offered here that the problem of violent and hateful men in American will come to an end.

A more complete rendering of the wartime mistreatment of Japanese Americans finally appeared in the 1999 film *Snow Falling On Cedars,* based on a 1994 novel by David Guterson. An American veteran, played by Ethan Hawke, returns from the war with a great deal of bitterness not only because he lost an arm fighting the Japanese but because he regrets the breakup of a relationship with a Japanese American girl before the war. When a local Japanese American man is put on trial in 1950 for a murder he did not commit, the veteran is forced to confront the legacy of his own hatred toward a former enemy and of discrimination in his hometown near Seattle. The trial of the innocent man serves as a device in which filmmakers can allow a defense attorney to recite the long history of discrimination toward Japanese Americans in this locale as an argument of why he was accused. It is at this moment that audiences get to see a rather full reenactment of the expulsion of these citizens during wartime and their somber march toward trains carrying them to internment camps. The entire episode convinces Hawke's character that he must put behind him legacies of hate from the past, and he produces evidence that proves the accused man is innocent beyond a shadow of a doubt.

The most powerful demand that the war be recalled as a quest for human rights and respect for all came in the 1961 feature *Judgment at Nuremberg.* In this story Nazi judges are put on trial for their complicity in helping Hitler rise to power and create an atmosphere of "racial pollution" that led to the deaths of so many innocent people. Richard Widmark, as an American prosecutor, is relentless here in attacking German defendants who in the name of the law sanctioned "murder, brutalities, torture, and atrocities." Certainly the fact that in this story Widmark's character was part of an American unit that had liberated some of the concentration camps drove some of his outrage. German defense lawyers argue that the responsibility for atrocities resided not with the German people or low-ranking officials but with the Nazi hierarchy. The German defense even links the killing of the Jews to the American killing of civilians at Hiroshima and Nagasaki. At dinner one evening, some Germans suggest to an American judge at the trial, played by Spencer Tracy, that the "little people" of their nation had also suffered with the loss of loved ones and knew almost nothing of what was happening to the Jews. The American jurist remains unconvinced, however, and he ultimately delivers a verdict that indicts the entire German nation for taking part in a "wide project of cruelty" and committing "crimes against humanity." He reasons that a nation cannot do just what it needs to do to survive but must stand for more noble ideals such as "justice, truth, and the value of a single human being."

Hollywood did much more than simply celebrate Americans and their war effort. Heroic individuals did move through the ranks of its fictional army, but so did men and women who were cynical, deceitful, and treacherous. Romantic views of the war generation and the ability of war to nurture character were affirmed and simultaneously challenged by countless feature films that stressed the costs of battle, the shadowy side of many Americans, and the futility of resorting to mass violence to solve political and social problems. Because this cultural debate was so nation-centered and linked to concerns of the nation's future, few efforts were made to probe the pain war had brought to those in other lands or to insist that the struggle had also been fought for the improvement of humanity. For Hollywood and for most Americans, the remembrance of the war was mostly about what they had done and what type of people they were. Movies left the distinct impression that Americans were not only gratified by the war experience but troubled as well.

CHAPTER SIX

THE OUTSIDERS

Sᴇɴᴛɪᴍᴇɴᴛᴀʟ ᴍʏᴛʜs ᴀɴᴅ ʜᴇʀᴏɪᴄ images often obliterated not only the tragic dimensions of the war but the sordid reality of racism and discrimination within America itself. When the nation went to war, it was forced to ask minorities to put aside their many grievances to join the effort to defeat foreign enemies. This request, of course, raised serious questions for both the white male majority that dominated the nation's politics and military and the members of minority groups themselves. National leaders had to find ways to integrate segregated people into the campaign for victory. Those consigned to forms of second-class citizenship, however, wondered how they could be expected to fight for liberal ideals abroad when they were denied fair treatment in their own country. Long before Pearl Harbor they had already found numerous reasons to be suspicious of authorities and to question righteous descriptions of the nation they inhabited.

Despite grounds for cynicism, the democratic rhetoric of the war years encapsulated in the promises of the Four Freedoms did have the effect of raising expectations among many minorities that their wartime sacrifices would translate into greater measures of equality and justice. Many minority leaders clearly saw the war not only as a dangerous period but as an opportunity that would allow them to make powerful claims for democratic rights in the postwar era. In time, African Americans, Mexican Americans, Japanese Americans, and women would invoke a remembrance of their wartime contributions to secure greater measures of equality and respect. Indeed, they worked, not to cover up critical memories of their unfair treatment and losses in wartime, but to resurrect them as a tactic in the long civil rights revolution that marked America in the postwar decades. Like street marches and pivotal court cases, war memories became valuable devices in helping minorities gain equality and claim space in the mythical community of World War II heroes.[1]

AFRICAN AMERICANS

America's longstanding racial problems did not evaporate during the massive mobilizations for World War II. To a remarkable extent racial violence and discrimination pervaded both military and domestic life during and after the war. Racism, in fact, permeated American thinking in a number of ways as the nation fought. John Dower has explained how racial hatred on the part of Americans and Japanese drove both sides to fight with a particular level of ferocity in the Pacific theater. At home racism inflamed passions as well, as millions of people moved from traditional homes into wartime jobs and military bases throughout the world. Tension around army camps or in booming cities frequently resulted in violent confrontations.

African Americans, like other minorities, were quick to see that patriotic service offered the prospect for long-term gains in civil rights. They noted the irony of being asked to sacrifice for America and being subjected to hostility and segregation at the same time. It was for this very reason that black leaders mounted the "Double V" campaign during the war that called upon blacks to fight for America in order to gain leverage in their quest for justice at home. As early as 1940, for instance, a black newspaper like the *Pittsburgh Courier* initiated a series of articles calling for an end to segregation among America's military forces. Some one million blacks served in the military during the war, and another million moved from the rural South to wartime industrial plants throughout the nation. The result of this contribution was, to say the least, substantial. Yet for most African Americans, their collective sacrifice would be meaningless if it did not help to end segregation and their inferior status in both military and civilian life.[2]

The mass movement of the black population not only proved to be disruptive but sometimes provoked efforts to minimize racial conflict both in factories and in military installations. In a study of wartime race relations, Daniel Kryder found evidence of new attempts to calm racial anger because such rifts threatened national unity and production goals. In looking at the files of the Fair Employment Practices Commission, he discovered that the government actually gave blacks opportunities to vent their frustrations over discriminatory hiring practices. Over time, attention to such grievances helped to assimilate them into the workforce, although clearly racial divisions were still incredibly powerful once the war ended. Similarly, military officials had to deal with huge waves of black anger and white hostility in the armed forces and only managed minor improvements over the course of the war. They did respond with efforts at amelioration such as the production of *The Negro Soldier,* an instructional film that stressed black contributions to America's wars and that was required viewing for troops of all colors by late 1944. Yet, clearly, the failure to integrate the armed forces in the early 1940s was a missed opportunity for promoting equality.[3]

Segregation in the wartime military was a source of great frustration to black soldiers and leaders who realized that the opportunity to fight was a way to gain greater measures of respect and justice. In his travels throughout various war zones, Walter White, a prominent leader of the National Association of Colored People (NAACP), noticed much frustration on the part of black soldiers who were trained to fight but kept from active combat roles because officials doubted their battlefield capabilities and because they feared angering white GIs. Much to the chagrin of black leaders, the War Department had concluded that they would not use the war as an attempt to alter the basic structure of race relations in the country. In an editorial in 1944, the NAACP criticized both the War Department and Franklin Roosevelt for not doing more to stop what they felt was mistreatment of black soldiers in both military and civilian life and demanded that "segregation in the armed forces should be abolished forthwith." But their pleas went unheard, and large numbers of African American soldiers were assigned to support roles in units such as the Corps of Engineers or the Quartermaster Corps instead of front-line action. Over time, manpower needs led to a more prominent role for blacks in combat. In several instances all-black fighting units such as the 761st Tank Battalion or the "Tuskegee Airmen" were created, but for the most part opportunities for African Americans to earn the highest form of public distinction from their war service was severely limited by the segregationist policies of the military.[4]

During the war the NAACP made a particular effort to monitor the state of race relations at American military bases. Generally, their investigators found some examples of accommodation between the races but many more instances of segregation and racial hostility, especially in the South. At the Aberdeen Proving Grounds in Maryland, NAACP representatives discovered that blacks and whites could use the same dispensary and that MPs treated black soldiers reasonably well. Similarly, at Camp Plauche, Louisiana, black officers were allowed to eat in the officers' mess hall, and the base commander was credited with trying to effect some improvements in race relations. Observers found an easing of segregation on army buses during the war years at Fort Benning, Georgia, and Fort Monmouth, New Jersey. Yet near the end of the war, in the summer of 1945, racial hostility remained strong, with many segregated theaters, sports facilities, and officers clubs. At Fort Benning, blacks and whites who took parachute training together were not allowed to swim together. And African American troops (but not white troops) at the fort were locked in a stockade prior to shipment overseas for fear of desertion. At Fort Bragg, North Carolina, segregation persisted on buses and in the dispensary. At a camp in Florida it was reported that white civilians working at the Post Exchange refused to serve black GIs until all of the whites were served. At MacDill Field in Florida the officer quarters and hospital wards were segregated. At Camp Livingston, near Alexandria, Louisiana, a considerable level of segregation was found at the base, and black and white prisoners were separated in the stockade. And at a naval air station near Corpus Christi, Texas, a black sailor told the NAACP just after the war was over that the racial situation was getting close to the "danger point" because blacks could not talk to the base commander and because some black sailors were being court-marshaled for simply defending their girlfriends and wives from "derogatory remarks" made by white sailors. The black seaman wrote that "we believe we have the right to democracy that we fought hard to preserve."[5]

African Americans in general drew a sense of determination to improve their condition in America from the experience of World War II. There would be years of struggle and violence ahead, but World War II, with its democratic rhetoric and calls to national duty, marked the beginning of the modern civil rights movement. Many black soldiers came home with a new resolve to resist discrimination and white violence. Between 1944 and 1950 hundreds of citizen committees and interracial councils were formed in American towns and cities, an indication that many whites sensed that a change was in the air. Coming home from the war, both black and white veterans felt that black sacrifice warranted better treatment in the postwar era and that a substantial part of the war effort was, in fact, a fight against racial intolerance everywhere. This did not mean that there was a consensus in America over this issue, however, and bigotry persisted. The point now was that the public inclination to end segregation and racial injustice was stronger than it had been before Pearl Harbor. Jackie Robinson's entry into white baseball in 1947 was a sign of this. So were attitudinal surveys of military personnel. In 1943 about 84 percent of white troops expressed support for a segregated military; eight years later less than half said they felt that way. Among black troops about 50 percent preferred segregated units in 1945, but almost none felt that way in 1951.[6]

There is substantial evidence, in fact, that military service heightened the determination of blacks to work for better treatment once they came home. In an excellent study of World War II veterans in the postwar South, Jennifer Brooks found that the experience of war and sacrifice had caused many veterans, both black and white, to imagine a "better America" once they returned. In looking closely at Georgia politics in the immediate postwar era, she noted that men of both races exhibited a new willingness to assert their political rights. She even found progressive liberal campaigns mounted by both black and white veterans and strong challenges to the old politics of white supremacy in the state. Sometimes this progressive spirit expressed itself in greater support for labor unions, because these veterans felt wartime service should translate into improved economic opportunities. Blacks, in particular, joined efforts to gain greater voting rights. Brooks quoted one black veteran who had been severely wounded in the war as saying that because he had lost "a portion of my body for this country" he was determined to vote when he returned home, regardless of the consequences. In Mississippi Medgar Evers came home after being wounded in France and began to work for the NAACP organizing efforts to improve black voting rights—a role he continued until his assassination in 1963. A fellow veteran, Aaron Henry, assumed the presidency of the state's NAACP office in 1959. In the North in the 1950s the NAACP mounted a number of attempts to help black veterans acquire housing in white suburbs. One former soldier and his family endured months of racial taunts after buying a home in the postwar suburb of Levittown, Pennsylvania, in 1957 but persisted in staying.[7]

In Alexandria, Louisiana, where racial turmoil during the war had helped to rejuvenate the local NAACP chapter, civil rights activists began to push for an increase in the number of blacks who could vote in 1944 and for a black community center once the war was over. Local blacks were also frustrated by what they felt was a shortage of descent jobs for African Americans after years of wartime service. David Illes, the principle of the local black high school, joined a group, hoping to form a new trade school in order to help black men gain employable skills. Inspired by the Supreme Court decision in *Smith v. Allright* (1944) that disallowed the practice of allowing only whites to vote in the Democratic Party primaries in the South, local activists soon brought pressure on voting registration officials in Rapides Parish and warned that they could face federal charges if they continued to restrict black access to the registration rolls. Soon local activists like Louis Berry and Spenser Bradley formed a committee of "pioneer applicants" that pushed harder for black registrants. By the end of the summer of 1944, however, there were still only seventeen African Americans registered to vote in the town, according to the local newspaper.[8]

In 1947 the local NAACP in Alexandria adopted a set of goals that included a desire to "educate Americans to accord full rights and opportunities to Negroes," to secure justice in the courts and full voting rights, and to stop the hideous practice of lynching. Furthermore, in order to improve the quality of life in the town, local black leaders insisted on the necessity of an African American community center. The town had purchased two buildings after the war that had been used for segregated white and black USO activities. Alexandria converted one structure into a community building for whites but leased the building used by blacks to a local industrialist. When the mayor told African Americans that they would have to raise funds to build a segregated center of their own, the local NAACP reacted angrily. They wrote the mayor to inform him that "colored citizens" had made "all the sacrifices which went along with the horrors of war" and had "sent their sons and daughters to fight the forces of evil and intolerance in far-flung battlefields, some of whom never returned." For their part in fighting the "forces of bigotry," African Americans now argued they deserved better treatment and a center at least the equal to that of whites in Alexandria. Eventually, the town provided them with the space they desired, but only after the minority group filed a law suit and after many delays by the mayor's office.[9]

Over time, the black community of Alexandria also sustained a remembrance of the war years that was more critical and less patriotic than the one that dominated the public culture of the nation. Blacks recalled not so much a story of the American victory but of the terrible riot that exploded on Lee Street in January of 1942. On a Saturday night, with thousands of troops on leave from several nearby bases, a fight erupted in the black section between African American troops and white military and state police. Many shots were fired, but immediately after the melee the local press took pains to report that no one was killed and denied a rumor that eighteen black soldiers were left dead from the affair. In fact, the local police chief indicated that if some black men were wounded it could have been from "stray shots" fired by black civilians. The press did admit—as did military authorities—that twenty-eight black soldiers were hurt and that police had used guns, tear gas, and sticks to quell the disturbance. If no one was killed, it was a miracle, for the local paper quoted one witness who said that "bullets were whistling and bricks were flying" and that it was as if "the Japs were attacking." Reports indicated that it took some sixty military police and thirty state officers to finally restore order to a section of town known as "Little Harlem."[10]

Over the next few years black leaders in Louisiana continued to press the War Department on the matter of the black deaths. Official War Department pronouncements stated that there were no fatalities in the riot, although the department admitted that "a total of thirty colored soldiers were hospitalized" and three were "critically wounded." War Department authorities investigated the matter on several occasions and further admitted that "civilian policeman and one military policeman had indulged in indiscriminate and unnecessary shooting." The department even sent a "special agent" from their counterintelligence unit to investigate the "underlying causes" of the disturbance. His report disavowed charges that there may have been subversive elements responsible for the riot but failed to mention that there had been a long pattern of police brutality toward black soldiers in the Alexandria area. The agent concluded that the fundamental cause of the riot was heavy drinking by black soldiers and fights over women.[11]

Black activists in Louisiana never did accept the government's version of the event and continued to argue that there had been African American deaths. Local NAACP officials wrote their national office, insisting not only that black soldiers died but that several innocent and "aged" black bystanders were killed by city police armed with sawed-off shot guns and that a white police officer was stabbed to death. Leon Lewis of the New Orleans Press Club wrote to the War Department in 1942, claiming that white undertakers were hired by the Army to embalm the bodies, which were then shipped out of town under the cover of darkness. In an article in *Colliers* several months after the riot, Walter Davenport, a roving political reporter for the magazine, stated categorically that "ten Negroes died" and described how racial strife and white police violence toward blacks in the South during the war was rampant. He reported that after the riot the area around Lee Street looked like it had been hit by an "aerial bombardment" and that it was an event like Pearl Harbor that should be remembered. Several members of the Alexandria branch of the NAACP also wrote to the War Department, charging that white MPs had even mistreated black women and children during the fight and appealing for an investigation of the "killings of black soldiers."[12]

In the decades after the war, the story of police brutality, black deaths, and a government cover-up continued to be told in the African American community of Alexandria. From time to time the black perspective was reinforced by testimony from various eyewitnesses who reported seeing black bodies in the streets. In 1994 William Simpson, a professor at a local college, published an article in *Louisiana History* that challenged the final report on the incident by the War Department that there were no black deaths. Using interviews he conducted with local black leaders such as Louis Berry and David Illes (who was slightly injured in the riot), Simpson showed that blacks still did not accept the government's version of events. He also conducted interviews with a white policeman who claimed he saw the death of at least one "black soldier" and a former city officer who claimed he saw a "lot of dead soldiers."[13]

In 2007 local blacks continued to insist on their version of the riots. In interviews and discussions held at the Arna Bontemps Museum in Alexandria, respondents were quick to discount the official memory of the riot. Heywood B. Joiner explained that his father, who had served on Guadalcanal, had been on Lee Street at the time violence erupted and recalled seeing black bodies loaded onto trucks and carried away. Robert Johnson, a member of the 367th Infantry during the war, was stationed at nearby Camp Claiborne during the riot but heard from friends who were there that there was widespread shooting and that black troops at the camp wanted to commandeer a tank and go into the town but were dissuaded from doing so. Johnson remembered that the Army's only black general, Benjamin O. Davis, was brought to the camp to soothe the widespread anger of black troops. Local black women also brought to the meeting at the Bontemps Museum an unpublished essay they had saved written by Stephen E. Henthorne, whose father, Ellis, had been on Lee Street during the riot. On his deathbed in 1978, Ellis Henthorne claimed he saw a black soldier shot dead and that the area looked like a "war zone littered with dead bodies . . . stacked up like cordwood."[14]

In recent years African Americans in Alexandria have mounted public commemorations of their local past on Lee Street. The images they have chosen to mark their history stand in stark contrast to the civic memorials that appear throughout the downtown area, however. A mural painted on the side of a building on Lee Street depicts local blacks who fought not only for their country in war but for civil rights—the "Double V." Thus, Louis Berry is included along with Amos Wesley, a local man who became a Tuskegee Airman. Even more striking is the wreath of flowers that stands in an empty lot on Lee Street that honors the "dead" from the 1942 riots. Etta Compton, an elderly black woman who lived near Alexandria during the war, placed the wreath there on her own and has replaced it for the past several years. At a more public space in front of Alexandria's municipal building, a Veterans' Memorial Plaza contains the seals of the major branches of the American armed forces and plaques mounted on stones that offer quotations from famous Americans on the need to be ready to fight for "freedom." John F. Kennedy asserts on one plaque that America will "oppose any foe to assure the survival and success of liberty." Daniel Webster is also invoked in words that ask God to "grant liberty only to those who love it and are always ready to defend it." On the same plaza stands a piece of abstract sculpture entitled "Wings of Peace." No names of war dead are listed at this site. A small park near the plaza contains a wall of murals painted by local school children called the "Peace Wall." And nearby stand several historical markers that recount the town's history. One marker recognizes the role Alexandria played in World War II but references only that important military maneuvers were held nearby before Pearl Harbor and that an air base operated in the area until 1992. It does not even say that anyone from the town died in the war. The largest war memorial in the town stands a few blocks away in front of the Rapides Parish courthouse. It is a column erected in 1914 by the local chapter of the Daughters of the Confederacy to the memory of the local Confederate war dead who were "enshrined in the hearts of the people." In front of the same building a memorial flame, ignited in 1970, now burns to honor "those who sacrificed so much in the defense of freedom."[15]

In the immediate postwar era, of course, there was a devastating tendency to return to prewar patterns of racial intolerance and violence. In the military, many black officers left after 1945, and the situation for black soldiers was generally seen as getting worse. In 1946 some black soldiers were so angry over continued segregation and hostility at an air base near Tampa that they rioted, seized weapons from white guards at the main gate and even took one white officer as a prisoner. The beating of Isaac Woodward, a black veteran just home from the South Pacific after three years in the service, drew national attention to the continued racism in the nation after years of African American sacrifice. A white police officer in South Carolina who beat Woodward so badly that he lost his eyesight was exonerated by an all-white jury. The incident did, however, spark a national wave of indignation, and it led to the creation of an ad hoc committee of citizens from various backgrounds called the National Emergency Committee Against Mob Violence. This action eventually helped to convince Harry Truman of the need to resolve the nation's immense racial problem. Truman formed a civil rights committee that issued a report in 1947 entitled *To Secure These Rights*. The report stated explicitly that the memory of the "war experience" had demonstrated that "the majorities and minorities of our population can train and work and fight side by side." The committee expressed particular concern over the "injustice" of asking men to fight for their nation and then returning them to lives as second-class citizens. One year later, Truman, acting upon the spirit of the report and the legacy of the war, issued an executive order calling for equal treatment and opportunity for all in the armed forces regardless of race, national origins, or religion. Risking criticism from southern Democrats within his own party, the president also created another committee charged with the responsibility of seeing that his decree was implemented.[16]

Racism in the wartime military and in the larger society was never a central part of the larger public discussion of the war and its remembrance that took place in the United States. In a celebration of the war effort such as Tom Brokaw's *The Greatest Generation* (1998), stories were told by blacks about their war years, but they stressed how they were able to overcome whatever discrimination they encountered. Thus, Martha Settle Putney, one of eight children in a black family, related how she volunteered for the Women's Auxiliary Corps (WAC) after finishing a college degree at Howard University and how she earned a doctorate after the war and became a teacher. To achieve her career goal, however, she first had to help integrate a swimming pool on a military base in Iowa and resist attempts of a train conductor during the war to seat her in the freight car rather than with the regular passengers. The war was recalled as part of a larger personal struggle against racism by Jonnie Holmes as well. In Brokaw's book, Holmes noted how, during training exercises in the 761st Tank Battalion, a soldier friend of his was found dead near a white neighborhood in Alexandria, Louisiana. He recalled that he and his fellow black troops did not believe official explanations that the man had been killed by a train while he was intoxicated. They suspected that their friend had been beaten to death by hostile whites, and they were prepared to take their weapons to the town to seek retribution but were dissuaded by their commanding officer.[17]

The importance of an African American remembrance of the war was, of course, that it tended—as did local expressions of grief and remorse—to resist efforts to sentimentalize completely what had taken place in the early 1940s. When Maggi Morchouse, the daughter of a white officer who commanded black troops in the 93rd Infantry Division, interviewed black veterans decades after the conflict, she heard a number of stories of racial conflict on or near military bases in the South. Several of her respondents told of a particular night at Camp Van Horn, Mississippi, when a full-scale fight broke out between black and white soldiers and nearly led to an order by a white colonel to fire upon black troops. Nelson Perry, a black veteran of the war, wrote in his autobiography in 1994 that as a young man in Minnesota he had been attracted to the idealism of the Young Communist League and had come to see Hitler as a danger that had to be defeated. He thus joined the Army, despite objections from his mother that she had not raised her sons to become "cannon fodder." Perry's idealism quickly subsided after several months in the segregated military. He recalled one moment when he was so angered at a white officer who referred to him as "boy" that he refused to follow any more orders until he received an apology. The apology actually came, but from another officer of lower rank. Perry saw this as something of a personal victory. He also documented problems black soldiers had once they left military bases. In Louisiana he noted that military police (MPs) often humiliated black couples by asking the women to show their "health cards," an affront that suggested they were certified to practice prostitution.[18]

A memoir of the black experience in World War II published by James Warren in 1996 focused on an even more dramatic aspect of the racial conflict that marked wartime military. Warren began his military career in 1943 as one of the original Tuskegee Airmen, an all-black flying group that saw considerable action in Europe. He recounted a particular story of racial turmoil that he and his colleagues encountered at Freeman Field near Seymour, Indiana, where tensions ran high. Black officers complained that they were bypassed for promotions, that they could not enter the all-white officer's club, and that they often had a hard time getting service at local taverns and restaurants. The wives of some black officers even charged that they could not always use local grocery stores.

In April 1945, African American officers at the base decided to mount an act of civil disobedience by organizing an effort to enter the officer's club. First, a small group of protestors went to the club, only to be—as expected—turned away. Warren was part of a larger second wave following the first group who were "determined that flagrant segregation and discrimination would not go uncontested." Included in this second group were Coleman Young, who would later serve as mayor of Detroit and a civil rights activist. Eventually, as a result of this protest, the base commander at Seymour had more than a hundred black officers arrested and sent to Graham Field in Kentucky, where they were incarcerated while arrangements were made for their court martial. Warren recalled that while imprisoned in Kentucky he told a legal clerk who was preparing for the trial of the men that he did not believe America should be fighting this war to preserve democracy and freedom in segregated groups and that he was certainly opposed to the fact that black bomber groups should be commanded by white officers. Fortunately, the public response by blacks to the arrest of the protestors was substantial and critical. Walter White argued to government officials that the arrest of the men was having a "devastating effect upon civilian and soldier morale" in the black community and called for the revocation of the arrest orders. Soon, in fact, all but three of the men were released. The three remaining in jail were tried for mutiny, but two were found not guilty and one received only minor penalties for "shoving a provost marshal." Warren felt his 477th bomber group came out of the episode "strengthened" because the unit's white command structure did not survive.[19]

In 1982 Robert Allen revived the memory of the Port Chicago mutiny of 1944. Allen acknowledged that he had been drawn to the incident from his experience as a draft-resister during the Vietnam War in the 1960s and a sense that his attitudes were different from men like his father, who were generally more supportive of war two decades earlier. Thus, he began to interview black servicemen who had been at Port Chicago during the war and noticed how many of his subjects remarked that no one had ever asked them about their experiences before.[20]

Located on the Sacramento River near San Francisco Bay, Port Chicago was a key naval loading facility for ordinance that was being shipped to the Pacific theater. In July 1944, a tremendous blast at that site totally obliterated two ships and killed 320 men, including 200 black ammunition loaders. Convinced that racism had consigned them to such dangerous jobs and that the Navy was indifferent to their needs for special safety precautions, black sailors refused to return to their positions after debris from the massive explosion had been removed. Some of the men felt they would have had a better chance of surviving in battle than on the docks at Port Chicago. Eventually, fifty black sailors were convicted by the Navy of mutinous conduct. The NAACP, while not allowed to be part of the actual judicial proceedings, objected strongly to the decision. Thurgood Marshall, who had attended the court proceedings and offered what assistance he could to the defense, publicly stated his belief that the men were largely victims of racial attitudes and complained to the Navy that they were never given proper training for their dangerous assignment. In 1945 the NAACP filed a brief seeking to set aside the convictions. Marshall again complained that in a trial that produced a transcript of some 1,400 single-spaced pages the judges deliberated for only eighty minutes. The civil rights lawyer calculated that each defendant received only about 1.5 minutes of consideration. Equally outraged, the black press erupted in anger over the treatment of black servicemen. The Chicago Defender called them "martyrs" and protested the assignment of so many black soldiers to loading docks. By 1947 the Navy released most of the men from prison and placed some on ships that wandered aimlessly through the South Pacific. When finally released from the service, the men were given a discharge under "honorable conditions," a category designed to indicate a status between "honorable" and "dishonorable."[21]

Allen's article on the incident and later book did lead to more public revelations over the episode. In 1990, a San Francisco television station produced a documentary of the Port Chicago disaster. Nine years later, NBC presented a television movie entitled Mutiny. The film clearly revealed the discrimination in the wartime Navy and portrayed the black sailors at Port Chicago as feeling they were generally treated "like trash." It even showed the practice of white officers wagering on which black loading gangs would pack more cargo and the indifference of the Navy to the need for specialized training for these men to perform the dangerous tasks they were assigned. Indeed, Thurgood Marshall's critique on the lack of proper training is a central theme of this postwar film. In the end, this program on a major network made it clear that black sailors were treated unjustly in World War II and denied the opportunity to fight and gain recognition in the way many whites did.

Political action also furthered the "rediscovery" of the Port Chicago disaster. In 1990 twenty-five members of Congress, including several from Northern California, asked the Navy to review the case in order "to ameliorate an unsavory chapter in the history of the segregated Navy." Some of the convicted men were still alive and stated publicly that they felt they had been treated unfairly. In January 1991, Congressman George Miller, whose district included Port Chicago and who had supported calls for a naval review, noted that at a time when blacks were again being asked to sacrifice for the nation in Operation Desert Storm, it was only right that these veterans of World War II receive justice from their own government. Eventually the Navy concluded from its review that racism did, indeed, exist in this branch of the service in the early 1940s but that prejudice did not influence the court martial proceedings. In 1992 Congressman Miller went even further by proposing a national memorial to the dead soldiers (both black and white) be erected at the site of the explosion to honor the men and reverse the "stereotype" that the sailors simply did not want to engage in dangerous work. What they wanted, Miller argued, was the right to be treated fairly and to fight overseas for their country. The congressmen stated unequivocally that it was racism that kept them from realizing their goals and "forced them into the least desirable jobs." Several years later, Miller led another large group of congressmen who called on President William Clinton to clear the records of the sailors because the court marital proceedings were racially biased—an argument that went against the Navy's conclusion on the matter.[22]

This interest in wartime racism took place, of course, in the wake of the modern civil rights movement. If Vietnam tended to make World War II appear nobler to some than it had been viewed in the 1940s, the civil rights agitation of the 1960s helped to expose more negative aspects of the war experience. Yet revelations of wartime injustice also led to efforts to construct new heroic stories of how such unfair treatment was overcome. No story of African Americans in World War II fit better into the process of crafting a virtuous tale from wartime racial hostilities than the account of the Tuskegee Airmen. In July 1941, the Army Air Force started to train African Americans as fighter pilots at an airfield in Tuskegee, Alabama. The decision to form such a unit in the first place resulted from Franklin Roosevelt's need to attract black voters during the 1940 presidential election, despite the attitude on the part of some Army officials that blacks could not be trained to be proficient pilots. Eventually, however, some one thousand men passed through the program, and hundreds flew combat missions in the European and Mediterranean theaters. By the end of the war, the men of the 332nd Fighter Group had proven themselves not only to be capable pilots but individuals who had earned the respect of their peers for flying missions that protected American bombers. Sixty-six of the flyers never returned home.[23]

On the fiftieth anniversary of the end of the war, HBO television brought to a national audience a film version of the story. Part fact and part fiction, the drama followed the young black pilots from basic training to combat in the skies over Europe. Although the characters in the movie were composite figures meant to portray the aspirations and experience of many African American men at the time, the feature made it clear that racism was prevalent in the Army Air Force and that many white officers and Southern politicians felt the time and energy that was being directed to training the men at Tuskegee could have been better spent on whites. The feature also indicated that important figures like Eleanor Roosevelt defended the project to train black flyers. In fact, her actual visit to Tuskegee to fly with one of the black pilots to demonstrate faith in their abilities is faithfully recreated in the film. The feature also presented the real life struggle of Lt. Col. Benjamin O. Davis to defend the program against racists in Congress who wanted to cut the budget and even terminate the entire effort. Davis, the son of the only black general in the Army at the time, had trained as a Tuskegee cadet himself and had led the airmen in their first combat assignments. Not all the black trainees could survive the rigors of training in the 1940s, yet the film makes it clear that those that did brought honor and distinction to their families. At the end of the film, photos of real airmen are displayed and viewers learn that the unit earned some 850 medals and that many were killed. Five decades after the war was over, the real-life struggles of black servicemen were now finally taking their place in the larger story of national honor that infused the remembrance of World War II.[24]

The HBO movie was based on a story conceived by Robert W. Williams, one of the actual airmen. Williams was driven by a strong feeling that the larger society should learn about the experience of the black flyers and saw this aspect of the war as very much a part of a long-term civil rights struggle. "This is a story about black people and our struggle as a people to get the right to fight with dignity for our country," he told reporters. For him it was a tale of "overcoming stupid racially motivated roadblocks and succeeding in spite of them." Amazingly, Williams had actually approached several Hollywood studios about making such a film as early as 1953 when he worked as an executive at *Ebony* magazine. The idea failed to gain any traction at the time, but Williams never lost sight of his goal and was finally able to find support in the 1990s, during a time when there was a distinct revival of interest in World War II.[25]

The rediscovery of the airmen led not only to more public revelations of their experience but to their inclusion in civic commemorations connected to the war as well. In 2001 Governor George Pataki of New York unveiled a full-scale replica of a P-51 Mustang fighter plane—the type, with their distinctive painted red tails, that the men had flown—at the American Airpower Museum on Long Island as a permanent tribute to the pilots. A news release from the governor's office claimed that he had always been in the "vanguard against racism in all its repug-nant forms" and that it should not be surprising that he had taken the lead in "creating this fitting tribute to all those who fought bigots some sixty years ago." The following year the Iowa Tuskegee Airmen Memorial was dedicated in Des Moines to honor the twelve airmen from the state. Leaders in this project in-cluded James E. Bowman, who had served as an official of the Des Moines school system and was a former Tuskegee airman. As in New York, the centerpiece of the memorial was the "Red Tail P-51 Mustang" plane the men flew. The Iowa trib-ute also included public recognition for Luther Smith, one of the Iowa airmen who had flown 133 combat missions during the war and who had been selected by President Clinton as one of seven veterans to accompany him to Europe for the fiftieth anniversary celebration of the end of World War II. In 2003 the Com-memorative Air Force Association, a group dedicated to restoring World War II–era planes "lest we forget that part of world history," decided to join an effort already underway by the Tuskegee Airmen, Inc. to find and restore Mustangs as a way to encourage minority youth to seek careers in aerospace and aviation. The airmen had already incorporated in 1973 to perpetuate comradeship among the veterans and promote their story as well as to raise funds for college scholar-ships. This national group was also responsible for the dedication of a monu-ment to the airmen at the United States Air Force Museum in Dayton, Ohio, in 1985 and the presentation of an eight-foot statue of a Tuskegee pilot at the U.S. Air Force Academy in 1988.[26]

The transition from stories of racial victimization to stories of heroic achieve-ment was evident in growing public recognition of the 761st Tank Battalion as well. In 1992 WNET-TV in New York presented a documentary, *The Liberators*, which recounted the story of the battalion and the complex battle it fought not only against the Germans but against racism at home. At a premier presentation, "prominent blacks and Jews" attended as a way of symbolizing the need for racial and ethnic harmony in the metropolitan area. Their attendance was also de-signed to serve as a reminder that both groups had suffered from racial hatred in the past and that blacks had also helped in the destruction of the Nazi regime that had decimated European Jews.

To some extent, the high-minded goals of the film were undermined when it was revealed that a depiction of the 761st as one of the American units that had directly helped in the liberation of Nazi camps at Buchenwald and Dachau was factually incorrect. Articles in a number of magazines and newspapers—some based on actual interviews with men who had served in the black tank unit—disclosed that these troops were nowhere near Buchenwald and Dachau, although they did help in freeing prisoners at a small camp that was part of the much larger Mauthausen camp system. A special investigation on the matter conducted by the American Jewish Committee, which conducted even more interviews with GIs from the battalion, affirmed the excellent fighting record of the men but did support the point that the film was mistaken as to their role at Buchenwald and Dachau.[27]

In 2004 legendary basketball player Kareem Abdul-Jabbar coauthored a popular account of the tank battalion entitled, *Brothers in Arms: The Epic Story of the 761st Tank Battalion, World War II's Forgotten Heroes*. Part of his motivation to do the book came from a chance encounter with an old friend of his fathers at the premier of *The Liberators*. Jabbar had known the man while growing up in New York City but never knew anything of the tank battalion or that his father's friend has served it as a "gunner." Impressed by the film and the discovery of his friend's service, the star athlete set out on his own to reconstruct this particular story from World War II.

Like many accounts of the war and the generation that fought it that were told in the 1990s, Abdul-Jabbar's book contained details of the men in battle but little record of the anguish many of them endured during or after the war. Brief glimpses of soldiers mourning their dead were mentioned in the story, but ultimately this book was a narrative of remembrance cast within a framework of the long African American struggle for equality and justice. It focused considerable attention on Jabbar's friend and a few of his comrades from basic training through the liberation of the "sub-camp" of Mauthausen. The author clearly depicts racism in the wartime military and describes some of the battlefield exploits of his subjects, especially in helping to free American forces who were trapped by the Germans at Bastogne during the Battle of the Bulge. Like other accounts, *Brothers in Arms* also makes it clear that these black men returned home with a renewed determination to resist discriminatory practices and that their record of service contributed to the ultimate integration of the armed forces.[28]

Jabbar's book also mentioned that the men of the 761st Battalion eventually received a Distinguished Unit Citation. The first request for such an award had actually been made in 1945, but it was denied by Third Army headquarters, despite a record that included the killing of 6,000 enemy soldiers. The issue languished for years until 1977, when an influential black congressman, John Conyers of Michigan, who had been one of the founders of the Black Caucus in 1969, elected to take up the cause of the fighting unit. Conyers wrote to the Secretary of the Army requesting the unit citation. The Army, now considerably more sensitive to the claims of its black troops than it had been in World War II, created a research group charged with looking into the matter. They found that racism had certainly existed in the wartime Army and that there had been "inadvertent neglect" in the 1940s when it came to considering medals for racial minorities. As a result of this research, President Jimmy Carter was able to present a Presidential Unit Citation for Heroism to the battalion in 1977. Soon more honors were given to the group. In 1993 a researcher at Ft. Hood, Texas, where many of the men had been trained, realized that the battalion was not mentioned at all in the base's museum. Immediately, officials at Ft. Hood erected a temporary monument at the main gate to the base. The following year, the base's processing center was named in honor of Reuben Rivers, a member of the tank battalion who would eventually receive a Medal of Honor for his battlefield exploits. In 1996 the mayor of nearby Killeen, Texas, invited surviving members of the group back to the town that had shown them considerable hostility during the war. Killeen even named one of its main streets after the 761st. Today at Ft. Hood a more permanent memorial commemorates the legacy of the tank fighters. The centerpiece of the memorial is a figure of an African American soldier kneeling on a granite base on which the words "Come Out Fighting" are inscribed. Surrounding the figure are several memorial tablets containing the names of the men from the tank unit who made the "supreme sacrifice," the text of the Presidential Citation for Heroism, and a picture of Reuben Rivers with an account of the actions that earned him the nation's highest award for bravery.[29]

The issue of whether African Americans had actually been denied the Medal of Honor in the 1940s because of racism ultimately led to a full review of the question by the military. In 1992 John Shannon, Secretary of the Army, created an independent commission to review archival records. The issue was important to African Americans not only because they resented the unfair treatment they had received during the war but because many white officers had questioned their ability to be effective warriors in battle when they did get the chance. In fact, in the 1940s the black press felt it necessary to affirm the courage and bravery of black soldiers in the face of public criticism over how they performed. The Army's investigation eventually concluded that the general (but not complete) exclusion of black soldiers from combat had severely restricted their opportunities to earn medals of distinction at the same rates as whites. It was also clear to the scholars that many "key commanders" were influenced by racial prejudice when evaluating the achievements of their troops. In fact, the report noted that World War II was the only war in which African Americans had failed to earn the Medal of Honor since its inception in the Civil War. One case the commission brought forward was the record of Reuben Rivers. In November 1944, while commanding a tank, Rivers was wounded and his leg was "slashed to the bone." Declining an injection of morphine or evacuation, Rivers helped push his company forward and continued to fight the Germans until he was killed. A white captain at the battle, David Williams, testified in 1994 that he had recommended Rivers for the Medal of Honor at the time of his sacrifice to an officer who had distinctly racist views. Although the modern research group could find no record of Williams's recommendation, it concluded that the dead soldier was fully deserving of this high honor.[30]

The Army investigation eventually led to the award of seven Medals of Honor to black troops. Six of the soldiers had already earned a Distinguished Service Cross in the 1940s, and researchers concluded that their previous achievements should now be elevated to a higher mark of distinction. A seventh award was given to Rivers, whom investigators concluded may have actually been recommended for the Medal of Honor for "heroism in battle" and who had long gone "unrecognized" for his deeds. In January 1997, at a White House ceremony, President Clinton presented six of the awards posthumously. One African American hero—Lt. Vernon Joseph Baker—still survived and was able to receive his medal in person. Clinton recounted the story of how he had wiped out two German machine gun nests and how the honor bestowed on the man was important because "history had been made whole." Arlene Fox, the widow of John Robert Fox, told those at the ceremony that the award to her husband was not only a tribute to him but to "black people everywhere" and that now a "tremendous wrong had been righted."[31]

MEXICAN AMERICANS

The experience of Mexican Americans in World War II was not entirely comparable to that of blacks. Like Native Americans, they had been accepted more fully into combat units and were able to earn battlefield distinctions during the war. But in the postwar era, they also argued that they had faced bias as well and now deserved a greater measure of honor and equality from their nation. Historically,

Mexican Americans, living largely in the southwestern portion of the United States, certainly faced all kinds of discrimination and segregation. Many worked in agricultural jobs that were highly transient and involved stays in squalid labor camps. And like other minorities, they found that their return home after the war failed to bring significant improvements in the way they were treated.

The discrepancy between their wartime service and their postwar status was brought into sharp relief in 1949 in the case of the reburial of Felix Longoria, a Mexican American infantryman who was killed fighting the Japanese in the Philippines four years earlier. Like other Americans who grieved over the loss of loved ones in the war, Longoria's widow, Beatrice, was asked by the government where she wanted her husband's remains to be interred. She expressed the wish that the body be brought back to his hometown of Three Rivers, Texas. She explained that she felt a "moral obligation" to see that he was put to rest in a place near where his parents lived and where he had shared his married life with her. Although there was little that was unusual in her decision, the repatriation of her husband eventually became a public controversy that illuminated the nation's longstanding problems with racial equality.[32]

Longoria's widow had asked a funeral home in Three Rivers for the use of their chapel for a memorial service for her fallen soldier. She had assumed his body would then be placed in the town's "Mexican cemetery," which was at that time segregated from a "white" cemetery by barbed wire. The funeral home denied her request, however, and its director claimed that he worried that local "whites would not like it." Upset by a decision that she felt dishonored a man who had fought and died for his country, Longoria conveyed her frustration to family members and friends in Corpus Christi. The issue struck a raw nerve in the larger Mexican American community of the city and reverberated with old grievances over housing segregation and other forms of injustice. Hector Garcia, a physician who had long campaigned for Latino civil rights in the Corpus Christi area and a war veteran himself, took up the reburial issue and began complaining to public officials. His pleas quickly caught the attention of the newly elected senator from Texas, Lyndon Johnson. The senator expressed his deep regret over what he called an act of "prejudice" and quickly made arrangements for the dead soldier to be buried in Arlington National Cemetery, "where the honored dead of our nation's wars rest."[33]

Johnson's actions brought national attention to the issue. Mexican Americans generally applauded his move, but many Anglos in Texas were outraged, for they thought the senator's actions had unfairly characterized the people of the state as racist. A front-page story in the New York Times informed a national audience of the rejection Beatrice Longoria had encountered and Garcia's charge that the actions of whites in Three Rivers constituted a "direct contradiction of those same principles for which this American soldier made the supreme sacrifice in giving his life for his country and for the same people who now deny him the last funeral rites of any American hero regardless of origin." The story also made it clear that Longoria's widow was profoundly grateful for Johnson's intervention and what she considered his "kindness in my hour of humiliation and suffering." An editorial in the *Santa Fe New Mexican* also noted that similar incidents of refusing to bury Japanese Americans soldiers had recently been reported in California and Chicago and that it was "distressing to learn that such stupid bigotry exists among us."[34]

Ultimately, the public response to the issue in Texas resulted not only in expressions of anger toward Johnson but in some attempts at reconciliation between Anglos and Latinos. In an "Open Letter to Senator Johnson," for instance, the Chamber of Commerce of Three Rivers claimed that he had acted much too quickly in what they called an "itchy trigger finger decision." They chastised him for harming the reputation of their community and were upset that many people in the town were now receiving "vile" letters criticizing them for their intolerance. They insisted that they did not necessarily defend the decision of the funeral home and claimed that Longoria could still be buried in the local cemetery—although they did not indicate in the letter that it was segregated. A Texas American Legion post also condemned the "hasty" actions of Johnson that brought "humiliation" to the "good people of the city of Three Rivers and the state of Texas." Other news articles were critical of Beatrice Longoria and her decision to allow her dead husband to be buried out of the state. There were, of course, many in Texas who supported Johnson and supported his stand against discrimination, and even some Legion posts in the state noted how inappropriate prejudice was. Eventually, the mayor of Three Rivers apologized to the Longoria family for the fact that the body had to be buried somewhere else and actually offered "one of the finest homes in the town" for use as a funeral site—an offer the grieving widow refused.[35]

The effects of the Longoria case proved to be longer lasting than the immediate controversy over Johnson's decision. The matter, along with Latino anger over discrimination, segregation, and access to health care, helped to expand the influence of the American G.I. Forum, a civil rights organization formed by Hector Garcia in 1948. The young physician and veteran was proud of his military service and his own rise from a lower-class minority family. Before the Longoria case he was already concerned over the fact that Latinos and other veterans in the

Corpus Christi area were unable to pay their bills and that many still lived in poverty. He also saw firsthand the many health problems these people faced, including high rates of tuberculosis, and was convinced that the naval hospital in Corpus Christi was ignoring veteran needs in general. In putting together the American G. I. Forum, Garcia and his supporters hoped to translate the legacy of Mexican American patriotism into distinct social and legal improvements. The group's constitution articulated a desire to "secure the blessings of American democracy through strictly non-violent means," to aid needy and disabled veterans, to advance understanding between citizens of various national origins and religious beliefs, to "secure and protect for all veterans and their families" their constitutional rights, and to defend the nation from "all enemies."[36]

Over the next decade, the Forum expanded its membership and influence substantially by adding over one hundred new chapters, mostly in the American southwest. Unlike earlier Mexican American groups, this organization was less interested in fostering ties to the homeland and more concerned with claiming their rights as American citizens, particularly in light of their war service. The organization continued to work for improved health care for veterans but also became an active civil rights organization, lobbying for improvements in conditions for migrant laborers and even for an end to discriminatory practices in public schools. For instance, by the early 1950s they brought to public attention the fact that although Mexican Americans constituted about 20 percent of the population of Texas, they held no representation on the Texas Selective Service Board. In New Mexico, Vincente Ximenes, a friend of Garcia's who had earned a Distinguished Flying Cross in North Africa, decided in 1950 to join the effort to help Latino veterans and helped found a chapters in Albuquerque and other towns in the state. In the 1950s the organization also initiated programs to teach English to Mexican American children and to challenge segregation in Texas schools. Hector Garcia, along with many others, had helped to raise funds that led to a successful court challenge to the segregation of Mexican American school children in a Texas district court in 1948. In *Delgado v. Destrop Independent School District*, the court ruled that the separation of children of "Mexican or Latin American descent" was unconstitutional. In a follow-up to the case, the state superintendent of public instruction declared that segregation "as mandated by the State Constitution" now only applied to African Americans.[37]

Reverberations from the memory of the Longoria case and the rising public sentiment against discrimination in the light of World War II could also be seen in the mass culture of the 1950s. Noted author Edna Ferber spent time with Garcia in Corpus Christi in 1950 and followed him to meetings of the Forum and on his visits to Mexican American neighborhoods as he attended to the health needs of the local population. In her novel *Giant* and its subsequent film version, she made a point of joining a story of the maltreatment of Mexican Americans in south Texas to a larger tale of the aggressive pursuit of power and wealth on the part of Anglos in the history of state. In the film version, men on the make, famously played by Rock Hudson and James Dean, stopped at nothing in chasing dollars and drilling for oil. Interestingly, Ferber's story frames the experience of World War II not as tale of democratic people taking on ruthless totalitarian regimes but as a time when ambitious (white) men used the huge wartime demand for oil to get rich and to keep a Mexican American working class in a perpetual state of second-class citizenship. The racist and greedy nature of Hudson's character is, in fact, counterbalanced in the story by the figure of his wife, played by Elizabeth Taylor, who hails from the East and whose liberalism allows her to take a more sympathetic stance toward the Latino population or, as they are called in the film, "wetbacks."

The Mexican American situation in Texas actually commands considerable space in the movie. Audiences see that they live in squalid conditions that bring illness and disease. They are even served by a young Mexican American doctor (a Hector Garcia–like character), and in one instance by Taylor herself, who sends her family doctor to save a sick Latino boy. The youth eventually goes off to fight for his country in World War II and is killed. He is buried among his impoverished people in a segregated cemetery where poor Mexican Americans stand to honor him and grieve for him. Later we see that a degree of liberalism has affected Hudson's character when he challenges a restaurant owner who refuses to serve Latinos. By now the Texas tycoon has a daughter-in-law and grandson of Mexican descent. Clearly, there is an argument in this popular story that the legacy of Latino sacrifice has rendered simple assumptions of continued racism unacceptable.[38]

Early in this century the specter of Felix Longoria was invoked again to plead the case for racial equality. In 2004 Santiago Hernandez, a federal prison guard, suggested that the name of the post office in Three Rivers should be named after the fallen soldier. Many Latinos in South Texas immediately supported the idea. Carolina Quintanilla, a Three Rivers resident, backed the proposal and felt it would stand as a "Rosa Parks monument" in the modern civil rights movement. The proposal, however, brought back old tensions. Susan Zamzow, whose father owned the funeral home that denied the use of its chapel to Longoria's widow, and others in the town saw Hernandez's suggestion as something that would only bring back an unwanted image of the community as racist. In fact, Felipe

Martinez, the Mexican American mayor of Three Rivers, did not like the idea himself and felt it would only divide the community he had to lead. Martinez claimed that supporters of Hernandez told him that he now had a chance to make history. But the mayor said he was more interested in uniting "all races" in the town. News commentary throughout Texas and elsewhere led to a recapitulation of the Longoria case but also to an explanation of how much race relations had improved since the war. Quintanilla admitted that social relations were better but still insisted that discrimination was a reality. Zamzow recalled that her family had received threatening letters in 1949 and still feared retribution over the matter to some extent. As of May 2007, the matter still had not been resolved, and a proposal to rename the post office facility was still stalled in Congress.[39]

In 2007 the matter of Latino sacrifice in the war erupted again when the Public Broadcast System (PBS) announced plans to present a fourteen-hour documentary on World War II produced by Ken Burns. The program was designed to feature an account of the war years that included interviews with local citizens in several selected American communities and also a fair amount of detail on the extent to which racism permeated wartime America. A firestorm of controversy erupted, however, when Latino civil rights groups learned that no one from their group was included in the various interviews in the program. Activists such as Maggie Rivas-Rodriguez, a professor at the University of Texas who had been directing an oral history project to document the Mexican American experience during the war; Marta Garcia, co-chair of the National Hispanic Media Coalition; and others quickly organized a campaign entitled "Defend the Honor." The idea was to show to the American public the vast participation of hundreds of thousands of Mexican Americans in the war in order pressure PBS and Burns to alter the content of his show. Latinos were particularly upset that one of communities featured in the program was Sacramento, where many of them lived. The "Defend the Honor" campaign was quickly joined by the American G.I. Forum. In a news release, the Forum called for a boycott of PBS shows and asked its members to withhold membership payments and monetary donations. The veterans organization also insisted that "heroic Hispanic Americans" needed to be accorded the same attention that the program was giving to African Americans and Japanese Americans. Members of the Hispanic Caucus in Congress also jumped into the fray and declared that they would "put the squeeze" on the broadcasters so that program content could be altered. Newspapers in the Southwest were filled with stories of discrimination Latinos faced in the 1940s. In New Mexico, articles were published that recapitulated the experience of local Latinos who had fought on Bataan. In Texas, the experience of Mario Garcia, a Medal of Honor winner who was refused service in a dinner in his hometown of Sugarland after the war, was reprinted several times.[40]

After direct meetings with representatives of "Defend the Honor," PBS announced that some alterations would be made to the Burns film. Paula Kerger, the chief executive of the broadcast corporation, wrote to Rivas-Rodriguez and outlined a plan whereby additional content would be added that acknowledged the wartime experiences of "Latino veterans" and Native Americans as well. PBS also promised that it would air a documentary that told the story of Hector Garcia and his fight for justice for Mexican Americans. And it stressed that many of its local affiliates would be producing additional programs focusing on veterans in their areas when the national presentation of the Burns film, *The War,* aired. It was also revealed that Burns would hire a Latino producer (Hector Galan) to help with creating the new content. The final product did not please Latino activists, however. In a documentary nearly fifteen hours long, the new material included only excerpts from interviews with two Latino war veterans and one Native American and lasted twenty-eight minutes. Representatives of "Defend the Honor" found the additions "disappointing" and complained that the material was not in any way integrated into the story in a "seamless manner." Roque Riojas, a veteran of campaigns in Italy and now living in Kansas City, asserted that there was no reason that Latinos should now "lick his [Burns's] boot because he added a piece at the end of a chapter."[41]

JAPANESE AMERICANS

Japanese Americans also reclaimed a more critical remembrance of their war experience to seek greater measures of equality and honor. On February 19, 1942, Franklin Roosevelt issued Executive Order 9066 directing the Secretary of War to remove from regions in the Western United States people deemed threats to national security. While the order did not mention Japanese Americans specifically, it allowed the government to forcibly remove them from their communities on the West Coast and place them into internment camps for the rest of the war. Some 120,000 citizens of Japanese descent were suddenly pulled from their homes, deprived of their constitutional rights to due process, and placed in ramshackle barracks surrounded by high fences and military guards. In *I Know Why the Caged Bird Sings,* Maya Angelou recalled that when she was a young girl living in San Francisco, the "Japanese disappeared soundlessly and without protest" and Southern blacks quickly moved into the neighborhoods they vacated.

Federal officials went to great lengths to downplay the extent to which this removal ruptured the lives of loyal American citizens. Their internment was explained as a "military necessity" and a measure that would actually ensure the safety of these people. A government-sponsored film entitled *Relocation* suggested that most of the evacuees—whether they were first-generation Issei immigrants or second-generation Nisei—were only too happy to cooperate in the massive round-up. What was not publicly revealed was that investigations by the Federal Bureau of Investigation and the Office of Naval Intelligence had informed government officials that no real military threat could be linked to these citizens and that the internees did not feel they needed any special protection. Nor did most Americans realize the true costs to the detainees, including the loss of their homes and businesses and the deplorable conditions that existed in many of the camps.[42]

In the immediate postwar years, Japanese Americans said more in public about the contributions they made to America's military effort and Nisei valor than they did about their victimization. Lon Kurshige has demonstrated that in 1949, when the celebration of Nisei Week was established in Los Angeles after an eight-year absence, the event was heavily infused with the veneration of Nisei soldiers who returned home and those who did not. At the same time, he found Nisei veterans, who now formed their own chapters of the American Legion and the Veterans of Foreign Wars, working to end legal forms of segregation such as the use of restrictive housing covenants in California. Their cause, moreover, was helped immeasurably by the release in 1951 of the Hollywood feature *Go for Broke*, which told the story of the all–Japanese American 442nd Regimental Combat Team that had fought hard and bloody battles against the Germans in Europe and which offered the American public a highly positive image of a minority group it had treated with derision during the war itself.[43]

Japanese American claims for redress over their wartime internment did not really materialize, however, until the modern civil rights movement began to make its mark on the nation's political culture. Textbooks in the 1940s and 1950s barely mentioned the event except to say on occasion that it was done out of "military necessity." In 1969, however, a small group of Japanese Americans began to make a "pilgrimage" to Manzanar, one of the camps located just east of the Sierra Nevada Mountains in California, as an act of remembering the injustice. The following year a much fuller discussion emerged within the Japanese American community over the wartime dislocations and the need to consider a possible call for restitution. In 1974 the Japanese American Citizen League (JACL), a national organization consisting mostly of Nisei, decided to organize a National Committee for Redress. Their goal was to seek payments for the losses the interned families suffered. Prospects that such an effort might succeed were enhanced by the fact that there were now four Japanese Americans serving in Congress. Daniel Inouye and Spark Matsunaga represented Hawaii, where Japanese American citizens had not been interned, in the Senate, and Norman Mineta and Robert Matsui represented California in the House. Mineta, in fact, had lived as a child in one of the camps and held vivid memories of his family's insurance business being closed and having to give away his dog during the evacuations.

In the early 1970s the JACL also initiated a process to get Manzanar declared a historic site by the state of California. Controversy over the proposal quickly ensued when Japanese American activists wanted to declare the site a "concentration camp." Members of the state's Historical Landmarks Commission rejected the terminology, and in the end the camp was referred to as "California Historical Landmark No. 850." In 1990s, when the National Park Service accepted the location as a National Historical Site, a similar dispute erupted. The federal agency again rejected the idea that it was a "concentration camp" and argued strongly that such a term implied gas chambers and systematic executions, none of which, of course, took place at any of the internment camps in the United States. Anger over the internment would not go away, however, and the words "concentration camps" eventually appeared on a "Go for Broke" Monument dedicated in Los Angeles in 1999 to Japanese American men who came from "Hawaii, the states, [and] America's Concentration Camps" to defend their country.[44]

The commemoration of the internment began to command considerable public attention in the Japanese American community by the late 1970s. Programs and pilgrimages were organized around a program called "Days of Remembrance," and the JACL now began to discuss in a more pointed fashion a plan for seeking redress. JACL officials admitted that Japanese Americans certainly were not slaughtered like the Jews had been, but they made it very clear that they were determined to seek some form of compensation for the fact that they were imprisoned by their own country and persecuted because of their "ancestry." In 1982 a group of Japanese American businessmen and World War II veterans also began to make plans for the building of a Japanese American museum in Los Angeles as a way to express pride in the group's accomplishments in America. Two themes drove the fund raising for this effort—the immigrant journey of the Issei, and the remembrance of the wartime evacuation. With grants from the state of California and the city of Los Angeles and private support, the museum opened in 1992 in an old Buddhist temple near the downtown area. The structure held special significance to the community because it had served in the years before the war as a religious center for immigrants, as an assembly point during the evacuations, and as a storage facility for possessions that many of the inmates had been forced to leave behind. One of its first major exhibits dealt with the art Japanese Americans produced while they were interned.[45]

Japanese American political pressure had already forced the government to create a Commission on Wartime Relocation and Internment in 1980. Charged with gathering information on the wartime evacuations, the commission called some 750 witnesses to testify at a series of public hearings in numerous cities. In its 1983 report, *Personal Justice Denied,* the investigative body concluded that government officials acted not out of military necessity but out of a sense of "hysteria" and "racial prejudice," a public declaration that undermined decades of official and unofficial rhetoric of the virtue of the American war effort. One factor contributing to the conclusion that the internment was racially motivated and unnecessary was the fact that people of Japanese descent in Hawaii, where they were less of a vulnerable minority, were allowed to remain free in their homes and to join the war effort. The report even documented the long history of racism toward the Japanese on the West Coast and the point that immigration from Japan was prohibited entirely in 1924. The commission's findings also noted the tremendous "human cost" as well as economic losses suffered by the internees and pointed out the irony that officials ignored the "repeated protestations of loyalty" during the war from the evacuees, even as many of them fought bravely for the nation. From all of this, the commission had little trouble in recommending a one-time payment of $20,000 (tax-free) to each survivor of the camp.[46]

Redress was achieved, of course, not only because of political pressure and the weight of evidence that documented injustice but because of the legacy of Japanese American valor. The story of the 442nd Regimental Combat Team had already been firmly established in the collective memory of the American war experience. Over 18,000 men served in the unit in seven major campaigns with some 600 giving their lives. This record of national service was reinforced by the fact that two U.S. senators from Hawaii, Inouye and Matsunaga, were veterans of the regiment and were each awarded the Distinguished Service Cross. Inouye's sacrifice was vividly on display when he took his oath of office and could not raise his war-damaged right arm like his peers. In fact, Japanese Americans, influenced by a newfound sense of power and righteousness and by a public culture now more sympathetic to minority claims, undertook their own campaign to review wartime records to see if even their battlefield achievements were in need of upgrading. There were sectors of the minority community that were displeased with promoting Japanese American loyalty at the expense of the legacy of those in the camps who had refused to sign a loyalty oath to the nation, but over time the memory of patriotism gradually effaced this record of dissent.

In 1995 Senator Daniel K. Akaka of Hawaii, persuaded by the recent effort to reconsider the intolerance of the war years and the awarding of medals to African Americans, called for a similar review for Asian Americans. His plan was to have military officials look again at Asian Americans who had earned the Distinguished Service Cross and "other equivalent awards." Support from the Clinton administration for such programs did evoke criticism with some citizens, who referred to the reviews as "pandering to minorities" and charged that such practices would devalue the Medal of Honor. Advocates argued, however, that the effort would not be a simple concession to minority grievances because it would be based on a reconsideration of men who had already won high levels of distinction. As a result of this review, the Army decided to award the Medal of Honor to twenty-two men, all but two of whom were Japanese American from the 100th Infantry Battalion and the 442nd Regimental Combat Team. Again, researchers found evidence of discrimination but also found "incontestable proof" of acts of valor. At a White House ceremony in 2000, while an army band played "Fanfare for the Common Man," seven living medal winners—including Inouye—received their awards from President Clinton. The chief executive spoke of the irony of having these men fight for their country "amid a piercing climate of discrimination against them." One of the recipients, George Sakato, whose family had been forced into the camps, said that he did not know how he earned such an award, but he certainly would accept it "for those who did not come back" and "for my fellow people."[47]

WOMEN AT WAR

Women too faced discrimination in the wartime military, despite the contribution they made to the victory. In the early 1940s both white and black women were compelled to leave home to find wartime jobs and join branches of the service. Some 36 percent of the domestic labor force was female during the war, and many women now found opportunities to make much better wages than they had before 1941. The civilian side of this wartime experience has often been symbolized by the figure of "Rosie the Riveter," an image that made women appear tough, independent, and patriotic. "Rosie" was also seen as a woman challenging conventional domestic role for females, a sign that many found disquieting. But the symbol was one very carefully cultivated during the war by the Office of War Information as a way to entice women into wartime factories.[48]

In the 1940s, war planners who promoted the image of "Rosie" assumed that she would be a middle-class woman who willingly left her domestic duties and children for a time to help win the war. The class assumptions here implied that she really did not have to work and that she would return to her household duties as soon as the shooting stopped. Motherhood was the real duty that women were presumed to desire. Such modes of thinking were not only at odds with the idea that women might actually want to work and to build long-term careers but also that many had no choice but to find work when they could. Research, in fact, has demonstrated that most women who entered wartime factories were from the latter category. And these women were eager to land the higher-wage jobs that suddenly opened for them after Pearl Harbor. For black women the new war jobs were appealing for the same reasons and were certainly seen as better than the traditional prospects they had in farm or domestic work. A study done at Ford Motor Company during the war found that 77 percent of the women who toiled there had already had at least one employer before 1941, a sign that their work patterns were driven not simply by wartime but by economic needs that predated the 1940s. Thus, "Rosie" was not only patriotic but practical, socialized in the on-going need to help provide for her family.[49]

The fact that after the war women were forced to leave these new industrial jobs, which many of them valued highly, was a sign that when it came to partici-pation in the workforce they too were viewed as second-class citizens and had to be "evacuated." In 1946 Frieda Miller, director of the Department of Labor's Women's Bureau, reported on the exodus of women from factory work during the reconversion to a peacetime economy and noted that the total number of fe-males in all types of employment dropped by some four million in the first year after the war. In the aircraft industry of Southern California the percentage of women workers dropped from 40 percent to only 12 percent by 1948. Moreover, Miller explained, many who did continue to work returned to non-industrial work and resented the lower pay scale they now found—again. The problem was exacerbated for black women because they realized what an economic break-through wartime jobs had been for them. When they were laid off, they had a difficult time going back to even more traditional working-class jobs such as in textiles that were dominated by white women. In a few years the rate of female participation in the workforce would begin to rise steadily, but this does not ne-gate the fact that immediately after the end of hostilities the assault on the female gains of the early 1940s was substantial.[50]

Little was said about "Rosie the Riveter" in the immediate postwar years. Without reading too much into it, a check of citations in the *New York Times* showed that "Rosie" was mentioned only about twenty times in the period of 1946 to 1959. In a similar thirteen-year period from 1968 to 1981—a period when there was a rising interest in civil rights and women's rights—there were three times as many references to "Rosie," and this was now more than two-and-a-half decades after the war. In 1981 a documentary entitled *The Life and Times of Rosie the Riveter* was shown at the New York Film Festival and continued to be featured at festivals and community events for years afterward. The film's producer, Connie Field, conducted over 700 interviews with wartime women for the feature and was assisted by government funds in the form of a grant from the National Endowment for the Humanities and by the Ford Foundation. Field explained that she was trying to dispel the myth that Rosie was simply a patriot and wanted people to understand that she also represented the issue of women's rights and opportunities in the workplace. In fact, she said she was inspired to do the film after working in Oakland, California, with an organization called "Jobs for Older Women" that had tried to find employment for women over age fifty. Her film focused essentially on five women—three black and two white—who had worked in wartime factories in the 1940s and the difficulties they had faced with a lack of child care facilities and racial and gender tensions. Her subjects expressed pride in their wartime roles in defeating Fascism but only regret that they had to relinquish those roles once the war ended.[51]

In the early 1980s a "feminist" scholar named Sherna Gluck, who said she was interested in seeing women gain greater access to opportunities outside the home, contributed to the growing public remembrance of "Rosie" by initiating an oral history project with women who had toiled in the aircraft industry around Los Angeles. While working on the project, Gluck told a local reporter that she believed many of her subjects had gained a new sense of independence from their wartime experience and that a record of that experience could encourage their daughters to seek even greater opportunities decades later. In the foreword to her book based on the interviews, *Rosie the Riveter Revisited: Women, the War, and Social Change* (1987), Gluck explained that by the late 1970s she had become angry over what she termed the "lost chances" women experienced at the end of the war and over the realization that so many of those women had wanted to keep working in "masculine domains." She hoped her project and book would help to "uncover the hidden history" of the war or the real experiences of women that had for decades been masked by the myth of "Rosie the Riveter." For her what now emerged from the "hidden" past was not a record of wartime trauma but a narrative of empowerment in which women told her the experience of working in factories and helping win the war had given them a new sense of confidence. They were especially elated that they were now doing work men did and that their contributions were seen as necessary. Gluck wrote that these women were "finally valued by others" and "came to value themselves more." Reviewers of the book were quick to seize on this point. An evaluation in the New York Times stressed that with "near unanimity" the war had taught these females that they could do "just about anything," and they now stood as symbols to future generations that women "have to fight for their rights."[52]

The war and its remembrance had not only raised issues of women's right to jobs but of the role they might play in the military. With the implementation of the first peacetime draft in 1940, a number of patriotic women's organizations such as the Women's Defense League of Chicago and the Oregon Women's Ambulance Corps were organized to instill values of loyalty and military-like discipline in women. By 1942 the government had formed an auxiliary group called the Women's Army Corps (WAC), which was integrated into the regular Army one year later, due to the particularly heavy demand for "manpower." The issue was controversial, however. Many people feared that women serving as soldiers would undermine the traditional differentiation in gender roles that envisioned men as "protector" and women as "protected," as historian Leisa Meyer has observed. Many also charged that women in the service would lower the moral standards of army life. In fact, as Meyer argues, there was a double standard in the Army when it came to sexuality. Women could be punished for engaging in promiscuous behavior, and their sexual activity was strictly governed by WAC officials. Sexual behavior on the part of men, on the other hand, was implicitly approved when they were officially issued condoms. By 1944 most Americans had become familiar with the sight of women in uniform, and eventually more than 350,000 entered active duty. Like industrial workers, many women did leave the military once hostilities ended, but the idea of their service roles had now been firmly established. In 1948, with the support of military leaders such as Dwight Eisenhower who still worried about meeting overall manpower and staffing needs, Congress passed the Women's Armed Services Act, which established units for women in the Army, Navy, Air Force, and Marines.[53]

Near the end of the twentieth century, as had other social groups who had commanded only limited amount of public attention in the remembrance of the war in its immediate aftermath, women too became more significant objects of commemoration. Mary Rose Okar, a Democrat from Ohio, introduced a measure in the House of Representatives calling for a "Women in the Service to America Memorial." The site chosen for the memorial was a structure near the entrance to Arlington National Cemetery called the Hemicycle, which had originally been built in 1930 to serve as the formal entrance to the national site but was no longer used for that purpose. The plan for the new memorial essentially consisted of putting a new museum inside the Hemicycle. The original design also called for thin glass pyramids to be placed on the roof of the structure with lighted candles shining through at night. In its final form, however, officials decided that the candles had to be eliminated because they might intrude upon the solemnity of the sacred ground at Arlington. Today flat glass panels sit on the roof of the Hemicycle with quotations etched into them that are projected onto the interior walls of the museum below when the sunlight is sufficiently strong enough to do so.[54]

The memorial is certainly a tribute to the role women have played in all of America's wars, but it also aspires to convey the message that women are the equals of men and can perform similar tasks. By 2007 there was a "Hall of Honor" in the museum that included a book containing photos and short biographies of women who had died in the war in Iraq. There were also small exhibits that told the story of women in World War II. One dealt with the recruitment and training of female soldiers, and another focused on the contributions of civilian females during the conflict. A third display concerning the war in the early 1940s looked at army and navy nurses serving overseas. Inscriptions from the glass panels above mostly reaffirmed the point that the loyalty of women to America was unquestioned. One quotation was from a woman who felt that she had to serve in World War II because America was "not just my brother's country" and "not just my father's country. It was my country as well." And an army nurse from the war is remembered as saying that she wanted future generations to remember that it was "women in uniform" that had guaranteed their freedom and that their resolve to win the war was just as great "as the brave men that stood among us."

The dedication ceremonies of the new memorial in 1997 turned out to be an extremely large celebration that lasted for several days. Patriotic rhetoric and female pride were themes that were repeated continuously. Togo West, Secretary of the Army, explained that "war was grim business" but that women have always met the challenge and that their record of service to the nation should never be forgotten. Military bands entertained the thousands of visitors who attended, and young college students marched in a line that performed the ideal that national loyalty would be exercised for generations to come. Popular entertainers sang a new song composed for the event that talked about how women had defended "our homes" and that "God" was on their side while they protected freedom. Women in uniform were ubiquitous at the various events. Air Force General

Wilma Vaught, who was considered a driving force in getting the memorial created, spoke of women's military achievements. And Vice-President Al Gore gave an address that stressed not only how the memorial celebrated patriotism but also the value of tolerance in our society because it showed that women deserve the same rights as men.[55]

In October 2000, the role of women in the war was commemorated again with the dedication of the Rosie the Riveter Memorial in Richmond, California. Over 200 former "Rosies" attended the ceremony, which was held at the site of a former wartime shipyard. Indeed, the general design of the memorial was based on the concept of a "Liberty Ship" under construction. As part of the "reconstructive process of human memory," porcelain panels were erected at the site, containing photos, letters, and other memorabilia from the experience of the women who worked there. Visitors could see that the women faced discrimination, hazardous working conditions, food rationing, and inadequate child care facilities as they tried to help win the war. Donna Powers, a film maker who made a documentary of the dedication event, remarked on how unusual it was to have a war memorial dedicated to females and expressed a sense of gratitude to the "Rosies" for having served as "pioneers of the women's lib movement." Interestingly, several of the women from the war who were interviewed in the documentary claimed that they never felt any sense of contributing to a women's movement as they worked at the shipyard. One said the "sisterhood she felt" was with her biological sister and never felt that her wartime work made any political statement.[56]

The very idea for the memorial came from Powers, a former vice-mayor of Richmond, who was driven by the need not only to help improve the community but also to advance the cause of giving women equal access to work and to jobs. In a speech at the dedication event, she exclaimed that she wanted to honor this older generation of women because she felt they were overly modest about their accomplishments. She claimed that these women revealed a sense of determination in going into the local Kaiser shipyards and reveled in the "excitement of being independent" and earning their own paychecks. The efforts of Powers to get the memorial built were strongly supported by her congressman, George Miller, who had already worked to commemorate the sacrifices of blacks who died in the Port Chicago explosion, which had taken place in his district as well, and who held fond memories of his own father working in the shipyards in the early 1940s. Congressman Miller continued the narrative of the war as a struggle for equal rights at home by stressing how both white and black women worked together in building ships. In his address he talked not only of the contributions of women but of the struggle of black soldiers to get proper recognition for their wartime roles and of the Port Chicago episode. For Miller the story of African Americans in the war and the account of women shipyard workers were all part of a larger (liberal) narrative about the rise of integration and fairness in American society. A similar theme was echoed by John Reynolds, who represented the National Park Service at the event and who explained that the women honored in Richmond helped to "build democracy" in the nation as much as ships.[57]

Over the long postwar era, accounts of wartime racism and minority heroism were summoned to demand equal rights for numerous minorities. Paradoxically, however, the evocation of this remembrance not only promoted some of the humanitarian sentiments that were first articulated in the Four Freedoms and exposed negative aspects of the war years, but they also reinforced traditional stories that saw all Americans as brave and innately patriotic. By the end of the twentieth century, the story of minorities in World War II turned out to be mostly a tale of how even mistreated citizens held fast to their love of the nation and were willing to fight for her survival. The legacy of their victimization and mistreatment remained but was getting more difficult to find as they now took their place in a fabled community of heroes.

CHAPTER SEVEN

THE VICTORS

TRADITIONAL THEMES OF AMERICAN decency and heroic individualism dominated the enormous public commemoration of the war that erupted near the end
of the twentieth century. Critical and humanitarian frames on the contest were
still evident, but they commanded only limited attention in the many fiftieth anniversary celebrations, books, films, and museum exhibitions that now marked
the nation's victory. There were clear reasons for this. The jumbled outlooks
of the wartime generation had now been simplified by the passage of time and
by the deaths of millions of those who lived through the war years. As reports appeared almost daily about the passing of the war's veterans, younger generations
looked back at honored ancestors with a sentimental gaze. Citizens who had no
direct knowledge of the war or the concerns of the 1940s acted as if they did in
mounting countless commemorations. And the American public in general
was more than ready to entertain highly laudable stories of national honor and
bravery as it began to erase the more troubling legacy of Vietnam and bask in the
afterglow of a Cold War victory.[1]

MODEL CITIZENS

The quintessential expression of the American myth of World War II in this period was Tom Brokaw's book, *The Greatest Generation*. It may have been pure coincidence that the book was listed just behind a volume entitled *Chicken Soup for
the Soul* on a list of best sellers for the 1990s, but it would not be too much to say
that its collection of personal stories from the wartime generation brought much
good feeling to the millions of readers of all ages. War did not lead to death and
destruction in Brokaw's book but mostly to the reinforcement of values such as
individualism, discipline, and self-sacrifice that created a great nation. He looked
at the war more like Henry Luce than like Norman Mailer. Derived in part by his
own recollections of himself as a boy living on an army base in South Dakota

during the war, Brokaw's memory—like that of many Americans who celebrated it in the 1990s—was deeply personal and nostalgic. It was grounded not only in private experience but in a longing for a time that was filled with heroic ancestors. He and his peers felt that the prosperity and freedom they enjoyed was the result of the sacrifices of the Americans that had won the war. The victory of these forebears was even imagined to be grounded more in their personal characteristics than in the mass mobilizations and productivity of American war effort. His heroes were extraordinary souls who ably managed the delicate task of defending traditional values and inflicting massive levels of violence without lapsing into moral transgressions themselves.[2]

While Brokaw sang the praises of people from many walks of life who served the nation in the 1940s, historian Stephen Ambrose focused his celebration on the men who fought in Europe. His immensely popular book *Band of Brothers* followed the exploits of the 101st Airborne from basic training through their battles against the enemy from the Normandy landings to the final destruction of Hitler's Germany. Certainly, the defeat of the Nazi regime was a story of good defeating evil. Yet this story was also personal, for the author drew on his own memories of seeing some of the men coming home from the service when he was a young boy in Wisconsin. Indeed, his history was grounded in stories told to him by hundreds of veterans, stories that he collected and transformed into a number of best-selling books. Ambrose was unabashed in his praise for these men. He referred to the soldiers in the 101st Airborne, for instance, as "idealists eager to merge themselves into a group fighting for a cause" and "actively seeking an outfit with which they could identify." As for Brokaw, war is uplifting for him, and his GIs benefit immensely from enduring hardships in life, whether surviving the Great Depression or fighting the Germans. Such experiences taught men the value of self-reliance, hard work, and the ability to take orders. They were able to blend an American sense of individualism with a cooperative spirit. Loyal to their country and to each other, to this author they were America's "finest youth."[3]

Mourning the dead—a key response to seeing war as tragic—commands almost no attention in either Brokaw or Ambrose, and the transition from war to civilian life is inevitably painless. Both stress that their subjects became incredibly successful in their civilian lives mostly because of the values they learned in the war. For the men of the 101st Airborne, Ambrose claimed that it was the Army that had taught them self-confidence and the lesson that they could endure more than they ever thought they could. When he describes the various battles with the Germans, he merely lists the names of the men who were killed at the end of chapters without any extended comment or display of emotion. There is a sense of triumph in Brokaw and Ambrose—on both a national and personal level—but no room for thinking that we should lament the war dead regardless of their nationality.[4]

One of Ambrose's central figures, Major Dick Winters, eventually produced his own book that also placed his wartime experiences within a mythical frame. Winters had gained a measure of fame when he was featured in the HBO television series *Band of Brothers* and because Ambrose, who had used his wartime diary in conducting research, continually praised him in public. The historian once told a television interviewer that that if he could have served in World War II he would have wanted to serve with Easy Company, 506th Parachute Infantry, 101st Airborne because it was led by Winters. The veteran returned the praise Ambrose lavished upon him by calling him "the leading historian of our time" and claiming that Ambrose had changed his life forever. In 2008 citizens could go to a Web site (www.majordickwinters.com) mounted by friends of Winters to sign a petition requesting that the Army award him the Medal of Honor for his actions on D-Day. In his own book, Winters demonstrated none of the cynicism or critical perspective on the war that was often found in the writings by soldiers in the 1940s, and he explained to his readers how the skill of leadership was demonstrated on the field of battle. He claimed, in fact, that his experience with Easy Company had "made me who I was" and that it had "brought out the best in me." Indeed, he felt that it was not until the experience of actual combat that he convinced himself that he had "measured up to my personal standard of leadership." His book, in fact, became a primer for managers of all kinds in American society, conveying the need for them to exhibit "character" and "courage, honesty, selflessness, and respect for our fellow man."[5]

Winters fortified his remembrance of war as a crucible of cherished values by including in his book a number of letters he had received from people who had watched the HBO series or heard him speak. A New York City police officer wrote him after the terrorist attacks on the World Trade Center to say that the television shows had inspired him to carry out his duties no matter what the circumstances. The officer indicated that he learned the "true meaning of dedication and courage in the face of insurmountable odds" from watching a story of the adversity soldiers had faced at Bastogne. Another man wrote that seeing the story of Easy Company had made him want to be a "better human being." A woman from North Carolina explained that watching the stories made her realize what men like Winters and her grandfather, a veteran of the Battle of the Bulge, had done and "how very blessed my generation is because of the sacrifices made by others." Winters even included letters from men who had fought along-side him during the war telling him he was the "greatest soldier" they had ever hoped to meet. The story of the "Band of Brothers" certainly contributed to the high esteem and legendary status the ordinary GI now enjoyed in contemporary America, but it is interesting to note that the HBO programs actually divulged more of the sense of anguish and regret many of the men felt when they lost a comrade in battle and the nightmares they suffered after the war than did the book Ambrose wrote on the same subject. The public triumph of the myth of the "good war" and good men that fought could never fully erase the personal sufferings many had endured.[6]

Popular books and television programs were not the only means by which Americans contributed to a reaffirmation of the heroic view of the war. Commemorative ceremonies at the time became extraordinary events. They began in 1991 with the fiftieth anniversary of the Japanese attack on Pearl Harbor. Echoes of wartime feelings quickly became entangled with contemporary perspectives as thousands of veterans made their way back to Hawaii to attend various ceremonies and visit the memorial to the sunken USS Arizona. Reporters were quick to notice the irony of so many American veterans passing large numbers of Japanese tourists who now flocked to the islands on a regular basis and who had become a mainstay of Hawaii's tourist economy. President George H. W. Bush, a veteran of the war himself, spoke at one of the anniversary events and stressed not so much the virtue of Americans who fought but the need to take from the experience of Pearl Harbor lessons for the future. Bush expressed pride that Americans had emerged victorious from two world wars and the Cold War in the twentieth century, but he warned against complacency and called for vigilance against any form of aggression that might threaten the security of the nation.[7]

Despite the fact that Japan and the United States had now been friendly allies for decades, the 1991 commemorations did expose lingering tensions from the wartime era. Calls were made in Japan again for the United States to apologize for the atomic bombings of Hiroshima and Nagasaki. During much of the postwar era Japan had used the bombings—and the suffering of its people—to claim a status as a war victim rather than a perpetrator in fashioning its own public remembrance. Opinion polls in Japan revealed that some 83 percent of the population felt such an apology was needed and that the bombings were "morally wrong" acts of war—a position that would obviously not resonate well with a romantic version of American identity. Thus, only 16 percent of Americans felt such an apology was needed, although a somewhat higher number suggested they might express regret for the bomb if Japan did the same for Pearl Harbor.

Contemporary studies also indicated that the issue of an apology was discussed much more widely in Japan than in the United States because of the widespread criticism it faced for its acts of aggression during the war from other Asian nations. Most of the American veterans at the ceremonies at Pearl Harbor, however, supported the thinking of their president, who told a television interviewer that America would not apologize for the bombings. Bush insisted that President Truman's decision to drop the bombs was justified because it had ended the war and ultimately saved millions of American and Japanese lives that would have been lost in a planned American invasion. He also recalled his own war experience in the Pacific, where his plane had been shot down, and the feeling of relief he felt when he heard the news of the atomic bomb. Aware of Bush's outlook, the Japanese parliament soon passed a resolution deciding not to offer any expression of regret over any of Japan's "World War II aggression."[8]

Some television productions attempted to present a more balanced perspective on the issue. This was certainly the case in *Pearl Harbor: Two Hours That Changed the World,* a joint production of ABC-TV and NHK, Japan's largest television network. The show informed viewers of the troubled relations between the two nations before the war and the problems the presence of an American fleet presented to military planners who wanted to spread Japan's influence and control throughout the far Pacific region. The show made a special effort, in fact, to feature interviews with men from both nations who joined the war effort. Thus, Japanese pilots who actually bombed Pearl Harbor revealed the sense of excitement they felt in carrying out the raid on behalf of their nation. American vets, on the other hand, recounted their feelings of anger over Pearl Harbor as they saw the destruction of naval vessels before them and the deaths of many of their comrades. One American soldier recalled that he could hear the sounds of men trapped beneath the hulk of the sunken battleship Arizona, where audiences were reminded that the remains of the dead still lay. Daniel Inouye, who lived in Hawaii at the time, remembered that when he learned that it was the Japanese that were mounting the attack he exclaimed, "You goddamn Japs!" And other vets made it clear that they still felt hostility toward the Japanese and rejoiced when they heard of the atomic bombings—a reminder in the late twentieth century that the "greatest generation" still carried traces of the emotions that were less than noble. At the end of the program, narrator David Brinkley noted that today Hawaii is a paradise again, as it was before Pearl Harbor, and that the Japanese have made substantial investments in the islands. Brinkley ended on a note of triumph, however, when he said that the United States vanquished both the Japanese and Germans in the war, put Western Europe back together, wrote a democratic constitution for Japan, and then was able to "stand off" the Soviet Union. In his estimation this was a "heroic performance by one of history's great countries."[9]

Three years later the focus of war celebrations tuned to the European theater of operations and the American landings in Normandy on D-Day, June 6, 1944. In fact, D-Day became a major centerpiece to the American victory celebration, commanding possibly more commemorative attention than almost any other aspect of the war and helping Americans emphasize their role in the defeat of the Germans more than the immense part played by the Soviet Union. It was D-Day that could more easily reinforce a legacy of victory and virtue with its direct connections to the downfall of Hitler. This event raised fewer questions than, for instance, the bombings that ended the war in the Pacific. Thus, even before the 1990s, presidents used the memory of D-Day to incite patriotic fervor and honor for the war effort and the men who fought. Historians have made it clear that Dwight Eisenhower benefited from the memory of D-Day in attracting voters to his presidential campaign in 1952, and Ronald Reagan helped his 1984 reelection bid immeasurably by giving a highly emotional and sentimental addresses at Normandy on June 6, 1984, which praised the heroism of the "boys" who stormed the beaches to liberate Europe—especially the rangers who climbed the cliffs at Pointe du Hoc. Reagan told stories of some of the men that were so touching that the daughter of one of them felt the president had given her dead father "immortality." Many veterans were more than ready to return again in 1994, lured by a desire to walk the beaches of Normandy as well as to visit the graves of fallen comrades who were interred in the massive American cemetery near the invasion beaches. Travel companies, recognizing the desire of many of the men to go back one more time, offered special packages to facilitate their return to France. One company, Galaxy Tours, promoted trips for veterans of particular units such as the 1st Infantry Division, the 749th Tank Battalion and the 82nd Airborne Division that took part in the landings. Another promotion included a cruise on the *Queen Elizabeth 2* to Europe and performances by wartime entertainers such as Vera Lynn and Bob Hope. The media coverage of the events at Normandy on June 6, 1994, was enormous. NBC-TV (with Tom Brokaw acting as one of its hosts) devoted some five hours of coverage to the Normandy commemoration. News magazines, including *Newsweek, Time,* and *U.S. News and World Report,* devoted cover stories to D-Day. *American Heritage* published a story on the landings and letters from American servicemen from the period and doubled its normal production run.[10]

The centerpieces of the 1994 ceremonies were the addresses given by President William Clinton. Widely known for the fact that he did not serve in the American military and for his criticism of the Vietnam War, the president eagerly embraced the mythical view of World War II in his speeches at this key battle site. He was as effusive in his praise of the American men who fought on D-Day as Ambrose and Brokaw had been. He later revealed much about the personal attachments he had to the war and to his father who served in it. In a formal address he celebrated the American role in liberating Europe. He explained the German defeat as primarily the result of the capacity of men raised in a democracy to defeat anyone who stood in their way, ignoring again the contributions of the Russians on the Eastern Front. In a talk on Utah Beach on June 6, he recounted the loss of young soldiers and the chaos that had existed among the men after they had landed, but he pointed out that victory was still achieved because "in the face of mayhem emerged the confident clarity born of relentless training . . . the guiding light of a just cause . . . and the democratic fury" of the GIs. As many others of his generation, he also raised the theme of gratitude and the issue of what the postwar generations owed the citizens that fought. He told the story of the mayor of a French town liberated by the Americans who continued to write letters to the families of the men who had fought and died to free her village each week for the rest of her life, noting that her son continued the task after she died in 1988. Admonishing his listeners that "we can do no less," Clinton declared that the living now had the responsibility to "turn the pain of loss into the power of redemption so that fifty or one hundred or one thousand years from now those who bought our liberty with their lives will never be forgotten."[11]

Later the same day at Pointe du Hoc, Clinton repeated the mythical theme that the American defeat of the Germans was grounded in the GI's special regard for freedom and their willingness to defend it. Like Ronald Reagan ten years earlier, he invoked the memory of the American rangers who scaled the "unforgiving cliffs" in the face of enemy fire to knock out German guns (which were later found to have been moved further inland) that could have threatened much of the invasion. Clinton asked the veterans of the ranger battalion in attendance in 1994 to stand and receive the grateful appreciation of all those who had assembled there that day. The president noted that most of the men in the landing force were new to battle when they landed in France, but "all were armed with the ingenuity of free citizens and the confidence that they fought for a good cause under the gaze of a loving God." He noted that Europe had longed for the day when men such as this would come to free it from the German tyranny and how the Germans never understood "what happens when the free unite behind a great and worthy cause." Raising the American myth of individualism to celestial heights, he claimed that "human miracles" begin with "personal choices" and that the end of the war in Europe could finally be imagined when free men came together "like the stars of a majestic galaxy." How different the remarks of Reagan and Clinton at Normandy were from those of Ernie Pyle, who refused to forget the human cost of war as he walked the beaches on the second day of the invasion in 1944 and wrote about seeing the "strong, swirling tides of the Normandy coastline" carrying "soldiers' bodies out to sea" and "covering the corpses of heroes with sand."[12]

The war-protestor-turned-president divulged more about his personal feelings toward World War II in private conversations and interviews with newsmen, revealing again how much the celebrations of the 1990s were driven by the personal ties so many younger Americans had to the men who had served in World War II. He told Tom Brokaw that he had been extremely moved by his visits to some of the American cemeteries in Europe and that he had not been prepared to have such an emotional reaction and "how it hits you." He was especially moved by seeing the Wall of the Missing at the cemetery near Cambridge, England, that included some 5,000 names, such as Glenn Miller and Joseph Kennedy, both of whom died in air crashes and were never found. He seemed to mourn the dead now in ways that were not evident in his public speeches. Brokaw asked the president if he ever regretted his decision to avoid military service in the 1960s. Clinton responded by saying that he had no regrets over his opposition to American policies regarding the Vietnam War, which he declared had done the nation more harm than good. But in the midst of the American victory celebrations of the 1990s he did admit that there were times when he wished that he had served his country. He claimed that he was a "child of World War II" and had grown up on war movies with John Wayne, John Hodiak, and Robert Mitchum and that for most of his life he had looked at a picture of his father— whom he did not know—in a World War II uniform. He acknowledged that his visit to Normandy had taken him back to his "roots in a very profound way."[13]

In another exchange with Wolf Blitzer, a reporter for CNN, Clinton expanded upon his ties to the "good war." He talked of another trip he had made to an American cemetery near Nettuno, Italy. This was for him a very personal journey, for his mother had often told him about his father serving in Italy performing maintenance on military vehicles. When he was old enough, he read more about the American campaign in Italy, and one account of his father's unit actually mentioned the elder Clinton. He felt this was the most "graphic account" he had ever read of his father's life and declared that it meant a great deal to him.

The president told Blitzer that he was very proud of his father's service. When the reporter asked again about his own experience with Vietnam, Clinton repeated his belief that his opposition was justified but said that "military service was an honorable thing and it is something that in a sense I wish that I had experienced."[14]

HIROSHIMA

The celebration of the war as romantic myth was grounded not only in the enduring appeal of the victory over evil forces but the equally strong impulse to disregard the darker legacy of the conflict. The moral implications of Allied bombing raids, which killed hundreds of thousands of civilians in Germany and Japan, for instance, were not always considered carefully by leading war planners like George Marshall and Dwight Eisenhower. Indeed, part of the gradual acceptance of such brutal tactics came from an amoral framework in which planners realized that the promise of precision bombing was not being realized and that such indiscriminate killing was unavoidable. Some even thought the mass bombing was a tactic to promote the importance of air power within the American military establishment. From this evolving context came the ferocious firebombing of Dresden and Tokyo—and, ultimately, the dropping of atomic bombs on Hiroshima and Nagasaki.

By 1945, in fact, few Americans had any moral reservations about the killing of enemy civilians, and most welcomed Truman's decision to drop the bombs because it eliminated the need for a costly invasion of Japan by American forces and ended the war. Over time, public approval was also reinforced by the fact that, for some twenty-five years after the bombings, the government kept from public view graphic film footage of the human destruction the new weapons caused. Indeed, Paul Tibbetts, the man who piloted the *Enola Gay*, the plane that dropped the first bomb, insisted after the war that he felt no remorse over the killing of civilians and was only interested at the time in contributing to the war effort. The attitude Tibbetts held might explain why in 2007 individuals could go to a Web site devoted to his career and purchase for $500 a ten-inch model of the Hiroshima bomb "made of solid mahogany" with a plate containing his signature.[15]

There were a few moments in the long postwar era after 1945, however, when critical memories of the bombings and the suffering they caused broke into the open and challenged the general level of acquiescence—and, for that matter, silence—Americans held toward the events. In these instances the public was confronted with a more human-centered rather than nation-centered perspective and with the troubling reality that even virtuous people could act in malevolent ways. The first major invocation of the atomic bombings as tragic rather than necessary acts took place in August of 1946 with the publication of John Hersey's interviews with Hiroshima survivors and their accounts of the calamity that followed the sudden blast. As a war correspondent who had visited battlefronts in Europe and the Pacific and the liberated concentration camps at Auschwitz and Bergen Belsen, Hersey had been able to acquire a unique perspective on the devastation war brought even before he arrived in the Japanese city. Some who read his interviews felt they sounded too much like a mere report of what had happened and did not express a sufficient amount of outrage over the mass killings. Others accused Hersey of being overly sympathetic to an enemy and argued that the Japanese asked for such retribution with their behavior at Pearl Harbor and Bataan. But a few commentators picked up the more serious implication of his story that Hiroshima was, indeed, a "human problem" and that, although it may have saved lives, it was still a "catastrophe" and a "monstrous" act. When published as a book, *Hiroshima* quickly became a best seller. The American Broadcasting Company offered readings over the radio on four consecutive evenings. Leading newspapers carried prominent features on the interviews. The *New York Times* even published a reproduction of a painting showing dead and wounded Japanese civilians along with an article that asserted that Hersey's book had "penetrated the tissue of complacency" Americans had built up over the war and over the bombs. Despite the sensational reaction his work provoked, however, it did not really upset public support for the bombings, a more heroic view of the war itself, or the inclination to build many more such weapons once it was learned the Soviet Union had built their version of the bomb in 1949.[16]

The suffering of Hiroshima returned to public consciousness in a vivid way again in 1955. In that year a group of American antinuclear and peace activists led by Norman Cousins, the editor of the *Saturday Review of Literature,* arranged for a group of twenty-five young Japanese women who had been disfigured by the first atomic blast to come to America for medical treatment. Known as the "Hiroshima Maidens," these women with scarred bodies appeared in numerous newspaper photos, allowing citizens to reflect again on the devastation of the bombings. Yet the overall media coverage failed to generate any real critical perspective on the events that ended the last war. In the end, it tended to serve American interests in the Cold War by stressing the generosity of Americans in trying to help these women and showing how intimate many of them had become with the American families that hosted them. The most poignant moment in their stay took place in front of a national television audience that watched the popular program *This Is Your Life* in May 1955. This particular episode featured the story of one of Hersey's respondents from 1946, Kiyoshi Tanimoto. The presentation included a dramatization of the moment the bomb hit, with the loud sound of a ticking clock counting down the time until detonation and dramatic music designed to mimic the explosion. Tanimoto was then greeted by a surprise guest, Robert Lewis, one of the men who helped fly the *Enola Gay*. Lewis seemed visibly shaken (Hersey later wrote that he thought he had been drinking) by the encounter with one of his victims but did present the Japanese guest with a check to help in the care of the maidens. At the end of the show American audiences could see two of the actual women who had come for reconstructive surgery but only in the form of silhouettes seated behind a screen that masked the full extent of their disfigurement.[17]

In the midst of the countercultural explosion of the 1960s, when critiques of the uses of American power were widespread, the legacy of Hiroshima was invoked again. Robert Jay Lifton brought the expertise of psychoanalysis to bear on the postwar lives of *hibakusha*, or Japanese survivors of the atomic blasts. In a remarkable book, *Death in Life* (1967), Lifton expanded knowledge considerably on how these atomic victims had to cope with their encounter with death. He explained the psychological process victims of the war faced long after peace treaties were signed and also raised awareness of the problem of public remembering that surrounded such momentous historical events. He had worked in Japan in the 1950s and first visited Hiroshima in 1962. He was struck by the fact that no one—not even the Japanese—had studied the psychological effects of the bomb on individuals and the tendency of those he called professionals in the "human sciences" to avoid the topic of "mass death and mutilation" that wars normally bring. He claimed that Hiroshima stimulated for him a sense of "resistance" to such avoidance. Lifton, who later became a harsh critic of the Vietnam War, was also coming to hold highly critical views of the Cold War nuclear arms build-up when he began to interview Japanese survivors in the early 1960s.

Lifton's portrait of the personal struggles of the *hibakusha* privileged the perspective of the victim over that of the perpetrator or warrior hero. He mapped out an elaborate process in which people who had faced the extraordinary experience of imminent death spent years afterward trying to restore a sense of stability and normalcy to their lives. War for them was in no way ennobling; in general, Lifton felt that despite all the talk that had taken place over Hiroshima people still did not understand what it was like to be a survivor or, as he put it, a "brutalized human being." Lifton's subjects at first coped with trauma through a process he called "psychic numbing," which tended to insulate them from reacting with horror to the mass death that they experienced. As he worked in Hiroshima, he even noticed that many in postwar Japan wanted to forget all that happened in the war and the suffering that still lingered; it was not only Americans who were reluctant to revisit the implications of Hiroshima. He noted the stark contrast between the "Peace Dome," which stood as a monument to the blast, and the new and gleaming city that grew up around it. Some civic groups and more than a few of the *hibakusha* even wanted to tear down the dome and erase all reminders of what had happened in 1945.[18]

In some ways it should not come as a surprise that it was Hiroshima that provoked the most controversial moment in the vast public celebration of the 1990s. Public support for Truman's actions and a highly traditional view of the war itself had never fully erased the questions many Americans had over the use of nuclear weapons on unarmed civilians. Lifton's work suggested as much, but so did earlier critiques issued by Hersey, by prominent leaders like Dwight Eisenhower, and by a number of religious spokesmen. Moreover, in the 1990s, in the aftermath of Vietnam and a conservative reaction to the 1960s—as historian Edward Linenthal has suggested—many Americans were more determined than ever to resist critical views of the national past that continued to permeate the culture. The matter came to a head in 1994 when the Smithsonian Institution's National Air and Space Museum (NASM) announced plans to build an exhibit around the *Enola Gay*. According to Richard Kohn, the former chief of history for the Air Force and a person who had worked with a planning committee, NASM officials were quite aware that such an exhibit had the potential to evoke a considerable amount of discord. Kohn revealed that a number of veterans groups had lobbied Smithsonian officials for years about their desire to display the plane but that the museum's Research Advisory Committee feared criticism from antinuclear activists would remind the public that the bombs had killed thousands of innocent civilians in Japan. By the late 1980s, however, the museum had come under the direction of scholars interested in exploring history in a more critical manner and moving away from what Kohn called "uninspired establishmentarianism." This was especially true of the museum's director, Martin Harwitt, who had been chosen over a retired Air Force general. When the initial script for the planned exhibit—"Crossroads: The End of World War II, the Atomic Bomb, and the Origins of the Cold War"—first appeared in January 1994, it evoked immediate criticism. The script duly acknowledged Japanese responsibility for starting the Pacific War but, in the eyes of critics, discredited the American war effort by focusing too much attention on the human devastation the bomb had caused in

Hiroshima and not enough on the suffering of the American soldiers in the Pacific war.[19]

The attack on the Smithsonian exhibit was led by the Air Force Association, a lobbying group set up just after the war to promote the views of the Air Force to Congress and the general public. The association charged that the script was "unpatriotic" and expressed outrage that the curators had wanted to portray some of the destruction the bomb had caused at "ground zero," including photos of Japanese dead and wounded. They were not pleased with suggestions in the text that Americans might have fought the Japanese mostly out of a desire for revenge. The association saw no reason to treat the nation's former enemies as "morally equivalent" to Americans or to demean in any way the motivations of American soldiers—a classic defense of a traditionalist or heroic view of war. It suggested that if the Smithsonian could not exhibit the *Enola Gay* "properly," it should turn the job over to an institution that could. Quickly, the essential nature of the association's critique was picked up by the American media—which by and large was highly supportive of the veterans. Newspapers and television commentators charged the Smithsonian with dishonoring the contributions of American fighting men, with being "antimilitary" and even anti-American. Many noted the curators had not served in the military themselves.

In subsequent months the Smithsonian became embroiled in a series of negotiations over the content of the script—sometimes on a line-by-line basis—with organizations such as the American Legion. Scholarly groups like the Organization of American Historians, on the other hand, strongly criticized a process whereby revisions were based on negotiations rather than on professional standards. Veteran support in Congress, however, was substantial. Soon the Senate passed a resolution calling for exhibits that reflected "positively" on the Americans who fought the Pacific War. In January 1995, a group of some eighty Republicans and Democrats called for Harwitt's dismissal. According to the *New York Times,* the lawmakers agreed with veterans who felt the planned exhibit would portray the United States as an aggressor and Japan as a victim of American racism. These critics called for more attention to Japanese expansionist policies in the Pacific before 1941 and the Japanese attack on Pearl Harbor. They also voiced anger that exhibition planners had revised downward the estimated number of American casualties that might have occurred if an invasion of Japan had been launched. William Manchester even joined the argument and told a reporter that he felt that the script seemed to be part of an ideological campaign to suggest that the dropping of the bombs was unnecessary. The debate ended not in any form of compromise but in a decision by the Smithsonian to cancel the exhibit and display only the fuselage of the plane without any historical debate on the bomb-ing or the casualties. The director of the Smithsonian, Michael Heyman, said the museum had made a mistake in attempting to "couple an historical treatment of the use of atomic weapons with the fiftieth commemorations of the end of the war."[20]

THE HOLLYWOOD SEQUEL

Not to be left out, Hollywood joined the late-century celebration as well in what amounted to a revival of the World War II films that had been so plentiful in the 1940s and 50s. No war film of the time captured more attention in this regard than Stephen Spielberg's *Saving Private Ryan* (1998). When he first read the script, Spielberg claimed that he thought immediately of his father, who had served in the war as a radio operator on a B-25 and how much such a movie would please him. He noted that it was his father that got him interested in the war itself and who helped jump-start his film career. In 2000 the prominent di-rector told an audience that in addition to honoring his father he wanted to make the film to recognize his "dad's generation." To him they were people who were selfless and willing to fight for "God and Country." He reasoned that the "baby boomers" of his generation were much more self-centered and were badly in need of the moral lessons the wartime generation could teach.[21]

Saving Private Ryan returns public attention to the European theater and to D-Day—a main ingredient in the American victory narrative. It does not shy away from presenting the brutal aspects of warfare and combat, but it focuses more on the suffering and dying of Americans than Germans. Relying on state-of-the-art technology, the opening of the film, which attracted enormous public attention, recreated the slaughter that took place on Omaha Beach as the men landed and, as such, was a critical appraisal of the war itself. Some reviewers even suggested that Spielberg's rendering of the horror of combat actually made the picture an antiwar film. But nothing could have been further from the truth. For the anguish of the GIs on the beach does not dominate the story: their per-sistence and courage in the face of enemy fire does. Consequently, the last part of the film is not so much about the horrors of war as it is a retelling of how the Americans won with daring and ingenuity, in this case boiled down to a small encounter with German tanks.

Although Spielberg remembers both the brutality of war and the victory of the Americans, the film is ultimately a morality tale that tends to transform the GIs of the 1940s into model men who are more loving than dangerous and are com-mitted to family and nation more than to violence and power. Indeed, the film is framed by opening and closing scenes at the American cemetery at Normandy, where Ryan—now a family man with children and grandchildren—returns to pay homage to the men who took him from the battlefields of France years ago. American officials had authorized his rescue when it was learned that his brothers had been killed in the war and that he was his family's last surviving male. In 1998, with tears in his eyes, he looks upon the graves of his comrades and wonders if he has "earned" the freedom they gave him by being a good father. No one who sees these scenes can avoid feeling that he is speaking directly to the postwar generation and making a plea for the restitution of traditional family values and forms of self-restraint that now appear in some disarray and are imagined to be at the very core of the heroic individuals who fought in the war. Indeed, the central actor in the film—Captain John Miller, played by actor Tom Hanks—is also a good family man and innately peace loving. He is a highly capable soldier but also a virtuous man who loves his wife and home and is repulsed by the violence around him. He is the standard that Ryan tried to emulate when he returned home after the war. A simple school teacher and part-time baseball coach from Pennsylvania, he disdains violence and says that every time he kills another man he feels "farther from home"—the traditional metaphor of American goodness in the movies of the 1940s. There are truly hints of regret over the killing in this statement—certainly more than in the attitudes of Truman and Tibbetts when it came to dropping the atomic bombs—but ultimately, at its rhetorical heart, this story supports the narrative of victory and virtue. The average American solider is a good man able to wage deadly warfare without becoming corrupted by the violence; he is the opposite of the brutal figures of Germans and Japanese that appeared in most Hollywood productions about the war. In the hands of Brokaw, Ambrose, and Spielberg, he is not only able to fight the good fight but to come away from the experience a better man.[22]

Public reaction to the film—to the extent that it can be gauged—seemed to focus more on the depiction of violence in the opening sequences than on the traditional story of beating the Germans that took up the later part. One veteran, who had fought on Iwo Jima and whose postwar nightmares were so vivid that he was able to smell the "putrid flesh" of dead bodies, cried uncontrollably for two days after seeing the movie—and then never had such troubling dreams again. Many individuals connected what they saw to their own family members—fathers, grandfathers, uncles—and the experience of these men in the war. The result—as is often the case when humans view the pain and suffering of others—was mixed. While some saw the sacrifices the men made and the horrors they endured as grounds for reverence, others concluded that such an experience could be ruinous and destructive as well. America Online actually set up a section of its Internet service to encourage viewers of the film to exchange their reactions. Many of the responses connected the sufferings of the soldiers to the heroic qualities attributed to the "greatest generation" to be sure. One person wrote about a father and an uncle who "hit the beach" during the war and how they now "love and honor them" for what they did. "I am forever grateful that those men fought for our country." Another wrote to tell of how their father lay wounded on a beach for sixteen hours during the war and that they now loved and revered him for what he endured. But a few focused only on the damage the war caused to men they knew and were less able to forget it in order to embrace heroic myths. The child of a man who fought at the Battle of the Bulge recalled after seeing the film that his father drank every night and never played with his children. The movie caused him to think that the effects of the war cost him the "ability to have a close family relationship." And another person revealed that for years after landing at Normandy his father drank heavily, endured nightmares, and often woke up "shaking and crying." Only a very few of the responders indicated that they regretted the war's human slaughter: "I mourn for the huge losses of WWII. Thirty million dead—just try to think of it. What carnage, what waste. Pain rippling out through lives and generations."[23]

The aspirations of Saving Private Ryan to frame the war in terms that were highly traditional and that downplay its ironic elements were repeated in Pearl Harbor (2001). The representation of the Japanese attack shows Americans suffering and dying during the assault—a spectacle that benefits a great deal from the modern technology of filmmaking, as does Ryan. Where the Spielberg film focused almost entirely on the battlefield, however, Pearl Harbor presents a love story as well. The story, focused on the relationships between an American nurse and two pilots, is obviously designed to attract audiences but also ends up making the Americans more human than the Japanese they are fighting. There is a touch of multiculturalism in the movie when audiences see an African American sailor, Dore Miller, picking up a gun to shoot at Japanese planes during the real attack. And there is no cynicism on the part of American soldiers toward the war or toward the military as was often the case during the 1940s. Even the initial defeat in Hawaii is reversed somewhat before the end of the movie, when audiences see a recreation of the bombing raid over Tokyo led by Col. James Doolittle that was staged only four months after Pearl Harbor to send a signal to the Japanese that they were not invulnerable.

Despite its patriotic leanings, American mass culture has always been characterized by crosscurrents and contradictions. As such it has frequently exposed both the best and the worst in the character of Americans and in the nature of all men and women. Before the modern celebration of World War II, Hollywood had a well- established track record, for instance, of producing films that were both pro-war and antiwar. Thus, even in the glow of the victory celebration of our times, it should come as no surprise that the tragic view of war—even of World War II—made a powerful appearance again. This can be demonstrated quite clearly in features such as *The Thin Red Line* (1998), *Flags of Our Fathers* (2006), and *Letters from Iwo Jima* (2006).

The critical nature of the *Thin Red Line* emanated from its origins as the second novel in the World War II trilogy authored by James Jones. Traditional motifs and the sentimental longings of the postwar generation fade here in the face of GI disdain for the war that pervaded the atmosphere of the 1940s. Moral ambiguity challenges virtue in this tale of the American encounter with the Japanese on Guadalcanal. Set in the paradise of the South Pacific, war is seen as an inversion of the settled and peaceful life these islands have known and not as a stage where men can demonstrate their loyalty and courage. The point is clearly made in the opening scene, in which American soldiers and local natives frolic in the ocean and on a beach on a warm and pleasant day. Here World War II becomes not the breeding ground for moral values but a place where men of all nations can demonstrate their capacity to face and even perpetrate evil. Americans soldiers in this recounting are filled with doubts over what they are doing. An American private concludes from his experience in battle that the entire world is really going to hell and that all one man can do is just look out for himself. An American officer represented in the figure of Captain Gordon Tall is even ready at a moment's notice to sacrifice the well-being of his men to achieve a strategic objective. Tall explains that this is his first war and he wants above all else to succeed. Both Japanese and American soldiers suffer in this story, and Americans demonstrate savage-like traits themselves as they charge into an enemy camp with fixed bayonets. War is not noble in this rendition but something that, in the words of one GI, "turns men into dogs." At the end audiences are left with the revelation that all men walk a thin red line between the loving and the barbaric parts of their souls.

The movement to establish a mythical view of World War II is further challenged in two films from director Clint Eastwood in 2006. Both *Flags of Our Fathers* and *Letters from Iwo Jima* focus on the bloody battle in the Pacific that took place in 1945. Yet while the first film directs its attention to the feelings of the Americans who fought, the latter makes a rare attempt to probe the emotions of the enemy. Both films also cross-examine the validity of seeing war in terms that are highly virtuous and patriotic. The combined effect of the two films is, in fact, to see the battle and its bloody consequences as something regrettable, because it brought pain and suffering not only to soldiers but to people who loved them in their respective homelands. In *Flags*, soldiers brought home to help sell war bonds have a difficult time accepting patriotic rhetoric of the nobility of the war they hear from civilians when they know their comrades are fighting and dying in gruesome conditions on Iwo Jima. In *Letters*, Japanese soldiers are conflicted as well over whether to see their sacrifice in terms of a traditional code of warrior honor or simply as meaningless. Some of them affirm the need and duty to die for the homeland; a few do not. Ironically, the portrait of the Japanese home front in *Letters* is more sympathetic than the one of the American home front in *Flags*. In the latter film, Americans civilians are seen as more prosperous during the war, more insulated from some of the harsh realities of warfare, and therefore more willing to see the war in terms of patriotic honor.

Both films empathize with the men who fought on the desolate island. In *Flags*, there is a clear effort to depict American troops as fighting mostly to protect each other and as men who are uncomfortable with all of the talk about patriotism that they encounter on the home front. In *Letters*, audiences are also asked to have compassion for men ensnared in the moral chaos of battle and—in the case of the Japanese—trapped in a situation from which there is no escape. *Letters* is particularly challenging to the mythical version of World War II in the United States because it dares to portray the Japanese as human beings who also have loving families and who possess a range of emotions. In humanizing the Japanese the film also humanizes the Americans, and that is why it is so threatening to the exceptionalist myth of the "good war." In fact, the film is based on the letters of General Tadamichi Kuribayshi, the Japanese leader on the island, who appears as a capable officer and loving husband. Another Japanese officer is even shown sparing the life of a wounded American in an act of mercy. And in a reversal of the sentimental version of the American triumph, American soldiers are shown killing two unarmed Japanese troops in cold blood after they had just surrendered. There is nothing in either film that says that Americans should not have fought World War II, but there is much to suggest that the costs were considerable and that the extent of human suffering on all sides needs to be recalled, not erased from the public remembrance.

THE HOLOCAUST

Part of the modern victory celebration was fueled not only by the veneration of the GIs but also by the gradual incorporation of the Holocaust into the American version of the war. Americans were certainly aware of the persecution of the Jews and other minorities in Europe during the early 1940s, but the full impact of the tragedy did not hit most citizens until they heard the news of the liberation of the camps in 1945 and saw newsreels of the Nazi atrocities. The discovery of the "death camps" did not spark a deep interest in what today is called the "Holocaust" or a public debate over genocide at the time, however. Rather, it was seen by most Americans as a manifestation of Nazi evil and an event that further justified the American war effort. The Nuremberg trials and the wide coverage they received in American society in the late 1940s downplayed the particular connection of the tragedy to the Jews and discussed it more as a crime against humanity and a piece of evidence in building a case for blaming the Germans for starting the war. The trials also served as an occasion to affirm the American commitment to a rule of law as compared to the evil ways of the Nazis. Over time and under the influence of Cold War pressures, Americans came to look more favorably on the German people and even their military when faced with the prospect of Soviet power in Europe, but in the late 1940s the focus was more on the nobility of Americans in contrast to German lawlessness.

Jewish Americans were too stunned and too heartbroken to be consoled by notions of American goodness, however. In synagogues, newspapers, school textbooks, and social organizations, extensive efforts were mounted to commemorate the millions of Jews who died and to reflect on the unprecedented tragedy that had just taken place. In this era the story of the Warsaw Ghetto, for instance, became a major topic of discussion among Jews in the United States. The term "Holocaust" appeared, but only as one descriptor along with others such as "Hitler's dark reign of terror." In some Jewish cemeteries in America, memorials were erected to those who died "under the rule of Nazi hordes." Well before the Holocaust became a fundamental part of the national remembrance, in other words, it became the firmly established as a central feature of American Jewish identity.[24]

The first popular treatment of the killings of the Jews to attract the attention of the American public appeared in 1950 with the publication of John Hersey's *The Wall*. Hersey again took up his human-centered remembrance of World War II as tragic by crafting a fictional account of Jews trapped in the Warsaw ghetto. He had actually passed through the ruins of Warsaw as he reported on the war, and he focused his fictional account on the daily struggle of Jews to survive and preserve aspects of their culture in the face of Nazi attempts to destroy it. His story is one of human devastation, despite the fact that a few Jews manage to avoid the trains to Treblinka to fight again. Yet much of the public reaction to the novel suggests that Americans were still disinclined to see the somber implications for all of humanity in both the war and the story Hersey wrote. Most reviews saw acts of Jewish resistance near the end of the book as a sign that the "human spirit" could triumph in the face of evil. In Charlotte, North Carolina, a rabbi, asked to review the book for a local paper, said he felt that Hersey wrote "magnificently of man's nobility in the face of death." In promoting the novel, the Book-of-the-Month Club claimed it contained a "great heroic theme of the human spirit defiant and unconquerable in the face of physical annihilation." Norman Cousins, however, noted that Hersey's depiction of the horror (which he felt could have been stronger) was important not because it celebrated any human spirit but because it disrupted what he felt was a public acceptance of mass violence that marked the immediate postwar era.[25]

Public awareness of the Holocaust in America was furthered just two years later with the publication of *The Diary of Anne Frank*. Unlike *The Wall*, the acute anguish of the victims is merely suggested in this story, which ends before the young girl, living in hiding in Holland under Nazi rule, is sent to a tragic death in a German camp. The story, in fact, is centered more on the personal feelings and emotions of a young woman coming of age and somewhat detached from the real war that raged outside her temporary sanctuary. When it was first published in Holland in 1946, it actually attracted little attention, as scholars such as Alvin Rosenfeld have pointed out, because it was too much of a grim reminder of all the agony that had just taken place. Inserted into the dynamics of American mass culture in the 1950s, however, it quickly gained a large audience for the opposite reason—that it managed to avoid a direct confrontation with the true cruelty of the war.[26]

As a book, a play, and a film, the story of Anne Frank became not so much a tragedy as an inspirational tale of hope. In the 1950s this story of a loving family in the midst of war was seen as a sign that the better side of human nature could still triumph over the darker impulses that lurked in the souls of men and women everywhere. At the end of the 1959 film, for instance, the young girl expressed the view that despite all that she had endured so far, "I still believe men are good." Astute observers have pointed out that such a perspective was readily accepted by Americans who wanted to retain faith in the ideals of liberal individualism and its central tenet that human nature would use liberty to gain what was best for all. Certainly Bosley Crowther, in a review in the *New York Times*, took a message of optimism from the movie and claimed he liked it because it showed the "magnificence of human endurance and compassion" during a time of turmoil and horror. Of course, neither he nor most of the American audience knew what researchers would learn years later—that Anne and her sister Margaret ended up in Bergen-Belsen, sickly and emaciated, and were simply thrown into a mass grave.[27]

By the 1960s the Holocaust was rapidly becoming central to the war remembrance and identity of both Jewish and American citizens. A new generation of Jewish Americans, even further removed from the tale of ancestors emigrating to America than their parents and the war itself, embraced the story of Hitler's destruction of the Jews as a vital part of who they thought they were and saw themselves as part of a global community whose fate was tied in part to the survival of the state of Israel. They were also imprinted by an American culture more focused than ever on the claims of victims for civil rights and redress.[28]

By the time Ronald Reagan was president in the 1980s, the Holocaust was important enough in the American memory of the war to stir passionate debate. In 1985 Reagan was planning a visit to Germany to strengthen ties with America's former wartime enemy. An alliance with West Germany, of course, was very much a part of American foreign policy during the Cold War. Problems for Reagan erupted, however, when he made the mistake of agreeing to make a ceremonial stop on this journey at a German cemetery in Bitburg that happened to contain a number of the graves of the notorious Waffen-SS troops who had been deeply implicated in the murders of the Jews. In a speech not long before he departed for Europe, Reagan stated that his purpose in going was to commemorate the postwar alliance that had developed between the two nations and not to revive memories of the Third Reich. He also expressed the idea that the Waffen-SS dead were victims just as much as the Jews.

Americans were outraged. Many veterans who had fought the Germans now joined with Jewish Americans to voice their anger over Reagan's plans, arguing that a visit to Bitburg not only paid homage to the perpetrators of the Holocaust but demeaned the sacrifices American soldiers had made in Europe in World War II. One rabbi claimed that such a visit would offer support as well to those who denied the Holocaust ever happened and noted that literature claiming the story of the tragedy was merely a hoax had recently been circulated in the schools of Northridge, California, where he lived. Elie Wiesel, a survivor of the death camps and a prominent thinker on the meaning of the Holocaust, wrote to Reagan expressing dismay and asked if the president could at least stop as well at the site of a former death camp. Senator Bob Dole wrote to suggest that Reagan pay a visit to Dachau in order to show that this nation was committed to never forgetting the violence perpetrated by the Nazis. Congresswoman Barbara Mikulski of Baltimore also wrote the president to tell him of her anger over the planned stop at Bitburg, claiming that it sent a "terrible message" to Gold Star mothers and

Holocaust survivors in her community. And the head of a veterans organization in Maryland wrote to say that "as veterans we cannot condone your denigration of the memories of our fallen comrades by laying a wreath" at Bitburg.[29]

In the end Reagan tried to please both sides. He put a stop at Bergen-Belsen on his itinerary and kept his appointment with German Chancellor Helmut Kohl at Bitburg, where he placed a wreath. In an address in Germany he said that he felt "great sadness that history could be filled with such great waste, destruction, and evil." He stressed, however, that responsibility for the evil resided not with the German people but with "a dictator" and his "fanatical followers"—thus preserving a mythical faith in human nature. "We do not believe in collective guilt," he asserted. To support his point he noted that many of the graves at Bitburg were those of teenage conscripts who were "forced" into battle during the "death throes" of the Nazi war machine. In fact, Reagan was so stung by the criticism he encountered over the visit that he moved quickly to get the Senate to ratify the United Nations Convention on Genocide, an action that the United States had resisted since its conception in 1948. For decades conservatives in Congress had been able to block approval of a number of UN treaties on human rights like this one because they feared such international agreements might infringe upon American sovereignty or even be used to foster racial integration at home. It was a striking bit of irony that a nation that had argued, in part, that it needed to fight World War II to foster human rights in the world rejected for years approving documents designed to do just that.[30]

By the 1990s the Holocaust had become a major subject of interest to Americans and certainly—like the story of D-Day—a central part of their victory narrative and celebration. Stephen Spielberg's film *Schindler's List*, appearing in 1993, was probably the most popular and widely viewed Holocaust story at the century's end and won an Academy Award for best picture. Spielberg's film, like Reagan's remarks, worked to restore faith in human nature and to overcome any perception that the Holocaust (or the war) should be seen as a sign of hopelessness. He focused his story not on the struggles of victims but on the deeds of a moral hero, Oscar Schindler, who saved Jewish lives by outwitting Nazi officials and getting them to assign Jews to work in his industries. This celebration of the individual hero probably contributed to the movie's popularity and was seen by some as an indication that the Holocaust had been truly "colonized" by an American culture fixated on optimism and exceptional people.[31]

Hollywood's earlier treatment of the Holocaust—beyond the story of Anne Frank—had actually differed significantly from the more positive take offered by Spielberg. Films such as *The Pawnbroker* (1964) and *Sophie's Choice* (1982) had not only highlighted the way war created victims rather than heroes but had connected the memory of the Holocaust to forms of discrimination that still existed in the United States itself, an indication that they were rooted at least partially in an older left-wing critique of American mythology that had driven filmmakers and writers like Mailer and Jones in the immediate postwar era. Both films were about Holocaust survivors who could not get beyond the trauma of losing loved ones in the war, and both depicted clearly that many people in America still suffered at the hands of oppression and injustice. In *The Pawnbroker*, actor Rod Steiger played Sol Nazerman, a man now living in Spanish Harlem in the 1960s but still obsessed with the loss of the family he loved in the "death camps." Nazerman had adopted something akin to a strategy of "psychic numbing" as he struggled simply to live day to day and to overcome recurring flashbacks of the horror he knew in Germany during the war. Life is grim in his pawn shop, where he watches a constant parade of desperate people and racial minorities in New York trying to survive by trading their meager possessions for a few dollars or engaging in all sorts of criminal activity. The film, like many other cultural products of the 1960s, refused to embrace a romantic view of American virtue.

In the same year that *Schindler's List* appeared, Americans further incorporated the Holocaust into the their story of the war by dedicating the United States Holocaust Memorial Museum near the National Mall in Washington, D.C. To Tim Cole this project was driven by the need for Americans to insert this tragedy into their own "fundamental tale of pluralism, tolerance, democracy, and human rights," which they were fond of telling. Certainly Cole had a point, but so did Elie Wiesel when he spoke at the museum's dedication and recounted the failure of many governments during the war, including that of the United States, to at least warn Jews in Europe of what was happening in the camps when they had knowledge that such atrocities were taking place. Wiesel declared that the "tale" of the Holocaust had to be communicated as part of the ongoing effort to see that human suffering anywhere could not be ignored again. The dedication was also another civic event of the 1990s that evoked an America-centered memory of the entire war. Both President William Clinton and Vice President Al Gore attended, and CNN broadcast the ceremonies throughout the world. At the same time additional events were held in the Washington area to mark the remembrance of the Holocaust. For instance, John Eisenhower, the son of the wartime general, read at Arlington National Cemetery a letter his father had written describing the horrors he found when he first saw the camp at Buchenwald.[32]

The idea for the museum actually originated in the administration of Jimmy Carter and was tied in part to Carter's interest in human rights in the late 1970s.

The president was also anxious to repair some damage he had done to his relationship with American Jews when he expressed support for the idea of a Pales-
tinian homeland. In its final form the museum—after much debate—became an
institution that presented to the public many of the most horrible details of the
catastrophe with an eye to educating audiences about the event. During the planning process some critics argued that the museum should tell the story of other
groups who suffered at the hands of the Nazis or who died in other instances of
genocide and not concentrate on the Jews alone. Jewish leaders in America remained adamant, however, that a broader focus would diminish the unique nature and impact of what happened to the Jews of Europe and that their story
alone was sufficient to evoke a more general sense of compassion for human
suffering in other times and places. Part of the final resolution of this debate was
a decision to present a large number of photographs of individual victims and
objects that they had possessed. The hope was that such displays would create a
more personal link between the dead and the living as they walked through the
museum. Despite the fact that the museum did offer some critical perspectives
on American inaction during the killings, it also offered visitors reminders that
Americans had liberated some of the camps. Indeed, the ability to link the theme
of American liberation to the entire story was compelling for many federal officials who supported the project. Interestingly, a memorial dedicated to the Holocaust in 1964 in Philadelphia consisted only of a piece of sculpture of victims
struggling through a ring of fire and did not raise the idea of American liberation. A statue to the same event dedicated in 1985 at Liberty Park in New Jersey,
however, pictured an American GI carrying a Holocaust survivor in his arms.[33]

The total impact that the museum makes on visitors cannot be known; however, evidence in recorded visitors' comments suggests that the role of Americans in liberating the camps does not impress most visitors as much as the overall theme of the sheer brutality and human suffering that the Holocaust
represents. More than most sites of remembering World War II in America, people seem to come away from the museum with the idea that at least this aspect
of the war was tragic and not conducive to nurturing positive values. The brief set
of quotations that follow, taken from thousands of responses visitors made between 2001 and 2007, can only hint at the theme:

The heart of God must break at what humans do to each other.

Taking a history class completely dedicated to these events does not prepare you for
this experience. I have been here before and it still amazes me that people could
commit such atrocities.

It's so sad what happened to the millions of innocent lives lost. The museum does a great job showing the truth of how horrible war making can be.

We are our own worst enemy. My heart goes out to all the people that lost their lives and to their families.

This experience has saddened me that people were capable of doing things to other human beings that I never imagined.

Never before did I understand the extent of human degradation, slaughter, and murdering to exhaust a race.

I will never forget my experience here. It is a reminder and remembrance.

The horrifying acts that man produces. Hopefully through the smoke and ashes mankind can learn from this.

In addition to seeing the destructive aspects of the war as a problem of human nature—a point that inferentially undermines efforts to make any group of people exceptionally virtuous—visitors to the museum also mention (with less frequency) the need for men and women in the future to practice tolerance. In this sense, the responses come closer to the human rights visions of the 1940s than many other remembrances of the war. Again, a few selected quotations cannot do justice to the full expression of this idea in visitor responses:

I am a devout Christian. My future son-in-law is Jewish. However, nothing matters but that we are all God's children and we need to always remember to treat each other with love.

You can never teach in a book what you can learn here about the persecution of the Jews and about human dignity, respect, and social injustice.

This is where I brought my family to teach my children never to hate or make fun of someone because of the nationality that they were born with.

This is a lesson of the results of intolerance and oppression. We must learn to respect and relish our differences and focus on what can unify us [as] one humanity."[34]

Visitor comments do not constitute elaborate interpretations of exhibits or even of the larger war experience, but they do offer hints as to how different presentations of the past and of the war tend to evoke varying responses. Most people who visit the United States Holocaust Memorial Museum (USHMM) appear to connect the evidence of the horrors and suffering they see to a larger issue of human nature—both how brutal it can be and the need to restrain that brutality by fostering attitudes of kindness and compassion. These responses suggest that visitors were connecting their exposure to the tragedy of war to a universal need for people to find ways to be kind and respectful to each other. We cannot, in fact, be sure what they think of the American victory or the many calls that permeate their world to emulate the patriotic valor and virtue of the American generation that fought the war, and of course some of the responses at the USHMM are from non-American citizens. The reactions from the USHMM become even clearer, however, when they are compared to similar responses collected at the National World War II Museum in New Orleans in recent years. There the reconstruction of the war experience is more focused on the American story and victory. The comments from New Orleans do suggest a different sort of reaction to a very different presentation of World War II.

The museum in New Orleans allows tourists to follow a basic American narrative from Pearl Harbor to ultimate victory. The entrance lobby is dominated by many of the weapons that Americans used to win—a military plane, for instance, and a Higgins landing craft. The latter are important to the New Orleans site because the Higgins boats were crucial in carrying American troops into beach landings in the Pacific and at Normandy on D-Day and because they were manufactured in New Orleans. The museum also offers selections from many oral histories from the wartime generations that offer glimpses of personal feelings from people who worked on the home front and many who served in the military. It quite consciously shows the multiracial character of the American fighting force.

The exhibit for the D-Day landing is probably the most extensive, with elaborate maps indicating the scope of the greatest amphibious assault in history and even a reconstructed German bunker offering tourists a view of the sea before the vast armada arrived. Less space is devoted to the Pacific side of the war, but throughout the museum death and suffering are depicted with photos of soldier dead and even the charred remains of Japanese civilians after Hiroshima. There is little to suggest that anyone regretted either the deaths of the Americans or the Japanese and almost no indication of what sort of impact the war deaths had on individual families. However, one can press a button and hear some of this, as in the case of one woman who remembered the grief her parents experienced when they learned of the death of her brother and her own feelings that she would have gladly traded his medals to have him come home alive.

The result of what is largely a straightforward account of the American victory is that visitors do not seem to link what they saw to universal questions of human violence and intolerance. Instead, they tend to state that they enjoyed the exhibits and that there is little they would change. Most surprisingly, they invariably like the exhibit on the Pacific War much more than the more extensive ones on Normandy. Clearly, the Pacific exhibit tends to register more heavily the brutality of war—especially with its account of the Bataan Death March, the photo of a severed head of a Japanese soldier carried on an American tank, and the human destruction at Hiroshima. It appears that the audience here is more accepting of the tragic dimensions of the war than the one at the Holocaust museum.[35]

The museum was originally named the National D-Day Museum when it opened in 2000. It was the brainchild of historian Stephen Ambrose, whose original inspiration came from listening to oral accounts of American veterans who landed at Normandy in 1944. Ambrose had begun to meet the veterans when taking educational tours of the European battle sites arranged by his good friend and colleague at the University of New Orleans, Nicholas Mueller. While working on the papers of Dwight Eisenhower and listening to the wartime hero discuss the importance of Andrew Higgins and his shipbuilding operation in New Orleans, Ambrose concluded that a museum needed to be constructed to recognize not only the American men of D-Day but the contributions of Higgins as well. It was at that point that Ambrose and Mueller set out on a vast fundraising campaign to raise the dollars needed to get the museum built. Their campaign was eventually joined by others who had gained some notoriety in the commemorations of the war in the 1990s, including Brokaw, Hanks, and Spielberg. Hanks was prominently featured on brochures that spread the appeal for funds, and in one instance he made the point that with the "last members of the 'Greatest Generation' passing away," it was imperative that "lessons" of their courage and sacrifice be preserved. Brokaw also appeared on such publications stating that the "duty, honor, achievement and courage" of the wartime generation "gave us the world we have today."[36]

The dedication ceremonies for the museum constituted one of the largest celebrations of the American victory of the modern era and reinforced completely the notion of American virtue. Thousands of people came to New Orleans to celebrate the triumph and the veterans of the various campaigns. Over the course of several days in early June 2000, participants could view reenactments of wartime skirmishes; attend dinners; listen to concerts featuring military marches and the popular music of the 1940s; hear speeches from prominent individuals such as Ambrose, Brokaw, and Spielberg; watch a massive parade of war veterans that featured several winners of the Congressional Medal of Honor; and tour the new museum. On the morning of June 6, 2000, the fifty-sixth anniversary of

the D-Day landings, NBC television featured an interview with Ambrose by Brokaw that stressed the high degree of importance Americans placed on the Normandy landings and what the GIs faced when they hit the beaches. Ambrose told
a national audience that he could not get enough of the stories from the veterans
and that he was "inspired" by them. Brokaw, in turn, praised the popular historian by calling him the "godfather" of the "Greatest Generation" and affirmed
that it was, indeed, D-Day that turned the course of the war.[37]

FDR

The celebration of American virtue that was at the heart of the public performance of the victory in the 1990s had privileged romantic myths about ordinary
individuals more than the contributions of wartime leaders like Franklin D.
Roosevelt. The legacy of FDR, the man who led America into the war and through
the war, was conspicuous by its absence in most of the modern commemorations. This represented a curious turn of events, since many Americans wrote to
his widow upon his death in 1945, expressing utter sorrow for the loss of a "great
good leader" and a man many felt was a "personal friend" who had helped them
in hard times and defended them in war. Ordinary citizens sent Mrs. Roosevelt
letters, cards, songs, and even poetry that revealed how strongly attached they felt
to the president and all that they had endured as a political community in the
1930s and 40s. In a poem entitled "Our Commander-in-Chief," a man from Cal
ifornia expressed the hope that someday "that better world for which we pray"
will be realized as FDR had hoped and that there would be "Four Freedoms then
for every man. Peace and Plenty in every land."[38]

This relative public neglect of Roosevelt and what he stood for would change
slightly in 1997 when a memorial to FDR, which had been planned and discussed for decades, was finally dedicated in Washington, D.C. The final design of
the monument suggested clearly why FDR's memory was attenuated in most of
the public celebrations that had so much more to say about the individual courage and loyalty of the ordinary American soldier. There were advocates for the
disabled who did not like the new Roosevelt memorial because it did not fully
reveal the fact that he was confined to a wheelchair, and some complained that
honoring him masked the fact that he did not do as much as he could have for
Holocaust victims.[39] But in another sense the memorial turned out to be a revelation of what most public celebrations of the 1990s themselves had covered up.
That is to say, the Roosevelt site evoked a remembrance of the more liberal version of World War II that had framed the struggle within the context of New Deal
welfare programs and human rights both for Americans at home and for men

and women throughout the world. There were few reminders of GI virtue at the memorial. Rather, the site actually disrupted the long effort to see the war as a ratification of individualism by suggesting that it had not worked in the United States in the 1930s, that many Americans had come to love a man and a welfare state that had helped them, and that the Four Freedoms and the birth of the United Nations—promoted not only by the president but his wife—were very much a part of why many in the 1940s thought the war should be fought. To the extent that the memorial ultimately failed to evoke the tragedy of war, it adopted a traditional frame on the past; but to the degree that it noticed the economic suffering of the "greatest generation," their attachment to the welfare state, and the liberal universalism of the 1940s, it emerged as another counter-memory, like stories of the war's victims, to the vast public celebration of the American victory.

In its final form the Franklin Delano Roosevelt memorial offered citizens a curious blend of realism and abstractionism. Designed by a landscape architect, Lawrence Halprin, the memorial presented a more literal reconstruction of the past than most prominent memorials by asking visitors to walk through the years of the Roosevelt presidency chronologically. Each of his four terms was covered in an outdoor "room," starting from this first term during the Great Depression and ending with his death and creation of the United Nations in his last term in office. The overall design was not nearly as majestic or as overpowering as the tributes to Jefferson, Lincoln, or Washington. Rather, like the Vietnam Veterans Memorial, it was more horizontal than vertical and was set in a garden-like setting that allowed it to incorporate the nearby landscape more than dominate it. Its rejection of height and grandeur signaled its refusal to become a traditional memorial with aspirations to erase the complexities of the past. Thus, the memorial site was populated with the figures of many people rather than a focus on one man. In addition to his wife, Eleanor, visitors could see statues of men who were out of work in the Depression and citizens listening to FDR on the radio as well as carvings of mourners following their dead president in a funeral cortege.

Despite its resistance to a classical tradition, the final memorial was still much grander than Roosevelt himself had wanted. In September of 1941 he had called Supreme Court Justice Felix Frankfurter to the White House to tell him that when the time came he desired only a simple memorial slab—about the size of his White House desk—placed somewhat unobtrusively in front of the National Archives building with a simple inscription such as "in the memory of" Franklin D. Roosevelt. Clearly, after this death the matter would move outside the control of the wishes of the president, however. Indeed, within months of his death close friends of the president, at the suggestion of Eleanor Roosevelt, had organized a private foundation to consider ways to memorialize him. Led by political allies such as Samuel I. Roseman and Robert Sherwood, this group categorically rejected the idea of building a memorial structure to the war leader and expressed a desire to honor him by promoting values and ideals such as the Four Freedoms for which he stood. Many in the foundation talked of the need to create "a living memorial" that would initiate educational programs designed to foster better relations between all the peoples of the world and hasten the global spread of economic security and political freedom. Sherwood told his colleagues in the foundation that both he and the president's widow felt there were simply too many economic and political problems in the postwar world to waste time and money planning a "bricks and mortar" monument. Others within the memorial group agreed. Isadore Lubin, a trustee of the foundation, argued that the major aim of the foundation should be the "improvement of human relations on a global basis" or what he called a monument "of mind and spirit." And Mary McLeod Bethune, a prominent African American educator, offered the view that the foundation should best concentrate on sustaining the "great humanitarian spirit and ideals" of Roosevelt, which included a legacy of "getting races, nations, and individuals to become better acquainted with one another."[40]

Part of this transnational legacy of the war was driven by a critical memory of what had taken place in the early 1940s. That is to say, many recalled the destructiveness of the war and the powerful weapons that scientists had created and that nations unleashed. Labor leader Walter Reuther told foundation members in 1948 that Roosevelt had been a true "architect in human relations" but that progress in such relations had not matched advances in the "physical sciences." To Reuther, there was a "moral lag between the two sciences," and more effort had to be expended to see that humans interacted more harmoniously or mankind would destroy itself. Another foundation member told a meeting of the group in 1949 that there was great anxiety in the world at the time over the possibility that the power of science would destroy civilization completely if men again resorted to "war over reason." Nearly everyone in the foundation therefore supported the idea of a new international order and the United Nations as a way to create a means to "abolish war" and the "unchecked pursuit of the national interest." And most understood that the achievement of better international relations would depend not only on the avoidance of war but on the realization of economic stability for men and women everywhere.[41]

By the early 1950s the liberal vision of the Roosevelt Foundation was grounded not only in a desire to keep alive the internationalism of the Four Freedoms but in a growing fear over the spread of McCarthyism in America. In a 1954 meeting trustees of the foundation worried out loud over how frightened most people were over communism and the methods congressional hearings used to "combat it." In that year calls were made for programs that would specifically promote educational endeavors centered on the importance of Freedom of Speech and Freedom from Want. Indeed, in their pursuit of programs that focused on the ending of deprivation, the foundation entered into a project with the Bureau of Labor Statistics to gather information that would allow them to measure the "social and economic cost of existing poverty in the United States and eventually in other parts of the world." Archibald MacLeish told the group in 1955 that failure to advance these freedoms would mean that they were "running away from the real battle." As part of their battle plan, in fact, Arthur M. Schlesinger Jr. proposed a program called the Four Freedom Awards as a way to recognize individuals from all walks of life—not just soldiers—who stood for the rights the group valued. Such recognition was important, Sherwood argued, to counter "retrogression and reaction at home" and the "forces of evil abroad."[42]

In 1946, some fifteen months after FDR's funeral, Congress also took up the issue of commemorating Roosevelt and passed a resolution creating a public commission charged with the responsibility of building a memorial to the fallen leader. The actual commission was not established until 1955, however, when it was led by the president's lawyer, Francis Biddle. The commission sponsored a design competition in 1958, and within two years had selected a plan by William Pedersen and Bradford Tilney of New York City, which consisted of eight soaring stone tablets—some rising as high as 165 feet—inscribed with quotations from Roosevelt's speeches. The design stirred considerable debate over the extent to which it sufficiently honored all that FDR stood for. A number of prominent architects joined a debate in *Architectural Forum* in 1961 and took a position on the Pedersen and Tilney design. Some lamented the movement away from the order and simplicity of classical monuments and referred to the proposed stone tablets or slabs as simply another version of Stonehenge and, consequently, an example of "primitivism." They felt Roosevelt deserved better. Yet there were prominent architects such as Philip Johnson who understood that the splendor and order that some desired was simply not possible in a postwar world marked by "unbelief" and "nonheroics." G. M. Kallmann, a professor of architecture at Columbia University, explained that modern design simply lacked "an authoritative language" because of the obsession most people now had with "individualistic expression rather than epic values." Kallmann argued that "modern man" was simply more uncertain about who he was or what he was like and therefore could not readily associate himself with the "heroic stance commonly associated with the monumental." Although many of the commemorations of the war in the United States in the 1990s and the new World War II Memorial dedicated in 2004 would attempt to restore the certainty and heroics Kallmann thought had been lost, his point did reveal a level of cynicism that characterized the more immediate post-war era. Once the family of the late president let it be known that they were not keen on the proposed design, however, it was dropped.[43]

The design of the "bricks and mortar" monument to Roosevelt that was finally erected in the 1990s certainly eschewed the motifs of heroism and tradition. Roosevelt does not sit high on a perch as do Jefferson and Lincoln nearby, al-though he is clearly venerated in this reworking of what he was about. Classical uniformity and abstractionism give way to something close to a history text that covers the years and events of the Roosevelt presidency. At this memorial site, World War II is not celebrated and the dead are not mourned. Rather, the war is framed by a larger story of the rise of mid-century liberal ideology. The design of this modern memorial, visited by some three million people annually, was actu-ally selected by the Roosevelt Commission in 1975, which at the time was under the leadership of two World War II combat veterans, Senators Mark Hatfield and Daniel Inouye. Hatfield, in fact, had been at Iwo Jima and at Hiroshima soon enough after the dropping of the atomic bomb and noticed that all of the bodies had not yet been recovered and that the "smell of decomposition" remained in the air.[44]

In the new memorial the blend of realism and abstractionism is spread evenly through the design. It is the Depression and Roosevelt's introduction of the wel-fare state that carried the burden of realism here; the depiction of World War II—despite its invocation of high idealism—is so abstract that it actually erases the experience not only of heroism but of suffering and dying. Three bronze sculptures in the first alcove devoted to Roosevelt's first term depict citizens in dire need. A farm family appears before a "crumbling house," five men in long overcoats stand in a Depression-era bread line, and another man listens intently by his radio for words of hope from the new president. Included here as well are a number of bas relief scenes from New Deal projects. Many commentators in 1997 noted the contrast between the political rhetoric of the 1990s, which sought to undermine the idea of the welfare state, and this depiction, which portrayed it as significant and much needed. Indeed, a number of people at the dedication told reporters expressly that they treasured the memory of Roosevelt because they recalled vividly how many of his programs helped their families. Senator Max Cleland of Georgia remembered that his father had never tasted whole milk or owned a suit of clothes until he got a job with the Civilian Conservation Corps. A visitor from Utah told of how his family was barely making ends meet until his dad obtained a job on a WPA road crew, and another came to the memorial site to remember the person he felt was "the greatest president of our lifetime" and one he thought of nearly every time his Social Security check arrived.[45]

As visitors move from the 1930s to the war, they can see blocks of granite strewn about on the ground. These are meant to allude to the devastation and chaos war can bring. Words etched in granite quote FDR as saying that he has seen war in his lifetime and the "dead in the mud" and that he hates war. Granite blocks are not the same, of course, as the names of the dead or even gold stars. And his references to seeing the dead and disliking war were actually about a brief trip he took close to the battlefront in World War I as the Assistant Secretary of the Navy and were used in a political speech he had delivered in 1936. They were not direct references to anything he had done or said in World War II. Indeed, the memorial, according to its designer Lawrence Halprin, deliberately avoided using any words from his famous statement that the date of the Pearl Harbor attack would "live in infamy" and any references to his deep hatred for the wartime states of Japan and Germany in order not to offend nations that were now America's allies.

The statue of FDR itself is anything but warlike or even statesmen-like and is simply a figure of the president wearing a long cape and sitting in his wheelchair with his friendly dog nearby. Visitors constantly touch the hand of the seated leader but get no direct reference to the savage nature of the war he waged and the enemy he faced. Nearby is another bas relief depicting mourners with their heads bowed walking behind the president's coffin as it is drawn by horses. Here we do get a glimpse of the deep national grief that his death evoked. This is not entirely surprising when one learns that the artist who executed the panel had been serving on a naval ship when the news of Roosevelt's death arrived and recalled how the news spread through the vessel like "fire." Even Halprin recalled Roosevelt's death and felt that, had he lived longer, the liberal dreams of the president would have had a greater chance of success. He felt there was great optimism about the power of liberal humanitarianism at the time but worried that "we'll never recapture that feeling again."[46]

Roosevelt is not only less warlike in this reconfiguration of World War II, but he is actually less commanding. He shared commemorative space with both his liberal ideals and his wife. While some might feel that the significant public life of Eleanor Roosevelt has been slighted here, she still merits a statue of her own near the spot where visitors see references to the Four Freedoms and the United

Nations. Certainly, this is a true picture of the powerful way in which she was
identified in the 1940s and 50s with such ideals. In fact, she not only pushed the
memorial foundation (from behind the scenes) to concentrate more on the promotion of the Four Freedoms than on building a memorial to the late president
but also allowed her public life to serve as a "living memorial" to the liberalism
of her husband's tenure in office. She appeared everywhere in the late 1940s and
50s in support of liberal causes. In her widely read newspaper column "My Day,"
she frequently criticized the denial of civil rights to black citizens in America,
praised organizations such as the American Veterans Committee for supporting
the "belief that all men are brothers and all human beings worth of respect," and
attended numerous dinners and events in which awards were given for the support of humanitarian causes. For a time in the early 1950s she even served as an
"honorary chairman" of the American Veterans Committee and in 1953 spoke to
the Washington chapter of the group on the topic of human rights.[47]

Americans continued to exhibit an enormous amount of interest in World
War II in the early years of this century. In the fall of 2007 public television stations presented a massive documentary produced by Ken Burns called *The War*
that ran more than fourteen hours. Traces of critical and humanitarian sentiments permeated the extraordinarily long feature, but in the end the virtue and
the victory stood above the rest. In this film the war is seen not so much as "good"
but as "necessary," a sign that it had tragic as well as noble outcomes. Unadulter-
ated celebration of the American struggle is moderated by interviews with ordinary citizens who frequently express sorrow for the loss of loved ones or recount
ugly incidents of wartime racism in America. A brief amount of time is even al-
located to the fact that some veterans—such as E. B. Sledge—were haunted by
nightmares once they returned home. Ultimately, however, the story is a sentimental one. Retrospective views on several American towns tend to reveal citizens who were primarily patriotic and supportive of the war effort and American
leaders like Roosevelt. An editor from Minnesota is quoted as noting the "quiet
dignity" of the local people he knew in contributing to the war effort; the Holocaust is invoked on several occasions to justify all of the sacrifice in ways that the
savagery of the Pacific theater could not; the legacy of the Four Freedoms is barely
hinted at. In the end most of the feature is taken up by rerunning film footage of
the war's battles, air attacks, and invasions that Americans had watched for
years.

As generations far removed from the actual experience of World War II took
control of its remembrance, romantic myths cast a longer shadow over the landscape of memory than they had ever done before. A half-century after the fight-

ing stopped, millions of Americans talked about the war as a character-building experience that transformed citizens into heroes and moral paragons. By then, however, the remaining members of the generation that experienced the war were more than willing to accept the accolades of their children and not ponder the conflicting crosscurrents that marked their past. Moreover, the passing of millions of witnesses meant that the vast emotional baggage of cynicism, confusion, sorrow, sober reflection, and even internationalism that coursed through the era of World War II simply commanded less public space. At the beginning of a new century, many Americans were more than ready to go to war again.

CONCLUSION

AMERICANS WHO EXPERIENCED World War II quarreled over its meaning while it was fought and for decades after it ended. Citizens from various backgrounds took justifiable pride in their victory over evil regimes and felt their achievement was worth all it had cost. Some readily embraced the idea that war bred character rather than tragedy and heroes rather than victims. They explained their own excursion into vicious actions as something that was thrust upon them against their will by wicked forces in the world. The traditionalists used this memory of the war to perform virtue and affirm a righteous identity for all Americans. However, heroic memories were grounded not only in traditional interpretations of the war experience but in the power of a political ideal that helped to hold together the American national experiment itself—personal independence. The extensive celebration of individual Americans from the war generation served not only to ennoble their deeds but to restore faith in the central political dream of the nation itself, a vision that was damaged by the realities of the war. How could one invest faith in any human being if humans had within them the potential for cruelty? The experience of war ratified this dim view of the soul of mankind. The heroic American memory of World War II denied it.[1]

Millions of soldiers and common people throughout the nation did, in fact, question the heroic myth. In books, films, local memorials, and political movements, Americans unwilling to be assuaged by patriotic honors, reluctant to let go of internationalist dreams, angered by their treatment as second-class citizens, and haunted by the horrors of warfare challenged the self-satisfaction of the romantics. These loyal Americans demanded that their losses be acknowledged, their exploitation be compensated, and the democratic implications of the struggle be fulfilled. They also saw in the unprecedented brutality of World War ll a reason to wonder whether those that suggested that Americans were some-how immune to the darker impulses of the human soul could be believed.

The gradual victory of tradition over both critical and even humanitarian per-spectives was not an easy one. For years, countless numbers of soldiers and civil-ians expressed their dissatisfaction with the war and much of what it entailed. Soldier-writers castigated military leaders who seemed indifferent to their best interests and maintained disparaging perspectives on the conflict and the dam-age it brought. Leading veterans organizations tended to sidestep questions about the harm the war brought and sought to uphold an ideal of a powerful and armed nation ready to go to war again and vanquish enemies. The differences in these views came to head in 1951, when millions of people cheered for Douglas MacArthur and others made it clear that they were not willing to follow leaders like him again in a quest for total victory. In towns and communities throughout the nation, critics insisted time and time again that memorials should reflect the sense of loss many felt and not simply the triumph. Hollywood itself felt com-pelled to register many of the doubts and regrets citizens felt for years after 1945 even as it took time to celebrate the American victory. At the end of the twentieth century, as many nations in the world were forced to come to terms with evil ac-tions that haunted their past, Americans were more inclined to use their lauda-tory memory of the war to reaffirm the noble sense of who they felt they were and to blunt efforts to analyze the complex record of their past. By then, however, most of the key witnesses had passed from the scene.[2]

The war years were also marked by intense racial conflict. Military bases and home front cities became sites not only of war mobilizations but of deadly con-flict and fighting. While postwar monuments and movies had little to say about such discord, the legacy of racism from the war era was never forgotten, and it eventually helped to propel powerful movements for social justice and equality at home. Although the public remembrance of the war often clouded from view the legacy of the fight for universal rights, a rising tide of minority claims for justice and compensation certainly kept alive aspects of this liberal dream. In the end, when it came to the memory of the war, minorities were welcomed into the imagined community of America not only because past injustices were acknowl-edged but because their victimization could now be refashioned into a story of heroism and virtue. This cultural revision certainly addressed bad practices from the past and helped to heal the ruptures of wartime, but it also erased or mini-mized the record of wartime hatred and reinforced the idea that Americans lacked the natural instincts toward brutality that afflicted the rest of mankind.

The power of virtuous myths and traditional memories so central to sustaining a legendary identity of the nation also diminished the legacy of domestic dis-content and human rights associated with other conflicts the nation fought. In the aftermath of the Civil War, an unprecedented encounter with death and trag-edy in American life, commemorations centered on the veterans from the North and the South who were recognized not so much for their suffering as for their valor on the field of battle. This formula not only served a need to reunite the na-tion but worked against determined attempts by African Americans to recall the war as one for equal rights for all. Moreover, it certainly mitigated a more "femi-nine" memory centered on the losses that were felt in small towns and marked in local graveyards.[3]

It took longer to establish the preeminence of virtuous accounts over critical and humanitarian ones when it came to World War I. Certainly Armistice Day and Memorial Day served as reminders that the sacrifices of World War I should be viewed in the most patriotic way. William Manchester vividly recalled as a boy watching his father don his Marine uniform and marching in Memorial Day pa-rades in Attleboro, Massachusetts. In 1921 the government dedicated the Tomb of the Unknown Soldier in which the remains of a dead American was placed "in honored glory." Yet by the late 1920s, Hollywood produced a number of movies that revealed many of the tragic aspects of the war, including *The Big Parade* (1927). And novelists of the time such as John Dos Passos, William Faulkner, and Ernest Hemingway crafted an entirely new genre of fiction called the "anti-war novel." It was not until nearly 1940 that Hollywood and others began to reinvigo-rate the more reverential look at the "Great War" in order to push public opinion toward supporting another American intervention into a European struggle.[4]

Tradition has even taken a greater hold of the American memory of Vietnam. At one time the war in Southeast Asia was seen mostly as a tragedy and as the complete opposite of World War II. This perspective still lives, but it is not as strong as it used to be. Consider the 2003 documentary *The Fog of War*, which focused on the recollections of Robert M. McNamara. By blending his recollec-tions of World War II and Vietnam, McNamara suspended critical judgments on war and mass slaughter by arguing that the killing was simply a rational re-sponse to an unfortunate situation. McNamara served his country by helping to design strategic bombing plans for the destruction of Japan in 1945 while a mem-ber of the staff of General Curtis LeMay and by acting as Secretary of Defense for Presidents John Kennedy and Lyndon Johnson during part of the Vietnam con-flict. He does not take a completely traditional view of American actions in both contests, and he acknowledges that the massive bombing campaigns waged upon innocent civilians in Japan and North Vietnam could be seen as immoral acts. What McNamara ultimately argues, however, is that these strategies were part of an approach to war that, far from being unethical, was simply normal and necessary. He stressed how LeMay would argue that the conduct of any war must be grounded in an ideal of efficiency. The general's logic was that the best war plan was one that would result in the killing of as many of the enemy as possible with only minimal losses for the American side. This is most likely why LeMay wanted to bomb Cuba with over 160 nuclear weapons during the Cuban missile crisis. In a sense, McNamara sought to rationalize war and slaughter in ways that soldiers often did in battle when they felt they were simply doing their job in destroying enemy combatants. Soldiers did this to temper the emotional crosscurrents many of them felt and to moderate deep feelings of vulnerability or qualms about killing. McNamara took normalization—and efficiency for that matter—further by turning them into virtues. In a sense, he confirmed the larger legacy of the twentieth century as a time when all men showed how "rational" they could be in destroying enemies and innocent civilians.[5]

Most veterans of World War II, including Lyndon Johnson and Richard Nixon, adhered to the necessity of destroying enemies in Southeast Asia and sacrificing men and materiel for an American victory. Leading veteran organizations such as the American Legion frequently mobilized rallies to support the war and counter the effects of antiwar demonstrators. Senator John Tower of Texas, who had served in the Pacific in World War II, told an "Honor America" gathering in Washington in 1969 that the war protestors should "know better" than to criticize American soldiers and the war itself. Samuel Stratton, a congressman from New York State who had served on MacArthur's staff in the South Pacific, also spoke at the event where many demonstrators carried posters proclaiming that "there is no substitute for victory."[6]

Not surprisingly, however, two of the most ardent opponents of the war in Vietnam and another crusade for total victory—Mark Hatfield and George McGovern—were also World War II vets. Like many of their generation, both men came home from war sobered by its harsh realities, skeptical of heroic views that privileged the achievements and losses of Americans over all others, and interested more in finding a path to world peace than a Cold War victory. Hatfield had been sent for a time to Vietnam in 1945 and came to sympathize with the Vietnamese struggle against French colonialism. McGovern served admirably as a bomber pilot in Europe but felt that ultimately World War II had demonstrated not so much the power and virtue of America but "man's inhumanity to man." He turned to ideals of internationalism and liberalism after the war in part because he felt a sense of "brotherhood" was necessary to restrain the cruel im-

pulses of mankind. It was this humanitarian perspective on the recently completed war that led him to come out strongly for Henry Wallace in 1948 and to
express admiration for his stand against militarism and nationalism. Drawing
on their memories of the "good war," these two senators became outspoken critics of the Vietnam War and in 1970 attempted to end the war by introducing a
measure in the Senate that would have cut off funding for American military operations in Southeast Asia and established a plan for withdrawing American
troops.[7]

By the 1980s it was already clear, however, that the public memory of Vietnam was moving away from damaging connotations of the destructive nature of
America and its warriors that had pervaded the late 1960s and early 1970s. Considerable attention was now directed to the issue of American POWs and to
charges that many of them were still missing and had been abandoned by their
government. The concern that these men were victims, in part, helped to move
the discussion over the war away from arguments that the nation had been a perpetrator of considerable violence upon the Vietnamese people. President Ronald
Reagan was at the forefront of this effort to revise the memory of Vietnam and
restore the myth of American innocence. During his run for the presidency in
1980, he had referred to Vietnam as a "noble crusade," a remark that evoked substantial public criticism at the time. But Reagan kept at it, and by 1988, in a Veteran's Day speech at the Vietnam Veterans Memorial, he felt confident enough
to present the case for incorporating the struggle in Southeast Asia into the same
mythical story that had already permeated the dominant public remembrance of
World War II. Intent on erasing any legacy of Americans as efficient killers, the
president referred to the men who fought in Vietnam as "gentle heroes" who "became champions of a noble cause." He acknowledged that citizens had been
deeply divided over the war, but he argued that, after a decade of seeing all of the
killing and turmoil that had taken place in Southeast Asia when Americans with-
drew, "Who can doubt that the cause for which our men fought was just?" Putting aside any critical version of war, he concluded that the soldiers who served
in Vietnam had left America a legacy of "love" for their families and for their
"buddies on the battlefield." And he proclaimed that the legacy and the nation's
love for its veterans was being reenacted every day with the placing of mementos
in front of the veterans memorial. McNamara would not invoke such sentimental language, but both men seemed ready to cast aside any idea that wars could
be simply tragic.[8]

Reagan's observation that the Vietnam memorial was now a site of national
healing at which the critical perspective on the war could be put aside was quite

astute. In a scholarly study of the effects of the Vietnam memorial, historian Patrick Hagopian found that a desire for healing and tempering the traumatic disruptions of the past continued well past its dedication in 1982. Thus he shows how the addition of statues near "the wall" dedicated to three fighting men of various races and a women's memorial served to bring representations of racial and gender accord to the public memory of the war and erase the reality of divisiveness that had dominated the political movements of the 1960s. Hagopian also found in many localities not only a replication of the practice of listing the dead—something that was quite common in World War II memorializations—but additional efforts to show unity such as statues of soldiers helping wounded comrades, females nurses helping injured men, and even letters exchanged between soldiers and those they cared about. He was also unable to find any mention of enemy dead, a pattern that would have been similar to World War II remembrances as well.[9]

From the perspective of our times, we can now also see that the men who fought in each of these contests ultimately tended to write about their experiences in similar ways. Many of the stories by Vietnam soldiers took the mythical version of World War II as a foil to construct their personal stories that they thought were in some ways unique. They assumed that the patriotic version of World War II was the only version that Americans held. Thus, many of them castigated the movies of John Wayne and Audie Murphy for giving them a false sense of what war was really like. Yet it is clear that soldiers in both wars saw their experience in critical terms and raised questions about heroic and patriotic views. In this regard, Philip Caputo is not so unlike James Jones. Caputo's account of his experience in Vietnam, A Rumor of War (1978), expressed a good deal of the cynicism that could be found in the works of earlier writers. Before he ever joined the Marines, Caputo remarked that he had already envisioned himself "charging up some beachhead like John Wayne in The Sands of Iwo Jima and then coming home a suntanned warrior with medals on my chest." In his autobiographical account of his Vietnam War experience, Ron Kovic explained that he had been duly impressed by watching Audie Murphy in To Hell and Back standing on a tank and firing at Germans troops. The movie version of Murphy's book was, indeed, a highly popular film in the mid-1950s. It is likely, however, that Kovic did not know that Murphy suffered trauma from his heroic actions and long years in combat. He kept his home filled with guns after 1945, often woke up in the middle of the night to fire them in a random fashion, and periodically turned the guns on his wife or himself without actually pulling the trigger. Murphy was also another World War II vet who held deep reservations over the war in Vietnam primarily because he feared that his two sons, who were approaching draft age in 1970, might want to go to Asia and try to replicate the heroics of their father.[10]

If the American public read books about the suffering of Vietnam veterans and heard speeches of the loving nature of the men who fought, over time they heard less and less about massive destruction Americans brought to Southeast Asia and terrible acts like the massacre at My Lai. Of course, such a pattern was consistent with the objectives of traditional forms of remembering that were always focused on the need to console citizens for their losses, enhance the reputation of the nation, and blunt the expression of empathy for all who suffered. My Lai had been the center of a huge public controversy when Americans learned that a unit of their troops had gunned down Vietnamese women and children in cold blood. William Calley, an officer in charge of the men implicated in the atrocity, was court-marshaled and convicted of murder in 1969. Like Hiroshima and Nagasaki, however, My Lai commanded less and less public reflection over time, and some scholars have argued that today it has virtually disappeared from the American memory of the war. Calley was let out of prison early. Even in Vietnam, references to the village where the killings took place cannot be found in tourist guides because officials do not want to lose some of the income American tourists can provide.[11]

Certainly, the remembrance of Vietnam still continues to resist complete absorption into a mythical story of American warfare. A trip to the National Museum of the Marine Corps in Triangle, Virginia, dedicated in 2006, underscores this point. The theme of "uncommon valor" is stressed in the space devoted to World War II. The central feature of the exhibit on this war is the battle of Iwo Jima, which is dominated by a wall of Marine Corps and Navy insignias—one for each man who fell. No photos of American casualties or listing of the names of the dead are to be found. Indeed, the entire external structure of the museum is designed to replicate the iconic image of the flag raising on the island in 1945. In contrast, the museum refers to Vietnam as a "political war" rather than a "military war," a reference to the belief that the nation's leaders did not allow the soldiers to pursue total victory. The centerpiece of the Vietnam exhibit is not about a victorious battle but about an episode whose outcome was more uncertain—the Marines' battle at Khe Sahn. Of course, it is still possible to see these wars in different ways at the national memorials in Washington that commemorate both events. The names of the dead stand out in the Vietnam Veterans Memorial; they do not appear at all in the memorial to World War II. Yet both memorials continue to serve, partially at least, as sites where individuals can come to heal past ruptures and derive a sense of honor.

Soldiers and veterans have dominated the public remembrance of World War II and, for that matter, most wars in modern America. In part, this is because they bore the brunt of the tragic aspects of the conflicts and witnessed much of the suffering and cruelty. The role they played as central agents of remembering was supplemented, however, by many other voices—including many who had no firsthand knowledge of the war at all. The desire to be part of a collective identity that was honorable was just as strong in the postwar generation as it was in the one that preceded it.

Generally sidetracked in this public remembering has been the issue of what war told anyone willing to listen about the problem of human nature. There were clearly moments in World War II when Americans performed honorably in fighting wicked forces in the world. Yet a true record of modern warfare—even in America—would make it clear that men and women everywhere were capable of unimaginable acts of brutality as well. Balanced perspectives, however, had a difficult time gaining traction in the public commemoration of World War II. Certainly, this was so because of the evil nature of enemy regimes. Yet the stark contrast between fascists and democrats was never enough to unify the outlooks of Americans on the war, and consequently the proponents of innocence and virtue had to mount a massive effort to quell the discontent, regret, and confusion that circulated through the hearts and minds of the wartime generation.

POSTSCRIPT ON IRAQ

THE INVASION OF IRAQ in 2003—like the war in Vietnam—brought another challenge to the long-term project to sustain a noble view of America and its wars. This was surprising in light of the fact that the assault on the dictatorship of Saddam Hussein began in a climate of patriotic unity and righteous vengeance after the terrorists attacks of September 11, 2001, on American soil. President George W. Bush was quick to place a moral frame on the terrorist act, a move that would immediately cast any American response into a mythical story of inno-cents facing evil forces in the world. And no better resource was available to him to bring clarity to the chaos of these events than the virtuous remembrance of World War II. Days after the assault, the president told Congress and a world television audience that the terrorists were antidemocratic forces that mankind had seen before in "all the murderous ideologies" of the twentieth century and fol-lowers of the "path of fascism, Nazism, and totalitarianism." Several months later, on the sixtieth anniversary of Pearl Harbor, he proclaimed that September 11, 2001, would now stand alongside December 7, 1941, as a moment in which "our way of life again was brutally and suddenly attacked." The chief executive urged citizens to remember the sacrifices of the "greatest of generations who de-feated tyranny" before as they embarked upon another struggle to "defend free-dom" and "secure civilization."[1]

Although the American government was quick to pinpoint the location of ter-rorist training camps in Afghanistan, President Bush retaliated for the attacks by sending the bulk of American forces to Iraq to topple the regime of Saddam Hussein, a brutal dictator whom the United States had already fought in 1991 in a successful effort to liberate Kuwait. Backed by support from the United King-dom, the Bush administration argued that the Iraqi dictator needed to be con-fronted sooner rather than later because he possessed weapons of mass destruction that could someday be used against the United States and because he had ties to al-Qaeda, the terrorist organization held responsible for the September 11 assault. Although Bush's preemptive strike against Iraq proved controversial, it was not an impulsive act. A doctrine of preemptive war—striking first to avert danger—had already been imagined and refined by conservative policy makers such as Bush's vice president, Dick Cheney, and his former aide, Paul Wolfowitz, after the Gulf War with Hussein in 1991. These conservative thinkers were devoted to one variant of the notion of American exceptionalism that was rooted in a belief that the unprecedented power the United States now held in world affairs after the fall of the Soviet Union required that it act unilaterally in any way it wished to ensure its own stability and advance its interests—even if it meant attacking another country.

The official rationales for war against Saddam and the surge of patriotism that followed the terrorists' attacks on American soil were soon challenged, however, by events in Iraq. No weapons of mass destruction were found, and no real evidence was produced that the dictator had meaningful ties to al-Qaeda. Furthermore, the assumption that the ending of a brutal dictatorship would lead to the emergence of democracy and freedom in Iraq was damaged by the emergence of an insurgency in the liberated nation that led to the deaths of thousands of American troops and many Iraqi civilians as well. There were even indications that many Iraqis were actually indifferent to the war, preferring to go about their own business as Americans, former loyalists to Saddam, and an influx of Islamic extremists went about killing each other. As the war in Iraq became more confusing and more costly, the virtue of the entire American effort was called into question. By 2008, officials who had called for the invasion in the first place were forced to defend their move, and others were looking for ways to withdraw American troops. Barack Obama was even running for the presidency, in part, on a platform that argued that Iraq was not the main front in the war on terror.

In our times critical perspectives on Iraq, less willing to justify American actions and human losses, have become widespread. The seeds of future debates over commemoration are already evident. For many Americans the invasion of Iraq came to resemble Vietnam more than World War II, a point that weakened rationales for why we had to fight. News of traumatic encounters with death on the part of American forces and Iraqi civilians served to undercut public support. Such cultural tensions are inevitable in war, of course. And in time, similar misgivings of citizens regarding both World War II and Vietnam gave way in varying degrees to traditionalist and patriotic outlooks. There is no reason, therefore, to believe that decades from now the same thing will not happen to the remembrance of Iraq. The War on Terrorism may eventually end in a way that is perceived as an American victory. Whether it does or not, the political and cultural imperative to remake all American wars into noble enterprises remains strong. And the demise of eyewitnesses will surely lessen the force of critical perspectives.

As with other wars, official views have been buttressed by the record of sacrifice and courage reflected by American servicemen. Popular support and sympathy for the troops has been strong. Sometimes, of course, individuals attempt to separate the merits of the war itself from the affection and concern they feel for those that fight, but this is not always an easy proposition. Patriotic ideals perform important functions in explaining why so many have to die. Thus, the connection citizens feel to the troops and their deeds has upheld and will continue to uphold virtuous frames on the war for years to come. An organization called Gathering of Eagles, for instance, has been formed to honor the men and women who served in Iraq and anywhere else on behalf of America. In its mission statement, the group asserted that it was impossible to back the troops and not support the wars they fought as well. The group also expressed a heroic view toward war memorials. They stated that memorial sites should be considered "sacred" places and not in any way convey an indictment of a conflict soldiers fought.

In 2007 in West Chester, Pennsylvania, a Navy veteran named Rich Davis began his own pro-war movement in response to local critics of the Iraq War. Davis, who said he had been raised to love his country and "not blame it," and his supporters congregated on a daily basis in public to wave American flags. In Flower Mound, Texas, in 2004, citizens organized a public celebration of the life of Marine Lance Corporal Jacob Lugo, the first serviceman from the town killed in Iraq, and renamed a local park in the fallen soldier's honor. And Mary Conboy, a mother who lost a son in Iraq, helped launch an organization called "Big Brothers-in-Arms," which attempted to pair up soldiers back from Iraq with veterans from former wars in an effort to help the returned warriors adjust and feel welcomed at home again.

As the war was being fought, books began appearing making the case for American warrior heroism. One powerful statement was Bing West's account of the battle for Fallujah. West was critical not so much of the war itself but of what he saw as indecisiveness on the part of American political and military leaders who delayed in giving clear orders to troops over whether to attack the Sunni insurgent stronghold of Fallujah in 2004. In part, the Bush administration wavered on this point for fear of negative publicity and possibly fueling support for the insurgents. The ultimate battle for the city was an intense one, however, featuring house-to-house fighting and the massive destruction of buildings and homes. West recorded the brave deeds of American forces not only in fighting insurgents but in saving their own comrades. He noted how the men were more than ready to fight for each other and for their nation's cause, and he lamented that it took authorities so long to give American troops a clear mission. He also regretted that the "Western press" gave more attention to wounded insurgents in the battle and the misconduct at Abu Ghraib prison than to "multiple incidents of bravery" exhibited by American soldiers. For this author and former Vietnam vet, one tragic remembrance of Fallujah was not the loss of life but the inattention paid to the nobility of the American fighters by the press; he worried that in commemorations to come "unsung, the noblest deed will die."[2]

The public's engagement with patriotic sacrifice and support for a war is always tenuous, however, and can easily shift into harsh criticism as losses mount or decisive victories fail to appear. Patriotic support can be sustained partially by minimizing knowledge about the human costs of the conflict. This was done fairly effectively in World War II. During the Iraq conflict, the government did attempt to do this to some extent by bringing the American dead back in secrecy to an air base in Delaware. At one point, a public affairs officer at Arlington National Cemetery actually lost her job because she tried to allow media coverage of funerals at the historic site. On balance, however, it was not difficult to find critical perspectives on the war in the American media, especially after revelations of torture of Iraqi prisoners of war by Americans at Abu Ghraib prison in 2004. Papers like the *New York Times* and the *Washington Post* mounted Web pages that listed the names (and many of the photos) of the American dead. The number of Iraqi civilians killed in the war became a public issue fraught with political implications as government and nongovernmental groups such as Iraq Body Count (a British-based organization), the Congressional Research Service, and the World Health Organization published various estimates of how many civilians were killed in Iraq.

Some Americans mounted individual protests against the war. In Brooklyn, New York, an empathetic artist named Carol Quint posted on line a drawing of a war memorial called "Iraqi women," which pictured grieving females standing in a "field of bones." Cindy Sheehan, the mother of an American soldier killed in Iraq, attracted considerable attention when she camped out near President Bush's ranch in Texas in 2005 to ask the commander-in-chief just what the "noble cause" was for which her son gave his life. Later, in a book, she recounted how some people can refuse to be consoled by patriotic language and see the sacrifice of loved ones in war not as a heroic act but as a rupture to their families and an irreplaceable loss. Defenders of traditional perspectives on war such as TV commentator Bill O'Reilly called Sheehan a "traitor," and other commentators called her a "nutcase." Yet Sheehan stood by her belief that the war was "illegal and immoral."[3]

Numerous other reports and books appeared that portrayed the conflict in Iraq not as a noble and justifiable war against evil terrorist but simply as a cauldron of chaos, death, and devastation. Reporter Dexter Filkins, offered an eyewitness account that stressed the extent to which many Iraqis were actually angry over the American presence in their land even after the fall of Saddam. Some Iraqis were further angered by what they saw as the indifference American troops displayed in the killing of innocent Iraq civilians, although Filkins documented remorse among some GIs over such deaths. Moreover, he made special efforts in his book to subvert the rhetoric he heard in Iraq from Bush administration officials like Paul Bremer about conditions improving, using his own interviews that documented the continued deaths, for instance, of Iraqi infants whose incubators shut down due to a lack of electricity. Home from the war, Filkins traveled to Arkansas to visit the family of an American soldier he had befriended. He noticed that photos of the fallen soldier had been placed on the red granite tombstone at his grave by parents who refused to forget the loss and pain of someone so "near and dear" and be comforted completely by official explanations for why he had to die.[4]

We cannot know how the Iraq War will be recalled in the decades to come, and we can only speculate as to what type of national memorial might be built to commemorate it. Certainly, the debate over remembering has already begun with the naming of parks, the placing of photos of the dead on local tombstones, and the publishing of both critical and noble accounts of what transpired. Events in Afghanistan may help shape the remembrance of Iraq in time; new perspectives may emerge—as the rise of Holocaust consciousness did—to reinforce more virtuous notions of what Americans fought for early in this century. Silences too may play a role, as they have in connection with Hiroshima and increasingly with My Lai. Abu Ghraib may become just a footnote in a larger story of victory over Islamic extremism. As long as America seeks to sustain its faith in the potential of the free individual and its sense of itself as a special nation among nations, powerful political and cultural forces will work to craft legendary tales of its wars and warriors and exonerate it from any sense of wrongdoing. There will be truth in these stories and evidence of noble and brave deeds. As these tales take their place in the long narrative of American memory, however, their power to persuade will hinge on just how much is forgotten.

Notes

INTRODUCTION

1. Kurt Vonnegut, *Slaughterhouse-Five, or the Children's Crusade: A Duty-Dance with Death* (New York: Delacorte, 1969). Vonnegut could not even be sure of how to title his novel of remembrance.

2. Candace Volker and Patchem Markall, "Introduction: Violence, Redemption, and the Liberal Imagination," *Public Culture* 15 (1): 1–10; Nancy Rosenblum, introduction to *Liberalism and the Moral Life* (Cambridge, MA: Harvard University Press, 1989), 5–7; Liah Greenfield, *Nationalism: Five Roads to Modernity* (Cambridge, MA: Harvard University Press, 1989), 400–402.

3. Kendall R. Phillips, introduction to *Framing Public Memory* (Tuscaloosa: University of Alabama Press, 2004), 3–9; Victor Turner, *Dramas, Fields, and Metaphors* (Ithaca, NY: Cornell University Press, 1974), 30–45; Richard Schechner, *Performance Theory* (New York: Routledge, 2003), xviii–xix, 186–87.

4. On the cultural celebration of the American victory and the "heroic individual," see Philip D. Beidler, *The Good War's Greatest Hits: World War II and American Remembering* (Athens: University of Georgia Press, 1998), 90–92; Thomas Englehardt, *The End of Victory Culture* (New York: Basic Books, 1995); Richard Slotkin, *Gunfighter Nation: The Myth of the Frontier in the Twentieth Century* (New York: Harper, 1992), 6. On public memory's importance to the sense of citizen attachment to the nation, see Carole Blair, Greg Dickson, and Brian Ott, "Rhetoric/Memory/Place," in *Memory Places: The Rhetoric of Museum and Memorials,* ed. Blair, Dickson, and Ott (Tuscaloosa: University of Alabama Press, forthcoming).

5. Jenny Edkins, *Trauma and the Memory of Politics* (Cambridge: Cambridge University Press, 2003), 10–19; Jay Winter, *Sites of Memory, Sites of Mourning: The Great War in European Cultural History* (Cambridge: Cambridge University Press, 1995), 1–6. Amy Kaplan, "Violent Belongings and the Question of Empire Today," *American Quarterly* 56 (March 2004): 1–18.

6. Drafts of Luce's unpublished book are located in box 83, folder 1, Henry Luce Papers, Library of Congress. A copy of his American Century essay can be found in *The Ideas of Henry Luce,* edited with an introduction by John K. Jessup (New York: Atheneum, 1969), 105–20.

7. Norman Cousins, *Modern Man Is Obsolete* (New York: Viking Press, 1945), 10–20; Reinhold Niebuhr, *The Irony of American History* (New York: Scribner's, 1952), 4–5, 19, 38. Niebuhr refers to a sense of innocence in the "official myth and collective memory" of the United States and other nations. Kevin Matson, *When America Was Great: The Fighting Faith of Postwar Liberalism* (New York: Routledge, 2004), 15–18. Luce did express recognition of the evil potential in human nature, but he used this idea to support continued military strength for the United States, which was apparently immune from this disease. See his speech "The Human Situation," box 72, folder 3, Luce Papers. On American identity, see also Rogers M. Smith, *Civic Ideals: Conflicting Visions of Citizenship in U.S. History* (New Haven, CT: Yale University Press, 1997), 1–5; Gary Gerstle, *American Crucible: Race and Nation in the Twentieth Century* (Princeton, NJ: Princeton University Press, 2001), 5. See Louis Hartz, *The Liberal Tradition in America* (New York: Harcourt, 1955) on the centrality of liberal individualism in American nationalism; Omer Bartov, *Mirrors of Destruction: War, Genocide, and Modern Identity* (New York: Oxford University Press, 2000), 16–17.

8. Slotkin, *Gunfighter Nation*, 91.

9. Studs Terkel, *"The Good War": An Oral History of World War II* (New York: New Press, 1984), 3–16; Paul Fussell, *The Great War in Modern Memory* (New York: Oxford University Press, 1975) and *Wartime: Understanding and Behavior in the Second World War* (New York: Oxford University Press, 1989). See the discussion on witnessing in Jay Winter, *Remembering War: The Great War between Memory and History in the Twentieth Century* (New Haven, CT: Yale University Press, 2006), 240–45. For an insightful discussion of the relationship between memory and accountability as a means to sustain claims of justice in the present, see W. James Booth, *Communities of Memory: On Witness, Identity, and Justice* (Ithaca, NY: Cornell University Press, 2006), 39–70. On the failure of traditional views to fully console people in Europe after World War I, see Susan Kingsley Kent, "Remembering the Great War," *Journal of British Studies* 37 (January 1998): 105–10. For an insightful discussion of the persistence of "traditionalism" in American cultural memory as a way to express nostalgia for a dream of individualism and self-reliance, see Michael Kammen, *Mystic Chords of Memory: The Transformation of Tradition in American Culture* (New York: Knopf, 1991), 299–301, 537.

10. John Bodnar, "Human Rights and the Legacy of World War II," *International Journal of the Humanities* 2 (2004): 137–46; Mary Ann Glendon, *A World Made New: Eleanor Roosevelt and the Universal Dream of Human Rights* (New York: Random House, 2001), 9–20; Kenneth Cmiel, "The Recent History of Human Rights," *American Historical Review* 109 (February 2004): 117–35; Samantha Powers, *A Problem from Hell: America and the Age of Genocide* (New York: Harpers, 2002), 54–83. Natalie Hevener Kaufman and David Whiteman, "Opposition to Human Rights Treaties in the United States Senate: The Legacy of the Bricker Amendment," *Human Rights Quarterly* 10 (1988): 309–37. On the utopian promises of nationalism to sanction violence in the pursuit of dreams, see Omer Bartov, *Mirrors of Destruction*, 154–57.

11. George Mosse argued that heroic myths had a more difficult time gaining traction in Europe after 1945 than after 1918 in "Two World Wars and the Myth of the War Experience," *Journal of Contemporary History* 21 (October 1986): 491–513; Catherine Merridale, *Night of Stone: Death and Memory in Twentieth Century Russia* (New York: Penguin, 2002),

22, 219; Michael Ignatieff, "Soviet War Memorials," *History Workshop Journal* 17 (Spring 1994): 157–63; Henry Rousso, *The Vichy Syndrome: History and Memory in France since 1944* (Cambridge, MA: Harvard University Press, 1991); Jeffrey K. Olick, "What Does it Mean to Normalize the Past? Official Memory in German Politics since 1989," in *States of Memory: Communities, Conflicts, and Transformations in National Retrospection*, ed. J. K. Olick (Durham, NC: Duke University Press, 2003), 259–88. On the power of patriotic forms of memory to heal wartime wounds, see Peter Lagrou, *The Legacy of the Nazi Occupation: Patriotic Memory and National Recovery in Western Europe, 1943–1965* (Cambridge: Cambridge University Press, 2000), 199, 211–17; Franziska Seraphim, *War, Memory, and Social Politics in Japan, 1945–2005* (Cambridge, MA: Harvard University Press, 2006), 1–20; Terry Eagleton, *Sweet Violence: The Idea of the Tragic* (London: Blackwell, 2003), ix–xvii.

12. On the stress on "human heroism," see Slotkin, *Gunfighter Nation*, 8–14, 347.

I. WARTIME

1. See Richard W. Steele, "American Popular Opinion and the War Against Germany," *Journal of American History* 65 (December 1978): 704–23; John Morton Blum, *V Was for Victory: Politics and Culture During World War II* (New York: Harcourt, 1976), 46. See also Kenneth D. Rose, *Myth and the Greatest Generation: A Social History of America in World War II* (New York: Routledge, 2008), 62.

2. Mark Kleinman, *A World of Hope, a World of Fear: Henry A. Wallace, Reinhold Niebuhr, and American Liberalism* (Columbus: Ohio State University Press, 2000, 1–7; Alan Dawley, *Changing the World: American Progressives in War and Revolution* (Princeton, NJ: Princeton University Press, 2003), 5–7; Louis B. Sohn, *The Human Rights Movement: From Roosevelt's Four Freedoms to the Interdependence of Peace, Development, and Human Rights* (Cambridge, MA: Harvard Law School Human Rights Program, 1995), 4–7; Elizabeth Borgwardt, *A New Deal for the World: America's Vision for Human Rights* (Cambridge, MA: Harvard University Press, 2005), 20; Susan A. Brewer, *Why America Fights: Patriotism and War Propaganda from the Philippines to Iraq* (New York: Oxford University Press, 2009), 88–90; see Francois Furet, "Democracy and Utopia," *Journal of Democracy* 9 (January 1998): 65–79.

3. Borgwardt, *A New Deal for the World*, 27–29.

4. Carol Anderson, *Eyes Off the Prize: The United Nations and the African-American Struggle for Human Rights, 1944–45* (Cambridge: Cambridge University Press, 2003), 14–19.

5. Robert B. Westbrook, *Why We Fought: Forging American Obligations in World War II* (Washington, D.C.: Smithsonian Books, 2004), 40–46; Susan Herbst, "Illustrator, American Icon and Public Opinion Theorist: Norman Rockwell and Democracy," *Political Communication* 21 (March 2004): 1–22. Not all artists saw the nation and the war in the same way. Thomas Hart Benton and Ben Shahn became "disillusioned" by the implications of the war for the idea of human progress. See Stephen Polcari, "Ben Shahn and Postwar American Art," in *Common Man, Mythic Vision: The Painting of Ben Shahn*, ed. Susan Chevlowe (Princeton, NJ: Princeton University Press, 1998), 67–109.

6. Allan M. Winkler, *The Politics of Propaganda: The Office of War Information, 1942–1945* (New Haven, CT: Yale University Press, 1978); Gary Gerstle, *Working-Class Americanism* (Cambridge: Cambridge University Press, 1989), 289. 310; Clayton R. Koppes and

Gregory D. Black, *Hollywood Goes to War: How Politics, Profits, and Propaganda Shaped World War II* (Berkeley: University of California Press, 1987), 66–70; Thomas Doherty, *Projections of War: Hollywood, American Culture, and World War II* (New York: Columbia University Press, 1993), 70–75; Barbara Diane Savage, *Broadcasting Freedom: Radio, War and the Politics of Race, 1938–1948* (Chapel Hill: University of North Carolina Press, 1999), 121–22; Michele Himes, *Radio Voices: American Broadcasting, 1922–1952* (Minneapolis: University of Minnesota Press, 1997), 230–43; Barry Schwartz, "Memory as a Cultural System: Abraham Lincoln in World War II," *American Sociological Review* 61 (October 1996): 908–27.

7. Cass R. Sunstein, *The Second Bill of Rights: FDR's Unfinished Revolution and Why We Need It More than Ever* (New York: Basic Books, 2004), 11–16.

8. Steele, "American Popular Opinion and the War Against Germany," 716; Sydney Weinberg, "What to Tell America: The Writers Quarrel in the Office of War Information," *Journal of American History* 55 (June 1968): 73–89.

9. John Morton Blum, *Liberty, Justice, and Order: Writings on Past Politics* (New York: Norton, 1993), 185; Winkler, *Politics of Propaganda*, 5–6, 50, 66–67, 73–77; Alan Nevins, "What Did the American People Think Once It Was in Process," in *While You Were Gone: A Report on Wartime Life in the United States*, ed. Jack Goodman (New York: Simon and Schuster, 1946), 17; Godfrey Hodgson, *The World Turned Right Side Up* (Boston: Houghton-Mifflin, 1996), 14.

10. Blum, *Liberty, Justice, and Order*, 173–74, notes that Wallace felt that Roosevelt was becoming more interested in winning the war as it dragged on than in promoting liberal dreams. Kleinman, *A World of Fear*, 7, 143–46, 172–73.

11. Archibald MacLeish, "For This We Fight" and "It Is What We Are," copies of speeches in box 43, MacLeish Papers, Library of Congress. Also see Clive Bush, "Left-Wing Isolationism, Literature, and Ideology in America during the Run-Up to World War II," *Comparative American Studies: An International Journal* 1 (2003): 131–52.

12. See Howard Jones, "One World: An American Perspective," in *Wendell Willkie: Hoosier Internationalist*, ed. James H. Madison (Bloomington: Indiana University Press, 1993), 165, 180–90.

13. See the letters to Willkie in "One World" file, Wendell Willkie Papers, Lilly Library, Indiana University, Bloomington. See also Donald Bruce Johnson, *The Republican Party and Wendell Willkie* (Urbana: University of Illinois Press, 1960), 236–60; David A. Hollinger, *Postethnic America: Beyond Multiculturalism* (New York: Basic Books, 2000), 52–53.

14. See Carol Anderson, *Eyes Off the Prize: The United Nations and the Struggle for Human Rights, 1944–1955* (Cambridge: Cambridge University Press, 2003), 80–82; 131–32; Mary Ann Glendon, *A World Made New: Eleanor Roosevelt and the Universal Declaration of Human Rights* (New York: Random House, 2001), xviii, 9, 19, 150–56. Mary Ann Dudziak, *Cold War Civil Rights* (Princeton, NJ: Princeton University Press, 2000), 5.

15. Mackinley Kantor, *Happy Land* (New York: McCann, 1942). See the following letters to Mackinley Kantor: A. Auhlke, Feb. 25, 1943; A. W. Foster, May 27, 1943; E. Bucke, July 5, 1943; F. Flack, Dec. 18, 1943; P. Kane, Feb. 28 1943; M. Plunkett, Aug. 13, 1943, in box 25, folder 5, Kantor Papers, Library of Congress. See also Dana B. Polan, *Power and Paranoia: History, Narrative, and the American Cinema, 1940–1950* (New York: Columbia

University Press, 1986), 124–30, 253. Robert B. Westbrook, "Fighting for the American Family: Private Interests and Political Obligation in World War II," in *The Power of Culture*, ed. Richard Wightman Fox and T. J. Jackson Lears (Chicago: University of Chicago Press, 1993), 195–221.

16. Polan, *Power and Paranoia*, 124–30, 253. Howard Blue, *Words at War: World War II Era Radio Drama and the Postwar Broadcasting Industry Blacklist* (Lanham, MD: Scarecrow Press, 2002), 2–3, 18, 167–74; see also Albert Wertheim, *Staging the War: American Drama during World War II* (Bloomington: Indiana University Press, 2004), 185–87; Jody Rosen, *White Christmas: The Story of an American Song* (New York: Scribner, 2002); Kathleen E. R. Smith, *God Bless America: Tin Pan Alley Goes to War* (Lexington: University of Kentucky Press, 2003), 9, 21–24.

17. Mark H. Leff, "The Politics of Sacrifice on the Home Front in World War II," *Journal of American History* 77 (March 1991): 1296–318. William M. Tuttle, *Daddy's Gone to War: The Second World War in Children's Lives* (New York: Oxford University Press, 1993), 49–51; Jerry Purvis Sanson, *Louisiana During World War II: Politics and Society, 1939–1945* (Baton Rouge: Louisiana State University Press, 1999), 218–19; Roger W. Lotchin, *The Bad City in the Good War: San Francisco, Los Angeles, Oakland, and San Diego* (Bloomington: Indiana University Press, 2003), 64.

18. See Eric Sevareid, *Not So Wild a Dream* (New York: Atheneum, 1946), 213–21; Richard R. Lingeman, *Don't You Know There's a War On: The American Home Front, 1941–1945* (New York: Capricorn, 1976), 72, 81, 281–82.

19. Louis Farichild, *They Called It the War Effort: Oral Histories from World War II Orange, Texas* (Austin, TX: Eakins Press, 1993), 2–5, 20–21, 111–18, 220.

20. Reuben Hill, *Families Under Stress: Adjustment to the Crises of War Separation and Reunion* (New York: Harper, 1949), 6, 50–63. Susan M. Hartmann, *The Home Front and Beyond: American Women in the 1940s* (Boston: Twayne, 1982). For an excellent discussion of "latchkey" children, see Tuttle, *Daddy's Gone to War*, 69–90.

21. Sheerie A. Kossoudji and Laura J. Dresser, "Working-Class Rosies: Women Industrial Workers during World War II," *Journal of Economic History* 52 (June 1992): 431–36; Maureen Honey, *Creating Rosie the Riveter: Class, Gender, and Propaganda during World War II* (Amherst: University of Massachusetts Press, 1984), 1–17.

22. See Susan Gubar, "This Is My Rifle, This Is My Gun: World War II and the Blitz on Women," in *Behind the Lines: Gender and the Two World Wars*, ed. Margaret Higonnet et al. (New Haven, CT: Yale University Press, 1987), 27–59.

23. Katherine Archibald, *Wartime Shipyard: A Study in Social Discontinuity* (Berkeley: University of California Press, 1947), 64–65; Lingeman, *Don't You Know There is a War On*, 77–78.

24. Lingeman, *Don't You Know There's a War On*, 329; Harvard Sitkoff, "Racial Militancy and Interracial Violence in the Second World War," *Journal of American History* 58 (December 1971): 661–81; James A. Burran, "Urban Racial Violence in the South during World War II: A Comparative Overview," in *From the Old South to the New: Essays on the Transitional South*, ed. Walter J. Fraser and Winfred B. Moore (Westport, CT: Greenwood, 1981); Adam Fairclough, *Race and Democracy: The Civil Rights Struggle in Louisiana, 1915–1972* (Athens: University of Georgia Press, 1995), 74–77; Barbara Dennis, "Second Front:

Racial Violence and Black Soldiers in Alexandria During World War II" (master's thesis, Louisiana State University, 1999), 36, 58–60; Luis Alvarez, "Zoot Violence on the Home Front," in *Mexican-Americans in World War II*, ed. Maggie Rivas-Rodriquez (Austin: University of Texas Press, 2005), 141–75; Mauricio Mazon, *The Zoot-Suit Riots: The Psychology of Symbiotic Action* (Austin: University of Texas Press, 1984), 64–69.

25. Archibald, *Wartime Shipyard*, 185–223.

26. Fairchild, *They Called It the War Effort*, 208–15; Thomas Saylor, *Remembering the Good War: Minnesota's Greatest Generation* (St. Paul: Minnesota Historical Society, 2005), 107–8; 116. Thomas Childers, *Wings of Mourning: The Story of the Last American Bomber Shot Down over Germany in World War II* (Reading, MA: Addison-Wesley, 1995), 203–19.

27. Peter Schrijvers, *The Crash of Ruin: American Combat Soldiers in Europe during World War II*, 57; Peter Kindsvatter, *American Soldiers: Ground Combat in the World Wars, Korea, and Vietnam* (Lawrence: University of Kansas Press, 2003), 8.

28. Samuel Hynes, *The Soldier's Tale: Bearing Witness to Modern War* (New York: Penguin, 1998), 14, 30, stresses the predominance of personal matters to the men over "big abstractions." Andrew Carroll, ed., *War Letters: Extraordinary Correspondence from American Wars* (New York: Washington Square, 2001), 199–200, 230–31.

29. Carroll, ed., *War Letters*, 197–98, 201–3, 214, 230–31, 310–11. On racial issues in the service, see Gwendolyn Hall, *Love, War, and the 96th Engineers* (Urbana: University of Illinois Press, 1995), 237.

30. Samuel A. Stouffer et al., *The American Soldier: Adjustment during Army Life* (Princeton, NJ: Princeton University Press, 1949), 1:431–32, 440.

31. Peter Schrijvers, *The GI War Against Japan: American Soldiers and the Pacific During World War II* (New York: New York University Press, 2007), 7–34; Craig Cameron, *American Samurai: Myth, Imagination, and the Conduct of Battle in the First Marine Division* (Cambridge: Cambridge University Press, 1994), 49, 74–76, 115–17.

32. Samuel P. Huntington, *The Soldier and the State: The Theory and Politics of Civil-Military Relations* (Cambridge, MA: Harvard University Press, 1957), 90–91; Gerald Linderman, *The World Within War: America's Combat Experience in World War II* (Cambridge, MA: Harvard University Press, 1997), 185–87; Benjamin Alpers, *Dictators, Democracy, and American Public Culture* (Chapel Hill: University of North Carolina Press, 2003), 165–66. For a critical perspective on the way war appeared to cheapen the value of the individual, see John Ciardi, *The War Diary of John Ciardi* (Fayetteville: University of Arkansas Press, 1988), 101.

33. Linderman, *World Within War*, 184–87; Fussell, *Wartime*, 79–81.

34. Barett McGurn, *Yank: The Army Weekly* (Golden, CO: Fulcrum Publishing, 2004), 55, 67–68, 109, 136–38.

35. Linderman, *World Within War*, 263–99; Joanna Bourke, *An Intimate History of Killing: Face to Face Killing in the Twentieth Century* (New York: Basic Books, 1999), 130; Fussell, *Wartime*, 3–18; William Manchester, *Goodbye Darkness* (Boston: Little, Brown, 1979), 39.

36. Bourke, *An Intimate History of Killing*, 13, 53, 169, argues that battle stories from Vietnam were more "confessional" and revealed a sense of guilt, whereas those from World War II showed less signs of regret. James Weingartner, "Massacre at Bari: Patton and an American War Crime," *The Historian* 52 (November 1989): 24–39; James Weingart-

ner, "Trophies of War: U.S. Troops and the Mutilation of Japanese War Dead, 1941–1945," *Pacific Historical Review* 61 (February 1992): 53–67; Schrijvers, *Crash of Ruin*, 75–79; Schrijvers, *GI War Against Japan*, 216; Laurence Leamer, *The Kennedy Men, 1901–1963: The Laws of the Father* (New York: Harper, 2001), 206–11.

37. John Costello, *Virtue Under Fire: How World War II Changed Our Social and Sexual Attitudes* (Boston: Little, Brown, 1985), 95–98; Schrijvers, *Crash of Ruin*, 177–83; Schrijvers, *GI War Against Japan*, 211.

38. Ernie Pyle, *Brave Men* (New York: W.W. Norton, 1944), 3; Bill Mauldin, *Up Front* (New York: Henry Holt, 1945), 3–5, 15; Todd DePastino, *Bill Mauldin: A Life Up Front* (New York: W.W. Norton, 2008), 117, 143; Philip Knightley, *The First Casualty: The War Correspondent as Hero and Myth-Maker from Crimea to Iraq* (Baltimore: Johns Hopkins University Press, 2004), 352–57.

39. Mauldin, *Up Front*, 6–9, 41. On Mauldin's treatment of the death of Marshall and Bradley, see Stephen Ambrose's introduction to the edition of *Up Front* published in 2000 by W.W. Norton. Pyle, *Brave Men*, 106–107.

40. Mauldin, *Up Front*, 7, 12–15; Pyle, *Brave Men*, 19, 124–40. John Hersey, *A Bell for Adano* (Garden City, NY: Knopf, 1944). On Pyle's cynicism, see Andrew J. Huebner, *The Warrior Image: Soldiers in American Culture from the Second World War to the Vietnam Era* (Chapel Hill: University of North Carolina Press, 2008), 276.

2. SOLDIERS WRITE THE WAR

1. Paul Fussell, *Thank God for the Atom Bomb and Other Essays* (New York: Summit Books, 1988), 53–81.

2. James Dawes, *The Language of War: Literature and Culture in the U.S. from the Civil War through World War II* (Cambridge, MA: Harvard University Press, 2002), 157–91, suggests how the experience of World War II left the impression on many that large organizations and bureaucracies would now limit the ability of the "rational, interest-seeking individual" to shape their own future. On bearing witness as resistance to forgetting, see W. James Booth, *Communities of Memory: On Witness, Identity, Justice* (Ithaca, NY: Cornell University Press, 2006), 72–83; Malcolm Cowley, "Two Wars—and Two Generations," *New York Times*, July 25, 1948, BR 1; Yuval Noah Harari, "Martial Illusions: War and Disillusionment in Twentieth-Century and Renaissance Military Memoirs," *Journal of Military History* 69 (January 2005): 43–72.

3. Dawes, *Language of War*, 32–45; Amy Kaplan, *The Social Construction of American Realism* (Chicago: University of Chicago Press, 1988), 11–12. On the point that modern literature tends to feature the contradictions and struggles of private life and therefore can subvert attempts to create a more mythical public image of the nation, see Simon During, "Nationalism's Other: The Case for Revision," in *Narrating the Nation*, ed. Homi K. Bhabha (London: Routledge, 1990), 138–53. *Life's Picture History of World War II* (New York: Time Inc., 1950).

4. On Mailer's own war experience, see Robert Jay Lifton and Greg Mitchell, *Hiroshima in America: Fifty Years of Denial* (New York: G. P. Putnam, 1995), 238. Norman Mailer to David Pressman, Nov. 16, 1948, correspondence folder 521.2, Mailer Papers, Harry Ran-

som Center, University of Texas, Austin. Norman Mailer, "The White Negro," *Dissent* (Fall 1957).

5. Norman Mailer, *The Naked and the Dead* (New York: Rinehart, 1948), 156–66, 223–29, 374–76.

6. See ibid., 174–75, for the discussion about a "Century of the Common Man." See A. Osil to Norman Mailer, May 8, 1948, general correspondence folder 520.8; M. Loeb to Mailer, June 24, 1948, correspondence folder 521.1; E. Neilsen, to Mailer, Oct., 1948, correspondence folder 521.2; D. Pressman to Mailer, Sept. 9, 1948, correspondence folder 521.2; R. Ruden to Mailer, Nov. 29, 1948, correspondence folder 522.3, all in Mailer Papers. The quote that the book reflects a "war without dignity" is from a review in *Time*, May 10, 1948, 106–109. The view that the book reflected the "brutality" of modern war is expressed in David Dempsey, "The Dusty Answer to Modern War," *New York Times*, May 9, 1948, BR 6.

7. James Jones, *From Here to Eternity* (New York: Scribner's, 1951), 850.

8. Ibid., 209, 264.

9. Ibid., 270–72.

10. James Jones, *The Thin Red Line* (New York: Charles Scribner's Sons, 1972), 74, 171–72, 291, 350.

11. James Jones, *Whistle* (New York: Delta, 1978), 49.

12. Ibid., 82–83, 132–34, 394, 410.

13. Joseph Heller, *Catch-22* (New York: Knopf, 1995), 213–14. See the incisive introduction to this edition by Malcolm Bradbury on war and fiction.

14. Ibid., 276–77.

15. William Bradford Huie, *The Execution of Private Slovik* (New York: Duell, Sloan, and Pearce; and Boston: Little, Brown, 1954), 27.

16. Ibid., 53, 132.

17. Reviews of Huie's 1954 book are collected in box 18, file 168 and 170, William Bradford Huie Papers, Ohio State University. On Huie's critique of Eisenhower, see the epilogue to the second edition (New York: Dell, 1970). Huie also critiqued Eisenhower in the *New York Times*, Feb. 28, 1963, 8. On the story of Frank Sinatra trying to make a movie of the film, see Ellen Cohn, "The Resurrection of Private Slovik," *New York Times*, March 10, 1974, 109. S. L. A. Marshall, "The Line of Duty," *New York Times*, April 25, 1954, BR 3; Mark Harris critiques Marshall in the *New York Times*, June 27, 1954. Huie continued to express reservations about the way the military conducted World War II in his 1959 book, which became a Hollywood film, *The Americanization of Emily*. For a recollection of the Huie point that argues that many American men deserted in the face of the oncoming enemy during the Battle of the Bulge where Slovik was stationed and thus that the decision to kill Slovik (despite his guilt) was unjust, see Benedict B. Kimmelman, "The Example of Private Slovik," *American Heritage* 38 (September/October 1987). Kimmelman was an army captain who was present at the actual court martial.

18. Claude Eatherly and Gunther Anders, *Burning Conscience* (London: Weidenfeld and Nicolson, 1961), 21, 38, 81. William Bradford Huie, *The Hiroshima Pilot* (New York: G. P. Putnam, 1964), 7–20, 160, 313.

19. James Gould Cozzens, *Guard of Honor* (New York: Harcourt Brace, 1948), 195, 216,

232, 237–41. See also Matthew J. Bruccoli, *James Gould Cozzens: A Life Apart* (San Diego: Harcourt, Brace, Jovanovich, 1983), 156–83.

20. Richard Brooks, *The Brick Foxhole* (New York: Harpers, 1945), 206, 237.

21. Audie Murphy, *To Hell and Back* (New York: Henry Holt, 1949), 83, 154, 177, 264, 273.

22. William Manchester, *Goodbye Darkness: A Memoir of the Pacific War* (Boston: Little Brown, 1979), 10, 246–48. Manchester's letters to his mother during the war reflect a much narrower and more personal frame on the war than his book that reflects more broadly on the many issues involving war and identity that circulated in the 1970s. See letters to his mother in 1943 in box 1, William Manchester Papers, University of Massachusetts, Amherst.

23. Manchester, *Goodbye Darkness*, 25, 28, 127.

24. Ibid., 67–68, 232–33, 391.

25. E. B. Sledge, *With the Old Breed: At Peleliu and Okinawa* (New York: Oxford University Press, 1981), 5, 16.

26. Ibid., 140–41.

27. Craig Cameron, *American Samurai: Myth, Imagination, and the Conduct of Battle in the First Marine Division, 1941–1951* (Cambridge: Cambridge University Press, 1994), 64–81. A more critical account of basic training can be found in Robert Leckie, *Helmet for My Pillow* (New York: Random House, 1957).

28. Sledge, *With the Old Breed*, 120–21.

29. Ibid., 100, 125, 143–47. See also Kenneth D. Rose, *Myth and the Greatest Generation: A Social History of America in World War II* (New York: Routledge, 2008), 61.

30. Sledge, *With the Old Breed*, 217–18, 235, 315. On Murphy's postwar nightmares and suffering, see Charles Whiting, *Hero: The Life and Death of Audie Murphy* (Chelsea, MI: Scarborough House, 1990), 240–41.

31. Paul Fussell, *Doing Battle: The Making of a Skeptic* (Boston: Little, Brown, 1996), 18–22.

32. Ibid., 96–105, 124.

33. Ibid., 124.

34. Ibid., 171–73, 245, 295.

35. John Horne Burns, *The Gallery* (New York: New York Review Books, 2004). This edition contains an insightful introduction by Paul Fussell.

36. James Michener, *Tales of the South Pacific* (New York: Macmillan, 1946), 119, 123, 142–43.

37. See Cameron, *American Samurai*, 75–79; Michener, *Tales of the South Pacific*, 193, 215, 378–79.

3. "NO PLACE FOR WEAKLINGS"

1. Michael Sherry, *In the Shadow of War: The United States since 1930* (New Haven, CT: Yale University Press, 1995), 123–36. Truman's reaction to what he saw in Berlin is noted in the *New York Times*, Aug. 10, 1945, 12.

2. *The Family of Man* (New York: Museum of Modern Art, 1955); Eric J. Sandeen, *Pic-

turing an Exhibition: The Family of Man and 1950s America (Albuquerque: University of New Mexico Press, 1995), 1–7; Sandeen states that the exhibit offered a rhetoric of "amelioration" (p. 159). Stephen J. Whitfield, *The Culture of the Cold War* (Baltimore: Johns Hopkins University Press, 1996), 59–60.

3. Paul Boyer, *By the Bomb's Early Light: American Thought and Culture at the Dawn of the Atomic Age* (Chapel Hill: University of North Carolina Press, 1994), 12, 258–65. John Bodnar, *Blue-Collar Hollywood: Liberalism, Democracy, and Working People in American Film* (Baltimore: Johns Hopkins University Press, 2003), 85–102. Laura McEnaney, *Civil Defense Begins at Home: Militarization Meets Everyday Life in the Fifties* (Princeton, NJ: Princeton University Press, 2000), 62–74, 119.

4. On the fear of another war, see Mark Silk, *Spiritual Politics: Religion and America since World War II* (New York: Simon and Schuster, 1988), 33; Diane Kirby, "Religion and the Cold War—An Introduction," in *Religion and the Cold War*, ed. Kirby (New York: Palgrave, 2003), 3. See also David Greenberg, *Nixon's Shadow: The History of an Image* (New York: Norton, 2003), chap. 2.

5. Jonathan Schoenwald, *A Time for Choosing: The Rise of American Conservatism* (New York: Oxford University Press, 2001), 8, 19–20, 31; Silk, *Spiritual Politics*, 31–33, 56.

6. See M. J. Heale, *American Anticommunism: Combating the Enemy Within, 1930–1970* (Baltimore: Johns Hopkins University Press, 1990), 3–4, 123–25, 143–45; John Fousek, *To Lead the World: American Nationalism and the Cultural Roots of the Cold War* (Chapel Hill: University of North Carolina, 2000), 16–18, 41–42. Bodnar, *Blue-Collar Hollywood*, 88.

7. "A Message from Erle Cocke Jr.," *American Legion Magazine* 49 (Nov. 1950): 38–39; Robert Bullard, "What We're Up Against," *American Legion Magazine* 34 (Jan. 1943): 1. See Athan Theoharis, "The FBI and the American Legion Contact Program, 1940–1960," *Political Science Quarterly* 100 (Summer 1985): 271–86; William Pencak, *For God and Country: The American Legion, 1919–1941* (Boston: Northeastern University Press, 1989).

8. See Jonathan M. Hansen, *The Lost Promise of Patriotism: Debating American Identity, 1890–1920* (Chicago: University of Chicago Press, 2003), 143–51. *American Legion Magazine* 35 (Sept. 1943); 34 (May 1944): 6.

9. Robert Eunson, "The Kid from Idaho," *American Legion Magazine* 35 (Dec. 1944): 25, 38; Kenneth Foree, "The Flag That Wouldn't Stay Down," *American Legion Magazine* 49 (June 1950): 11–13, 48–49.

10. On the postwar repression of gay men, see David K. Johnson, *The Lavender Scare: The Cold War Persecution of Gays and Lesbians in the Federal Government* (Chicago: University of Chicago Press, 2004); see also Allan Berube, *Coming Out Under Fire: The History of Gay Men and Women in World War II* (New York: Free Press, 1990), 57–65. J. Shea, "To the Boy Back Home," *American Legion Magazine* 34 (Jan. 1943): 3; H. M. Forgy, "Faith Under Fire," *American Legion Magazine* 37 (July 1944): 1, 13. Lawrence S. Wittner, *Rebels Against War: The American Peace Movement, 1933–1983* (Philadelphia: Temple University Press, 1984), 100–101. Richard H. Palmer, "Moral Re-Armament Drama: Right-Wing Theater in America," *Theater Journal* 31 (May 1979): 172–85; *New York Times*, Feb. 2, 1953, 13.

11. David Camelon, "I Saw the G.I. Bill Written," *American Legion Magazine* 47 (Sept. 1949): 11–13, 46–50. Jennifer D. Keene, *Doughboys, the Great War and the Remaking of America* (Baltimore: Johns Hopkins University Press, 2001), 186–97, 205–12. Lizabeth

Cohen, *A Consumers Republic: The Politics of Mass Consumption in Postwar America* (New York: Vintage, 2003), 137; Margot Canaday, "Building a Straight State: Sexuality and Social Citizenship under the 1944 G.I. Bill," *Journal of American History* 90 (Dec. 2003), 935–57. Suzanne Mettler, *Soldiers to Citizens: The G.I. Bill and the Making of the Greatest Generation* (New York: Oxford University Press, 2005), 6–7, 136–43, noted that some blacks who became active in the postwar civil rights struggle benefited from the educational and job training aspects of the bill.

12. Henry J. Taylor, "How to Win the Peace," *American Legion Magazine* 36 (Jan. 1944): 14–15. Tom Connally, "The Charter Declares Peace," *American Legion Magazine* 39 (Oct. 1945): 3, 9, 29–30. Wythe Williams, "Breathing Time—How Long?" *American Legion Magazine* 42 (Dec. 1947): 14–15; Erle Cocke, "Who Is Letting Our G.I.s Down?" *American Legion Magazine* 50 (May 1951): 29–30.

13. Justin Gray, *The Inside Story of the Legion* (New York: Boni and Gaer, 1948), 191–204.

14. Joseph Walwik, *The Peekskill, New York, Anti-Communist Riots of 1949* (Leiston: Edwin Mellen Press, 2002), 2–3, 53–64. Philip Jenkins, *The Cold War at Home: The Red Scare in Pennsylvania, 1945–1960* (Chapel Hill: University of North Carolina Press, 1999), 41–56. Richard Fried, *The Russians Are Coming, the Russians Are Coming* (New York: Oxford University Press, 1998), 51–58; 67–77. Samuel G. Freedman, *The Inheritance: How Three Families and the American Political Majority Moved from Left to Right* (New York: Touchstone, 1996), 130, noted that the local Legion post in nearby Crotonville, New York, chose not to participate in the action in Peekskill because they were too busy with "local projects."

15. Charles Bolte, *The New Veteran* (New York: Reynal and Hitchcock, 1945), 92–97; Robert L. Tyler, "The American Veterans Committee: Out of a Hot War and into the Cold," *American Quarterly* 18 (Fall 1966): 419–36.

16. *Bulletin of the American Veterans Committee*, June 15, 1945, copy in box 33, National Association for the Advancement of Colored People (NAACP) Papers, Library of Congress; Tyler, "The American Veterans Committee," 419–361; Bolte, *New Veteran*, 92–97; 101, 104–105.

17. Chat Paterson to Walter White, March 3, 1947, box B3, NAACP Papers. Mauldin's views are expressed in an AVC news release, Feb. 22, 1953, box 2, William H. Mauldin Papers, Library of Congress. Bolte discussed an episode in Oregon in 1944 in which a American Legion post removed the names of Japanese American servicemen from a local honor roll, an act repudiated by the national Legion office in Bolte, *New Veteran*, 54–77. See also *New York Times*, Dec. 12, 1944, 13.

18. P. Indritz to Thurgood Marshall, Aug. 2, 1954, box B3, NAACP Papers.

19. F. Williams to O. Bradley, Nov. 18, 1946, box B207; D. J. Dupuy to Thurgood Marshall, May 18, 1944; R. Jeanette Ivy to Thurgood Marshall, May 12, 1944; Emory Jackson to Thurgood Marshall, May 5, 1944; Donald Flascoff to Julia Baxter, May 18, 1944, box B2, NAACP Papers.

20. Donald Becker, "The Veteran: Problem and Challenge," *Social Forces* 25 (Oct. 1946): 95–99; R. Alton Lee, "The Army Mutiny of 1946," *Journal of American History* 53 (Dec. 1966): 555–71; Robert E. Humphrey, *Once Upon a Time in War: The 99th Division in*

World War II (Norman: University of Oklahoma Press, 2008), 307; Michael Gambone, *The Greatest Generation Comes Home: The Veteran in American Society* (College Station: Texas A&M University Press, 2005), 42; *Washington Post*, March 2, 1946, 5.

21. On the Haverhill parade, see Haverhill War Records Committee, *Haverhill in World War II* (Haverhill, MA, 1946). Eliza K. Pavalko and Glen K. Elder, "World War II and Divorce," *American Journal of Sociology* 95 (March 1990): 1213–34; David Gerber, "In Search of Al Schmid: War Hero, Blinded Veteran, Everyman," *Journal of American Studies* 29 (1991): 1–32; Thomas Childers, *Soldier from the War Returning: The Greatest Generation's Troubled Homecoming from World War II* (Boston: Houghton Mifflin Harcourt, 2009); Freedman, *The Inheritance*, 130–34; Tom Matthews, *Our Father's War: Growing Up in the Shadow of the Greatest Generation* (New York: Broadway Books, 2005), 13–28, 231–33; Lori Rotskoff, *Love on the Rocks: Men, Women, and Alcohol in Post-World War II America* (Chapel Hill: University of North Carolina Press, 2002), 136–37, explains the growth of Alcoholics Anonymous. Robert Havighurst et al., *The American Veteran Back Home: A Study of Veteran's Readjustment* (New York: Longmans, Green, 1951), 24–32, 51, 71, 142–43, 206–14.

22. John Kiernan, "UMT—A Must," *American Legion Magazine* 40 (March 1946): 9, 62–63; Rupert Hughes, "Make the Training Military," *American Legion Magazine* 38 (March 1945): 20, 29–30; Edward C. Elliott, "An Educator Looks at UMT," *American Legion Magazine* 38 (April 1945): 19, 46.

23. *Universal Military Training*, February 1945, and *World Peace is a Possibility if UMT is Obtained and Maintained*, February 1952, Pamphlet File, American Legion Archives, Indianapolis. See the argument that UMT would make the U.S. more "warlike" in Booth Tarkington, "Opposing UMT," *American Legion Magazine* 39 (April 1945): 23, 72–73.

24. On the "selling" of the Korean War as a limited war, see Steven Casey, *Selling the Korean War: Propaganda, Politics, and Public Opinion in the United States, 1950–1953* (New York: Oxford University Press, 2008), 4–5, 244–63. McCarthy is quoted in David Oshinsky, *A Conspiracy So Immense: The World of Joseph McCarthy* (New York: Free Press, 1983), 32–33. See Paul M. Edwards, *To Acknowledge a War: The Korean War in American Memory* (Westport, CT: Greenwood Press, 2000), 16, 64.

25. *New York Times*, April 10, 1951, 6; April 12, 1951, 5; April 23, 1951, 4.

26. E. G. Canady to Truman, April 12, 1951; J. Campbell to Truman, April 16, 1951; A. J. Crispell to Truman, April 11, 1951; A. Wagener to Truman, April 11, 1951; B. Cradit to Truman, April 11, 1951; M. Langevin to Truman, April 12, 1951; M. Linder to Truman, April 16, 1951, RG 584, box 1440, Official File, Truman Library.

27. H. Cook to Truman, April 12, 1951; J. J. Carey to Truman, April 12, 1951; C. Clough, J. Etter, and S. Russell to Truman, April 11, 1951, RG 584, box 1440, Official File, Truman Library.

28. On MacArthur's reputation, see William Manchester, *American Caesar: Douglas MacArthur, 1880–1964* (Boston: Little, Brown, 1978), 7, 236–37; 389. On John Kennedy's views, see Robert Dallek, *An Unfinished Life: John F. Kennedy, 1917–1963* (Boston: Little, Brown, 2003), 92–93. Moss to Truman, April 12, 1951; M. McCoy to Truman, April 20, 1951, box 1422; L. MacBride to Truman, April 11, 1951; H. Ray to Truman, April 11, 1951, box 1426, RG 584, Official File, Truman Library.

29. C. Marriott to Truman, April 16, 1951; E. Cibel to Truman, April 10, 1951; G. Mor-

ris, April 21, 1951; J. Adaline, May 7, 1951; G. Morris to Truman, April 21, 1951, RG 584, Official File, Truman Library.

30. See Manchester, *American Caesar*, 648–59. Lawrence H. Suid, *Guts and Glory: The Making of the American Military Image in Film* (Lexington: University of Kentucky Press, 2002), 30.

31. *Washington Post*, April 17, 1951, 1; April 2, 1951, 23; April 20, 1. Kurt Lang and Gladys Engle Lang, "The Unique Perspective of Television and Its Effect: A Pilot Study," *American Sociological Review* 18 (Feb. 1953): 3–13, argued that the parades and celebrations for MacArthur appeared to be even more solemn on television than they were in the streets, where high levels of crowd noise and confusion made it hard to see and hear what was going on.

32. See *Revitalizing a Nation: A Statement of Beliefs and Opinions, Policies Embodied in the Public Pronouncements of the General of the Army Douglas MacArthur* (Chicago: Heritage Foundation, 1952). See also Morris Janowitz, *The Professional Soldier: A Social and Political Portrait* (New York: Free Press, 1960), 215–20.

33. Dodd's speech is reprinted in Lawrence S. Wittner, ed., *MacArthur* (Englewood Cliffs, NJ: Prentice Hall, 1971), 25–29.

34. See *Duty, Honor, Country: A Pictorial Autobiography* (New York: McGraw Hill, 1965), 213. *Time*, April 10, 1964.

35. *New York Times*, Sept. 11, 1981, A11; Oct. 20, 1984, 2.

36. See Robert Griffith, "Dwight D. Eisenhower and the Corporate Commonwealth," *American Historical Review* 87 (Feb. 1982): 87–122; Geoffrey Perret, *Eisenhower* (New York: Random House, 1999), 412–18. See the insightful comparison between Eisenhower and MacArthur campaign buttons in Christine Scriabine, "American Attitudes toward a Martial Presidency: Some Insights from Material Culture," *Military Affairs*, December 1983, 165–72.

37. Hanson W. Baldwin, "Two Generals: The Climax of the Drama," *New York Times*, July 6, 1952, SM3. T. Harry Williams, "The Macs and the Ikes: America's Two Military Traditions," *American Mercury* 75 (1952): 32–39.

38. *Time*, April 4, 1969; *Washington Times Herald*, April 2, 1969, A22.

39. Louis Harris, "Eisenhower Always Highly Regarded by the American Public," *Washington Post*, April 1, 1969, A14; "Nixon Eulogy," *Washington Post*, March 31, 1969, A1; George Wilson, "McGovern on Defense: A Disciple of Eisenhower," *Washington Post*, June 25, 1972, B1; Blanche Wiesen Cook, "Eisenhower—Military Master Who Feared Militarism," *Los Angeles Times*, Nov. 1, 1972, D7; David Broder, "Ike on 'Man Against War'" *Washington Post*, Sept. 8, 1983, A17.

4. MONUMENTS AND MOURNING

1. Avishai Margalit, *The Ethics of Memory* (Cambridge, MA.: Harvard University Press, 2002), 7–9, 27, 77–79; Benedict Anderson, *Imagined Communities: Reflections on the Origins and Spread of Nationalism* (London: Verso, 1983), 9–11. Both James E. Young, "Germany's Memorial Question: Memory, Counter Memory and the End of the Monument," *South Atlantic Quarterly* 96 (Fall 1997): 1–26, and Jay Winter, *Sites of Memory, Sites of*

Mourning: The Great War in European Cultural History (Cambridge: Cambridge University Press, 1995), discuss the difficulty of trying to build traditional memorials that efface the pain and suffering of war after the massive scale of killings in World War I. See also Jenny Edkins, *Trauma and the Memory of Politics* (Cambridge: Cambridge University Press, 2003), 13–15.

2. James Mayo, *War Memorials and the Political Landscape: The American Experience and Beyond* (New York: Praeger, 1988), 3–5.

3. Ron Robin, *Enclaves of America: The Rhetoric of American Personal Architecture Abroad* (Princeton, NJ: Princeton University Press, 1992), 3–6, 122–26.

4. Raymond Halloran describes his wartime experiences and postwar struggles in an oral history interview. See Interview with Raymond Halloran by Bill Alexander, March 15, 1998, in the Admiral Nimitz Museum and University of North Texas Oral History Collection, No. 1250, especially pp. 101–31. Elizabeth Nishiura, *American Battle Monuments: A Guide to Military Cemeteries and Monuments Maintained by the American Battle Monuments Commission* (Detroit, MI: Omnigraphics, 1989), 6–12, 230–56. Kurt Piehler, *Remembering War the American Way* (Washington, DC: Smithsonian Institution, 1995), 129–31. "Meeting Minutes and Agendas, 1923–1993," June 5, 1947, May 4, 1949, Nov. 9, 1949, box 1, Records of the American Battle Monuments Commission, RG 117, National Archives.

5. Karl Ann Marling and John Wetenhall, *Iwo Jima: Monuments, Memories, and the American Hero* (Cambridge, MA: Harvard University Press, 1991), 15, 75, 125, 237; Albert Boine, *The Unveiling of the National Icons: A Plea for Patriotic Iconoclasm in a Nationalist Era* (Cambridge: Cambridge University Press, 1998), 181–82.

6. John Bradley, *Flags of Our Fathers* (New York: Bantam, 2000), 259; "Ira Hayes—Our Accuser," *Christian Century*, Feb. 9, 1955, 166–67; Albert Hemingway, *Ira Hayes: Pima Marine* (Lanham, MD: University Press of America, 1988), 2–3, 149–58.

7. The *Johnstown Tribune Democrat*, March 31, 1945, announced his death; Ted Potts, "Strank Recalled as Tough Marine," Feb. 24, 1985, May 16, 1986, May 14, 2006, clippings in Strank File, Cambria County (PA) Library. I thank Jennifer Pruchnic for her help in obtaining this material.

8. Interview with Mary Pero by John Bodnar, Davidsville, Pa., June 1, 2006. See also *Washington Post*, Feb. 18, 2005. I thank Matt Bodenschatz of the *Johnstown Tribune Democrat* for helping me to locate Mary Pero.

9. Edward T. Linenthal, *Sacred Ground: Americans and their Battlefields* (Urbana: University of Illinois Press, 1991), 181–85; Joy Waldron Jasper, James P. Delgado, and Jim Adams, *The USS Arizona: The Ship, the Men, the Pearl Harbor Attack, and the Symbols That Aroused America* (New York: St. Martins, 2001), 176–77. On the USS *Missouri*, see ww.uss missouri.com.

10. Linenthal, *Sacred Ground*, 179–80; Emily S. Rosenberg, *A Date Which Will Live in Infamy: Pearl Harbor in American Memory* (Durham: Duke University Press, 2003), 33.

11. Geoffrey M. White, "Moving History: The Pearl Harbor Films," in *Perilous Memories: The Asia Pacific Wars*, ed. Takashi Fukitani, Geoffrey M. White, and Lisa Yoneyama (Durham, NC: Duke University Press, 2001), 267–98.

12. Bob Dole, *One Soldier's Story: A Memoir* (New York: HarperCollins, 2005), 269–70.

Nicolaus Mills, *Their Last Battle: The Fight for the National World War II Memorial* (New York: Basic Books, 2004), 1–2, 92, 105. *Save Our History: The World War II Memorial,* video-cassette (History Channel, 1999).

13. Douglass Brinkley, ed., *The World War II Memorial: A Grateful Nation Remembers* (Washington, DC: Smithsonian Books, 2004), 7–9; Mills, *Their Last Battle,* 143–45; Christopher Thomas, *The Lincoln Memorial and American Life* (Princeton, NJ: Princeton University Press, 2002), 23; John Bodnar, "Monuments and Morals: The Nationalization of Civic Instruction," in *Civic and Moral Learning in America,* ed. Donald Warren and John J. Patrick (New York: Palgrave/Macmillan, 2006), 215–18.

14. The information on Red Oak, Iowa, is drawn from interviews by the author with Dennis Wolfe, Red Oak, Iowa, July 29, 2008, and Elwin Diehl, Red Oak, Iowa, July 30, 2008. See also Milton Lehman, "Red Oak Hasn't Forgotten," *Saturday Evening Post,* Aug. 17, 1946. Lehman's article actually shows that right after the war citizens in the town held differing views over how best to commemorate the dead. To one local pastor, the deaths of the men demanded that the living work to improve racial tolerance in the world. For others, some of the dead were simply memorialized in small shrines with photos and American flags in private homes.

15. *Discovering Pittsburgh Sculpture* (Pittsburgh: University of Pittsburgh Press, 1983), 84; Martha Norkunas, *Monuments and Memory: History and Representation in Lowell, Massachusetts* (Washington, DC: Smithsonian Institution Press, 2002), 167. I thank Martha Norkunas for sending me copies of much of her research data from Lowell. Jennifer Wingate, "Over the Top: The Doughboy Statue in World War I Memorial and Visual Culture," *American Art* 19 (2005): 26–47; Anton Rajer and Christine Style, *Public Sculpture in Wisconsin: An Atlas of Outdoor Monuments, Memorials, and Masterpieces in the Badger State* (Madison: University of Wisconsin Press, 1998), 18.

16. Piehler, *Remembering War the American Way,* 116–22; *Washington Post,* Nov. 12, 1921, 1.

17. David Glassberg and Michael Moore, "Patriotism in Orange: The Memory of World War I in a Massachusetts Town," *Bonds of Affection: Americans Define Their Patriotism,* ed. John Bodnar (Princeton, NJ: Princeton University Press, 1996), 166, 173–74. Michele Bogart, *Public Sculpture and the Civic Ideal in New York City, 1890–1930* (Chicago: University of Chicago Press, 1989), 271–93. J. M. Bartlett and K. M. Ellis, "Remembering the Dead in Northrup: First World War Memorialization at Welsh Parish," *Journal of Contemporary History* 34 (Jan. 1999): 324, claimed that the listing of the names of the dead suggested the point that the men who died should not have died at all.

18. Andrew M. Shanken, "Living Memorials in the United States during World War II," *Art Bulletin* 84 (March 2002): 130–47; Mayo, *War Memorials as Political Landscape,* 113; *Recreation* (May 1945): 39, 74, 109. Harry P. Jeffrey, "Legislative Origins of the Fulbright Program," *Annals of the American Academy of Political and Social Science* 491 (May 1987): 36–47; *Christian Century,* May 1, 1946, 551; *Ladies Home Journal* 65 (May 1948): 23, 230–31. Randall Bennett Woods, *Fulbright: A Biography* (Cambridge: Cambridge University Press, 1995), 108, 129–30.

19. The promotional brochure for the fund drive in Milwaukee, entitled "Which Will

It Be?" is located in a file for the Milwaukee War Memorial in the Milwaukee Country Historical Society.

20. *Los Angeles Times,* Dec. 11, 1944, 4.

21. *Los Angeles Times,* March 4, 1946, A1. James Fraser, "Let Our Monuments Inspire-Endure," *The Rotarian* 8 (Feb. 1946), 24–25, 51–52; C. Rothschild, "What Lives in a War Memorial," *Saturday Review of Literature,* June 1, 1946, 25–27. Margaret Cresson, "Memorial's Symbolic," *New York Times,* July 22, 1945, 80.

22. Edward Steere and Thayer M. Boardman, *Final Disposition of World War II Dead, 1945–1951* (Washington, DC: Office of the Quartermaster General, 1957), 16–17, 188–89, indicated that some 70 percent of the bodies were brought home. *Life,* Nov. 3, 1947, also noted that 70 percent were brought back. David Cohn, "The Soldier Dead Come Home," *Atlantic Monthly* 179 (May 1947): 66–68, felt that 70 percent was higher than a similar figure for World War I, which he placed at 60 percent.

23. *Tell Me About My Boy,* a 1946 pamphlet published by the Quartermaster Corps for the relatives of dead soldiers can be found at www.qmfound.com/about_my_boy.htm; Steere and Boardman, *Final Disposition of World War II Dead,* 1–16.

24. Katherine Verdery, *The Political Lives of Dead Bodies: Reburial and Postsocialist Change* (New York: Columbia University Press, 1999).

25. "Should Our War Dead Be Brought Home?" *Life,* June 18, 1945, 23; Harold Martin, "They Lie Where They Would Wish to Be," *Readers Digest* 48 (March 1946): 77–78; *Washington Post,* March 11, 1947, 6; David L. Cohn, "The Soldier Dead Come Home," *Atlantic Monthly* 179 (May 1947): 66–68.

26. Rev. William Brewster to Truman, telegram, Feb. 8, 1946, file 190 E, Official File, Truman Papers, Truman Presidential Library.

27. Mrs. Paul Tucker to Truman, Dec. 17, 1946; Mrs. Ralph Bell to Truman, Dec. 21, 1946; James Barnett S.J. to Truman, April 15, 1947; William Hassett to Truman, May 1, 1946; Anna Parsons to Truman, Sept. 9, 1946; Lucile Douglas to Truman Sept. 23, 1946; J. D. Mitchell to General Vaughn, Nov. 17, 1947, file 190 E, Official File, Truman Papers.

28. Brief on Behalf of the Next of Kin of Stephan C. Lautenbach, Aug. 21, 1947, file 190 E, Official Files, Truman Papers.

29. Albert Miller to Truman, June 6, 1946; L. C. Deibler to Truman, April 18, 1946; Loretta Keil to Truman, April 7, 1946; Frances Gagliardi to Truman, May 8, 1946; Harry Hodson to Truman, May 17, 1946; A. Eiser to Joseph Epstein, April 29, 1947, file 190 E, Official File, Truman Papers.

30. *New York Times,* Oct. 27 , 1947, 1, 3. This particular report featured photos of women weeping in public.

31. Steve Rajtar and Frances Elizabeth Franks, *War Monuments, Museums, and Library Collections of the 20th Century Conflicts* (Jefferson, NC: MacFarland, 2002); Mayo, *War Memorials as Political Landscape,* 7–70; *New York Times,* Oct. 27, 1947, 1; Steere and Boardman, *Final Disposition of the World War II Dead,* 682–83; *Detroit News,* Aug. 15, 1948, 1.

32. *Life,* July 19, 1948, 33–36.

33. *Kansas City Times,* Nov. 6, 1948, 1; *Springfield (Mo.) News Leader,* Nov. 4, 1948, 1; Louella Dulin interview by John Bodnar, Brookline, Mo., Feb. 1, 2007. Dulin, Henry Wright's daughter-in-law, said he was "broken in spirit."

34. Louella Dulin interview by John Bodnar, Brookline, Mo., Feb. 1, 2007, typescript of story in author's possession.

35. Stephen Wright interview by John Bodnar, Hurley, Mo., Feb. 1, 2007.

36. Copy of poem in author's possession.

37. "Dedication Program," box 1, Virginia War Memorial Records, Virginia State Library. In 1981 the names of 1, 289 soldiers from Virginia who were killed in Vietnam were added to the site.

38. *Omaha World Herald*, June 6, 1948, 1.

39. Ibid., Aug. 23, 1948, 1; Michael Kelly, "Our Memorial Is Still a Beauty," ibid., May 22, 1998, 48.

40. Ibid., June 6, 1948, 1.

41. James Martin Davis, "Families and Omaha Remember," *Omaha World Herald*, Aug. 21, 1998, Aug. 22, 1948, June 3, 1948, clippings in Memorial Park file, Douglas Historical Society, Omaha.

42. Lajba's views are expressed in a pamphlet entitled *The 50th Anniversary World War II Memorial*, copy in Memorial Park File, Douglas County Historical Society.

43. Alvin Sunseri and Kenneth Lyfgot, *Commemorative Story of the 1988 Rededication* (Waterloo: Friends of the Waterloo Library, 1988); *Waterloo Daily Courier*, Jan. 12, 1943, 1, announced the men were missing and carried photos of the entire family and the home in which they lived.

44. See John Bodnar, *Blue-Collar Hollywood: Liberalism, Democracy and Working People in American Film* (Baltimore: Johns Hopkins University Press, 2003), 80–82.

45. *Waterloo Daily Courier*, Nov. 4, 1988, B1; Nov. 10, 1988, A1–2; Apr. 20, 1997.

46. John R. Satterfield, *We Band of Brothers: The Sullivans and World War II* (Parkersburg, Iowa: Mid-Prairie Books, 1995), 169–73, 199–201; *Waterloo Daily Courier*, Nov. 4, 1988, B1; Nov. 10, 1988, A1–2.

47. Alex Kershaw, *The Bedford Boys: One American Town's Ultimate D-Day Sacrifice* (Cambridge, MA: De Capo Press, 2003), 73–80, 97–98, 208.

48. Ibid., 205–207. See Bruce C. Smith, *The War Comes to Plum Street* (Bloomington: Indiana University Press, 2005), 219–21, for another account of how news of D-Day casualties came slowly to New Castle, Indiana.

49. Kershaw, *Bedford Boys*, 290–91.

50. *Bedford Bulletin*, May 2, 1946, 6.

51. Kershaw, *Bedford Boys*, 220–23; James Morrison, *Bedford Goes to War: The Heroic Story of a Small Virginia Community in World War II* (Lynchburg, VA: Warwick House, 2001), 245. I thank James Morrison for sending me information on the windows in the Bedford Christian Church. Draper's Web site is www.rjgieb.com/heroes/draper/draper/html.

52. *Bedford Bulletin*, June 10, 1954, 1.

53. *Lynchburg News Advance*, June 3, 2001, I 3; *Roanoke Times*, June 6, 1999, 1.

54. "Their Sacrifice, Our Freedom," videotape of Dedication Ceremonies, June 6, 2001; taped by WDBJ TV, Roanoke, and sold at the gift shop of the National D-Day Memorial. On Macie Hoback's lifelong grieving over her dead sons, see Kershaw, *Bedford Boys*, 232. See Douglas Brinkley, *The Boys of Pointe du Hoc: Ronald Reagan, D-Day, and the U.S. Army 2nd Ranger Battalion* (New York: William Morrow, 2005), 227–28.

55. *Bedford Bulletin*, May 26, 2006, 1, 4, treats the dedication of the Eisenhower statue.

56. See Donald Knox, *Death March: The Survivors of Bataan* (San Diego: HBJ, 1981). John W. Dower, *Embracing Defeat: Japan in the Wake of World War II* (New York: W.W. Norton, 19990), 449, 616; "Ruin Japan! Is Cry," *New York Times*, Jan. 29, 1944, 1–2; "Kin of Prisoners Ask for Revenge," *New York Times*, Jan. 29, 1944, 3.

57. *Chicago Tribune*, Sept. 13, 1943, 11; Sept. 19, 1954, 5; March 24, 1985, H11; "Philippine Epic: General MacArthur and His Men Make a Thermopylae of Bataan," *Life Magazine*, April 13, 1942, 25–36.

58. See Richard Slotkin, *Gunfighter Nation: The Myth of the Frontier in Twentieth Century America* (New York: Harper, 1992), 218–26.

59. *Life*, July 6, 1942, clipping in Bataan file, Harrodsburg Public Library, Harrodsburg, Kentucky. For a view of one Bataan survivor who felt an obligation to keep alive the story of prisoner "abuse," see Tony Bilek, *No Uncle Sam: The Forgotten of Bataan* (Kent, OH: Kent State University Press, 2003), xi, 252–53.

60. *Harrodsburg Herald*, May 8, 1942, 2; *Life*, July 6, 1942, clipping in Bataan file, Harrodsburg Public Library.

61. *Harrodsburg Herald*, June 19, 1942, 2. The report from the *New York Times* was reprinted in the *Harrodsburg Herald*, June 19, 1942, 7.

62. Ibid., May 1, 1942; Oct. 16, 1942, 7; June 18, 1943, 1; June 25, 1943, 1; Jan. 14, 1944, 1; Jan. 26, 1945, 1; Feb. 2, 1945, 1.

63. Ibid., June 14, 1946, 4; June 21, 1946, 1; July 12, 1946, 4.

64. *Louisville Courier Journal*, May 28, 1961, clipping in Bataan file, Harrodsburg Public Library; James Russell Harris, "The Harrodsburg Tankers: Bataan, Prison, and the Bonds of Community," *Register of the Kentucky Historical Society* 86 (Summer, 1988): 230–79, used interview material collected from the men in 1961 and 1985–86.

65. *Lexington Herald Leader*, May 25, 1981, clipping in Bataan file, Harrodsburg Public Library; Studs Terkel, *The Good War: An Oral History of World War II* (New York: New Press, 1984), 69–79; Harris, "Harrodsburg Tankers," 230–79.

66. "Minutes," 192nd Tank Company Auxiliary Records, 1946, Rock County Historical Society, Janesville.

67. Ibid.

68. *Wisconsin State Journal*, March 26, 1967, sec. 4, p. 1.

69. Donald Knox, *Death March: The Survivors of Bataan* (New York: Harcourt, Brace, Jovanovich, 1983), 474–80. Knox told the story of the American prisoners strangling comrades to Tom Doherty. See Doherty, "Too Little, Too Late: Janesville's Lost Children of the Armored Force," *Wisconsin Magazine of History and Biography* 75 (1992): 272.

70. Knox, *Death March*, 478–81.

71. Dave Kenney, *Minnesota Goes to War: The Home Front during World War II* (St. Paul: Minnesota Historical Society, 2005), 226–27; *Brainerd Daily Dispatch*, Aug. 9, 1981, 1. I thank Lucille Kirkeby of the Crow Wing Historical Society for sending me this clipping. Another account of the postwar struggle of a Bataan survivor can be found in Thomas Saylor, *Long Hard Road: American POWs during World War II* (St. Paul: Minnesota Historical Society, 2007), 246.

72. See Ben Steele oral history, 2001, Moorhead State University library, Moorhead, Minnesota. A transcript of the interview can be found at www.mnstate.edu/heritage/ VETERANS/index.htm. Also see Dan Murr, *"But Deliver Us From Evil": Father Duffy and the Men of Bataan* (Jacksonville Beach, FL: Murr Publishing, 2008), 88–112.

73. Alan Newberg, ed., *Ben Steele: Prisoner of War* (Billings: Eastern Montana College, 1986) contains reproductions of many of his drawings. See also Ben Steele interview, 2001, Moorhead State University Library. Steele described his nightmares of fighting Japanese guards in a telephone interview with the author, Sept. 3, 2008. For more on Steele's experience as a prisoner, see Michael Norman and Elizabeth M. Norman, *Tears in the Darkness: The Story of the Bataan Death March and Its Aftermath* (New York: Farrar, Straus, and Giroux, 2009).

74. *Deming Headlight*, May 1, 1942, 1; *Albuquerque Tribune*, March 8, 2002, 1. Eva Jane Matson, *It Tolled for New Mexico: New Mexicans Captured by the Japanese, 1941–1945* (Las Cruces, NM: Yucca Tree Press, 1992), 95–97. I thank Rick Padilla, museum director, for allowing me to tour the museum.

75. Ibid., 86.

76. *Colors of Courage: Sons of New Mexico/Prisoners of Japan*, videocassette produced by the Center for Regional Studies, University of New Mexico, copy located in Center for Southwest Studies, University of New Mexico. *Albuquerque Journal*, April 10, 2004, clipping in World War II file, Center for Southwest Studies. I thank Nancy Martinez Brown for helping me locate this material.

77. Dorothy Cave, *Beyond Courage: One Regiment against the Japanese, 1941–1945* (Las Cruces, NM: Yucca Tree Press, 1992), 385–87. *Albuquerque Tribune*, April 15, 1946, 2; April 12, 1946, 1. *Pilgrimage to Chimayo: Contemporary Portrait of a Living Tradition* (Santa Fe: Museum of New Mexico Press, 1999).

78. *Santa Fe New Mexican*, Oct. 28, 1999, A1–2; *Corpus Christi Times*, Oct. 25, 1999. Everett R. Rogers and Nancy R. Bartlit, *Silent Voices of World War II: Sons of the Land of Enchantment Meet Sons of the Land of the Rising Son* (Santa Fe, NM: Sunstone Press, 205), 81–82; Matson, *It Tolled for New Mexico*, 82–86.

5. THE SPLIT SCREEN

1. Mark Feeney, *Nixon at the Movies: A Book about Belief* (Chicago: University of Chicago Press, 2004), 65–68. See Michael Rogin, *Ronald Reagan: The Movie and Other Episodes in Political Demonology* (Berkeley: University of California Press, 1988), 32–34.

2. Sheri Chinen Biesen, *Blackout: World War II and the Origins of Film Noir* (Baltimore: Johns Hopkins University Press, 2005), 2–9; J. David Slocum, "Cinema and the Civilizing Process: Rethinking Violence in the World War II Combat Film," *Cinema Journal* 44 (Spring 2005): 35–63. On left-wing moviemakers and Cold War repression, see Lary May, *The Big Tomorrow: Hollywood and the Politics of the American Way* (Chicago: University of Chicago Press, 2000), 226–38. For a discussion on the marketing of violent and pornographic images in postwar culture, see Carolyn Dean, *The Fragility of Empathy after the Holocaust* (Ithaca, NY: Cornell University Press, 2004), 1–15. Dean sees, over time, a trivialization of tragedy and a numbing effect on the capacity to empathize with the suffering of others.

3. See especially, Jan Herman, *A Talent for Trouble: The Life of Hollywood's Most Acclaimed Director* (New York: G. P. Putnam, 1995), 278–83. See Marilyn Ann Moss, *Giant: George Stevens, a Life on Film* (Madison: University of Wisconsin Press, 2004), 119–23, 180–81, for a discussion of the war's impact on the Stevens and how it was expressed in films like *Shane* (1953), which appeared to retreat into a prewar past where individuals really could stand up alone to (mythically) stop evil in the world.

4. Michael E. Birdwell, *Celluloid Soldiers: Warner Bros. Campaign against Nazism* (New York: New York University Press, 1999). On the variety of depictions of American soldiers in war films, see Martha Bayles, "Portraits of Mars," *Wilson Quarterly* (Summer 2003): 12–19. Christine Gledhill, "The Melodramatic Field of Investigation," in *Home Is Where the Heart Is*, ed. Gledhill, (London: British Film Institute, 1987), 5–42. See also Richard Schechner, *Performance Theory* (New York: Routledge, 2003), xix, for the point that performance does not so much reflect life as essentialize it.

5. Jeanine Basinger, *The World War II Combat Film: Anatomy of a Genre* (New York: Columbia University Press, 1986), 9–42, 58, 79.

6. Lary May, "Making the American Consensus: The Narrative of Consensus and Subversion in World War II Film," in *The War in American Culture: Security and Consciousness During World War II*, ed. Lewis Erenberg and Susan A. Hirsch (Chicago: University of Chicago Press, 1996), 71–104. Clayton R. Koppes and Gregory D. Black, *Hollywood Goes to War: How Politics, Profits, and Propaganda Shaped World War II Movies* (Berkeley: University of California Press, 1990), 64–70.

7. Lawrence Suid, *Guts and Glory: The Making of the American Military Image in Film* (Lexington: University of Kentucky Press, 2002), 8, 123–24, 183–89.

8. On Wayne's manly character, see Gary Wills, *John Wayne's America* (New York: Touchstone, 1997), 12–27.

9. See Richard Slotkin, *Gunfighter Nation: The Myth of the Frontier in Twentieth Century America* (New York: Athenaeum, 1992), 334–43, 447–91.

10. Basinger, *World War II Combat Film*, 169.

11. On the postwar debate over human nature, see John Bodnar, *Blue-Collar Hollywood: Liberalism, Democracy, and Working People in American Film* (Baltimore: Johns Hopkins University Press, 2003), 90–94.

12. See Christian G. Appy, "We'll Follow the Old Man: The Strains of Sentimental Militarism in Popular Films of the Fifties," in *Rethinking Cold War Culture*, ed. Peter G. Kuznick and James Gilbert (Washington, DC: Smithsonian Press, 2001), 74–105.

13. See George F. Custen, *Twentieth Century's Fox: Darryl F. Zanuck and the Culture of Hollywood* (New York: Basic Books, 1997), 360–65.

14. "The Screen," *Commonweal*, Oct. 26, 1962, 124; Margot A. Henriksen, *Dr. Strangelove's America: Society and Culture in the Atomic Age* (Berkeley: University of California Press, 1997), 317–19; Stephen Whitfield, *The Culture of the Cold War* (Baltimore: Johns Hopkins University Press, 1996), 220–25.

15. Jeanine Basinger, *A Woman's View: How Hollywood Spoke to Women, 1930–1960* (Middletown, CT: Wesleyan University Press, 1993), 6–13; Dana Polan, *Power and Paranoia: History, Narrative, and the American Cinema, 1940–1950* (New York: Columbia University Press, 1986), 248–49.

16. *New York Times*, Feb. 10, 1944, 19.

17. James Agee, "Death Takes a Powder," *Nation* 158 (May 1944): 549.

18. Polan, *Power and Paranoia*, 253.

19. See John Huston, *An Open Book* (New York: Knopf, 1980), 110–28. An earlier Huston documentary for the army, *The Battle of San Pietro* (1945) also depicted gruesome scenes of American casualties. Huston's 1951 film *The Red Badge of Courage* used a story set in the Civil War to extend his antiwar sentiments. See Guerric DeBona, "Masculinity on the Front: John Huston's 'Red Badge of Courage' Revisited," *Cinema Journal* 42 (Winter 2003): 57–80. On the impact of World War II on outlooks toward war-related stress, see Paul Wanke, "Psychiatry and Its Role among Ground Forces in World War II," *Journal of Military History* 63 (Jan. 1999): 124–46; Ellen Dwyer, "Psychiatry and Race during World War II," *Journal of the History of Medicine and Allied Sciences* 61 (Aug. 2006): 117–43.

20. MacKinley Kantor to J. Riley, March 4, 1946; D. Gottlieb to Kantor, Nov. 13, 1945; C. Sussman to Kantor, Dec. 11, 1945, box 25, folder 7, Kantor Papers, Library of Congress. The experience of visiting the relatives of dead soldiers and how it affected the writer is recorded in the author's notes in box 70, folder 5, Kantor Papers. Herman, *A Talent for Trouble*, 278–305. Many reviews of the film liked it for its willingness to expose the cynicism and destructiveness of the war; see "Pursuit of Happiness," *Commonweal*, Dec. 13, 1946, 230. James Jones charged that any movie that suggested that war built character was "phony" in "Phony War Films," *Saturday Evening Post*, March 30, 1963, 129. See also Bodnar, *Blue-Collar Hollywood*, 99–101.

21. Paul Buhle and Dave Wagner, *Hide in Plain Sight: The Hollywood Blacklistees in Film and Television, 1950–2002* (New York: Palgrave-Macmillan, 2003), 163–67.

22. Stephanie Coontz, *The Way We Never Were: American Families and the Nostalgia Trap* (New York: Basic Books, 1992), 54–55, has argued that in postwar America family life became idealized and envisioned as a site of ideal love because of the spread of individualism and market principles in the rest of society. The loving family and marital relationship were now often seen as a unique place in life where the "rationality and cost benefit analysis" of the marketplace could be left behind. While this is an intriguing suggestion, it is also true that the ruptures of wartime and the need to restore them also promoted a highly idealized understanding of what married life was and could be.

23. See Emily S. Rosenberg, "Foreign Affairs after World War II: Connecting Sexual and International Politics," *Diplomatic History* 18 (Winter 1994): 59–70.

24. Bodnar, *Blue-Collar Hollywood*, 147–49; 160–62.

25. See James Naremore, *More than the Night: Film Noir in its Contexts* (Berkeley: University of California Press, 1998), 6–12, 34–43; Sheri Biesen, *Blackout: World War II and the Origins of Film Noir* (Baltimore: Johns Hopkins University Press, 2005), 74, 124–27.

26. See also *Somewhere in the Night* (1946), the story of a veteran who returns with a case of amnesia and finds decay and moral disorder in a seamy section of Los Angeles.

27. Samuel Fuller, *A Third Face: My Tale of Writing, Fighting, and Filmmaking* (New York: Applause Theater and Cinema Books, 2002), 180, 475–83.

28. See Robert A. Ray, *A Certain Tendency of the Hollywood Cinema, 1930–1980* (1985).

29. Naremore, *More than the Night*, 114–15.

30. See Naoko Shibusawa, *America's Geisha Ally: Reimagining the Japanese Enemy* (Cambridge, MA: Harvard University Press, 2006), 255–67)

6. THE OUTSIDERS

1. Not all racial minorities can be treated in this chapter, but it is important to note that Native Americans began to receive some public tribute during and after the war for some of their heroic exploits. These Americans were willingly let into combat units, and there is evidence that they volunteered in relatively large numbers. Some, like Ernest Childers of Oklahoma, earned the Medal of Honor and public respect. There was also considerable interest in Ira Hays, who was part of the flag-raising team on Iwo Jima and in Navajo Code Talkers who helped to outwit the Japanese. Native Americans may have benefited during the war years from an older stereotype in the minds of whites who saw them as brave warriors. After the war some Native Americans and as well as white politicians worked to improve the situation on Native American reservations and to reduce government control over their lives. See Tom Holm, "Fighting a White Man's War: The Extent and Legacy of American Indian Participation in World War II," *Journal of Ethnic Studies* 9 (1981): 69–81; Alison R. Bernstein, *American Indians and World War II* (Norman: University of Oklahoma Press, 1991), 134–39, 159–65. On how the war raised the expectations for justice on the part of blacks, see Thomas J. Sugrue, *Sweet Land of Liberty: The Forgotten Struggle for Civil Rights in the North* (New York: Random House, 2008), 54, 84. On turning victims into heroes in postwar Europe, see Pieter Lagrou, *The Legacy of Nazi Occupation: Patriotic Memory and National Recovery in Western Europe* (New York: Cambridge University Press, 2000). See also Tony Judt, "The 'Problem of Evil' in Postwar Europe," *New York Review of Books*, Feb. 14, 2008, 33–35. On the function of myths, see Roland Barthes, *Mythologies* (New York: Hill and Wang, 1972), 143–46. Barthes sees mythical speech as opposing "political speech," which would tend to see the past as a product of conflict and not as something as flowing from eternal truths and values such as presumptions that most Americans are inherently virtuous and patriotic. On the positioning of genealogy against the liberal and universal dream of human rights, see Wendy Brown, *Politics Out of History* (Princeton, NJ: Princeton University Press, 2001), 21.

2. Lee Finkle, *Forum for Protest: The Black Press during World War II* (Rutherford, NJ: Fairleigh Dickinson Press, 1975; John W. Dower, *War Without Mercy: Race and Power in the Pacific War* (New York: Pantheon, 1986).

3. Daniel Kryder, *Divided Arsenal: Race and the American State During World War II* (Cambridge: Cambridge University Press, 2000), 2–9, 89–90, 134–37. Gary Gerstle, *The American Crucible: Race and Nation in the Twentieth Century* (Princeton, NJ: Princeton University Press, 2001), 187–237, also suggests that the maintenance of a segregated military during the war was a missed opportunity.

4. Walter White, *A Man Called White* (Bloomington: Indiana University Press, 1948), 253–58; 288. *Crisis*, Aug. 6, 1944, copy in "Editorials in *Crisis*, 1941–1945" file, box F6, NAACP Papers, Library of Congress. Sherie Mershon and Steven Schlossman, *Foxholes and Color Lines: Desegregating the U.S. Armed Forces* (Baltimore: Johns Hopkins University

Press, 1998), 52–57; Maggi M. Morehouse, *Fighting in the Jim Crow Army: Black Men and Women Remember World War II* (Lanham, MD: Rowan and Littlefield, 2000, 5–11.

5. See "Camp Investigations," boxes G1 and G2, NAACP Papers, Library of Congress.

6. Charles C. Moskos, *The American Enlisted Man: The Rank and File in Today's Military* (New York: Russell Sage, 1970), 119. Mershon and Schlossman, *Foxholes and Color Lines*, 175; Morehouse, *Fighting in the Jim Crow Army*, 200–201.

7. Jennifer E. Brooks, *Defining the Peace: World War II Veterans, Race, and the Remaking of Southern Political Tradition* (Chapel Hill: University of North Carolina Press, 2004), 3–13. For more on how military service raised the political expectations of black men, see Greta de Jong, *A Different Day: African-American Struggles for Justice in Rural Louisiana, 1900–1970* (Chapel Hill: University of North Carolina Press, 2002), 146. Sugrue, *Sweet Land of Liberty*, 212, 224–25. John Ditmer, *Local People: The "Struggle for Civil Rights in Mississippi* (Urbana: University of Illinois Press, 1994), 1–18, also locates the beginnings of a modern civil rights struggle in the experience of World War II. Suzanne Mettler, *Soldiers to Citizens: The G.I. Bill and the Making of the Greatest Generation* (New York: Oxford University Press, 2005), 55–56; 136–38; 142, shows that blacks were more likely to use the benefits for vocational training than college. Edward Humes, *Over Here: How the G.I. Bill Transformed the American Dream* (Orlando, FL: Harcourt, 2006), 215–21.

8. Mark V. Tushnet, *Making Civil Rights Law: Thurgood Marshall and the Supreme Court, 1936–1961* (New York: Oxford University Press, 1994), 126–27; *Alexandria Daily Town Talk*, Aug. 12, 1944, 1.

9. J. M. Murphy to J. A. Blackburn, March 4, 1947; T. Caudle to R. Carter, May 13, 1947, box B60, NAACP Papers, Library of Congress. Interviews with Gwendolyn Iles-Foster and Alice Faye Belman, Alexandria, May 22, 2007; *Alexandria Daily Town Talk*, Aug. 12, 1944, 1. Greta de Jong, *A Different Day*, 140; Judith Rollins, *All Is Never Said: The Narrative of Odette Hines* (Philadelphia: Temple University Press, 1995), 134–35. On voting drives in Louisiana in the 1940s, see Adam Fairclough, *Race and Democracy: The Civil Rights Struggle in Louisiana, 1915–1972* (Athens: University of Georgia Press, 1995), 78, 102–103.

10. *Alexandria Daily Town Talk*, Jan. 12, 1942, 1.

11. T. R. Greene, "Memorandum to the Office in Charge," March 12, 1942, "Alexandria Louisiana Disturbance" file, Records of the Office of the Secretary of War, RG 107, National Archives and Record Administration, College Park, Maryland (hereafter NARA).

12. James LaFourche to Walter White, Jan. 19, 1942; L. Lewis to Wm. Hastie, Feb. 5, 1942; Georgia Johnson to Wm. Hastie, Jan. 24, 1942; David Bell and S. Bradle to Wm. Hastie, Jan. 24, 1942, "Alexandria Louisiana Disturbance" file, Records of the Secretary of War, RG 107, NARA.

13. William M. Simpson, "A Tale Untold? The Alexandria, Louisiana, Street Riot (January 10, 1942)," *Louisiana History* 35 (Spring 1994): 133–48. The Iles injury is confirmed in an interview with Gwendolyn Iles-Foster by John Bodnar, May 22, 2007.

14. Interviews with Heywood Joiner Jr., Robert Johnson, Gwen Iles Foster, Amos Wesley III, Alice Faye Belman, Alexandria, May 22, 2007. Stephen E. Henthorne, "A Short Trip South: Based on Deathbed Statement of Ellis Henthorne, 27 March 1978," unpublished paper in author's possession.

15. Interview with Etta Compton, Alexandria, May 22, 2007.

16. *To Secure these Rights* (Washington, DC: Government Printing Office, 1947), 47; Alan L. Gropman, *The Air Force Integrates, 1945–1964* (Washington, DC: Office of Air Force History, 1985); Mershon and Schlossman, *Foxholes and Color Lines*, 158–86; Bernard C. Nalty, *Strength for the Fight: A History of Black Americans in the Military* (New York: Free Press, 1981), 218–44; Walter White, *A Man Called White*, 325–27.

17. Tom Brokaw, *The Greatest Generation* (New York: Random House, 1998), 186–99.

18. Morehouse, *Fighting in the Jim Crow Army*, 101–02; Nelson Perry, *Black Fire: The Making of an American Revolutionary* (New York: Free Press, 1994), 126–29; 133–85.

19. James C. Warren, *The Freeman Field Mutiny* (Vacaville, CA: Conyers Publishing, 1996), 6, 95–99, 187. Coleman Young and Lonnie Wheeler, *Hard Stuff: The Autobiography of Coleman Young* (New York: Penguin, 1994), 61, 76. Gropman, *Air Force Integrates*, 22–27. A fictionalized account of the Freeman Field mutiny was included in James Gould Cozzens's postwar novel *Guard of Honor*. See James Allison, "Mutiny at Freeman Field," (unpublished paper, 1995) in the collections of the Indiana Historical Society. Benjamin O. Davis Jr., *Benjamin O. Davis, American: An Autobiography* (Washington, DC: Smithsonian Press, 1991), 143–44, noted that he found low morale among black troops in part because they had trouble getting promoted. Davis took over the command of the 477th in June 1945.

20. Robert Allen, "Injustice Upheld in Port Chicago Mutiny Trial," *Black Scholar* (Summer 1982).

21. Robert Allen, *The Port Chicago Mutiny: The Story of the Largest Mutiny Trial in U.S. History* (San Francisco: Equal Justice Society/Amistad Press, 1989). See Thurgood Marshall to James Forrestal, Oct. 19, 1944; News Release, April 5, 1945, Court Martial file, box B21, NAACP Papers. Lee Finkle, *Forum of Protest: The Black Press during World War II* (Rutherford, NJ: Fairleigh-Dickinson University Press, 1975).

22. Allen, "Injustice Upheld in Port Chicago Mutiny Trial," 24, 56–60; *San Francisco Chronicle*, June 28, 2002. Studs Terkel, *"The Good War": An Oral History of World War II* (New York: New Press, 1984), 392–400.

23. Gropman, *Air Force Integrates*, 6–10.

24. See William Alexander Percy, "Jim Crow and Uncle Sam: The Tuskegee Flying Units and the U.S. Army Air Forces in Europe during World War II," *Journal of Military History* 67 (July 2003): 773–810.

25. "Flying in the Face of Discrimination," *New York Times*, Aug. 20, 1995, TE 5. In 1999 a play, *Black Eagles*, performed in New York, was also based on the story of the airmen. Several of the original flyers attended and were introduced to the audience. See *New York Times*, April 22, 1999, C13. In 2006 William F. Holton, a historian of the Tuskegee Airmen, Inc., modified any tendency to completely mythologize the airmen by admitting that a point made repeatedly in association with their records, that no bombers they had ever escorted in battle were ever lost, was not completely accurate.

26. Lena Williams, "Flying in the Face of Discrimination," *New York Times*, Aug. 20, 1995, TE 5, 34.

For an interview with Luther Smith, see Yvonne Latty, *We Were There: Voices of African American Veterans from World War II to the War in Iraq* (New York: Amistad, 2004), 16–21.

27. *New York Times*, Feb. 12, 1993, B1.

28. Kareem Abdul-Jabbar, *Brothers in Arms: The Epic Story of the 761st Tank Battalion: World War II's Forgotten Heroes* (New York: Broadway Books, 2004), 242, 261.

29. Ibid., 267–68; Studs Terkel, *"The Good War"*, 261–67.

30. Elliott V. Converse, et al., *The Exclusion of Black Soldiers from the Medal of Honor in World War II* (Jefferson, NC: McFarland and Co., 1997), 4–5, 11, 70–71. See also Thomas St. John Arnold, *Buffalo Soldiers: The 92nd Infantry Division and Reinforcement in World War II, 1942–1945* (Manhattan, KS: Sunflower Press, 1990), 179, 183. On the controversy over the effectiveness of black troops in battle, see the excellent book by Robert F. Jefferson, *Fighting for Hope: African American Troops of the 93rd Infantry Division in World War II and Postwar America* (Baltimore: Johns Hopkins University Press, 2008), 229.

31. *Washington Post*, Jan. 14, 1997, 1.

32. See the excellent account of the Longoria case in Patrick J. Carroll, *Felix Longoria's Wake: Bereavement, Racism, and the Rise of Mexican-American Activism* (Austin: University of Texas Press, 2003), 4–6, 55–56. See also Ignacio M. Garcia, *Hector P. Garcia: In Relentless Pursuit of Justice* (Houston: Arte Publico Press, 2002), 104–39.

33. Carroll, *Felix Longoria's Wake*, 66. George N. Green, "The Felix Longoria Affair," *Journal of Ethnic Studies* 19 (Fall 1991): 25.

34. *New York Times*, Jan. 13, 1949, 1; *Santa Fe New Mexican*, Jan. 14, 1949, clippings in Longoria Correspondence, box 3, Lyndon B. Johnson Library, Austin, Texas (hereafter LBJ Library). On controversies surrounding the reburial of Nisei GIs in Santa Ana, California, see *Pacific Citizen*, Nov. 20, 1948, 1; on similar disputes in Chicago, see *Pacific Citizen*, Nov. 27, 1948, 1. I thank Ellen Wu for references to the *Pacific Citizen*.

35. See *Three Rivers News*, Jan. 20, 1949, clipping in Felix Longoria file, box 3; "Resolution of Bexar Country Central Council American Legion," San Antonio, Jan. 27, 1949, Felix Longoria file, box 2; Pre-Presidential Confidential File, LBJ Library; Carroll, *Felix Longoria's Wake*, 70–71. S. Dyer and M. Knighten, "Discrimination after Death: Lyndon Johnson and Felix Longoria," *Southern Studies* (Winter 1978): 423. Robert Dallek, *Lone Star Rising: Lyndon Johnson and His Times* (New York: Oxford, 1991), 369, argues that Johnson was not always a staunch defender of civil rights but was sincerely outraged over the refusal to bury Longoria.

36. Ignacio M. Garcia, *Hector P. Garcia: In Relentless Pursuit of Justice* (Houston: Arte Publico Press, 2002), 5–6, 77–78. Henry A. J. Ramos, *The American G.I. Forum: In Pursuit of the Dream, 1948–1983* (Houston: Arte Publico Press, 1998). "Hector Garcia Oral History Interview" by David McComb, July 9, 1969, LBJ Library.

37. See Ramos, *American G.I. Forum*, 5–9, 19–31, 51. Carroll, *Felix Longoria's Wake*, 105, 192–93. Guadalupe San Miguel, "The Struggle Against Separate and Unequal Schools: Middle-Class Mexican-Americans and the Desegregation Campaign in Texas, 1929–1957," *History of Education Quarterly* (Autumn 1983): 343–59.

38. On Ferber's visit to Garcia, see Ramos, *American G.I. Forum*, 24–25.

39. See *Los Angeles Times*, June 27, 2004; and *Corpus Christi Caller Times*, April 12, 2004, clippings posted on http://arlingtoncemetery.net/longoria.htm.

40. See http://defendthehonor.org.

41. *Washington Post*, Sept. 22, 2007, C1. For a celebration of Mexican American valor in World War II, see Raul Morin, *Among the Valiant: Mexican Americans in World War II and Korea* (Los Angeles: Valiant Press, 2002).

42. *Personal Justice Denied: Report of the Commission on Wartime Relocation and Internment of Civilians* (Seattle: University of Washington Press, 1997), 149–53, 241–42. Mitchell T. Jaki, Harry H. L. Kitano, and Megan Berthold, *Achieving the Impossible Dream: How Japanese Americans Obtained Redress* (Urbana: University of Illinois Press, 1999), 2.

43. Lon Kurshige, *Japanese-American Celebration and Conflict: A History of Ethnic Identity and Festival, 1934–1990* (Berkley: University of California Press, 2002), 119–35. For more on the reception to *Go for Broke*, see Ellen Dionne Wu, "Race and Asian American Citizenship from World War II to the Movement" (Ph.D. diss., University of Chicago, 2006), 150–80. See T. Fujitani, "*Go for Broke:* The Movie: Japanese-American Soldiers in U.S. National, Military, and Racial Discourses," in Geoffrey M. White, and Lisa Yoneyama, *Perilous Memories: The Asia-Pacific Wars* (Durham, NC: Duke University Press, 2001), 239–66. For more on how the image of the Japanese also improved in the United States in the 1950s as part of the need to embrace Cold War allies, see Naoko Shibussawa, *America's Geisha Ally: Reimagining the Japanese Enemy* (Cambridge, MA: Harvard University Press, 2006).

44. Robert T. Hayahi, "Transfigured Patterns: Contesting Memories at the Manzanar National Historic Site," *Public Historian* 25 (Fall 2003): 51–71; Laura Hein and Mark Selden, "The Lessons of War, Global Power, and Social Change," in Hein and Selden, *Censoring History: Citizenship and Memory in Japan, Germany, and the United States* (Armonk, NY: Sharpe, 2000), 36. Roy L. Brooks, "Japanese American Redress and the American Political Process: A Unique Achievement," in *When Sorry Isn't Enough: The Controversy Over Apologies and Reparations for Human Injustice*, ed. Brooks (New York: New York University Press, 1999), 157–58. See Caroline Chung Simpson, *An Absent Present: Japanese Americans in Postwar American Culture* (Durham, NC: Duke University Press, 2001).

45. Brooks, "Japanese American Redress," 157–59; Tsung Chi, *East Asian American and Political Participation* (Santa Barbara: ABC CLIO, 2005), 53–54. Damon Freeman, "A Closer Look at the Japanese American National Museum," www.oah.org/meetings/2001/janm.html. *Los Angeles Times*, Aug. 23, 1985, B6.

46. *Personal Justice Denied*, 3–5; Brooks, "Japanese American Redress," 157–58; Leslie T. Hatamiya, "Institutions and Interest Groups: Understanding the Passage of the Japanese American Redress Bill," in *Japanese Americans: from Relocation to Redress*, ed. Roger Daniels, Harry H. L. Kitano, and Sandra C. Taylor (Seattle: University of Washington Press, 1991), 219–21.

47. James C. Naughton, Kristen E. Edwards, and Jay M. Price, "Incontestable Proof Will Be Exacted: Historians, Asian Americans, and the Medal of Honor," *Public Historian* 24 (Fall 2002): 11–33. *Washington Post*, June 2, 2000, 1. For belated recognition of Native Americans or, specifically, Navajo Code Talkers, see Adam Jevec, "Semper Fidelis, Code Talkers," *Prologue Magazine* 33 (Winter 2001), and the film *Windtalkers* (2002). Elements of the Japanese American community wishing to base their claims of redress more on past injustice than on patriotic deeds are discussed in Alice Yang Murray, *Historical Memories of*

the Japanese American Internment and the Struggle for Redress (Stanford, CA: Stanford University Press, 2008), 1.

48. Maureen Honey, *Creating Rose the Riveter: Class, Gender, and Propaganda during World War II* (Amherst: University of Massachusetts Press, 1984), 1–17. Sherrie A. Kossoudji and Laura J. Dresser, "Working-Class Rosies: Women Industrial Workers During WWII," *Journal of Economic History* 52 (June 1992): 431–46.

49. Kossoudji and Dresser, "Working Class Rosies," 431–36.

50. See Sherna Berger Gluck, *Rosie the Riveter Revisited: Women, the War, and Social Change* (New York: New American Library, 1987), 16–17; *New York Times*, May 5, 1946, SM11; Karen Tucker Anderson, "Last Hired, First Fired: Black Women during World War II," *Journal of American History* 69 (June 1982): 82–97.

51. *New York Times*, May 2, 1981, 13.

52. Gluck, *Rosie the Riveter Revisited*, xiii–xiv; *New York Times*, June 14, 1987, A1.

53. Leisa D. Meyer, *Creating GI Jane: Sexuality and Power in the Women's Army Corps During World War II* (New York: Columbia University Press, 1996), 2–6, 100–107; Jeanne Holm, *Women in the Military* (Novato, CA: Presidio Press, 1982), 21–56; 103.

54. See www.arlingtoncemetery.net/womens.htm.

55. *Women in the Military Service to America*, videocassette of dedication ceremonies, October 18, 2007, sold at the museum's gift shop.

56. *Rosie the Riveter Memorial Dedication, October 14, 2000*, videocassette produced by KCRT TV, Richmond, California. See also www.rosieriveter.lrg/memdes.

57. Ibid.

7. THE VICTORS

1. On the ability of mythic symbols to "engulf subjectivity" and reinforce authority, see Frank Mort, "Social and Symbolic Fathers and Sons in Postwar Britain," *Journal of British Studies* 35 (July 1999): 353–84.

2. Tom Brokaw, *The Greatest Generation* (New York: Random House, 1998), xiv–xxx; 43–51, 268, 329–31; The list of best sellers of the 1990s is to be found in *USA Today*, March 3, 2004, D1.

3. Stephen Ambrose, *Band of Brothers: E Company, 506th Regiment, 101st Airborne from Normandy to Eagle's Nest* (New York: Touchstone, 2001), 2–11, 82.

4. Ibid., 218–19; 402, 403.

5. Major Dick Winters, *Beyond Band of Brothers: The War Memoirs of Major Dick Winters* (New York: Berkley Publishing Group, 2006), 258, 266, 285–93.

6. Ibid., 268–73. In the HBO series soldiers can be seen not only traumatized at times but expressing criticism of officers and even killing unarmed German prisoners. See Part III: "Carentan" and Part VII: "The Breaking Point."

7. *New York Times*, Dec. 8, 1991, 24.

8. *New York Times*, Dec. 7, 1991, 9; Dec. 8, 1991, 24, 26.

9. *Pearl Harbor: Two Hours That Changed the World*, ABC-TV special, 1991.

10. *New York Times*, Jan. 9, 1984, SM12; April 17, 1994, 16; May 30, 1994, 35; June 7,

1994, 1, 10. On Ronald Reagan's Normandy speeches in 1984, see Douglas Brinkely, *The Boys of Pointe Du Hoc: Ronald Reagan, D-Day, and the U.S. Army 2nd Ranger Battalion* (New York: William Morrow, 2005), 186–92; 216–17.

11. "Remarks on the 50th Anniversary of D-Day at Utah Beach, June 6, 1994," *Public Papers of William J. Clinton,* I (1994), www.gpoaccess.gov/pubpapers/search.html

12. "Remarks on the 50th Anniversary of D-Day at Pointe du Hoc in Normandy, June 6, 1994," ibid. See James Tobin, *Ernie Pyle's War: America's Eyewitness to World War II* (New York: Free Press, 1997), 177–78.

13. "Interview with Tom Brokaw, June 5, 1994," *Public Papers of William J. Clinton,* I (1994).

14. "Interview with Wolf Blitzer, June 5, 1994"; "Interview with Harry Smith, June 5, 1944," ibid.

15. On the rise of civilian bombing as a tactic, see Michael S. Sherry, *The Rise of American Air Power: The Creation of Armageddon* (New Haven, CT: Yale University Press, 1987), 256–64; A. C. Grayling, *Among the Dead Cities: The History and Moral Legacy of the WWII Bombing of Civilians in Germany and Japan* (New York: Walker, 2006), 1–8. Mike Wallace, *Mickey Mouse History and Other Essays on American Memory* (Philadelphia: Temple University Press, 1996), 270–85; Paul Fussell, *Thank God for the Atomic Bomb and Other Essays* (New York: Summit Books, 1988), 14–37; Robert Jay Lifton and Greg Mitchell, *Hiroshima in America: Fifty Years of Denial* (New York: G. P. Putnam, 1995) explain Truman's "official view" that the bombs saved some one million lives. Mailer's view of the bomb is quoted on page 238. Tibbetts's view of the bombing is discussed in Bob Greene, *Duty: A Father, a Son, and the Man Who Won the War* (New York: Harper Collins, 2001). Tibbetts is also quoted in the *Houston Chronicle,* Jan. 22, 2005, B2. For a study that shows that high school textbooks in America almost never questioned the use of the bomb, see Carol Anne Harrison-Wong, "Educational Significance of How U.S. History Textbooks Treat Hiroshima" (Ph.D. diss., Teacher's College, Columbia University, 2003). See also Thomas Cripps, "So Their Eyes Won't Glaze Over: How Television News Defined the Debate over the Smithsonian's *Enola Gay* Exhibit," *Wide Angle* 20 (April 1998): 77–104.

16. John Hersey, *Hiroshima* (New York: Knopf, 1946); Charles Poore, "The Most Spectacular Explosion in the Time of Man," *New York Times,* Nov. 10, 1946, G7; "Hiroshima," *Washington Post,* Sept. 15, 1946, B1. For a critique of Hersey's moderate presentation of his accounts and his lack of outrage, see "Hersey's Hiroshima," *Politics* 3 (Oct. 1946): 308. John P. Diggins, "The American Writer, Fascism, and the Liberation of Italy," *American Quarterly* 18 (Winter 1966): 599–614. Paul Boyer, *By the Bomb's Early Light: American Thought and Culture at the Dawn of the Atomic Age* (Chapel Hill: University of North Carolina Press, 1994), 204–207 discusses the impact of Hersey's book. Michael J. Yavenditti, "John Hersey and the American Conscience: the Reception of 'Hiroshima'" *Pacific Historical Review* 43 (Feb. 1974): 24–49.

17. Norman Cousins, "The Maidens are Coming," *Saturday Review of Literature,* April 9, 1955, 24; Cousins, "Interim Report on Maidens," *Saturday Review of Literature,* Oct. 15, 1955, 22–23. An excellent account of the *This is Your Life* program can be found in Rodney Barker, *The Hiroshima Maidens: A Story of Courage, Compassion and Survival* (New York: Viking, 1985), a book authored by an individual who lived in a family that hosted some

maidens when he was a boy. Film of the episode can be seen in *White Light/Black Rain: The Destruction of Hiroshima and Nagasaki,* a documentary film produced by Steven Oka-zaki in 2007. Also see Caroline Chung Simpson, *An Absent Presence: Japanese-Americans in Postwar American Culture, 1945–1960* (Durham, NC: Duke University Press, 2001), 115–23. Hersey's remark on Lewis is made in a 1985 edition of *Hiroshima.*

18. Robert Jay Lifton, *Death in Life: Survivors of Hiroshima* (New York: Random House, 1967), 3–10, 13–27, 275–81. For an insightful discussion of Lifton's anti-nuclear and later antiwar actions regarding Vietnam, see Kirsten Fermaglich, *American Dreams and Nazi Nightmares: Early Holocaust Consciousness in Liberal America* (Hanover, NH: University Press of New England, 2006), 141.

19. See a full account of the controversy in Richard Kohn, "History and the Culture Wars: The Case of the Smithsonian Institution's 'Enola Gay' Exhibition," *Journal of American History* 82 (Dec. 1995): 1036–63. Also see an extended treatment of the issue in Edward Linenthal, "Anatomy of a Controversy," in *History Wars: The Enola Gay and Other Battles for the American Past,* ed. Edward Linenthal and Tom Engelhardt (New York: Henry Holt, 1996), 9–62; Wallace, *Mickey Mouse History,* 278–79. Kyoto Kishimoto, "Race and History Wars in the 50th Anniversary of the End of World War II" (Ph.D. diss., Bowling Green State University, 2001), 46–64. Kishimoto notes that in Japan the issue was known as the "Atomic Bomb Exhibition controversy" and not the "Enola Gay controversy."

20. Wallace, *Mickey Mouse History,* 281; *New York Times,* Jan. 26, 1995, A12; Feb. 5, 1995, E5. Kohn, "History and the Culture Wars," 1050–55; Linenthal, "Anatomy of a Controversy," in *History Wars,* 35.

21. See Stephen Dubner, "Steven the Good," *New York Times Magazine,* Feb. 14, 1999, 38–43, 66, 75. Spielberg's remarks on his "dad's generation" can be seen on "The Grand Opening Ceremonies of the National D-Day Museum, June 3–6, 2000," videotape, sold by the museum, now called the National World War II Museum, located in New Orleans.

22. For an argument critical of any film that claims one can derive positive traits from the experience of war, see James Jones, "Phony War Films," *Saturday Evening Post,* March 30, 1963. For a celebration of the fighting ability of common American men, see Norman Corwin, "On a Note of Triumph," script available from Lodestone, 627 North Morton St., Bloomington, IN 47404.

23. The reaction of the Iwo Jima veteran is recalled in Danny Thomas Oral History Interview, Feb. 26, 1999, North Texas University Oral History Collection. Selections from the America Online responses can be found in Jesse Kornbluth and Linda Sunshine, eds., *"Now You Know": Reactions after Seeing Saving Private Ryan* (New York: New Market, 1999), 16,19–20, 24, 32, 39–40, 47, 76.

24. The efforts among American Jews in the immediate postwar era to see the tragic slaughter for what it was is described best in Hasia R. Diner, *We Remember with Reverence and Love: American Jews and the Myth of Silence after the Holocaust, 1945–1962* (New York: New York University Press, 2009). See also Donald Bloxham, *Genocide on Trial: War Crimes Trials and the Formation of Holocaust History and Memory* (Oxford: Oxford University Press, 2001), 11, 129–32; Ronald Smelser and Edward J. Davies, *The Myth of the Eastern Front: The Nazi-Soviet War in American Popular Culture* (Cambridge: Cambridge University Press, 2008), document the more favorable attitude toward the German army during

the early years of the Cold War. See Tim Cole, *Selling the Holocaust: From Auschwitz to Schindler: How History Is Bought, Packaged, and Sold* (New York: Routledge, 2000), 3–7; Peter Novick, *The Holocaust in American Life* (Boston: Houghton-Mifflin, 1999), 1–8, 20. On American opinion toward Nuremberg, see William J. Bosch, *Judgment at Nuremberg: American Attitudes Toward the Major German War-Crime Trials* (Chapel Hill: University of North Carolina Press, 1970), 87–99; 117–25. Interestingly, Bosch's book, published in 1970, does not contain the term "Holocaust" in its index.

25. For the reaction to *The Wall*, see *Charlotte Observer*, March 5, 1950; *New Haven Register*, Feb. 26, 1950; *New York Times*, Feb. 27, 1950; and Norman Cousin's review in the *Saturday Review*, March 4, 1950, clippings in box 24, Hersey Papers, Yale University. A copy of the Book-of-the-Month-Club ad is found in box 10. See also David Sanders, *John Hersey Revisited* (Boston: Twayne, 1991).

26. Alvin H. Rosenfeld, "Popularization and Memory: The Case of Anne Frank," in *Lessons and Legacies: The Meaning of the Holocaust in a Changing World*, ed. Peter Hayes (Evanston, IL: Northwestern University Press, 1991), 243–78.

27. The 1959 movie *The Diary of Anne Frank* was directed by George Stevens, whose own memory of the war included service in the Signal Corps as he shot footage of the liberation of Dachau. *New York Times*, March 19, 1959, 40; Judith E. Doneson, "The American History of Anne Frank's Diary," *Holocaust and Genocide Studies* 2 (1987): 149–60; Cole, *Selling the Holocaust*, 35; Rosenfeld, "Anne Frank and the Future of Holocaust Memory" (Washington, DC: Holocaust Memorial Museum Occasional Paper, 2005), 9. I thank Professor Rosenfeld for giving me a copy of this paper.

28. Novick, *Holocaust in American Life*. Hasia Diner, "Post–World War II American Jewry and the Confrontation with Catastrophe," *American Jewish History* 91 (Sept.–Dec. 2003): 439–67; Lawrence Baron, "The Holocaust and American Public Memory, 1945–1960," *Holocaust and Genocide Studies* 17 (Sept. 2003): 62–88.

29. Solomon Rothstein to Reagan, Feb. 11, 1985; Elie Wiesel to Reagan, Jan. 31, 1985; Bob Dole to Reagan, Feb. 11, 1985; Barbara Mikulski to Reagan, April 19, 1985, Stanley Aranoff to Reagan, April 16, 1985, Joseph McCloskey to Reagan, April 19, 1985, White House Office of Records Management, TR 123-01, Reagan Presidential Library. See Edward Linenthal, *Preserving Memory: The Struggle to Create America's Holocaust Museum* (New York: Viking, 1995), 130.

30. *New York Times*, May 6, 1985, A8; *Washington Post*, April 17, 1985, A1. On the reluctance of the United States to endorse UN human rights treaties after World War II, see Samantha Power, *"A Problem from Hell": America and the Age of Genocide* (New York: Harper, 2002), 70–83, 165; Natalie Hevener Kaufman and David Whiteman, "Opposition to Human Rights Treaties in the United States Senate: The Legacy of the Bricker Amendment," *Human Rights Quarterly* 10 (1988): 309–37.

31. Yosefa Loshitsky, introduction to *Spielberg's Holocaust: Critical Perspectives on Schindler's List* (Bloomington: Indiana University Press, 1997), 2–3. Cole, *Selling the Holocaust*, 1–19. Allison Landsberg has argued that no matter how much the media may distort actual historical events, they can still stimulate important emotions such as empathy that help to sustain a degree of human compassion not normally seen in most public rituals. See Landsberg, "America, the Holocaust, and the Mass Culture of Memory: Toward a Rad-

ical Politics of Empathy," *New German Critique* 71 (Spring/Summer 1997): 63–86. For an excellent discussion of how some Americans used a remembrance of certain aspects of World War II to critique American military and racial policies in the late 1950s and early 60s, see Fermaglich, *American Dreams and Nazi Nightmares*, 1–23.

32. See Linenthal, *Preserving Memory*, 1–3, 263.

33. *New York Times*, May 31, 1985, B1; Richard Handler, "Lessons from the Holocaust Museum," *American Anthropologist* 96 (1994): 674–80.

34. All of the quotations are taken from visitor responses culled from comment books in the United States Memorial Holocaust Museum for the period from 2001 to 2007. I thank Jeffrey Carter and Larry Garfinkle of the museum for sending me this information.

35. Visitor observations are drawn from "Visitor Survey Results" compiled between 2003 and 2006. I thank Gordon Mueller, CEO of the museum, and Sam Wegner, the museum's director of educational activities, for providing me with this material.

36. Gordon Mueller interview with John Bodnar, May 24, 2007, New Orleans; Stephen Ambrose, "The D-Day Museum," *American Heritage* 51 (May/June 2000): 38–48.

37. *The Grand Opening Ceremonies of the National D-Day Museum, June 3–6, 2000*, videotape sold at the gift shop of the National World War II Museum, New Orleans.

38. On expressions of sorrow over the loss of "our commander-in-chief," see "Condolence Correspondence," boxes 3225 and 3226, Eleanor Roosevelt Papers, Franklin D. Roosevelt Library. For criticisms of the memorial in 1997, see Alida Black, "Struggling with Icons: Memorializing Franklin and Eleanor Roosevelt," *Public Historian* 21 (Winter 1999): 63–72.

39. Justice Felix Frankfurter, "The Memorial to F.D.R: What the President Wanted," *Atlantic Monthly* 207 (March 1961): 39–40. David Dillon, *The FDR Memorial Designed by Lawrence Halprin* (Washington, DC: Spacemaker Press, 1998), 22–27, 30.

40. See "Board of Trustee Minutes, 1947–1954," and "Verbatim Report, Third Annual Meeting of Board of Directors, Mar. 19, 1948," box 1, Franklin D. Roosevelt Memorial Foundation Papers, FDR Presidential Library, Hyde Park, New York.

41. "FDR Memorial Foundation Memorandum on Next Steps, Oct. 12, 1949, Programs Considered, #3," box 17, FDR Foundation Papers; "Verbatim Report, Third Annual Meeting of the Board of Trustees, March 19, 1948," box 1, FDR Memorial Foundation Papers, FDR Library.

42. "Report of the Executive Committee, May 18, 1954," box 2, FDR Foundation Papers; "Minutes of Board of Trustees, May 18, 1954," box 2, FDR Foundation Papers. On fears of McCarthyism, see James Loeb to George Elsey, Nov. 28, 1952; A. Schlesinger to W. A. Harriman, "Proposal for Awards for Achievement in Support of Four Freedoms," box 17, FDR Foundation Papers.

43. Dillon, *FDR Memorial*, 22–27, 30. "The F.D.R. Memorial Competition—pro and con," *Architectural Forum* 114 (April 1961): 187–88.

44. Dillon, *FDR Memorial*, 30. Hatfield recounts his war experiences in an interview with David Isenberg at ADM Online, March 16, 1997, www.cdi.org/adm/1027.

45. See *Washington Post*, May 3, 1997, A1; Francis X. Clines, "Memorials That Forget," *New York Times*, Oct. 27, 1996, E2.

46. Francis X. Clines, "Memorial Recaptures Roosevelt Era," *New York Times*, May 2, 1997, A2; see *Washington Post*, May 3, 1997, A1; Nicolaus Mills, "Monumental Correct-

ness: The New FDR Memorial," *Dissent* 44 (Fall 1997); Leon Wieseltier, "Immemorial," *New Republic*, June 9, 1997, 50.

47. See, for instance, "My Day" for July 10, 1948; Sept. 29, 1953. The columns are reproduced on the Web site of the Eleanor Roosevelt and Human Rights Project at George Washington University; see www.gwu/~erpapers/myday. Also see American Veterans Committee file, box 3400, Eleanor Roosevelt Papers, FDR Library.

CONCLUSION

1. See Daniel Marcus, *Happy Days and Wonder Years: The Fifties and Sixties in Contemporary Politics* (New Brunswick, NJ: Rutgers University Press, 2004), 67, 196–97. An incisive discussion of how memories of war and trauma lose their critical edge the more they are shared in public is to be found in Joanna Bourke, "Introduction: 'Remembering' War," *Journal of Contemporary History* 39 (4) (2004): 473–85.

2. Marcus, *Happy Days and Wonder Years*, 67, uses the term "nation-defining." Peter Fritzsche, "Specters of History: On Nostalgia, Exile, and Modernity" *American Historical Review* 106 (Dec. 2001): 1587–618.

3. See Dorothy Ross, "Lincoln and the Ethics of Emancipation: Universalism, Nationalism, Exceptionalism," *Journal of American History* 96 (Sept. 2009): 379–99. David W. Blight, *Race and Reunion: The Civil War in American Memory* (Cambridge, MA: Harvard University Press, 2001), 2; Gaines M. Foster, *Ghosts of the Confederacy: Defeat, the Lost Cause, and the Emergence of the New South* (New York: Oxford University Press, 1987), 198. The triumph of a patriotic memory of the war over one more focused on personal loss is stressed in Cecilia Elizabeth O'Leary, *To Die For: The Paradox of American Patriotism* (Princeton, NJ: Princeton University Press, 1999). Drew Gilpin Faust, *The Republic of Suffering: Death and the American Civil War* (New York: Knopf, 2008), 100–101, 264, reveals that the encounter with mass death during the Civil War also provoked a divided response somewhat similar to World War II that was torn between irony and sentimentality. In her estimation, sentimentality tried to sustain the idea that the individual dead mattered to some extent. The ironic view inferred that in modern warfare they did not.

4. Leslie Fiedler, *Waiting for the End* (New York: Dell, 1965), 20–31; William Manchester, *Goodbye Darkness: A Memoir of the Pacific War* (Boston: Little Brown, 1979), 25–28, 127.

5. *The Fog of War: Eleven Lessons from the Life of Robert McNamara* is a documentary film by Errol Morris produced in 2003. Information on LeMay's plans for Cuba is drawn from Barrett Tillman, *LeMay* (New York: Palgrave McMillan, 2007), 73, 161, 158–59. On the recognition of evil in the twentieth century, see Susan Neiman, *Evil in Modern Thought: An Alternative History of Philosophy* (Princeton, NJ: Princeton University Press, 2002), 1–13, 282.

6. See *New York Times*, Nov. 9, 1969, 57; *Washington Post*, Nov. 12, 1969, A13.

7. George McGovern, *Grassroots: The Autobiography of George McGovern* (New York: Random House, 1977), 30–31, 43–45. Robert Sam Anson, *McGovern: A Biography* (New York: Holt, Rinehart, Winston, 1972), 57–60. Thomas J. Knock, "'Come Home America': The Story of George McGovern," in *Vietnam and the American Political Tradition: The Poli-*

tics of Dissent, ed. Randall B. Woods (Cambridge: Cambridge University Press, 2003), 82–120. Tom Brokaw, *The Greatest Generation* (New York: Random House, 1998), 333–39.

8. Marcus, *Happy Days and Wonder Years,* 81–82. See also Carlos Rowe and Rick Berg, introduction to *The Vietnam War and American Culture,* ed. Rowe and Berg (New York: Columbia University Press, 1990), 1–17. Reagan's speech is available on line from the Presidential Speech Archives of the Miller Center for Public Affairs at the University of Virginia.

9. Patrick Hagopian, "America's Offspring: Infanticide and the Iconography of Race and Gender in Commemorative Statuary of the Vietnam War," *Perspectives: An Annual of American Cultural Studies* 26 (2001): 537–74.

10. Philip Caputo, *A Rumor of War* (New York: Ballantine Books, 1978), 6; Ron Kovic, *Born on the Fourth of July* (New York: McGraw-Hill, 1976), 54. Don Graham, *No Name on the Bullet: A Biography of Audie Murphy* (New York: Penguin, 1989), 189–90. For another reference to the impact of Wayne and, in this case, of a father who had served in World War II and Korea, on a young soldier, see Lewis B. Puller, *Fortunate Son: The Autobiography of Lewis B. Puller* (New York: Bantam, 1991), 37. For an insightful comparison of stories soldiers wrote from several wars, see Tobey C. Herzog, *Vietnam War Stories: Innocence Lost* (London: Routledge, 1992), 6, 25–33, 93–96.

11. Kendrick Oliver, *The My Lai Massacre in American History and Memory* (Manchester, UK: Manchester University Press, 2006), 237, 276–77, 325.

POSTSCRIPT ON IRAQ

1. See George W. Bush, "Proclamation 7511—National Pearl Harbor Remembrance Day, Dec. 5, 2001." Erika G. King and Robert A. Wells, *Framing the Iraq War Endgame: War's Denouement in an Age of Terror* (New York: Palgrave Macmillan, 2009), 33.

2. Bing West, *No True Glory: A Frontline Account of the Battle of Fallujah* (New York: Bantam, 2005), 184–85, 319–24.

3. Cindy Sheehan, *Peace Mom* (New York: Atria Books, 2006).

4. Dexter Filkins, *The Forever War* (New York: Vintage, 2008), 91, 93, 145.

Selected Bibliography

ARCHIVE AND MANUSCRIPT COLLECTIONS

American Legion Archives, Indianapolis, Indiana
  Pamphlet File
Beinecke Library, Yale University, New Haven, Connecticut
  John Hersey Papers
Cambria County Library, Johnstown, Pennsylvania
  Michael Strank File
Center for Southwest Studies, University of New Mexico, Albuquerque, New Mexico
  World War II File
Douglas County Historical Society, Omaha, Nebraska
  Memorial Park File
Harrodsburg Public Library, Harrodsburg, Kentucky
  Bataan File
Lyndon B. Johnson Library, Austin, Texas
  Senate Papers
Library of Congress, Manuscript Division, Washington, D.C.
  Henry Luce Papers
  Mackinley Kantor Papers
  Archibald MacLeish Papers
  William H. Mauldin Papers
National Association for the Advancement of Colored People (NAACP) Papers
Lilly Library, Indiana University, Bloomington, Indiana
  Wendell Willkie Papers
Milwaukee County Historical Society, Milwaukee, Wisconsin
  Milwaukee War Memorial File
National Archives and Records Administration, Archives II, College Park, Maryland
  Record Group 117, American Battle Monuments Commission
  Record Group 107, Secretary of War Records
Ohio State University Library, Rare Books and Manuscripts
  William Bradford Huie Papers
Harry Ranson Center, University of Texas, Austin, Texas
  Norman Mailer Papers

Ronald Reagan Library
  White House Office of Records Management
Franklin D. Roosevelt Library, Hyde Park, New York
  Eleanor Roosevelt Papers
  Franklin D. Roosevelt Memorial Foundation Papers
Rock County Historical Society, Janesville, Wisconsin
  192nd Tank Company Auxiliary Records
Harry S. Truman Library, Independence, Missouri
  Official File
      RG 584 (MacArthur Dismissal)
      File 190 E (repatriation)
Virginia State Library, Richmond, Virginia
  Virginia War Memorial Records
W. E. B. Du Bois Library, University of Massachusetts, Amherst
  William Manchester Papers, 1941–1988

DOCUMENTARIES/VIDEOS

Band of Brothers. HBO TV mini-series. 2001.
The Battle of San Pietro. Documentary film. John Huston, director. 1945.
Colors of Courage: Sons of New Mexico, Prisoners of Japan. Video. Center for Regional Studies, University of New Mexico, 2002.
The Fog of War: Eleven Lessons from the Life of Robert McNamara. Documentary film. Errol Morris, director. 2003.
The Grand Opening Ceremonies of the National D-Day Museum, June 3–6, 2000. Video. National World War II Museum, New Orleans, 2000.
Pearl Harbor: Two Hours that Changed the World. ABC-TV special, 1991.
Rosie the Riveter Memorial Dedication, October 14, 2000. Video. KCRT TV, Richmond, California, 2000.
Save Our History: The World War II Memorial. Video. History Channel, 1999.
Their Sacrifice, Our Freedom. Dedication Ceremonies, June 6, 2001. Video. WDBJ-TV, Roanoke, Virginia. National D-Day Memorial, 2001.
White Light / Black Rain: The Destruction of Hiroshima and Nagasaki. Documentary film. Steven Okazaki, producer. 2007.
Women in Military Service for America. Dedication ceremonies for the Women in Military Service for America Memorial, Arlington National Cemetery, October 18, 2007. Video.

FEATURE FILMS

A Foreign Affair (1948)
Air Force (1943)
All My Sons (1948)
All Quiet on the Western Front (1930)

Americanization of Emily (1964)
An Apartment for Peggy (1945)
A Streetcar Named Desire (1951)
A Walk in the Sun (1945)

Bad Day at Black Rock (1954)
Battleground (1949)
Best Years of Our Lives (1946)
Big Red One (1980)
Boy with the Green Hair (1948)
Blue Dahlia (1946)
Caine Mutiny (1954)
Crossfire (1947)
Cry Havoc (1943)
Command Decision (1949)
Confessions of a Nazi Spy (1939)
Dead Reckoning (1946)
Diary of Anne Frank (1959)
Dr. Strangelove, or How I Learned to Stop
    Worrying and Love the Bomb (1964)
Fighting Seabees (1944)
Flags of Our Fathers (2006)
Fort Apache (1948)
From Here to Eternity (1953)
Gentlemen's Agreement (1947)
Go For Broke (1951)
Guadalcanal Diary (1943)
Homecoming (1948)
Home of the Brave (1949)
I'll Be Seeing You (1944)
Judgment at Nuremberg (1961)
Letters from Iwo Jima (2006)
Longest Day (1962)
MacArthur (1977)
Miracle at St. Anna (2008)
Mister Roberts (1955)
My Foolish Heart (1950)
No Down Payment (1957)

Patton (1970)
Pearl Harbor (2001)
Pride of the Marines (1945)
Purple Heart (1945)
Sands of Iwo Jima (1949)
Saving Private Ryan (1949)
Sayonara (1957)
Schindler's List (1993)
Sergeant York (1941)
She Wore a Yellow Ribbon (1949)
Since You Went Away (1944)
Snow Falling on Cedars (1999)
Somewhere in the Night (1946)
Sophie's Choice (1982)
South Pacific (1958)
Strategic Air Command (1955)
Story of GI Joe (1945)
Task Force (1949)
Tender Comrade (1943)
The Clock (1945)
The Great Raid (2005)
The Man in the Grey Flannel Suit (1955)
The Men (1950)
The Pawnbroker (1964)
The Victors (1963)
The Young Lions (1958)
They Were Expendable (1945)
Thin Red Line (1998)
Till the End of Time (1946)
Twelve O'Clock High (1949)
War Lover (1962)
White Christmas (1954)
Windtalkers (2002)

ORAL HISTORY INTERVIEWS

Belman, Alice Faye. Interview by John Bodnar, May 22, 2007. Alexandria, Louisiana.

Compton, Etta. Interview by John Bodnar, May 22, 2007. Alexandria, Louisiana.

Diehl, Elwin. Interview by John Bodnar, July 30, 2008. Red Oak, Iowa.

Dulin, Louella. Interview by John Bodnar, February 1, 2007. Brookline, Missouri.

Garcia, Hector. Interview by David McComb, July 9, 1969. Lyndon Baines Johnson Library.

Halloran, Raymond. Interview by Bill Alexander, March 15, 1998, no. 1250. Admiral Nimitz Museum and University of North Texas Oral History Collection.

Iles-Foster, Gwendolyn. Interview by John Bodnar, May 22, 2007. Alexandria, Louisiana.

Johnson, Robert. Interview by John Bodnar, May 22, 2007. Alexandria, Louisiana.

Joiner, Jr., Heywood. Interview by John Bodnar, May 22, 2007. Alexandria, Louisiana.

Mueller, Gordon. Interview by John Bodnar, May 24, 2007. New Orleans, Louisiana.

Pero, Mary. Interview by John Bodnar, June 1, 2006. Davidsville, Pennsylvania.

Steele, Ben. Interview by John Bodnar, Sept. 3, 2008. Billings, Montana.

Thomas, Danny. Interview by Richard Byrd and Peter Love, Feb. 25, 1999. University of North Texas Oral History Collection.

Wesley, III, Amos. Interview by John Bodnar, May 22, 2007. Alexandria, Louisiana.

Wolfe, Dennis. Interview by John Bodnar, July 29, 2008. Red Oak, Iowa.

Wright, Stephen. Interview by John Bodnar, Feb. 1, 2007. Hurley, Missouri.

NEWSPAPERS AND MAGAZINES

Albuquerque Journal

Albuquerque Tribune

Alexandria (LA) Daily Town Talk

American Heritage

American Legion Magazine

American Mercury

Atlantic Monthly

Bedford (VA) Bulletin

Brainerd (MN) Daily Dispatch

Charlotte (NC) Observer

Chicago Tribune

Christian Century

Commonweal

Corpus Christi (TX) Caller Times

Corpus Christi (NM) Times

Crisis

Deming (NM) Headlight

Detroit News

Harrodsburg (KY) Herald

Houston Chronicle

Johnstown (PA) Tribune Democrat

Kansas City (MO) Times

Ladies Home Journal

Lexington (KY) Herald Leader

Life

Los Angeles Times

Louisville (KY) Courier Journal

Lynchburg (VA) News Advance

Nation

New Republic

New Haven (CT) Register

New York Review of Books

New York Times

New York Times Magazine

Omaha (NE) World Herald

Pacific Citizen

Readers Digest

Recreation

Roanoke (VA) Times

Rotarian

San Francisco Chronicle

Santa Fe New Mexican

Saturday Evening Post

Saturday Review of Literature

Springfield (MO) News Leader

Three Rivers News (TX)

Time

USA Today

Washington Post

Washington Post Times Herald

Waterloo (IA) Daily Courier

Wisconsin State Journal

Index